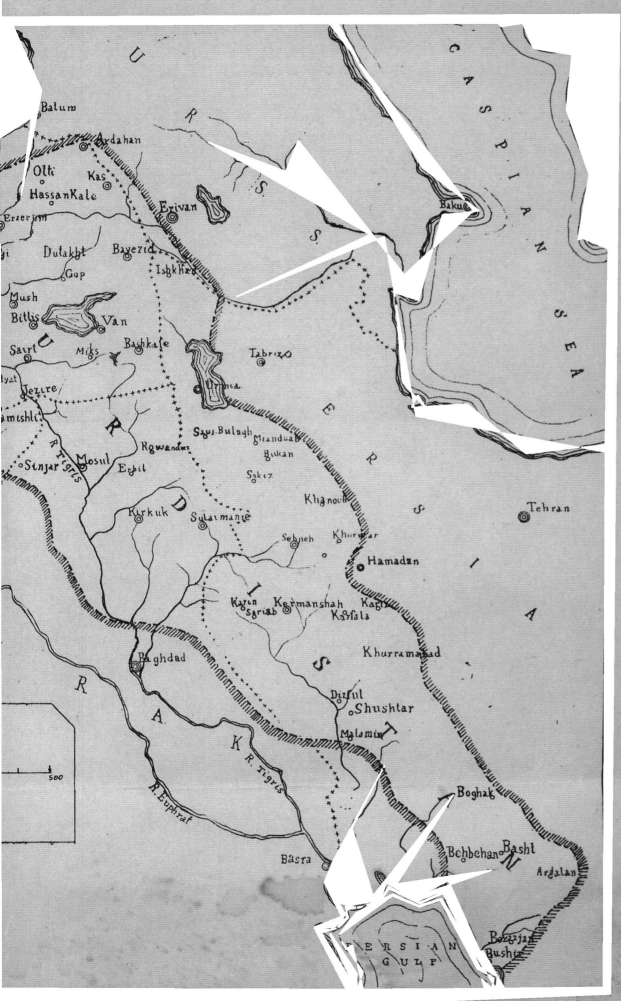

Map presented by the
Kurdish League Khoybun to
the San Francisco Conference
on March 30, 1945

Courtesy Mme. Roger Lescot

KURDISTAN

*After the death of the great Persian king Jamshid, the
tyrant Zahhak usurped the throne and established a reign
of terror. Besides being cruel by natural inclination, he
suffered from a strange disease that made him even more
of an oppressor. Two snakes grew out of his shoulders and
caused him severe pain, which could only be alleviated by
feeding the snakes human brains each day. So every day
Zahhak had two young persons killed and their brains fed
to the snakes. The man charged with slaughtering the
two young people taken to the palace each day took pity
on them and thought up a ruse. He killed only one person
a day, replacing the other by a sheep and mixing the two
brains. One young person's life was thus saved every day;
he was told to leave the country and to stay hidden in
distant inaccessible mountains. The young persons thus
saved gradually came to constitute a large community;
they married among themselves and brought forth offspring.
These people were named Kurds. Because during many
years they evaded other human company and stayed away
from the towns, they developed a language of their own.
In the forests and the mountains they built houses and
tilled the soil. Some of them came to own property and
flocks, and spread themselves over the steppes and deserts.*

From the *Sharafname*, a history of the Kurdish tribes,
written by the Kurdish emir Sharafuddin of Bitlis, 1597

Mountains of northern Iraq
Susan Meiselas/Magnum

Kurdish refugees fleeing Saddam Hussein's attacks in northern Iraq head toward the border of Turkey, April 1991

Coşkun Aral/Sipa Press

Qala Diza, town of 70,000 Kurds in
northern Iraq, destroyed in a 1989 border
"cleanup" operation during the Anfal campaign
Susan Meiselas/Magnum

Graves of those killed during the 1988 chemical bombing of the village of Goktapa, northern Iraq
Susan Meiselas/Magnum

KURDISTAN

In the Shadow of History

SUSAN MEISELAS

With Chapter Commentaries by
Martin van Bruinessen

RANDOM HOUSE
NEW YORK

CONTENTS

Istanbul, Turkey: December 1991

In a bookstall squeezed into a crowded alley, I see a postcard entitled "Kurde noble." I ask myself, Is the man in the picture really a Kurd? I know that turn-of-the-century studios routinely offered their clients exotic costumes to wear when being photographed. The name of the noble Kurd does not appear on the back.

It is assumed I am a tourist until I ask to buy this card. Then, immediately, the shopkeeper finds me suspect.

This image from 1895 celebrating Kurdish identity, produced for and sold to early travelers, is now forbidden. The Kurdish language is outlawed; Kurdish history cannot be taught in Turkish schools.

One hundred years after this picture was taken, Turkey is again at war with the Kurds.

Kurde noble.

Postcard, Sebah & Joaillier/
Courtesy Pierre de Gigord

New York City: January 1997

After six years of working with the Kurdish community and handing the postcard to nearly everyone I met, someone finally identified the "Kurde noble." A Kurdish scholar tells me that the image is of the infamous Kurdish chief Musa Beg, known to have pillaged an Armenian village in 1889 and kidnapped a young Armenian girl named Gulizar. Though the Turkish sultan tried to protect him, Musa Beg's trial became a cause célèbre in Europe. He was sentenced to exile in Mecca.

Only insiders know this history—who he was, what he did, the enmity he raised in the Armenian community. Like all outsiders, I am utterly dependent on those who can inform and interpret.

INTRODUCTION

Qala Diza, Northern Iraq: April 1991

At every mountain pass, another village leveled; stone houses are now piles of rubble. No electricity, no running water, little food. People living under slabs of concrete within the ruins of their former homes. They have chosen to stay in this wasteland rather than face exile in either Turkey or Iran.

When the Gulf War began, I, like most Americans, knew little about the Kurds. My first visit to the region was brief. Pleased to have the Western press witness the Kurds' pressing need for humanitarian aid, Iran facilitated access to the Kurdish refugee camps. I was given a five-day visa—barely time to leave Paris, cross the Iranian border, and get to the "liberated" zone within northern Iraq. While the world's attention was concentrated on the flight of the Kurds, I was drawn to the places from which they'd come. I drove in along the same road upon which many Kurds were still fleeing. I was stunned by what I saw. I had never witnessed such a complete and systematic destruction of village life, even in ten years of covering the conflicts in Central America.

Although few Western observers had been inside northern Iraq for nearly a decade, reports periodically leaked out through the Kurdish network about Saddam Hussein's 1988 "Anfal" campaign, a brutal attempt at annihilation. Nearly 100,000 Kurds were said to have "disappeared." After reports that mass graves had been uncovered inside the Kurdish enclave, the group Human Rights Watch sent a mission into the territory to investigate. It was an opportune moment, since no one knew just how long it would take Saddam to regain military strength and reassert control over the region.

I was asked to join Dr. Clyde Snow, a forensic anthropologist well known for his exhumation of the mass graves in Argentina and Chile. My task was to photograph the sites of evidence—scars on survivors, unmarked graves, the clothes that had once wrapped bodies now buried anonymously, the bullet holes in skulls—the visible remains. That the Anfal campaign had ended three years before did not reduce the urgency with which we worked. I was part of an international team building a legal case against Saddam Hussein's brutality. Working with a small group of Kurds, we excavated where the gravediggers remembered burying the dead. Meticulously, earth was shoveled and then brushed away by hand, until finally the skull of a male teenager appeared, a synthetic cloth blindfold still wrapped around it. Needing no instruments, the experienced Dr. Snow measured the holes to determine range, caliber, type of weapon. He concluded that the boy was the victim of an execution.

These were not the first mass graves I had documented. This time, however, I was coming in at the end of the story. I had no connection to the Kurds and even less sense of why these killings had occurred. I felt strange—photographing the present while understanding so little about the past. Now I realize that the unearthing of these graves led me to years of further digging.

Paveh, Iran: September 1991

In the window of a small photo studio, there are typical pictures of the town's weddings and recent births. Alongside the familiar is one image—quite horrific—of men bearing the impaled heads of Kurds on long spikes. I question the owner and am told that he does not know when the image was made or where he found it. Nor does he have any idea whose heads they were.

The studio owner, a Kurdish man, knows little about these events, yet he keeps the picture as a symbol of his people's suffering, as a piece of the past, as evidence of a history. Not knowing quite why, I ask if I can make a copy of the print. I am struck by the role of the local photographer—as keeper of the collective archive—reproducing an image from his world to share with a total stranger.

Today "Kurdistan" does not exist on the map. Since 1918, the Kurds' homeland has remained divided among Turkey, Iraq, Iran, Syria, and what is now the former U.S.S.R. In each country the Kurds have been continuously threatened with either assimilation or extermination. But as a place, Kurdistan exists in the minds of more than twenty million people, the largest ethnic people in the world without a state of its own.

An isolated image in a window would seem to pose little threat, but that local shopkeeper is surely a man of courage. An accessible repository of Kurdish images is impossible anywhere in the Middle East. It is no accident that the Kurds do not have a national archive.

Some Kurds know a lot about those who passed through their lands over the last century. The names of Western travelers, missionaries, military officers, and colonial administrators float among the names of their own Kurdish heroes. My friend Bakhtiar Amin told me about a Major Noel, who in 1919 advised the British to be careful to distinguish between the Kurds and their Middle Eastern neighbors. Though Noel's diary could be found in the Public Record Office in London, it has only recently been published in Kurdish. Other Kurds told me that they had read some of the Western memoirs written about them. Dusty books, sparsely illustrated, long out of print, were taken off back shelves in their homes and proudly shown to me as treasured accounts. Thumbing through the pages, I thought about all the photographs that had been made and then taken away from Kurdistan.

I, too, have been such a traveler. I began to wonder where those early photographs were, imagining the route of their travel—carried by hand as glass or nitrate negatives, or shipped in trunks—to be pasted into albums or relegated to archives, or to disappear into attics. I wanted to retrace the paths of those earlier Western travelers and find the souvenirs and recollections of their journeys.

New York City: September 1992

Archives are strange lands, each with its distinct organization. Photographs frequently inhabit files without record of date, name, place, or event. At the Bettmann Archive I am allowed to pore through the manila folders (the archive is not yet fully computerized). In the "Iran" folder, I find an image of a dignified man sitting on a chair placed on a carpet in the middle of a stark landscape, men in Kurdish dress behind him. This picture could never have been discovered without browsing—its caption identifies him as a general but makes no reference to the Kurds.

Finding a photograph is often like picking up a piece from a jigsaw-puzzle box with the cover missing. There's no sense of the whole. Each image is a mysterious part of something not yet revealed.

In Western archives, the word "Kurdistan" is rarely indexed. The Kurds are cataloged according to the countries in which they live as minorities; most often they appear in archival indices as "ethnic types." In each collection the classification varies; the photograph is seen as ethnographic description or aesthetic object, especially if it was made by a renowned photographer. Rarely is there any historical information about the people who are pictured and then categorized. But the image still stands as evidence of an encounter.

Every picture tells a story and has another story behind it: Who's photographed? Who made it? Who found it? How did it survive? I wonder what we can know of any particular encounter by looking at such a picture today. We have the object, but it exists separated from the narrative of its making.

What interested me was the intersection and interplay between those who shaped Kurdish life and the lives of the chroniclers who pictured them—the photographers and those photographed, the points of cultural exchange, how the various protagonists crossed one another's paths. Both left their marks on Kurdish history.

Diyarbakır, Turkey to Arbil, northern Iraq: October 1992

Crossing the border again into Iraq, this time to travel with As'ad Gohzi, a former peshmerga fighter who is not just a translator but truly a guide. Within bare rooms, men sit on carpets with their backs against walls, drinking tea; the women are hidden, along with their stories. Only because we are Western women are we welcome to join the men.

As'ad knows whom to approach and how to appreciate the gracious and extended Kurdish rituals. Custom requires celebrating our visit with a meal. Several hours later, the photo albums and bags full of pictures appear from the closets, evoking spontaneous memories. Teaching Kurdish history and language is illegal in schools throughout Turkey and Iran. So stories passed down within families carry much of what is known about the past, preserving it for generations.

I can't escape the tradition of the colonial foreigner. I travel and collect, take and treasure, classify, consume and possess. Yet I also feel the need to repatriate what I uncover as I attempt to reconstruct the past from scattered fragments.

With photocopies of pictures from Western archives, my assistant, Laura Hubber, and I returned to northern Iraq. We moved from house to house seeking assistance in the identification of a familiar face, a facade, or simply the date that a costume or custom might disclose. We annotated as we went. With As'ad, we first visited the homes of powerful aghas and shaikhs and then began to trace the genealogies of families known to have played important roles in Kurdish nationalist history.

Over time, my role divided between maker and collector. I stopped taking photographs, except to reproduce existing family photos with a Polaroid system. I felt immense pleasure sitting with families, first peeling off a positive image (the back of the print served as a perfect reference card for notations), then watching with my host as the negative appeared in the tray of sodium solution. Their precious originals stayed with them, but they allowed us to make copies to take away. These were privileged moments: to be invited inside, to listen to the storytellers, then to eat and sleep on their floors. Everywhere we were strangers, yet we were welcomed with trust as soon as people understood that they were contributing to a collective memory.

Arbil, northern Iraq: April 1993

A Kurdish scholar living in New York gave us the name of a well-known photographer, now dead. In Iraq, the photographer's son greets us uncertainly, at first cautious about speaking of his patrimony. After tea, he disappears to the back of the house and returns carrying little orange boxes crammed with glass negatives. He shows us what remains of his father's distinguished work.

Making prints is complicated logistically and must be done discreetly. We borrow a small darkroom in town, mix homemade chemicals, and use paper I've brought from New York. Formal portraits of families and notables, private and public events appear. One image leaps out: a group of Kurds behind someone in official dress, the Persian flag hanging above them. A significant moment—a brief interim before power became centralized in Persia? An image suggesting the hope that Kurds could control their ancestral lands? Or does this photograph memorialize yet another lost possibility, tribal chieftains betraying other rival chiefs? There's no way to know yet.

After I finish printing, the photographer's son reburies the glass plates somewhere in his backyard, to make sure that whatever might happen in Iraq, the images will somehow survive.

Our next few trips were driven by active pursuit—to try to rephotograph those pictures too dangerous for the Kurds to carry across any borders. Even a family portrait can be considered subversive if interpreted by officials as an expression of Kurdish identity and thereby linked to a nationalist movement. Of the nearly half million Kurdish refugees now living in Europe, I wonder how many of them had to leave their photographs behind.

As military operations intensified in the Kurdish provinces of Turkey, I wanted to pick up my camera and shoot or at least witness what was happening—villages being burned and thousands of Kurdish families forced to evacuate. But mobility in the area was restricted: journalists—especially photographers—were obliged to report to local authorities and were not permitted to wander. The Kurds could no longer afford to talk to strangers or speak about a history that had long been publicly denied.

Eventually, the Turks closed the border with northern Iraq, cutting down the flow of nongovernmental workers and limiting visas for the foreigners who had previously crossed freely. This meant that I could not photograph in the "militarized zone" or continue to collect anywhere in Kurdistan. The only possibility was to resume research in the archives and to keep up the work within the exile community.

New York City: June 1993

People keep sending material. A package arrives from the grandson of Percival Richards, who accompanied Major Noel to Kurdistan in 1919. Heaped together with the pictures are a few letters scribbled in pencil by Richards to his wife, along with his marriage license, a passport, and the bill for his coffin, detailing its size and cost—a man's life now contained in a yellow plastic bag.

My studio is filled with stacks of images made by men and women whom I've never met, most of whom died before I was born.

New York City: September 1993

There's a book in the library, The Kurdish Republic of 1946, *detailing the brief moment in history when the Kurds had an independent state. Within a year, the Iranian army attacked the central city of Mahabad. The Kurds destroyed all their own records and photographs in fear of further reprisals.*

I learn that the book's author, William Eagleton, is now the special coordinator for the United Nations in Sarajevo. In the fifties he served as the American consul in Iran and collected interviews and existing documentation about the Mahabad Republic. I write to him, asking after the pictures that appeared in his book.

New York City: November 22, 1994

Received word from Eagleton—the Vienna warehouse where he'd stored all his papers has burned down. Everything has been lost except the pictures he sent us a few months ago. He writes, "I wish to know that they are safe, since they are the only things that remain of my adventures in Kurdistan."

How arbitrary the survival of such evidence can be.

Most of the images and written artifacts about the Kurds that survive, survive in the West. In part this is because the Kurds have little security and limited funds to maintain museums and libraries or to protect private collections. Ironically, interpretations of their culture offered by outsiders—missionaries, colonial administrators, and early travelers—have become indispensable sources of written and visual information.

In the present work I've tried to re-create the Kurds' encounter with the West and ask readers to engage in the discovery of a people from a distant place without knowing exactly where that process will lead. In no way is this a definitive history of the Kurds. Texts and images are presented as fragments, to expose the inherent partiality of our knowledge. This is a book of quotations, with multiple and interwoven narratives taken from primary sources—the raw materials from which history is constructed.

Excerpts from diaries and documents make public what was often a personal record or private exchange. Suggesting the randomness by which history gets made, newspaper clippings and selected bits of memoirs reveal what was presented by the media and commonly believed at the time. Kurdish oral histories interspersed throughout contest the Western perspective of Kurdish life, as well as the view of

the local regional powers. The book's design reproduces the images with all the markings of age and travel, so that the surface itself reveals the history of survival. I emphasize the photograph as object, as artifact, once held, now torn and stained. A photograph is a document that resists erasure.

Rather than emerging as a completed puzzle with every piece fitting neatly together, this book project has revealed a mosaic—only from a distance is there a shape to discern. This is a reconstruction based on what remains and has been retrieved; we cannot know what is gone. Certainly, much is missing.

New York City: December 1996

A phone call just before Christmas day—As'ad Gohzi is in Guam. The U.S. military airlifted him out of northern Iraq along with other employees of U.S.-funded nongovernmental organizations who could be in danger if the Iraqi army returns. He arrived with his family and nearly five thousand other Kurds. The most recent round of infighting between the Kurdish parties triggered Saddam's August invasion. Once again, families are ripped apart as the Kurds war among themselves.

New York City: July 16, 1997

Mustafa Khezry, with whom I first traveled to Iran, has just called. He has finally discovered the documents I wanted, in Baku, Azerbaijan.

I think about my two earlier trips there. It was impossible for me to access the KGB files. I knew there was likely to be some material regarding the Russian relationship to the Kurdish Republic of Mahabad. I asked if there was anything about the deportations of the Kurds under Stalin. He couldn't tell me.

It was hard to tell him that the book was going to press in two weeks' time and that I couldn't add anything else.

There will always be more to uncover.

In the same way that a collection of unearthed bones can reveal concealed events, these photographs cannot be denied. But like scattered bones, these images would have remained disconnected from the skeleton of the narrative without knowledge of the people and place from which they've come.

For Westerners, I hope that this book can create a presence of those who continue to be distant, linking the headlines of the future with the Kurdish past.

For the Kurds, I hope that this book serves as a sourcebook of a suppressed history that can now be repossessed, though not without risk.

—SCM
July 1997

Postcard of the City of Arbil, ca. 1900
Unknown/Courtesy Azad Mukriyani

Travelers and Missionaries as Witness

Kurdistan, "land of the Kurds," is mentioned by European travelers from the fifteenth century onward: a mountainous, wild land of ill-defined extent between Persia in the east and Asia Minor and Syria in the west. Kurdistan never was a state by itself, and in fact at most times it was divided between two or more neighboring states. It was recognized as a distinct region because its most conspicuous inhabitants, the Kurds, appeared so different from their neighbors. For many centuries they have been present in the same region and have had an awareness of being a single people in spite of great diversity and of frequent conflicts placing one tribe against another.

A modern sense of nationhood emerged relatively late among the Kurds, and only as a consequence of dramatic changes of their traditional world. These changes were largely due to the impact of the West, which greatly increased in the nineteenth century.

The nineteenth century was a period of intense imperialist competition for control of the weakening Muslim states of Persia and the Ottoman Empire (which between them incorporated Kurdistan). Britain and Russia, and to a lesser degree France and Germany, vied for political and economic influence and territorial control at the expense of these Muslim empires.

Especially after Napoleon's temporary conquest of Egypt in 1798, Britain made efforts to secure its grip on the Ottoman Empire in order to safeguard its communications with India. From that year on, the East India Company had a permanent Resident in Baghdad, who also established political contacts with the major Kurdish chieftains of southern Kurdistan. Russia was inexorably expanding southward, conquering the Crimea peninsula by the middle of the century and most of the Caucasus in the following decades. In the Russian-Turkish war of 1877–78, Russian troops penetrated deep into Asia Minor, occupying large parts of Kurdistan. It was only due to pressure from rival European powers at the Berlin Congress in 1878 that Russia had to relinquish most of Asiatic Turkey again.

Kurdistan, like all of the Ottoman Empire and Persia, was an ethnic mosaic, where various religious and linguistic minorities lived interspersed among the Kurds. Most of the Kurds were Sunni Muslims, but perhaps a quarter or a third adhered to heterodox varieties of Islam that preserved traces of earlier religions. Armenians, Nestorian and Jacobite Christians, and Jews were the largest non-Muslim communities. In the nineteenth century, missionaries of many nationalities visited the Christian communities living among the Kurds and elsewhere in the region, building schools and hospitals for them and making efforts to convert them to their own national churches. Members of these minority communities felt encouraged to throw off the yoke of inequality under which they had long lived—aspirations that were repeatedly to provoke some of their Muslim neighbors to massacre.

Throughout the nineteenth century, the European powers exerted considerable influence on Ottoman affairs, pressing for administrative reform and protection of the Christian minorities. Reform-minded Ottoman bureaucrats, who controlled the Empire during the so-called Tanzimat ("Reforms") period, 1839–76, legislated an end to discrimination against non-Muslims, upsetting the traditional order and provoking resentment among sections of the Muslim population. Other reforms aimed at centralization; previously autonomous Kurdish districts were brought under direct central control.

Sultan Abdulhamid II (1876–1909) greatly distrusted the European powers and their ostensible allies, the reformist bureaucrats and the Christian minorities. His concerns were shared by Kurdish traditional leaders who feared, especially after the Russian occupation of 1877, that the local Armenians might with Russian support establish a Christian state. This situation appears to have brought about, for the first time, the idea of a Kurdish state. In 1880, the religious leader Shaikh Ubaidullah led an uprising of Kurdish tribes on the Persian-Ottoman border. While the shaikh kept proclaiming his loyalty to the Ottoman Sultan, he wrote to the English missionary Cochran at Urmia that the Kurds were a nation apart and wished to be their own masters.

Sultan Abdulhamid suppressed Ubaidullah's rebellion and exiled the shaikh to Mecca, but not much later he concluded a convenient alliance with the major Kurdish chieftains. He enlisted Kurdish tribesmen, commanded by their own chieftains, as irregular militias (called Hamidiye) to protect the ancien régime against the Russian threat outside and the twin threats of administrative reform and Armenian nationalism within. Armed by the sultan, the Hamidiye regiments could terrorize their Christian and Muslim neighbors with impunity. In 1894, when Armenians in Sasun district rebelled against double taxation, Hamidiye regiments carried out a massacre there. Other serious massacres of Armenians took place in various parts of the Empire in 1895 and 1896; this time, however, the Hamidiye appear to have played only a marginal part.

In 1908, reform-minded Young Turks imposed a constitution upon Abdulhamid; the following year they forced him to resign and placed his son Mehmed Reshad on the throne. The Hamidiye remained loyal to their founder; the commander of the strongest regiment, Ibrahim Pasha of the Milan tribe, led an unsuccessful rebellion against the Young Turks. The new regime disbanded the Hamidiye but soon established its own Kurdish tribal militias.

The Young Turks initially reasserted the equality of all Ottoman citizens, irrespective of language or religion, but gradually drifted to a pan-Turk, pan-Islamic position. In the First World War they allied themselves with Germany and, in an almost suicidal impulse, declared war on the old enemy Russia and persuaded the sultan to issue the call for jihad, "Holy War." The Armenians, considered potential collaborators with the Russian enemy, were evicted from their villages and towns and dispatched toward Syria. A high proportion of them never arrived but were murdered, in large-scale massacres apparently orchestrated by the Young Turks' secret service. With the Armenians gone, and the other Christians reduced, the region had become more homogeneous, and the idea of a Kurdish nation state conceivable—but Islam continued to command stronger loyalties than ethnicity.

—*MvB*

Postcards, ca. 1895
Courtesy Pierre de Gigord

در کردستان زنهای ارامنه و اکراد کیرا درست میکنند

famille Kurde

En Kurdistan, le nettoyage de la gomme adragante.

Mercredi 14/9/04 - Chère Mademoiselle - Vous devez savoir qu'en Turquie chaque mosquée possède sa fontaine pour les ablutions que sont obligées de faire les musulmans avant leur prière. Les pigeons par centaine y instruisent leurs nids

A Koordish Chief. — Representative of a people (estimated 3,000,000) occupying the highlands of EASTERN TURKEY and beyond. Sultan Abdul Hamid II, recognizing the valor of these bold mountaineers, organized them as his personal troops to guard his Eastern domain. AMERICAN BOARD missionaries come in contact with this virile and capable people at many points in the EASTERN TURKEY field, and Christianity is finding freer access in the new times.

Fille Kurde   Salut de Constantino

comme la religion musulmane ne permet pas de toucher à ses oiseaux ils en paix et s'apprivoisent facilement. Voilà pourquoi Mademoiselle, les alentours de sont toujours envahis par des pigeons. Sincères Salutations

Vieux Kurde. Mademoiselle. Souvenir de

For the Use of Travellers and Residents in Uncivilized Lands

The following are the instruments of precision recommended to be used by travellers who cannot burden themselves with much baggage:—

1. Callipers. . . .
2. Measuring tapes. . . . If not washable, several should be taken, as they are soon rendered illegible by the grease and filth of the subjects measured.
3. Jointed measure of wood, at least 1 yard or 1 metre in length. . . .
4. Medical Thermometer. . . .
5. Seconds Watch.
6. Dotted papers, for testing distance and clearness of vision. . . .

Dr. Beddoe, F.R.S., Notes and Queries on Anthropology, 1st Edition, 1874
Royal Anthropological Institute, London

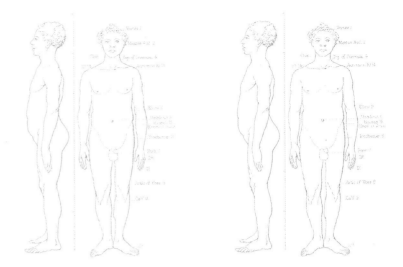

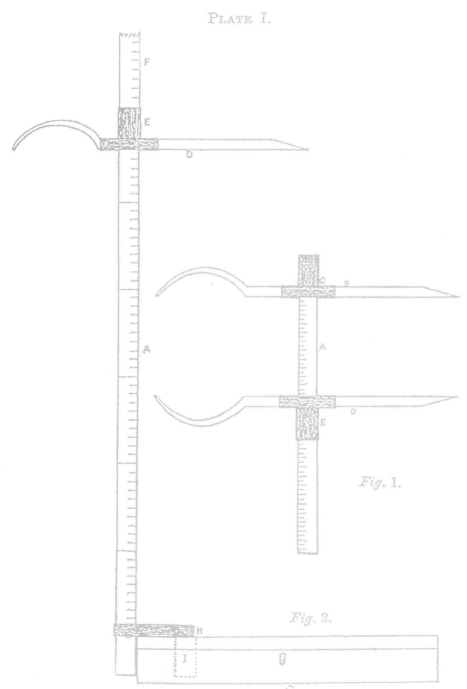

PLATE I.

Fig. 1.

Fig. 2.

There is one branch of work that should always be put off until the people are confident that the investigator's intentions are at least harmless, viz., anthropometry; physical measurements are almost invariably regarded with suspicion.

Most natives are susceptible to patriotic flattery. If the investigator says that . . . the great ones of his country really desire to know how they do various things and what they think, he is almost certain to get some response. . . . It is important that not even the slightest expression of amusement, incredulity, or dissent should ever be displayed at the description of ridiculous, impossible, or disgusting features in custom, cult or legend. . . .

The natives should feel that you are inquiring not out of mere curiosity but because of a real desire to understand their mode of life both now and in the past, and that people at home are equally desirous to have this information. It may be advisable to tell them something about our forefathers in the stone ages, how rudely and simply they lived. . . .

Without permission, you should not touch, photograph or sketch anything which may possibly be sacred. . . . People of rude culture are so unaccustomed to any . . . evidence of sympathy with their ways of thinking and acting that such care on your part will go far to break down the reticence which they naturally show in speaking of their religious ideas. . . .

In approaching timid or shy natives with a view to establishing friendly relationship and confidence, it is very useful to seek out one who has been wounded and to render "first aid" to him. Other natives will be curious to see what is being done and will gradually gather round, and when they recognize that the visitor is doing something to help them, they are liable to become reassured and friendly. A surgical bandage and disinfectant may frequently be the means of establishing friendship. . . .

When trying to photograph shy natives, it is well to conceal the fact that the real lens is pointing at them. A dummy lens fixed at the side of the camera and pointed away at right angles to the natives, will make them think that they are safe, the real lens being concealed by the hand until the last moment. . . .

It is hoped that this book will be largely used by missionaries. . . . A missionary who studies the native religion sympathetically will not only discover the real nature of those he wishes to improve, he will not only reach the hearts of the best members of the community, but he will also find himself in a position to effect far more vital and fundamental reforms.

Notes and Queries on Anthropology, 5th Edition, 1892
Royal Anthropological Institute, London

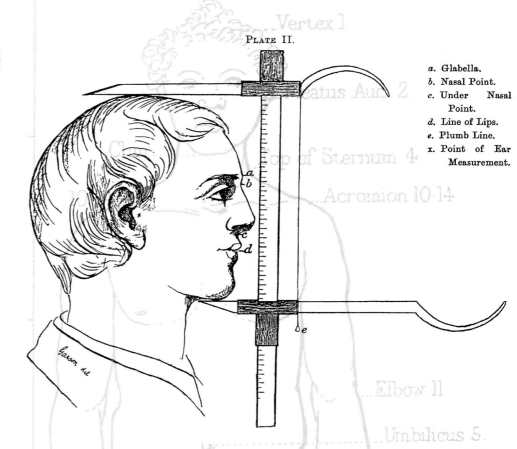

PLATE II.

a. Glabella.
b. Nasal Point.
c. Under Nasal Point.
d. Line of Lips.
e. Plumb Line.
x. Point of Ear Measurement.

We cannot tell you who Mr. Vane was, although I believe those two photographs were made here at the Smithsonian. It was a fairly common practice to have people model garments, often so that lay figures could be prepared for exhibits. Sometimes the models seem to have had special knowledge of the cultures involved. At other times, however, I suspect it may have simply been a question that the clothing fit a given person.

Excerpt from letter by
James R. Glenn, Senior Archivist
National Anthropological Archives,
National Museum of Natural History,
Washington, D.C., September 28, 1993

Portraits of Mr. Vane in dervish costume

Unknown/Smithsonian Institution

Background:
Royal Anthropological Institute, London

Ernest Chantre

French Anthropologist
Photographs by Captain Barry,
French Photographer

The Kurdish type I established after studying 332 individuals (62 women) can be summarized as follows:

The physiognomy of the Kurds breathes savagery: their characteristics are hard, their eyes, of a fierce brightness, are small and sunken under the orb. The men are most commonly dark, tall, and lean and have uncommon strength. They wear hardly anything except for a mustache and they cover their heads with a turban that is sometimes of gigantic proportions. Their step is firm, they hold their heads up with pride, and their look has a supreme arrogance. They do not laugh or talk much.

Ernest Chantre, *Les Kurdes: Esquisse Historique et Ethnographique*, 1897

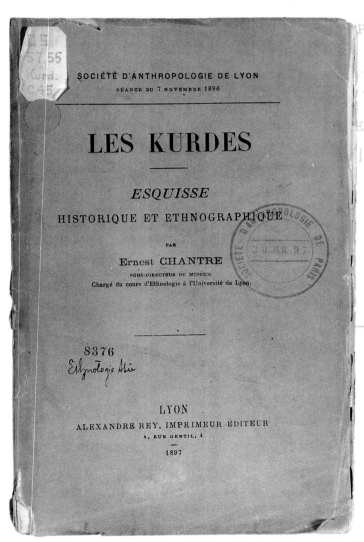

Courtesy Musée de l'Homme, Paris

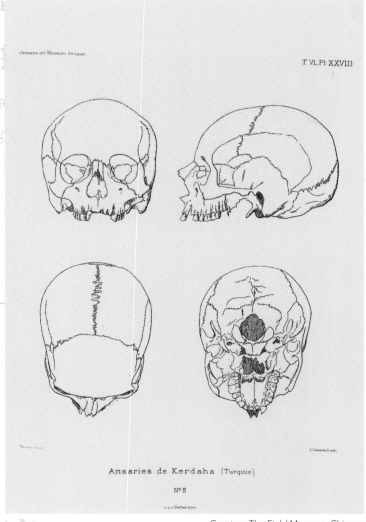

Ansaries de Kerdaha (Turquie)
Nº 5

Courtesy The Field Museum, Chicago

"Examined from this point of view, these skulls present a much more elongated oval than that found on the Armenians. . . . The forehead is large and slightly rounded; the frontal bumps are moderately pronounced even in male subjects."
—Ernest Chantre

1890s

E. Chantre photog 1890

Héliogravure Dujardin

Kurdes Bourouki d'Airidja

Le Cheikh Atach et sa femme

Imp. J. Saillard Lyon

Ernest Chantre, *Missions Scientifiques en Transcaucasie, Asie Mineure et Syrie 1890–1894, Archives du Muséum d'Histoire Naturelle de Lyon*, 6th Volume, 1895/Courtesy The Field Museum, Chicago

The eyes are black (66%), of an astonishing acuity, never narrow or oblique, fairly separated. The hair is black (204 brown, 118 medium, 10 blond). The nose, of a firm, bold line, defines their physiognomy. Not crooked and absolutely aquiline, it is straight (37%), most often convex (50%), though sometimes concave (18%), on the men. For the women, the proportion of straight noses is 66%. The nose is long. The women wear a metal stud in their nostrils. The ears tilt forward.

The face is narrow, the chin is strong. The waist is high and difficult to ascertain. The head is longer than it is wide. They are mesaticephalous (60%) but there are enormous variations according to certain localities where they have been compared with certain peoples. Hence the tribes of Armenian origin are often brachycephalous, whereas others (like the Yezidi of gypsy origins) are dolichocephalous like their neighbors, the Persians and the Arabs.

Ernest Chantre, *Les Kurdes: Esquisse Historique et Ethnographique*, 1897
Courtesy Musée de l'Homme, Paris

The general physiognomy and morphology of an individual, of a family, or of a race can without a doubt be established through direct observation and can be described with the help of qualifications, as well as by numerous photographs all taken with the same aspect— that is to say, frontal or head on, and profile of well-chosen subjects. Yet these documents, which must be thought of as indispensable, would remain incomplete if not accompanied by multiple and rigorous measurements. The proportions of the body, the shape of the eyes, of the nose, of the face, and of the head in general, can only be known and studied thanks to anthropometric research.

Ernest Chantre, *Missions Scientifiques en Transcaucasie, Asie Mineure et Syrie 1890–1894, Archives du Muséum d'Histoire Naturelle de Lyon*, 6th Volume, 1895
Courtesy The Field Museum, Chicago

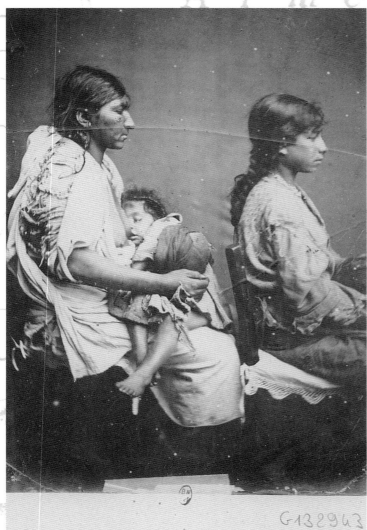

Kurdes Zazas. Diarbekir. (Kurdistan)

Kurdes Zazas. Diarbekir. (Kurdistan)

Kurdes Zazas. Diarbekir. (Kurdistan).   Kurdes Zazas. Diarbekir. (Kurdistan).

Kurdes Eydéranly. Vallée de l'Abaga. (Kurdistan)   Kurdes Eydéranly. Vallée de l'Abaga. (Kurdistan)

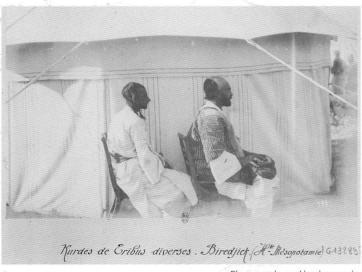

Kurdes de tribus diverses. Biredjick. (Hte Mesopotamie)   Kurdes de tribus diverses. Biredjick. (Hte Mesopotamie)

Photographs and background map from *Mission Scientifique de Mr. Ernest Chantre dans la Haute Mesopotamie, le Kurdistan et le Caucase*, "Kurdistan, de Diarbekir à Hazu, Mars à Septembre, 1881"/Bibliothèque Nationale de France, Paris

OTTOMAN EMPIRE

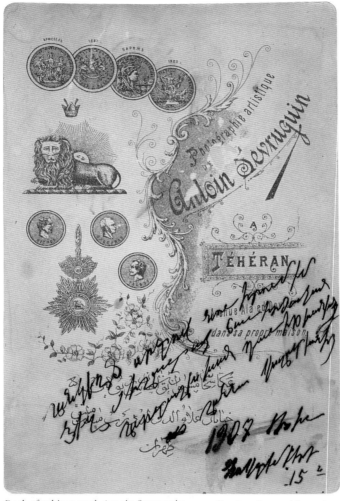

Back of cabinet card, Antoin Sevruguin   Courtesy Emanuel Sevrugian

Antoin Sevruguin
Armenian Photographer

My grandfather Antoin had the idea to start a photographic documentation of the ethnography, landscapes, and architecture of Persia. However, in those days, to put to work such an idea was quite a difficult and adventurous task. So Antoin managed to convince his two brothers . . . to join him. They started out for Persia, probably sometime in the 1870s, together with many other helpers and a big caravan. (Since they had to have separate tents for their "dark laboratory" to prepare the chemicals with which to furnish the glass-plates, etc.) . . . Finally they turned to Tehran, their birthplace, where the three brothers soon established a prosperous photographic studio, Antoin being the artistic heart of the business. . . .

When the well-known German scholar, the archaeologist Professor Sarre, from Berlin, came to Tehran, he originally intended to travel to the South of Persia himself. . . . However, at that time many southern tribes were in turmoil and the German Embassy of Tehran dissuaded him from such a dangerous expedition, but they recommended Sarre to contact my grandfather, who had the reputation to be quite an audacious man and last not least, for having good relations with many tribal chieftains (many . . . were his customers and guests whenever visiting Tehran, with many he exchanged mutual presents on Nowrooz-day; e.g., the "Kurdish girl" is the picture of the young wife of a prominent Kurdish chieftain).

Whatever Sarre did not find in the large collection of Antoin's studio he ordered from him by a formal contract. . . . Sarre used all the photographs done by Antoin under his own name (possibly because he thought it to be within his own right since he had paid for the pictures

and also had financed the expedition, although he himself had stayed in the safety of the capital). . . .

Although my grandfather had earned several prizes and medallions in international photographic exhibitions of his time, he, as well as my father, were bitter about the fact that most European scholars and tourists whenever publishing his photographic works did so either under their own names or anonymously. . . . Most of the serious or artistic photography published in European books and brochures on Iranian life and customs of the late 19th and early 20th century derived from my grandfather's studio. . . .

The destruction of the main body of Antoin's collection was a severe financial blow to the family. . . . The looting, burning and destroying were performed by Loor-tribesmen whom Mohammed Ali-Shah had called into Tehran in order to terrify and check the Constitutionalists of Tehran. . . . My father remembers well that he as a youngster and his uncle Emanuel (my grandfather's brother) kept the inventory of far more than 7,000 glass-plate negatives. However, after the house was put to sack they could collect or could restore by immense patience only about two thousand glass-plate negatives from the debris (my grandfather Antoin himself, being too heartbroken, did not participate in that tremendous work of assembling the remainders). . . .

During the reign of Reza Shah I . . . the remaining two thousand glass-plate negatives of the original collection were officially confiscated, since the Shah did not want any traits of the pre-modern Persia to exist.

Letters from Emanuel Sevrugian, grandson of Antoin Sevruguin,
to the Freer Gallery of Art, November 5 and 27, 1990

1890s

"Juive," wife of a Kurdish chieftain, ca. 1890–95

PERSIA

Mr. Young reported that the Segruvian [sic] negatives, a famous collection known to all Persian scholars, have been given by Segruvian's heiress to the American (Presbyterian) Mission in Tehran with instructions that they be sold for the benefit of the Mission. . . . Segruvian was court photographer to Nasr al-Din Shah and his immediate successors; he accompanied the Shah on his royal progresses and recorded personages, monuments, costumes, types and manners. . . . [T]hey form a precious record of a fast-disappearing way of life.

Myron Bement Smith, Chairman, Committee for Islamic Culture,
Minutes of Fourth Meeting, September 15, 1951
Courtesy Freer Gallery of Art and Arthur M. Sackler Gallery Archives

My working method has been to expand and to enrich my geographical, chronological, and subject files with whatever pertinent information comes to eye. Whenever in my reading I see a statement that may have bearing on a monument, a document, or a problem, I type its text or import as a note . . . and drop it in the file beside the field note or the photograph. . . .

The purpose behind this juxtaposition of datum and opinion is to create an aura of history around each document, to enhance its identity, and to relate it to problems which scholars have proposed or believe they may have solved. . . .

The central document in the Islamic Archives is the photograph. . . .

What is needed, therefore, is a central repository. . . . There the photographic documents . . . can be assembled and inter-filed with typed and other documents—extended captions, bibliographies, field notes, excerpts from the literature, notes on problems, etc., supplementing the information in the photographic image. . . . Such a photograph collection . . . can offer scholars and students the intellectual stimulus of ideas without walls, a fresh educational resource not bounded by words.

"The Islamic Archives: Genesis, Philosophy, and Significance," from Myron Bement
Smith to the First World Congress of Iranologists, Tehran, September 5, 1966
Courtesy Freer Gallery of Art and Arthur M. Sackler Gallery Archives

The Sevruguin family, undated

Kurdish chiefs, undated

1890s

"Kurdesse," ca. 1890–1910

Camp opposite the village of Shamsabad

Isabella L. Bird
British Traveler

Kurdistan is scarcely a "geographical expression," and colloquially the word is used to cover the country inhabited by the Kurds. They are a mysterious people, having maintained themselves in their original seats and in a condition of semi-independence through all the changes which have passed over Western Asia. . . .

In the evening . . . two other Persian-speaking Kurds hovered so much about my tent that I invited them into the veranda and had a long and pleasant talk with them. . . . They said they had heard of Europeans travelling in Persia to see mines, to dig among ruins for treasure, and to collect medicinal herbs, but they could not understand why I am travelling. I replied that I was travelling in order to learn something of the condition of the people, and was interested likewise in their religion and the prospects of Christianity. "Very good, it is well," they replied; "Islam never recedes, nor can Christianity advance. . . ."

The subject of Christian missions in Persia is a very interesting one, and many thoughtful minds are asking whether Christianity is likely to be a factor in the future of the Empire? As things are, no direct efforts to convert Moslems to Christianity can be made, for the death penalty for apostasy is not legally abolished, and even if it were, popular fanaticism would vent itself upon proselytes.

Meeting Dr. Cochrane

The profession of Dr. Cochrane [missionary doctor] opens to him homes and hearts everywhere. All hold him as a friend and benefactor, and he has opportunities, denied to all others, of expounding the Christian faith among Moslems. A letter from him is a safe-conduct through some parts of the Kurdish mountains, and the mere mention of his name is a passport to the good-will of their fierce inhabitants. . . .

He and some of the younger missionaries were born in Persia, their fathers having been missionaries before them, and after completing their education in America they returned, not only with an intimate knowledge of etiquette and custom, as well as of Syriac and Persian, but with that thorough sympathy with the people whom they are there to help and instruct, which it is difficult to gain in a single generation, and through languages not acquired in childhood. Dr. Cochrane has had many and curious dealings with the Kurds, the dreaded inhabitants of the mountains which overhang the beautiful plain of Urmi, and a Kurd, who appears to be in perpetual "warpaint," is the gatekeeper at the Dispensary. . . .

When Obeidullah Khan, with 11,000 Kurds, laid siege to Urmi . . . Kahn sent for Dr. Cochrane, saying that he wished to know his residence and who his people were, so as to see that none of them suffered at the hands of his men. Not only this, but he asked the names of the Christian villages on the plain, and gave the Hakim letters with orders that nothing should be touched which belonged to them. . . .

Obeidullah kept his word, and for the sake of the Hakim and his healing art, not only was not a hair on the head of any missionary touched, but the mixed multitude within the gates and the herds were likewise spared.

Isabella L. Bird, *Journeys in Persia and Kurdistan*, Vol. II, 1891

"The southern end of the Kuh-i-Jehanbin (the world-viewing mountain) is seen to the right. . . . The mules are eating their morning chopped straw, on which they will march 30 miles, carrying 300 to 400 lbs. without touching anything again till sundown. . . . Breakfast is cooking, and the village cattle are beginning to file over the foot bridge, making for the spring pastures a little way up the mountain slopes. . . . Elevation 6,600'." —Isabella L. Bird

PERSIA

Dr. Joseph Plumb Cochran
American Missionary Doctor

A riding whip serves to stir a village patient's potion

Dr. Cochran working in the Urmia mission

Two weeks ago I returned from a trip to Nochea, a district in Kurdistan, two and a half days distant. I went to pay a visit to Sheikh Obeidullah, who considers himself the third man in ecclesiastical rank in Islam. He is also the civil monarch of the Kurds. He has seemed disposed for some years past to get into closer relations with us and the civilized world. . . . He has several times sent to us, asking that we put him in a way of getting such help from the British government. Last year before entering on a campaign against the Turks, to whom he had up to that time paid tribute, he sent confidential agents to us repeating this request. . . . After inflicting considerable damage on the Turkish frontier, an understanding was come to by which the Sheikh and his people were made practically independent of that government. . . .

For a number of years this Sheikh has appeared very friendly to us, often sending kind messages and invitations to have us visit him. A few weeks ago he was taken severely ill, and therefore sent, asking me to make him a visit. . . . After a ride of five hours . . . we rode up to the Kurdish mosque, we were met by a large number of the villagers who welcomed us among them. I was guided into the quarters set apart for us. To get to this apartment I followed my leader through numerous dark passages. . . . A most stifling, highly-perfumed moist air, greeted us. Groping my way in the darkness, I found myself a seat in a corner. Into this room were brought some of our horses, baggage, and saddles, and soon after supper was served. A sheepskin was brought in for the table, and in it was the bread. Spreading the skin on the floor, roasted lamb, cheese, honey, and milk were placed on it. After supper we sat around a flickering light. . . . I described to my companions the conveniences and luxuriance of some of the American hotels, and we all strove to imagine ourselves quartered in one of those palaces. . . .

During the week that I stayed at his house, I had many very pleasant talks with him. He was very much interested in hearing about the new inventions and other wonders of the Western world. . . . The majority of the people whom I saw came to me, as well to be treated, as to see me for curiosity or other reasons, so that I saw and treated a very large number of Kurds in my absence from home.

Dr. Cochran, quoted in R. E. Speer,
The Foreign Doctor, 1911

August 2, 1880—*The Sheikh's son sent word that he would come Saturday at sundown. So we sent for the Mussulman cooks; they only can prepare pillau; then we had about ninety pounds of rice picked over, two lambs killed, ice brought, etc. We set the table in the parlour. . . . It was a strange sight, at least it would have been to you, these wild Kurds, very richly dressed, and all armed with swords and pistols, sitting down to a table daintily arranged with flowers and silver, and with ladies, for the first time, I presume. Those near the Sheikh's son behaved well, and did well with knives and forks, and napkins, but those at the opposite end played and mussed like little children. . . .*

October 11—*The Governor of the city was here to call. He says the Persians are determined to fight it out with the Sheikh. We are placed in a rather difficult position. Of course we ought to maintain a neutral position, being friends of both parties, but the Sheikh keeps sending Joe letters, which makes the Persians think that we are in league with him, and of course if we betray anything to the Governor, the Sheikh would be displeased. . . .*

The report is now that 150 villages were sacked by the Sheikh's son . . . and the inhabitants massacred, and over 4,000 people must have perished in all. And to think that the man who ordered all this cruelty sat at our table at Seir a few months ago! . . .

October 18—*Yesterday a letter came from the Sheikh's brother-in-law, who is in command of the army now advancing, saying that he was responsible that no non-combatants, Nestorian or Mussulman, should be hurt, that it was not his design to harm the people of the country. This was in reply to a letter Joe sent him, asking him to abstain from any violence to the people. He also asked that we send him a little tea, but I fear that the Persians would consider this giving aid to the enemy. . . .*

November 12—*It's worse than trying to serve both God and Mammon, this endeavouring to keep on good terms with both Persians and Kurds. . . .*

Letter from Dr. Cochran's wife to her family, quoted in R. E. Speer, *The Foreign Doctor*, 1911

Dr. Cochran with Kurdish chieftain

We are also a nation apart. We want our affairs to be in our own hands, so that in the punishment of our own offenders we may be strong and independent, and have privileges like other nations; and respecting our offenders, we are ready to take upon ourselves that no harm or damage shall accrue to any nation.

*Yusuf Bey of Köshk, Kurdish chief,
eastern Turkey, 1893*

H.F.B. Lynch/The British Library, London

H.F.B. Lynch
British Traveler

*A shower of soft rain was falling as we entered Köshk at four o'clock. . . .
Köshk is distinguished by a single house in the proper sense, a two-
storeyed building of stone. It is the abode of Yusuf Bey, chieftain of the
Sipkanli, whose portrait I was allowed to take. His followers gathered
round us, a throng of Kurdish warriors, prepared at any moment for
a fight. Besides knives, each man carried a rifle; a band of cartridges
was fastened across the breast. I examined several weapons; all
bore the Russian marks and letters. They told me that they were
procured from the Russian soldiers, probably Cossacks, in the frontier
districts of Kagyzman and Erivan. . . .*

*Yusef Bey . . . and his brother are men of more than ordinary
proportions, and both are true types of the Kurd. He told me that they
were in daily expectation of attack from Hoseyn Pasha of Patnotz. This
miscreant, although under the ban of justice, had been given the title
of Pasha by the Turkish Government, partly in order to recruit their
new irregulars among his tribe, and partly as a recompense for his
bribes. He had quite recently burnt some villages of the Sipkanli, and
had reduced the clan to poverty. Judging from the finery which was
displayed by the inhabitants of Köshk, I could only accept the latter
part of this statement in a very relative sense. . . .*

*Among the forty tenements which constituted this particular
settlement we were astonished to find that six were inhabited by
Armenians. Imagine the condition of these poor people, in the very
jaws of their enemy, who just allows them to exist and no more! The
Turkish authorities, a long way distant, would be quite powerless to
assist them, even if they had the desire.*

*A poor stableman told us beneath his breath that their lot was
desperate, and that some of his countrymen had contrived to escape
to Russia.*

H.F.B. Lynch, *Armenia: Travels and Studies*, 1901

*Kurd of Köshk in gala dress with his subterranean
village in the distance, eastern Turkey, 1893*

Young Kurd woman at Gotni, Mush Plain, 1893

1893

Hamidiye cavalry at Gumgum, 1890

Eyub Pasha (seated), Hamidiye officers

Encounter with the Hamidiyeh

The Kurdish village of Gotni . . . situated at the foot of the southern border range . . . was the first village inhabited by Mohammedans in which I was allowed to photograph the women. I obtained this favour by dint of considerable cajolery and judicious presents to the elders and to the ladies themselves. . . .

One of my models was a damsel of no little beauty—a full-blooded, strapping girl. It was evident that she was the belle of the whole settlement, and she was certainly an exception and a contrast to the lank creatures who were her comrades. . . . (My photograph of the belle of Gotni displays such a lack of good features that I must refrain from reproducing it for fear of belying my impression. In its place I offer a picture of one of the best-looking of her less flourishing comrades.)

The fashionable amusement of the day were the Hamidiyeh. A

luxurious coffee-house had just been built for their delectation; their name was on every tongue. . . . The Hamidiyeh are irregular cavalry, who owe their origin to the endeavour of the Sultan Abdul Hamid to emulate the example which gave to Russia her Cossack troops. They are recruited for the most part among the Kurdish tribes; the name of yeomanry expresses the nature of their military service, but cannot be applied to the class to which they belong. . . .

Some of the principal officers are represented in my illustrations; and I would beg my reader to observe the seated Kurd in the Georgian dress—it is Eyub Pasha with his son and nephew. Behind him stands his principal henchman, who, although a Kurd, has seen service with regular troops.

H.F.B. Lynch, *Armenia: Travels and Studies*, 1901

OTTOMAN EMPIRE

Emma Barnum
American Missionary

You have no doubt heard already of our trials, and I trust of our personal safety, through the Papers. And now I will try to give you an account of what has taken place.

All this fall there were rumors which made the Americans fear greatly for their lives. The Turks intimated that something was to take place. It was reported that arms were secretly given out to the Turks by the Government. Koords attacked villages, first only to carry off the sheep belonging to Armenians, then they grew bolder and plundered the houses, carrying off everything that the poor people possessed and killing many. They told the Armenians that they were carrying out the orders of the Sultan. Riots and massacres occurred in the large cities, and as the Koords came nearer and nearer to the City the people were in great terror. . . .

We were told that the Turks had the impression that we had 500 martini rifles, and a great deal of dynamite and bombs, that Papa had photographed the refugees who had come in, and that it was he who was causing this fear in the City. He went out at once to some of the chief men and denied the charges. He invited them to come and search our houses for weapons, although it was contrary to regulations—and said he was willing to do anything to help in restoring confidence. . . .

We hear that the Sultan has given orders that we are to be protected. We have had four telegrams from our Minister. He seems in earnest to secure our safety, and we feel that it is insured, but it will take a long time for the country to settle down.

The Turks have brought great pressure upon the Armenians to deny their faith, telling them that if they do not at once accept the Turkish religion they would be killed at once and their wives and children would be taken to Turkish harems. Thus many have died a martyr's death and many others have denied their Savior. Of course there can be no more school, at least for this year. If we can only get the funds we have a great relief work opened to us. Our life and work has been suddenly changed, and I don't see how we shall ever be able to go back to the old life again. God has spared our life, and He must have something for us to do. We can trust Him for the future, however dark it does seem now.

We hear that the Turks have sent a telegram to Constantinople which they obliged many Armenians to sign, saying that the American Missionaries were the cause of the massacre and riot, and asking to have us removed. But it would be a sad day for the Christians if we should be obliged to leave. . . .

It is bed time and I must say goodnight, and send my love to the dear Aunties and friends who will see this letter.

We are in God's keeping and we can trust Him for our own safety and future, and that of all our dear friends. I know you will pray for us and these poor people. Remember especially those who have denied Christ, and pray that the doors may soon be opened for us to carry the Truth to the Turks.

Very lovingly yours,
Emma Barnum

Letter from Emma Barnum, November 18, 1895
Manuscript Division, Library of Congress, Washington, D.C.

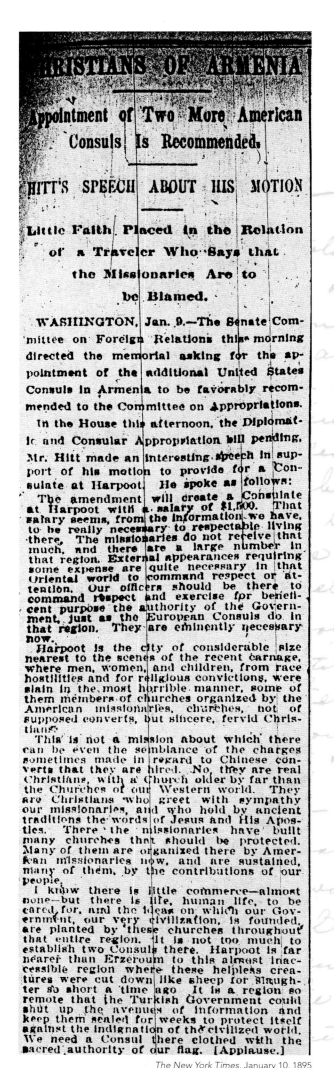

CHRISTIANS OF ARMENIA

Appointment of Two More American Consuls Is Recommended.

HITT'S SPEECH ABOUT HIS MOTION

Little Faith Placed in the Relation of a Traveler Who Says that the Missionaries Are to be Blamed.

WASHINGTON, Jan. 9.—The Senate Committee on Foreign Relations this morning directed the memorial asking for the appointment of the additional United States Consuls in Armenia to be favorably recommended to the Committee on Appropriations.

In the House this afternoon, the Diplomatic and Consular Appropriation bill pending, Mr. Hitt made an interesting speech in support of his motion to provide for a Consulate at Harpoot. He spoke as follows:

The amendment will create a Consulate at Harpoot with a salary of $1,500. That salary seems, from the information we have, to be really necessary to respectable living there. The missionaries do not receive that much, and there are a large number in that region. External appearances requiring some expense are quite necessary in that Oriental world to command respect or attention. Our officers should be there to command respect and exercise for beneficent purpose the authority of the Government, just as the European Consuls do in that region. They are eminently necessary now.

Harpoot is the city of considerable size nearest to the scenes of the recent carnage, where men, women, and children, from race hostilities and for religious convictions, were slain in the most horrible manner, some of them members of churches organized by the American missionaries, churches, not of supposed converts, but sincere, fervid Christians.

This is not a mission about which there can be even the semblance of the charges sometimes made in regard to Chinese converts that they are hired. No, they are real Christians, with a Church older by far than the Churches of our Western world. They are Christians who greet with sympathy our missionaries, and who hold by ancient traditions the words of Jesus and His Apostles. There the missionaries have built many churches that should be protected. Many of them are organized there by American missionaries now, and are sustained, many of them, by the contributions of our people.

I know there is little commerce—almost none—but there is life, human life, to be cared for, and the ideas on which our Government, our very civilization, is founded, are planted by these churches throughout that entire region. It is not too much to establish two Consuls there. Harpoot is far nearer than Erzeroum to this almost inaccessible region where these helpless creatures were cut down like sheep for slaughter so short a time ago. It is a region so remote that the Turkish Government could shut up the avenues of information and keep them sealed for weeks to protect itself against the indignation of the civilized world. We need a Consul there clothed with the sacred authority of our flag. [Applause.]

The New York Times, January 10, 1895

Harpoot, Turkey —
November 18, 1895.

My dear Aunties.

It seems a long, long time since I have written you, so much has happened. I could only send you a hurried note last week as I had a good deal of writing to do for my father. I wonder whether all our letters have reached you and whether this even will go through.

You have no doubt heard already of our trials, and I trust of our personal safety, through the Papers. And now I will try to give you an account of what has taken place.

All this fall there were rumors which made the Armenians fear greatly for their lives. The Turks intimated that some thing was to take place — It was reported that arms were secretly given out to the Turks by the Government — Koords attacked villages. first only to carry off the sheep belonging to Armenians, then they grew bolder and plundered the houses. carrying off every thing that the poor people possessed and killing

ASIA

TURKISH ASIA
Kurdish Tent

The Kurds are nomadic Muslims who live in Armenia. They do not get along with the Armenians, who are Catholics. They massacred Armenians to such an extent that many of the latter emigrated on their own to Europe.

The price of the album is 3 francs. To collect these lovely pictures, buy at your local store for ■ francs, the superb album entitled ASIA, published by PUPIER CHOCOLATES. Nice gifts will be given to the collectors who present one or several completed albums to us.

Translation of inserted card

Armenian Massacre: The Capuchin fathers of Malatia are held prisoner

ARMENIAN MASSACRE

The Capuchin Fathers of Malatia, Prisoners in a Barracks
(29 October–9 November 1895)

The Christian inhabitants of all the localities within the vilayet of Mamouret have partly been massacred. Those who were able to escape were forced to convert to Islam. In Malatia, the Kurds and the Turks threw themselves on the Christians, and the massacres and looting continued for six days. The Armenians took refuge in churches to escape the looting and burning. The Catholic Capuchins were ill-treated and beaten. Their house, their school, and their church were burned. Transported to a barracks, they remained there without food for three days and three nights, objects of the mockery and insults of their guards.

The monastery of Our Lady of Aiguebelle, established in the year 1045, is situated in an isolated valley in the province of Drôme. The celebration of the HOLY OFFICE, MANUAL LABOR, and STUDY divide the Trappist's day. Manual labor is, in our time, for the religious of the Trappists, not only a rule of law, but also an absolute necessity. Their only resources derive from farming and more specifically from the production of AIGUEBELLE CHOCOLATE.

Translation of inserted card

Cards inserted in boxes of chocolate manufactured by Capuchin fathers

Translated by Stuart Alexander/Courtesy Pierre de Gigord

1895

Armenian Massacre: The death of Franciscan father Salvatore

ARMENIAN MASSACRE

The Defense of Gurun by the Armenians
(12 November 1895)

Armenian Massacre: The Armenians defend Gurun

In a ten-kilometer radius around Gurun most Armenian villages were destroyed and their inhabitants massacred. Finally, the city of Gurun was laid siege to by two thousand Kurds who are now believed to have been in disguise. The besieged, numbering four thousand—old people, men, women, and children—resisted for four days; a thousand of them, hidden in a church, gave up their arms and were spared. One does not know the exact number of victims, but we know that on November 28 *(fourteen days after the massacres)* twelve hundred corpses lay in the streets; a thousand Armenian homes had been burned; and five hundred pillaged, as well as all the churches, and one hundred and fifty women or young girls had been kidnapped by the Kurds.

Translation of inserted card

Armenian Massacre: Removal of the victims in Galata

The Riots in Constantinople

Every despatch from Constantinople brings fresh details of the massacres of Armenians that followed on the seizure of the Ottoman Bank by Armenian revolutionaries. On August 26, about two o'clock in the afternoon, some forty Armenians seized the premises of the Ottoman Bank, killing the gendarmes who were on guard and the porters at the entrance. . . . A correspondent, who was an eye-witness of the riot and of the subsequent massacres, says that the fight at the bank went on until one o'clock. . . . Amid the crowd in the streets which had quickly collected were seen groups of Mussulmans and Kurds, all armed with bludgeons, iron staves, or clubs, and acting under the direction of men in turbans, who were evidently Softas. These gangs chiefly sought out Armenians, but often they struck down passers-by indiscriminately. The scene soon resembled that of the carnage of last September. In all quarters of the city Armenians were brutally murdered. One of our correspondents sent a sketch of massacres in the streets of Galata, where the Mussulman thirst for blood seemed to reach a climax; and another of some Armenian porters who tried to escape from the savage Kurds by throwing themselves into the sea opposite the Custom House at Stamboul. While in the water these wretched men were clubbed to death by the Mussulman boatmen. In front of the guard-house at the Galata end of the bridge the rabble was slaughtering Armenians in the most cold-blooded fashion in the presence of the commander of the troops, several aides-de-camp of the Sultan, and last, but not least, the general commanding the Hamidieh regiment which recently arrived here. . . . During Wednesday night and the whole of Thursday the city was given over to the Mussulman populace, who murdered and pillaged Armenians without hindrance from the police. . . . The representatives of the Powers have sent a collective note to the Forte demanding an inquiry, and that the guilty parties shall be punished. The Forte, replying to the note, threw all the responsibility on the Armenians. The Embassies merely acknowledged the receipt of the note, and declined to discuss it. . . . Sir Philip Currie, the British Ambassador, arrived in Constantinople at the end of last week, and has at once joined with the other representatives in their Note urging the Sultan to punish those guilty of the shocking crimes which have disgraced Turkey in the eyes of Europe.

The Graphic, British weekly magazine, September 12, 1896
Courtesy *The Illustrated London News*, London

DRAWN BY W. SMALL

The Hamidieh Cavalry, formed five years ago out of the unmanageable Kurdish tribes, was incorporated in the Turkish Army, it is said, for the purpose of checking the too rapid advance of the Armenian race, and the history of last winter shows how effectively they performed their duty. The Sultan is now desirous to have peace in Asia Minor, and hearing from

Shakir Pasha, the Gener dinate and still thirsted f large number of these tro is glad to have these ru

THE RIOTS IN CONSTANTINOPLE: THE

FROM A SKETCH BY AN EYE WITNESS

ARRIVAL OF THE HAMIDIEH CAVALRY FROM ARMENIA

pector in Armenia, that the Kurds were inclined to be insubor- odshed and plunder, thought to ease the situation by ordering a to come to Constantinople. Another reason why Abdul Hamid near him is that he is suspicious of the guards around his palace.

His own safety depends on the mutual enmity of his guards and these Kurds. The Hamidieh Regiment is regarded with suspicion by the European residents in Constantinople, who remember the disorderly behaviour of their officers when the first regiment was formed

Sir Mark Sykes
British Officer

The Pasha, whom I had visited before, came out to meet us, and embraced me after the Bedawin fashion—that is, by kissing my right shoulder. I was immediately led into the great tent, which was supported on over 100 poles and measured 1,500 square yards of cloth. Coming from the glare of the mid-day sun it was at first difficult to distinguish anything clearly in the recesses of this vast tabernacle, but at the farther end about 150 men were standing around the low divan on which Ibrahim sits. He led me to the divan, which was placed before a camel-dung fire, on which stood the usual number of coffee-pots.

The Pasha was a tall, slimly-built man, with a purely Kurdish face with a large lumpy nose, rather piercing inquisitive eyes, a fairly high forehead, and a large mouth. In repose his face had a rather sinister expression, being fixed in that settled frown common to all tent-dwellers who live in a sunlit desert; and this grim and thoughtful look was not lessened by a sword-cut under the eye, which caused the lower lid to droop. In conversation, however, his continual smile was open and pleasing, and his manner almost genial. In curious contrast to his face, his hands and feet were extremely small and delicately formed. In the course of conversation he showed a wonderfully accurate knowledge of the affairs of Europe, England's relations with Ireland, and many matters which pointed to other sources of information than Turkish newspapers, of which of course he has a plentiful supply.

Sir Mark Sykes, *The Caliph's Last Heritage: A Short History of the Turkish Empire*, 1915

IBRAHIM. PASHA.

"His photograph will give you some idea of the man. Ibrahim Pasha's mother was an Arab of the noblest race, his father a Kurdish chieftain of renown. In Ibrahim we find the racial characteristics of both his parents—the constructive and practical powers of the Kurd combined with the mental faculties and humanity of the Arab."
—*Mark Sykes*

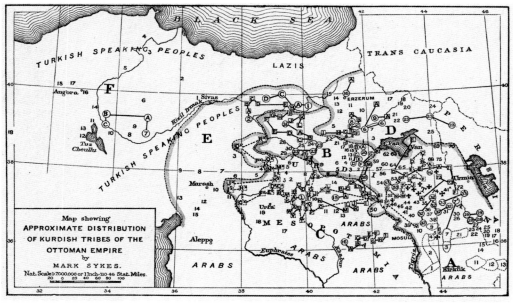

Unknown/Lilly Library, University of Indiana

"The materials collected in the ensuing pages are the results of about 7,500 miles of riding and innumerable conversations with policemen, muleteers, mullahs, chieftains, sheep drivers, horse dealers, carriers and other people capable of giving one first hand information. The results, I fear, are extremely meagre, but I hope they may prove of use to future travellers. . . . In preparing the following list of the various tribes of the Kurdish race . . . I have decided for the purposes of this work to break up the regions inhabited by Kurds into six zones [A–F]; . . . the zones marked on the map are not ethnological but merely a convenient form of grouping."
—*Mark Sykes*

Dear Mr. Scott Keltie,
I am very sorry to hear that you think the tribe list insufficient. . . . At present the Kurds as a people are "terra incognita"—this as far as I know is the first attempt to get them into any kind of order—as you see I have barely scratched the surface. . . .

The work I have in hand will not be published for at least 18 months and I should be sorry to think that travellers should be debarred from having a rough sketch of the Kurdish people with which to start operations of investigation. . . . I have shown the list to many consuls and others who all agreed that it would have been very useful to them. Further it is quite sound from a scientific point of view as I have neither theorised nor romanced. . . .

Yrs very sincerely,
Mark Sykes

P.S. To make detailed investigations of the Kurds will take 30 savants about 15 years.

Letter, March 15, 1907,
Royal Geographical Society, London

1907

Ibrahim's first remarks were very characteristic—Had the Algeciras conference really broken down? And was it true that Sarah Bernhardt's theatrical travelling tent was larger than his? . . .

It was not long after the close of the Russo-Turkish War that Ibrahim began to give proofs of his ability and foresight. His first act was to make firm friends with the sturdy little colony of Circassians at Ras-el-Ain, and then to gather under his dominion the lesser Shaykhs of the surrounding tribes, and to part them from their own people, in this way securing parties of 100 and 200 tents at a time. . . . Ibrahim's policy consisted in being friendly to the strong, conciliating the weaker, and bullying only the weakest. . . .

Ibrahim, together with some other Kurdish chiefs, was enrolled in the Hamidieh, and after visiting Constantinople was promoted to the rank of Brigadier-General and given the rank of Pasha. After this his policy grew bolder. . . . He encouraged Christians (Armenians and Chaldaeans) to take refuge in the vicinity of Viranshehr, and established a bazaar in that town, which rapidly increased in size. While other tribes and chiefs plundered and massacred Armenians, Ibrahim protected and encouraged Christians of all denominations. It is estimated that during the great Armenian massacres he saved some 10,000 Armenians from destruction. . . . He has spies in every town in the district, and in his camp has established a refuge for robbers and evil-doers on condition that they behave themselves while in his district.

Ibrahim Pasha is a very strange character. . . . In him we see the feudal baron and the eastern despot and the nomadic chief; amid his tents we may glean some idea of the life in the camps of Timur and Attila; in his rise to power, there is some suggestion of the early success of the Osmanlis—in his weakness and strength, some of the faults and qualities of Mithridates. . . .

When, perchance, a man appears whose craft is only equalled by his political astuteness, then we see the extraordinary phenomenon of a feeble invalid, such as Ibrahim, ruling a host of divided and untamable peoples.

The day following our arrival the Pasha gave orders to strike camp and move. The whole of the baggage train, which numbered no fewer than 2,000 animals, was on the march in an hour and a half from the issuing of the order, a little more than that time being required to pitch the camp. . . . On the march the Pasha rode a young white dallul (trotting camel) at the head of the caravan, accompanied by 50 horsemen of his private staff and a pack of about 15 couple of gazelle dogs—the whole forming a sufficiently striking picture.

During the whole of my five days' sojourn with Ibrahim, affairs were continually being carried on in the great tent. . . . Horsemen with messages, letters, and despatches were continually coming and going on all kinds of business, which the Pasha transacted with extraordinary celerity, never seeming to have to pause to think and always appearing certain of his own mind.

Sir Mark Sykes, *The Caliph's Last Heritage: A Short History of the Turkish Empire*, 1915

Sir Mark Sykes/British Public Record Office, Kew
F078/5395

1 Ibrahim Pasha's youngest son—
2 " " " eldest son & probable successor
3 Ibrahim Pasha
4. His Chief Officer
5. His Doctor.
6. Circassian A.D.C.
7. Haiderauli Refugee
8. Kurdish Agha
9. Shammar Arab
10. Armenian Merchant

Ibrahim Pasha & myself.

Monastery of Mar Behnam (twelfth to fourteenth century), 1909

Gertrude Bell
British Archaeologist

I have written of politics & of commerce, of steamships & of locomotive engines but I have not pronounced the word which is the key note of the 'Iraq. It is romance. Wherever you may look for it you shall find it. The great twin rivers, gloriously named; the huge Babylonian plains, now desert, which were once a garden of the world; the story stretching back into the dark recesses of time—they shout romance. No less insistent on the imagination & no less brilliantly coloured, are the later chapters in the history of the 'Iraq. The echoing name of Alexander haunts them, the jewelled splendours of the Sasanian King of Kings, the clanging fame of the Mohammedan Khalifate, the tragic dissolution of the Mongol invasion, & last (to English ears not least) the enterprise, the vigour, the courage of our seamen & merchants who forced their path through the gates of the 'Iraq & brought the Pax Britannica into the torrid seas of the Persian Gulf.

Chapter of an unfinished, unpublished, and undated manuscript by Gertrude Bell
Miscellaneous 20; The Robinson Library, University of Newcastle-upon-Tyne

January 29, 1909
There is a moment, too, when one is newly arrived in the East, when one is conscious of the world shrinking at one end and growing at the other till all the perspective of life is changed—after a few days it becomes a common place and one notices it no more. Existence suddenly seems to be a very simple matter and one wonders why we plan a scheme, weary ourselves with hurrying—after nothing . . . when all we need do is to live and make sure of a succeeding generation.

Letter from Gertrude Bell in Port Said to her mother, Florence Bell,
The Robinson Library, University of Newcastle-upon-Tyne

1909

*Some day, I hope the East will be strong
again and develop its own civilization,
not imitate ours, and then perhaps
it will teach us a few things we once
learnt from it and have now forgotten,
to our great loss.* —Gertrude Bell

May 4, 1909

*I . . . rode through blazing heat across the plains of Assyria, deep in
corn. The peasants were harvesting the barley and close on their heels,
the locusts alas! were harvesting the wheat, which is still green. It was
so hot that I had to go into a house, in a village I passed, to lunch. Early
in the afternoon we came to Mar Behnam where there is a wonderful
Jacobite monastery, an ancient mound with a round pool at its feet,
and a little village. I photographed and took notes in the monastery all
the afternoon. My tents were pitched on the slopes of the mound and I
sat and watched the people watering their flocks at the pool while the
moon rose over Assyria and found it, I expect, very little changed.*

Gertrude Bell Letters, The Robinson Library,
University of Newcastle-upon-Tyne

MESOPOTAMIA

Gateway between courts U and V, W Arch,
Palace of Khusrau, Iran, 1911

Friday, March 24, 1911
Exquisite morning. I got out to the ruins about 6:30. . . .
Worked till 2 at the small palace. Fattuh sending me
out lunch. . . . Then moved over to the big palace where
Daoud Khan's son came to see me. Worked till 5 while
the Kurds amused themselves with rifle practice.
——Gertrude Bell

1911

32

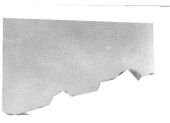

Tuesday, March 28, 1911
About 1 o'clock we reached Kasri Shirin which stands most beautifully on the river Helwan, a straggling street climbing the hill side, the great fort of Kerim Khan standing on top. . . . I interviewed the Khans (there were a great many of them) and told them I was going to work in the ruins . . . a couple of great Sassanian palaces. . . . I found my servants camping near the first palace and a little upset because two bullets had whizzed past their ears while they were riding up to it. . . .

A good many people came out to see me in the course of the afternoon and they all assured me that we should be greatly troubled by thieves if we spent the night there. I remained skeptical as to the thieves, but there was no doubt about the rifle bullets, and it is almost as annoying to be shot by accident as on purpose. . . . I worked for the next two days at the palaces without so much as turning round. I went out to the ruins at 6 a.m. and remained there till 9 p.m. and I never stopped for a moment drawing, measuring and photographing except when Fattuh sent or brought me lunch and tea. It is almost more than the human frame can bear when you have got to struggle through such an undertaking single-handed, and I wished several times that the Sassanians had never been born.

Lady Bell, *The Letters of Gertrude Bell*, 1927

Fattuh drinking tea, near Altun Kenpra, Iraq, 1911

Gertrude Bell/University of Newcastle-upon-Tyne

Yezidi sanctuary at Lalish

We were now entering the country which is the headquarters of the Yezîdîs, who, from their desire to conciliate or propitiate the Spirit of Evil, are known to Moslem and Christian as Devil Worshippers. By Moslem and by Christian they have been placed beyond the bounds of human kindness, and while the Mohammadan has been unremitting in his efforts to bring them, by methods familiar to dominant creeds, to a sense of their short-comings, the Christian has regarded the wholesale butchery which has overtaken them from time to time as a punishment justified by their tenets. . . . I carried a letter to 'Alî Beg, the head of the sect, and proposed to visit him in his village of Ba'adri and to see, if he would permit, the most sacred of all Yezîdî shrines, Sheikh 'Adî.

The Yezîdîs, being of Kurdish race, do not differ in appearance from the rest of the population, except in one particular of their attire: they abhor the colour blue and eschew it in their dress, but red they regard as a beneficent hue, and their women are mostly clothed in dark-red cotton garments.

The village of Ba'adri clings to the green slopes of the foot-hills, and 'Alî Beg's whitewashed house stands over it like a miniature fortress. The beg received me in his divan with the utmost cordiality. . . . The Yezîdî women are neither secluded nor veiled, and when 'Alî Beg took me to see his wife we found her in the midst of her household, male and female, giving orders for my entertainment. . . . Meantime the beg had made preparations for my visit to Sheikh 'Adî, whither two Yezîdi horsemen and all my four zaptiehs were ordered to accompany me, lest we should meet with Kurdish robbers in the hills. 'Alî Beg with a dignified retinue of elders, watched our departure. . . .

After a climb of close upon two hours, we reached the summit of the hill and the path dipped down through sturdier oak woods, into a secluded valley, out of the heart of which rose the fluted spires of Sheikh 'Adî, a sanctuary and a tiny village embosomed in planes and mulberries and ancient fig-trees. The khatun . . . came to meet me with a black cap upon her head and a heavy linen veil thrown over it and drawn tightly under her chin. . . .

We passed through a doorway into a small paved court, still and peaceful and half-shaded by mulberries. The further side was bounded by the wall of the shrine, which opens into the court by a single door. Upon the wall near the door a snake is carved in relief upon the stones and painted black. With a singular magnetic attraction it catches and holds the eye, and the little court owes to its presence much of the indefinable sense of mystery which hangs over it as surely as hang the spreading branches of the mulberry-trees.

Gertrude Bell, *Amurath to Amurath*, 1911

The khatun at the door of Sheikh Adi

Gertrude Bell/University of Newcastle-upon-Tyne

MESOPOTAMIA

Saring Mahmoud

Yezidi Chief

My father, Saring Mahmoud (Farizian Sarink Mahmoudovich), was the head of several villages in the Kars region. They had cattle, but he was not a farmer. At that time, there was great pressure from the Turks to become Muslim. The territory around us was Kurdish. Our families did not marry them, but we didn't fight each other. In the same village as my father, lived Janghir Agha, the great Yezidi leader, who began to fight the Turks in the early 1900s.

My mother was from the Armenian village of Mirak. She was fourteen years old when someone came from her village and told my father about her. At that time, it wasn't difficult to cross the border. My father went to get her, and brought some jewels. Her family accepted him, he, of course, paid something, and so she left with him.

Still today, relatives make the negotiations and still must pay. A man can have four wives.

In 1914, Turkish troops came to the region. My father fled with his whole family to the village of Sarghez in Soviet Armenia where his aunt lived. The village was in the mountains. There were only a few Armenians, but the school, of course, was in the Armenian language.

Interview with Akim Saringovich Farizian,
Yezidi agronomist living in Georgia, July 1996

Background: *Yezidis during morning prayer, Yerevan province*
Dmitri Yermakov

Saring Mahmoud, 1915

Saring Mahmoud with his family, undated
Courtesy Akim Saringovich Farizian

Zakho Kurds

Zakho Kurds

Zakho Kurd

Albert Kahn
French Banker

Mr. Kahn would like to make, while there still is time, something called the "Archives of the Planet," that is to say, "originate a kind of photographic inventory of the earth's surface, as occupied and ordered by man, such as it appears at the beginning of the twentieth century." Mr. Kahn said he wants "to freeze once and for all, aspects, practices and ways of human life whose fatal disappearance is only a matter of time."

Letter from Emmanuel de Margerie to Jean Brunhes, who became the director of the Archives of the Planet, January 26, 1912

Bahznani Yezidi cemetery

> *Life has to be seized wherever it may be, in all places, at all moments, abroad, in the street, everywhere.*
>
> Albert Kahn, cited by Georges Wormser in *Autour du monde: Jean Brunhes, regards d'un géographe, regards de la géographie*, 1993

Priest in Mar Ya'qub

Frédéric Gadmer/Musée Albert Kahn, Département des Hauts-de-Seine, Boulogne

Yezidi chief in Bachiqua

Kurdish Jew

Marian O'Connor

British Traveler

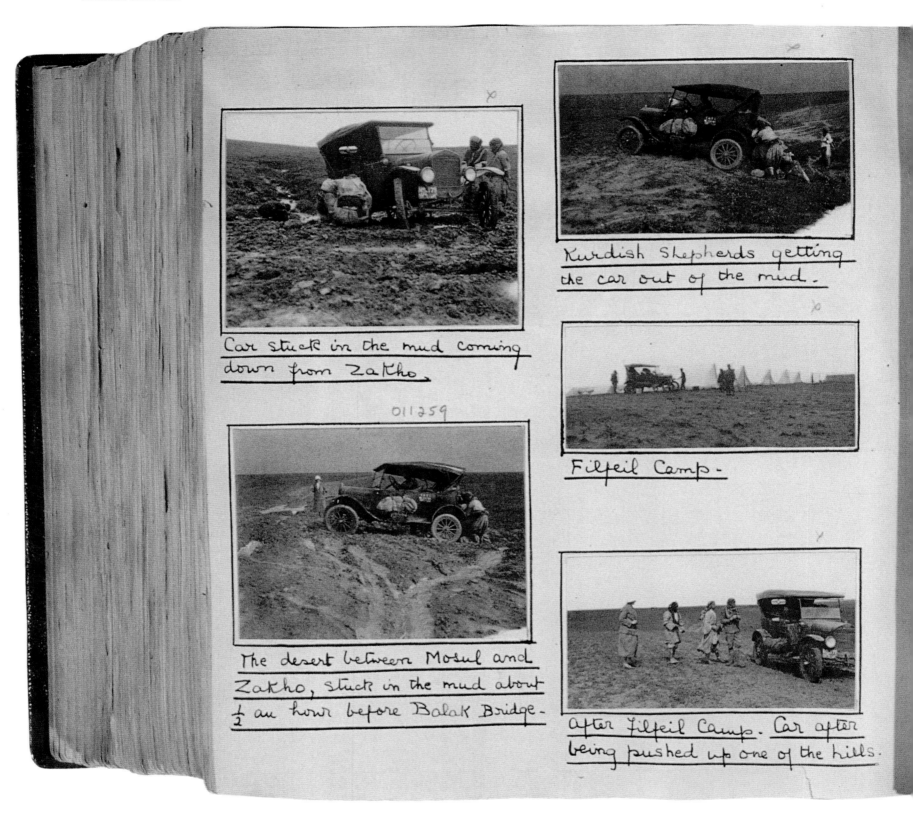

Car stuck in the mud coming down from Zakho

011259

The desert between Mosul and Zakho, stuck in the mud about $\frac{1}{2}$ an hour before Balak Bridge.

Kurdish Shepherds getting the car out of the mud.

Filfeil Camp.

After Filfeil Camp. Car after being pushed up one of the hills.

Whole 2
Pages
A 32493a

011260

The Desert
between Zakho
and Mosul.

Kurdish Shepherds who rescued us. A. 32492

Coming down from Zakho. A. 32493

011261

Kurdish shepherds wearing thick
felt 'abas. A. 32494

Undated album from southern Mesopotamia, ca. 1919
Marian O'Connor/Royal Geographical Society, London

68

A group of "Yezidis" or Devil-worshippers (on right).

Turkis

XX

70

71

A Khurdish village dug into the hill side. The people in this country are Troglodytes, living in houses underground, with a long shaft to let in light & air, I spent two nights in these underground dwellings.

A Khurdish peasant with native carpet.

peasants ploughing.

72

27

a group of Kurds with a caravan.

Pages from the photo album of M. Philips Price/Royal Geographical Society, London

M. Philips Price

Britïsh Journalist

After some days at Erzerum, I hired four horses and with my servant and an escort of Turkish soldiers lent to me by the governor-general, I rode out of the city eastwards towards the Turco-Persian frontier. . . .

I saw a few Khurdish nomads, the majority living in a semi-settled, semi-nomad state, indicating clearly that they were in an intermediate state preparatory to settling. All through this country the relations, not only between Mohammedan and Christian, but even between nomad and settled, were amicable. It was not till I reached the Persian frontier that the truculent attitude of the nomads became apparent. . . .

Skirting the end of the ridge which marked the frontier about nightfall, I observed an encampment of felt tents, which I knew were those of some Tartar nomads. . . . At the edge of the encampment I met two Khurds who came out to see who I was. They had large black turbans, hooked noses, hanging cheeks, and an expression which suggested that they would cut anyone's throat for very little.

I explained that I was an Englishman going to Persia and that I had heard of the wonderful people called Khurds so I had come all the way to see them. This little oriental blarney worked like a charm, I was invited into the camp, and in a few minutes I was squatting cross-legged on the floor of the tent, while a few black-eyed ruffians squatted round me eyeing me like a prize bull. When once their suspicion was allayed, two of them went off to fetch a sheep to kill for me, and I settled down in comfortable quarters in the corner of this felt tent. The women, who live in a separate quarter of each tent but are unveiled and have quite handsome features, brought me some of their embroidery work. Nomad shepherds of this type are chiefly monogamous. It is only the chieftains or the more wealthy flock owners who go in for polygamy. The price of a wife ranges from ten to twenty horses apiece, and appears to vary according to the price of horses. Women are not by any means oppressed however, and within the precincts of the tent their word is law. Anything to do with external policy such as the migration of the tribe, the position of the tent, the safety of the flocks is unreservedly in the men's hands. I found that the native language of these people was Khurdish, but most of them spoke Turkish which is the dialect running all through this part of the country, whether on the Turkish or the Persian side of the frontier. . . .

During supper, I discovered that these Khurds were nothing else than professional robbers, who supplemented the produce of their flocks by occasional sheep raiding in Turkish territory, and looting caravans which entered Persia from the Black Sea. They belonged to a tribe ruled by a famous Khurdish chieftain called Sinko, a notorious brigand about whom I had heard great complaints from the Turkish governors in Armenia.

The Khurdish chiefs on the Turco-Persian frontier claim the right to protect many of the Khurds now settled in the villages on the Turkish side, and also some Armenian villagers too. The consolidation of Turkish authority in the districts west of the frontier has caused these Khurdish chieftains to lose many of their retainers, and their chieftains now find amusement in distracting the Turkish authorities by periodically reviving their old claims and putting them into force by systematic raids and caravan looting. A war between nomad and settled population goes on all over the country. It is not a religious war, because the Khurds are nominally Mussulmen and are more bitter against the Turkish authorities and the settled Moslem natives in Armenia than they are against the Armenians themselves.

M. Philips Price, *A Journey Through Turkish Armenia and Persian Khurdistan;*
Journal of the Manchester Geographical Society, Vol. XXX, 1914

Dispatch to 3rd Army, Erzurum, September 19, 1914

To All Units

According to reliable information from the Armenians in the Caucasus, the Russians have provoked Armenians living in our country, by promises that they will be granted independence in territories to be annexed from Ottoman land, and that they have brought many of their own men disguised as Turkish peasants to the Armenian villages in our country, that they have stored arms and ammunition in many places to be distributed to Armenians, and moreover, the Russian General Loris Melikow went to the Van region for the same purpose.

Military History Documents, published by the Military History and
Strategic Studies Department of the Turkish General Staff, December 1982

Official Proclamation

Our Armenian fellow countrymen, who form one of the Ottoman racial elements, having taken up with a lot of false ideas of a nature to disturb the public order, as the result of foreign instigations for many years past, and because of the fact that they have brought about bloody happenings and have attempted to destroy the peace and security of the Ottoman state, of their fellow countrymen, as well as their own safety and interests . . . have to be sent away to places which have been prepared in the interior vilayets, and a literal obedience to the following orders, in a categorical manner, is accordingly enjoined upon all Ottomans:—

1. With the exception of the sick, all Armenians are obliged to leave, within five days from the date of this proclamation, and by villages or quarters, under the escort of the gendarmery.
2. Although they are free to carry with them on their journey the articles of their movable property which they desire, they are forbidden to sell their landed and their extra effects, or to leave them here and there with other people. . . .
3. To assure their comfort during the journey, hans and suitable buildings have been prepared, and everything has been done for their safe arrival at their places of temporary residence, without their being subjected to any kind of attack or affronts.
4. The guards will use their weapons against those who make any attempts to attack or affront the life, honor, and property of one or of a number of Armenians. . . .
5. Since the Armenians are obliged to submit to this decision of the Government, if some of them attempt to use arms against the soldiers or gendarmes, arms shall be employed only against those who use force, and they shall be captured dead or alive. . . .
6. As the Armenians are not allowed to carry any firearms or cutting weapons, they shall deliver to the authorities every sort of arms, revolvers, daggers, bombs, etc., which they have concealed in their places of residence or elsewhere. . . .
7. The escorts of soldiers and gendarmes are required and are authorized to use their weapons against and to kill persons who shall try to attack or to damage Armenians in villages, in city quarters, or on the roads for the purpose of robbery or other injury.
8. Those who owe money to the Ottoman Bank may deposit in its warehouses goods up to the amount of their indebtedness. . . .
9. Large and small animals which it is impossible to carry along shall be bought in the name of the army.
10. On the road the vilayet, leva, kaza and nahieh officials shall render possible assistance to the Armenians.

Enclosure to a dispatch from the American consul at Trebizond to the
embassy at Constantinople, dated June 28, 1915. State Department translation of
law of deportation handed by the Turkish governor of Trebizond to U.S. consul
Oscar Heizer, reproduced in the appendix of The Slaughterhouse Province, 1989

Armenian deportations as seen through the window of the American consul

Leslie A. Davis/Melissa Media Associates, New Rochelle

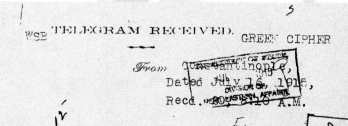

TELEGRAM RECEIVED.

WSB   GREEN CIPHER

From Constantinople,
Dated July 16, 1915,
Rec'd. 80 8:10 A.M.

Secretary of State,
Washington.

858, July 16, 1 p m.

Confidential. Have you received my 841? / Deportation of and excesses against peaceful Armenians is increasing and from harrowing reports of eye witnesses it appears that a campaign of race extermination is in progress under a pretext of reprisal against rebellion.

Protests as well as threats are unavailing and probably incite the Ottoman government to more drastic measures as they are determined to disclaim responsibility for their absolute disregard of capitulations and I believe nothing short of actual force which obviously United States are not in a position to exert would adequately meet the situation. / Suggest you inform belligerent nations and mission boards of this.

AMERICAN AMBASSADOR,
Constantinople

Deciphered by

Melissa Media Associates, New Rochelle

Armenians being deported from Harput

Leslie A. Davis/Melissa Media Associates, New Rochelle

Leslie A. Davis
American Consul

June 30, 1915
I have the honor to report to the Embassy about one of the severest measures ever taken by any government and one of the greatest tragedies in all history. . . .

As stated in [previous] despatches, a revolutionary movement on the part of some of the Armenians was discovered and severe measures were taken to check it. . . . These were undertaken in a wholesale manner, little distinction being made between people who were entirely innocent and those who were suspected of being participants in the movement. Practically every male Armenian of any consequence at all here has been arrested and put in prison. . . . Several hundred of the leading Armenians were sent away at night and it seems to be clearly established that most, if not all, of them were killed. . . .

Another method was found, however, to destroy the Armenian race. This is no less than the deportation of the entire Armenian population, not only from this Vilayet, but, I understand, from all six Vilayets comprising Armenia. . . . The full meaning of such an order can scarcely be imagined by those who are not familiar with the peculiar conditions of this isolated region. A massacre, however horrible the word may sound, would be humane in comparison with it. . . . I don't believe it possible for one in a hundred to survive, perhaps not one in a thousand. . . . The fate of these people can readily be imagined. The method is perhaps a little more cultured than a massacre, but it will be far more effective and thorough. It is quite probable that many of them will be robbed and murdered en route, as the roads are now filled with bands of pillaging Kurds.

July 24, 1915
Any doubts that may have been expressed in previous reports as to the Government's intention in sending away the Armenians have been removed and any hope that may have been expressed as to the possibility of some of them surviving has been destroyed. . . . It was apparent that very few would ever survive the journey from here to Ourfa or to any other place at this season of the year. As a matter of fact, it has been quite unnecessary to consider the difficulties of such a journey. It seems to be fully established now that practically all who have been sent away from here have been deliberately shot or otherwise killed within one or two days after their departure. This work has not all been done by bands of Kurds but has for the most part been that of the gendarme who accompanied the people from here or of companies of armed "tchetehs" (convicts) who had been released from prison for the purpose of murdering the Armenian exiles.

That the order is officially and nominally to exile the Armenians from those Vilayets may mislead the outside world for a time, but the measure is nothing but a massacre of the most atrocious nature. It would be that even if all the people had been allowed to perish on the road. As the greater part of them, however, have been actually murdered and as there is no doubt that this was done by order of the Government, there can be no pretense that the measure is anything else but a general massacre.

Leslie A. Davis, U.S. Consular Dispatches From American Consulate, Mamouret-ul-Aziz (Harput), Turkey, To Honorable Henry H. Morgenthau, American Ambassador, Constantinople, reproduced in the appendix of *The Slaughterhouse Province*, 1989

MISSION BOARD TOLD OF TURKISH HORRORS

Correspondents Confirm the Reports of the Wiping Out of Armenians.

SCATTERED OVER EMPIRE

Christian Cities Cease to Exist as Such and Inhabitants Are Driven Far from Home.

Under the caption "In Darkest Turkey," the American Board of Commissioners for Foreign Missions says that it has at hand "abundant and undeniable evidence" confirmatory of the newspaper reports concerning the persecution of the Christian subjects of the Ottoman Empire.

"This evidence," says the board, "does not come through letters from the missionaries; they write briefly and of their own affairs; they refrain from discussing political affairs. They seek to maintain a neutral attitude in this time of strife.

"But from other sources, in roundabout but absolutely reliable ways, come to the board rooms accounts of proceedings in many parts of Turkey that are so appalling as to be almost beyond belief. They indicate a systematic, authorized and desperate effort on the part of the rulers of Turkey to wipe out the Armenians.

"Apparently the uprising of Armenian revolutionists at Van, which paved the way for Russian occupation of that city without resistance, has been seized by the Turks as a pretext for a general attack upon the Armenians everywhere. In some cases by massacre, more often through torture and exile, they are being eliminated from the field; they are being put where they need no longer be considered.

"Along the track of the Russian armies toward the Persian border, from Van to Moush and Bitlis, in the cities of Eastern Turkey, such as Diarbekir, Harpoot and Mardin, and especially in Central Turkey and the region stretching to the south, this cruel, relentless persecution has been for some time under way.

Report by a British Resident.

"A British resident of Constantinople who had left that city and was temporarily at a Mediterranean port beyond the reach of the censor, writes as follows:

You have probably learned something of the sad condition of the Armenians from the papers, but probably nothing gets through that in any adequate way portrays the desperate straits in which these poor people find themselves.

You may have heard that Zeitoon has ceased to exist as an Armenian town. The inhabitants have been scattered, the city occupied by Turks and the very name changed. The same is true to a large extent of Hadjin, except, I believe, the name has not been altered. The Armenians of the regions of Erzrum, Bitlis and Erzingen have, under torture, been converted to Islam. Mardin reports 1895 conditions (the year of the infamous massacre) as prevailing there. The tale is awful to the last degree.

The most horrible scene I have ever witnessed, one not surpassed by any in Dante's "Inferno," was the group of those who remained at the first camp after the majority of the exiles had gone. The first time I saw this group was in the dusk of the evening. There were several hundred of the dead and dying scattered about the camp, the most of whom were under a clump of trees at one end of it. One or two gendarmes were on guard, but they made no objection to walking among them. . . . All in the camp were beyond help. Within a few feet of them was a long trench and each day those who were dead, or thought to be dead, were gathered up by the gendarmes and dumped into it. The exiles themselves were compelled to dig this trench as long as any of them were able to work. Hundreds of Armenians were buried in this field in the summer of 1915. Today there is hardly a trace of the camp left, but whenever I have ridden past it I have always thought of the hellish scenes that took place there during the "deportation" of the Armenians. . . .

Many of the Armenians were massacred by the Kurds at the instigation of the Turkish Government; but, on the other hand, many Kurds kept Armenians in their villages and protected them in various ways. The Dersim Kurds were most active in helping them. . . .

In the summer of 1916 all of the Armenians who had been hiding in the Dersim succeeded in escaping to Russia and others began fleeing from Harput and Mamouret-ul-Aziz to the Dersim in the hope of getting away. . . . The Kurds came from the mountains and took them to the Dersim in large parties, charging some of them substantial amounts and taking others for comparatively small sums. . . . It was dangerous, of course, for the missionaries or for me to help them escape. I do not know what the others may have done, but I did help a great many with money and in some cases took them away myself and delivered them to the Kurds. It would have been very bad if I had been caught, but nothing of that kind happened and some were thus enabled to get away who could not otherwise have done so.

Report of Leslie A. Davis, American Consul, Formerly at Harput, Turkey, on the Work of the American Consulate at Harput since the Beginning of the Present War, February 9, 1918, Reproduced in *The Slaughterhouse Province*, 1989

Director of the Near East Relief for Turkey and Syria and Mrs. George M. Beck of Michigan City, Indiana, distributing bread to Armenian refugees, 1915

Unknown/Mission Album Collection, United Methodist Church Archives, Madison

The New York Times, September 17, 1915

58326. Starving Armenians who have fallen by the wayside. Armenia.

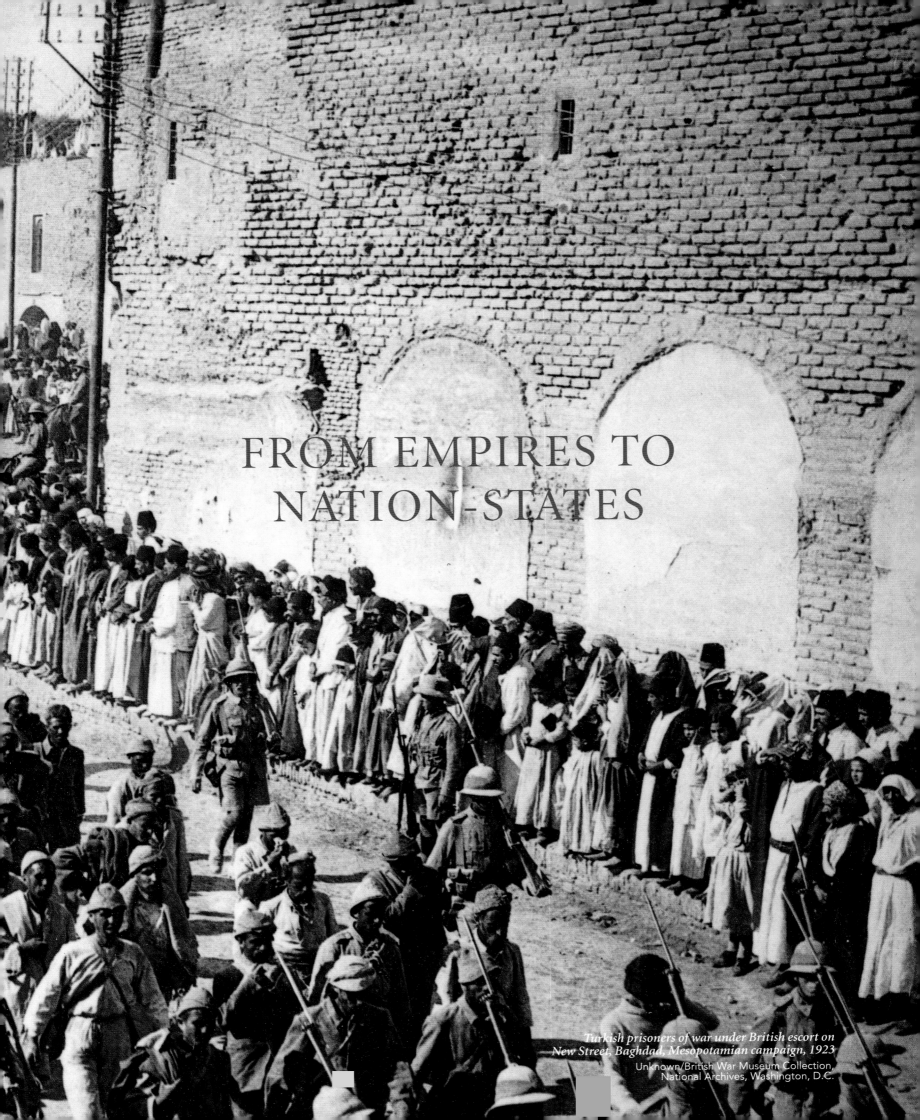

FROM EMPIRES TO NATION-STATES

Turkish prisoners of war under British escort on New Street, Baghdad, Mesopotamian campaign, 1923

Conflicting Claims on Eastern Turkey

Throughout the First World War, the Kurds remained loyal to the Ottoman sultan and heeded the call for jihad, holy war against the infidel enemy. Kurdish nationalists were as yet few in number; most of them were urbanized and educated members of the aristocracy, and their ideas held little appeal to the other Kurds. Even by the time the Ottomans were losing on all fronts—when British troops occupied southern Mesopotamia (i.e., the southern and central parts of present-day Iraq), when Arab armies were cutting Syria loose from the empire, and while Woodrow Wilson spoke of self-determination for the empire's peoples—the Kurds remained unmoved.

By the time the armistice was signed on October 31, 1918, what remained of the empire was in ruin. Debates on its future inevitably involved the future status of the Kurds and Kurdistan. In the old capital, Istanbul (which Europeans insisted on calling by its Greek name, Constantinople), educated Kurds established a voluntary association with the aim of raising the Kurds' national awareness and of representing Kurdish interests in the political debate. They sought contact with the British High Commissariat, which represented the victorious Entente (i.e., Britain, France, Italy, and Greece) and was therefore the real powerholder, as well as with the postwar Ottoman government (which had been purged of Young Turk hard-liners). Most of these Kurds thought of little more than a measure of administrative decentralization and collective Kurdish representation in a restored Ottoman sultanate. One strong faction within the association, however, dominated by the Bedirkhan family, strove for Kurdish independence and attempted to get European support for this project. At the Paris Peace Conference this nationalist tendency was represented by the Kurdish aristocrat Sherif Pasha, a former Ottoman diplomat who had joined the opposition in exile.

In eastern Anatolia, Armenians who had survived the massacres, mostly behind the Russian front lines, attempted to carve out the independent state that they felt entitled to by Woodrow Wilson's principles and for which they expected international support. They were well-armed after Russian troops had withdrawn from the region and had left many of their arms behind. The Armenians sought revenge on those whom they blamed for the massacres, and in turn expelled many Muslims from their villages. Local Muslims, mostly Kurds and Turks, whose turn it was to be threatened with expulsion if not worse, organized resistance groups that fought the Armenians for control of territory. They were aided by remnants of the Ottoman army in the region.

In May 1919 the Istanbul government dispatched the highly respected general Mustafa Kemal to the east to take care of the orderly demobilization and disarmament of the Ottoman troops, as demanded by the victors. Once in Anatolia, Kemal reorganized the army instead and set about coordinating the Muslim resistance. When Greek armies invaded western Anatolia, also in May 1919, the fighting spread all over the country. At a national congress in Sivas in September, where the various regions were represented, Mustafa Kemal firmly established his leadership of what was now a movement to preserve the last remnants of the empire, the provinces with non-Arab Muslim (i.e., Turkish or Kurdish) majorities.

At that time the southern part of Kurdistan was occupied by the British; in the north there appeared to be considerable, though by no means uniform, support for the Kemalist movement. In several towns there were associations of Kurdish nationalists, but their ideas did not yet cause much enthusiasm among the population at large. An American fact-finding commission, led by General James Harbord, toured the country in September 1919 and recommended an American mandate over all of Asia Minor as a solution for the rapidly escalating ethnic (mostly Muslim-Christian) conflicts. Soon after, however, America withdrew from the Peace Conference, and the idea of an American mandate, which had appealed to certain sections of the Turkish public, vanished into thin air.

Around the same time the British officer Noel, a would-be Lawrence of the Kurds, made a less official tour of the Kurdish districts to gauge the strength of tribal support for the idea of Kurdish independence or for some form of British mandate. He was accompanied by two young Kurdish nationalists, members of the Bedirkhan family. The Kemalists, not unnaturally, perceived his presence in the region at the time of the Sivas Congress as a British attempt to incite Kurdish tribes against their incipient liberation movement. Mustafa Kemal was formally a rebel against the sultan's government, which was ultimately under British control. At this time the loyalties of provincial authorities and population still were uncertain.

Soon, however, the Kemalist movement, which made Ankara into its new capital, appeared to have won the sympathies and loyalties of most Muslims of the country. But it was the Istanbul government that took part in the Peace Conference and in 1920 signed the Treaty of Sèvres, which explicitly allowed for an independent Armenian state and left open the possibility of a Kurdish state if a strong demand for such an entity were to emerge. By that time, however, it was no longer the Istanbul government that controlled most of the country but the Kemalists in Ankara, and the Sèvres Treaty remained a dead letter. In August 1922, the Kemalists won their final victory over the Greeks and henceforth controlled all of Asia Minor. A new peace accord was negotiated between the Entente powers and the Ankara government, and was signed at Lausanne in 1923. It recognized a new Turkey, approximately within its present borders, and no longer mentioned Armenia or Kurdistan.   —*MvB*

British Desiderata in Turkey in Asia Report

The Kurds have no sense of nationality of any kind whatever. They have a subconscious sense of race and certain tribal instincts, but they are entirely uninfluenced by the idea of nationality as modern Europeans understand the word. . . . There is a tradition of an Armenian nation and a Jewish nation which once formed a State; this tradition the Kurds have not got. No Kurd repines over his lost Empire. The Kurdish national songs do not tell of the palmy days when Kurdistan was really Kurdistan. . . .

A consolidated Kurdistan is an impossibility. There is no reason why the distribution of the Kurds should dictate frontiers or why Kurds should be regarded as a people who require consolidation.

Lieutenant Colonel Sir Mark Sykes, "Proceedings and Appendices of a Committee Appointed by the Prime Minister," March 15, 1915/British Public Record Office, Kew
CAB27/1

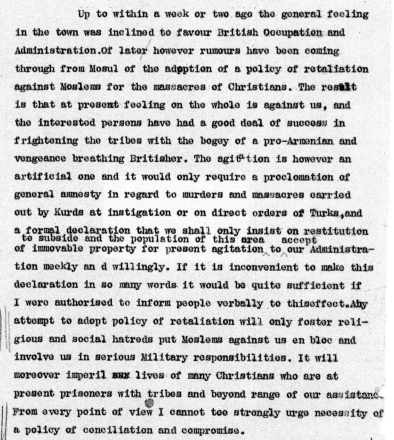

Telegram.

From. Major Noel.Nisibin.

To. Political Baghdad.

No 54.

Dated and received 24th April 1919.

****

Up to within a week or two ago the general feeling in the town was inclined to favour British Occupation and Administration.Of later however rumours have been coming through from Mosul of the adoption of a policy of retaliation against Moslems for the massacres of Christians. The result is that at present feeling on the whole is against us, and the interested persons have had a good deal of success in frightening the tribes with the bogey of a pro-Armenian and vengeance breathing Britisher. The agitation is however an artificial one and it would only require a proclomation of general amnesty in regard to murders and massacres carried out by Kurds at instigation or on direct orders of Turks,and a formal declaration that we shall only insist on restitution of immovable property for present agitation to our Administra- to subside and the population of this area accept tion meekly an d willingly. If it is inconvenient to make this declaration in so many words it would be quite sufficient if I were authorised to inform people verbally to thiseffect.Any attempt to adopt policy of retaliation will only foster reli- gious and social hatreds put Moslems against us en bloc and involve us in serious Military responsibilities. It will moreover imperil any lives of many Christians who are at present prisoners with tribes and beyond range of our assistance. From every point of view I cannot too strongly urge necessity of a policy of conciliation and compromise.

The movement in favour of Kurdish independence rests on no natural foundation. Without the fear of retaliation and the dread of a pro-Armenian policy the Kurdish national propoganda would never have attained the success it has. The Kurdish tribes of this area have become debased and spoilt by long contact with Arabs ansd do not possess those national characteristics and instincts which distinguish tribes round Sulaimaniah and Rowanduz ends.

****

Ruined bazaars in Khanigin, southern Mesopotamia, 1918

British Public Record Office, Kew
AIR 20/714

Unknown/Imperial War Museum, London

Woodrow Wilson's Twelfth Point

The Turkish portions of the present Ottoman empire should be assured a secure sovereignty, but the other nationalities which are now under Turkish rule should be assured an undoubted security of life and an absolutely unmolested opportunity of autonomous development.

The twelfth point of fourteen points outlined to a joint session
of Congress by President Woodrow Wilson, January 8, 1918

Memorandum on the Claims of the Kurd People

In virtue of the Wilsonian principle everything pleads in favour of the Kurds for the creation of a Kurd state, entirely free and independent. Since the Ottoman Government has accepted Mr. Wilson's fourteen points without reservation, the Kurds believe that they have every right to demand their independence, and that without in any way failing in loyalty towards the Empire under whose sovereignty they have lived for many centuries, keeping intact their customs and traditions. . . .

We demand that independence which is our birthright, and which alone will permit us to fight our way along the road of progress and civilization, to turn to account the resources of our country and to live in peace with our neighbours. . . .

We beg the Peace Conference to name an international commission, charged with tracing the frontier line in accordance with the principle of nationality so as to include in Kurdistan all those territories where the Kurds are in a majority; on the clear understanding, that if in the districts allotted to Kurdistan, sufficiently large agglomerations of other nationalities be found, provision shall be made for them in a special statute in conformity with their national traditions.

General Sherif Pasha, president of the Kurd delegation
to the Peace Conference in Paris, March 22, 1919
Courtesy Kurdish Institute of Paris

General Sherif Pasha
Unknown/Courtesy Naci Kutlay

The entire country within its national frontiers is an undivided whole.

In the event of the Ottoman Empire being split up, the nation will unanimously resist any attempt at occupation or interference by foreigners.

Should the Government be incapable of preserving the independence of the nation and the integrity of the country, a provisional Government shall be formed for the purpose of safeguarding these aims.

National Congress of Turkish Provinces, Erzurum, July 23, 1919,
from *A Speech Delivered by Mustafa Kemal Atatürk*, 1927

Section 1

"All the News That's Fit to Print."

The New Y

VOL. LXVIII. NO. 22,436.

NEW YORK, SUNDAY, JUNE 29, 1919. 12

PEACE SIGNED. EN

Armenians hold sign for "The Wilson Principles" at a reception for Major General Harbord at Erzurum, Turkey, September 25, 1919

Major General James G. Harbord
American Military Officer

The principal interest of our mission centred around the Armenian vilayets of Turkey and the provinces of Russian Armenia. Our journey was therefore planned with the double purpose of paralleling the old international boundary to satisfy ourselves as to whether or not the Turks were massing troops in that region, and to see as much as possible of that Armenia which the Armenians are still hoping to see erected into a separate state. . . .

Few Americans, except missionaries, have ever been seen on the Mardin-Sivas highway, and we had no unattended moments except when remote from settlements. We were as unconventional and interesting to the native inhabitants as they were to us. There are no secrets of the toilet nor of any of the ordinary processes of life in a motor car caravan halted near a village in Asiatic Turkey. . . .

Sivas had an especial interest for our mission. In the early part of the summer of 1919 many stories had come out of Trans-Caucasia regarding a great congress of the Nationalist Party of Turkey which met at Erzurum in July. Its meeting was foretold as a Pan-Turanian movement calculated to unite all of Turanian blood in a common cause, and again as Pan-Islamic intended to bring together representatives of the Moslem faith from all over the world to preserve the Turkish Empire and protect the Caliph in his ancient seat at Constantinople. Mustapha Kemal Pasha, an officer of high reputation in the Turkish army who had commanded an army corps with distinction and great gallantry at the Dardanelles and Gallipoli, had, after the Armistice, been sent as Inspector-General to Anatolia and the Armenian vilayets, charged with the responsibility for the old international frontier between Turkey and Russia and the command of the troops in the eastern region. His headquarters were at Erzerum. . . .

Briefly, the movement stands for the integrity of the Ottoman Empire under the mandate of a disinterested great power, preferably America. . . . Their idea of a mandate differs from ours, however, in that they conceive it as advice and assistance from a big brother, with such slight exercise of authority as not to interfere with their interior government or their foreign relations.

U.S. Major General James G. Harbord, "Mustapha Kemal Pasha and His Party," *The World's Work*, Vol. 40, June 1920

ork Times.

THE WEATHER | Section
Fair and continued cool Sunday; fair Monday; moderate winds.
For full weather report see Page 18.
1

PAGES. In Nine Parts.

FIVE CENTS In Greater New York

OS THE GREAT WAR:

*The Bedirkhan family: Emin Ali Bey (father of Celadet, Kamuran, and Süreya),
Ali Shamil Pasha, and Bahri (seated L-R); standing behind (L-R) Murat Ramzi Bey,
Hasan, Miqdad Midhat Bey, and Kamil, ca. 1880*

Unknown/Courtesy Saif T. Badrakhan

The Bedirkhans

Kurdish Family

*Bedr Khan begot 90 sons. This enormous family has been constantly
identified with insurrectionary movements against the Ottoman
Government. There is a special group for Bedr Khan in the Turkish
secret cyphers. All Bedr Khans of any ability and energy have suffered
exile and imprisonment.*

Diary of Major Noel on Special Duty in Kurdistan, 1919
Oriental and India Office Collections, The British Library, London
L/P+S/10/818

In the name of God the merciful and the compassionate, I feel for the
Kurds. The Kurds are more sensitive and intelligent than a lot of
other peoples, they are chivalrous and strong, and they hold on
firmly to their religion. But they are not well educated like other peoples, and they are not rich. They do not know what happens in the
world; they have no idea of what their neighbor Moscow is like and
what it does. Well, with God's consent I have now written this journal
and, God permitting, I shall write new issues once every two weeks. I
gave it the name of *Kurdistan*.

In this journal I shall speak of the beauty of knowledge and learning; I shall show the Kurds where people study and where there are
good schools; and I shall explain where there are wars, what the great
powers are doing, how they wage war and how they engage in trade.

Editorial in *Kurdistan*, the first Kurdish newspaper (right), published by Miqdad
Midhat Badr Khan in Cairo, April 22, 1898, translated by Amir Hassanpour
Courtesy Dr. Celile Celil

1919

56

Major E.W.C. Noel
British Officer
Photographs by Percival Richards, British Administrator

June 14–August 23
It was decided that I should visit Constantinople with a view to meeting the Bedr Khan family, and taking one or more of them as well as other influential Kurds, on a mission to Kurdistan, with the object of counteracting the Pan-Islamic propaganda of the Turks and their efforts to turn all Kurds against us by frightening them with the bogey of an Armenian domination backed by British bayonets. . . .

We left early on a two days' march to the tents of Yakub Pasha, the chief of the other big Kurdish tribe in this area, the Atmi, or as the Turks have it the Atmali.

On the right Badr Khan Beg
On the left Jelal Eddin Ali Khan Beg
both sons of the rightful ruler of
Kurdistan — they accompanied us on
the latter stages of our trip — The turks
tried very hard to get them — but nothing
doing — They look rotten in European dress
don't they?

Snow in July!!

It may be remarked that the nomenclature of this country, as shown on our maps, is mainly Turkish. This is due to the fact that the maps are based partly on Turkish ones and partly on reports of travellers who did not know Kurdish, and were invariably chaperoned by a couple of Turkish gendarmes. In point of fact the original nomenclature is Kurdish and has been Turcified by the Government.

Diary of Major Noel on Special Duty in Kurdistan, 1919
Oriental and India Office Collections, The British Library, London
L/P+S/10/818

Courtesy Richard Hesketh

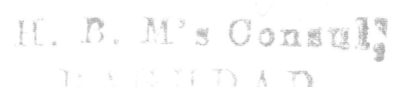

A dinner to which Noori Pasha entertained us — I forget now wether it was 17 or 19 Courses!!

Interior of Tappu Aghas Summer residence

August 27

After a long march of 12 hours we reached the residence of Tappu Agha, the head of the Sinamilli Kurds. . . . Tappu has built himself a very pleasant Summer residence. The big room in which we sit, with its huge open fireplace, stone-flagged floor, spring of crystal water in the centre flanked by a broad divan covered with bright silks, and its well-built gable roof of massive juniper beams, gives a most pleasing impression. It is certainly the best residence of any Kurdish chief I have yet seen, and denotes the possession of some culture and taste. In this connection Sir Mark Sykes refers to the Sinamilli as a fine handsome people, good farmers, literate, and very artistic in the painting of their houses.

From Tappu I learnt further details regarding the assistance given by his tribe to Armenian refugees. . . . The Sinamilli gave a refuge to some 60 people who remained with them till the British occupation of Marash. The befriending of the Armenians came to the knowledge of higher Turkish officials, who at one time actually decided as a punishment to deport the Kurds in the same way as the Armenians.

Diary of Major Noel on Special Duty in Kurdistan, 1919
Oriental and India Office Collections, The British Library, London
L/P+S/10/818

1919

The Character of the Kurds As Illustrated by Their Proverbs and Popular Sayings

There is a great deal to be said for the contention that national character expresses itself in popular sayings and proverbs. That the latter are sometimes paradoxical and tend to extremes cannot be denied. Truth is, however, often seen at her best on the tight rope. . . .

The Kurds are a mountain race, with all the characteristics of mountaineers—love of freedom, violent passions and a clannish feeling of pride. These primary traits dispose the Kurds to fly to arms at small provocation, and engage with zest in bitter blood feuds. . . . Enmity and feuds are generally of a very implacable and uncompromising nature. The Kurd is a good hater.

DIZHMIN A BABE NABITA DUST A KURRE.
"The enemy of the father will never be the friend of his son."

RRAI DEBINA B'HOST DIZHMIN NABINA DOST.
"Roads may be short but enemies won't be friends."

MIRUF KHUNDAR BIT QARRDAR NABIT.
"It is better to have blood on one's hands than to be in debt."

KHALON KHWARZA RRA KIRRIN MAMA BRAZA CHAL KIRRIN.
"Uncles are ready to help the sons of their sisters, and to bury those of their brothers."

This refers to the fact that feuds often arise between brothers, whereas marriage is a favorite means of making up quarrels. A bride may take the place of blood money. . . .

What has been taken for treachery is really the result of the hard physical conditions in which the Kurd lives, the constant and bitter inter-tribal feuds, and the fact that his country has for centuries been overrun and subdued by foreign invaders, who have never shown the least sympathy or consideration for the subject race. . . .

The hardness in the character of the Kurd, and the fact that he has for centuries revolted against the yoke of the conqueror, has given a trait of great independence and aloofness to his character. . . .

NANE HUR KA AVE MINAT A KHALQE PAWA.
"Better to live on bread and water than to be under an obligation."

MIRUF DIKE RUZHEKI BIT BILA MIRISHKA SALEKI NABIT.
"One crowded hour of glorious life is worth an age without a name (better to be cock of the roost for a day than a hen for a year)."

SARE HATA B'RINI NAYAITI KIRRINI.
"A head that is to be cut off cannot be ransomed."

In Kurdish there is no word for a prostitute. In the Eastern districts she is euphemistically referred to as a Persian; in the North as a Russian; in the South as an Arab; and in the West as a Turk. . . .

The Kurd feels nothing but the deepest and bitterest antipathy to the Turk and all his ways. For the Persian the feeling is one of good-natured contempt and dislike of his deceitfulness. The Kurd's dislike of the Arab is that of the patrician for the plebeian. For the Armenian the feeling is much similar to that against the Jews in Eastern Europe and the East End of London. The Kurd looks on the Nestorian as a Kurd.

NAV BYN A MA WA MUYEKA NAV BYN A MA WA FELLAH CHIAYEKA.
"Between us (i.e., the Nestorians and the Kurds) there is but a hair's breadth, but between us and the Armenians a mountain."

Percival Richards/Courtesy Richard Hesketh

An old Kurdish (Kermanji) lady winnowing grain

August 28
It has often been said that the Kurdish language is nothing more than a patois which varies from valley to valley. It is true that the language of S. E. Kurdistan, i.e., Baba Kurdi, is considerably different from Kermanji, but it is untrue to say that the variations of Kermanji show very fundamental differences. I have with me men from the Boutan, Diarbekir, and Hakkiari. All of them can well understand and make themselves clearly understood in this the extreme West of Kurdistan. . . .

The Sinamilli Kurds are not nomads in the same sense as the tribes in Eastern Kurdistan, such as the Herki and the Jaf. All of them own land in the "Dasht" (Winter quarters), and about ¾ of them own houses as well. In the Summer quarters (Zozam) they also possess their own land on which they settle instead of roaming about in search of pasture as true nomads do. . . .

The intensity of sowing, which is a measure of the fertility of the soil, is shown by the number of seeds which falls on a bullock's hoofmark. The number varies from 15 to 2.

Diary of Major Noel on Special Duty in Kurdistan, 1919
Oriental and India Office Collections, The British Library, London
L/P+S/10/818

*Turkish escort and Servants
On day of "Wind up"*

After a most wonderful trek over trackless mountains, stopping with
different Kurdish tribes on the way, we arrived very tired and travel
worn at Malatia, where I went into the American hospital suffering
with a nasty abscess, caused by long hours in the saddle. It was while
in hospital that I got the first news that the Turks were after us. One
night I was in a most comfortable sleep (about 10:30) when I was
roughly awakened, and found Pollard whispering excitedly in my ear
"Come on Dick, the Major wants you on time, there are 100 Cavalry
and 400 machine guns on the way from Sivas to arrest us. . . . Needless
to say, I was out of bed in "one time," and down at the camp in "two
time." The Major greeted me with, "Are you fit to ride, Sir?" "Well
Sir," I answered, "if it comes to a choice twixt riding on a wound or
being made a prisoner by Bolshevik Turks and probably shot, well
I'm for the ride."

Letter from Percival Richards in Halabja, Kurdistan,
to his wife, December 20, 1919
Courtesy Richard Hesketh

September 3

On nearing Malatia we were met by the Muttessarif, the Mayor and
other prominent officials.

The Muttessarif, Khalil Bey, one of the Bedr Khan family, is the
uncle of the two Bedr Khans who accompany me. He is an ardent
Kurdish nationalist, in fact, the founder of the Kurdish Club and
newspaper at Constantinople.

September 4

To-day I sent the following telegram which summarises the political
situation and attitude of the Kurds as deduced by my journey from
Aintab to Malatia: . . . I found nearly everywhere a very lively sense of
Kurdish nationality, antipathy to the Turk, and a great hatred of
the Government. There is a general disposition to revolt against the
Government, but at present it is held in check by the fact that the
tribesmen have been thoroughly cowed during the war. It would not,
however, require a great stimulus from outside to start an
insurrectionary movement.

September 9

The G.O.C., 13th Corps, who is an Arab named Jowdet Bey, issued
today the following circular telegram. . . .

"The mission which has arrived at Malatia under the presidency
of a British officer harbours evil designs on our fatherland. . . .
Oh honourable people! For the last 600 years the supporters of Islam
have consisted of four peoples—the Kurds, the Turks, the Albanians
and the Arabs. Previous to the Balkan war the Albanians were
deceived by the lure of independence. To-day, when speaking of
small nations, the word Albania is not even mentioned. . . . The
Arabs by deceit have been separated from us. Now they wish by a
repetition of that deceit, to separate the Kurds. However . . . this
British officer, who calls himself a Colonel but is really only a Major,
was previously Political Officer at Sulaimaniyah where he deceived
Shaikh Mahmoud, the same Mahmoud who is still valiantly struggling against the British. . . .

"Turks and Kurds are brothers and the unique mainstay of Islam.
The day they separate, Islam will grow feebler. The Turks can live
without the Kurds, but the Kurds who are neighbours with the Arabs,
Persians and Armenians, can never exist alone."

September 10

When we had been on the move for an hour we realized that we were
being pursued. The cavalry, about 40 in number . . . worked round our
flank and surrounded us in a narrow broken ravine. . . . The only thing
was to bluff it out. The Turkish officer sent two men forward to call on
me to surrender. I replied by asking him to come forward himself to
meet me. He meekly complied and found himself covered by the rifles
of our party. Ostentatiously cocking my revolver I walked up to him
with one of the Bedr Khans as interpreter.

"I do not want to arrest you," he said, "but only the Kurds who are
with you."

"That will mean we shall have to fight," I replied. . . .

He blurted out that we could pass:

Diary of Major Noel on Special Duty in Kurdistan, 1919
Oriental and India Office Collections, The British Library, London
L/P+S/10/818

1919

From the Turkish Army Corps to the Sultan

September 11, 1919

The [Constantinople] Government has conspired to shed the blood of Mohamedans in a fratricidal war, by planning a sudden attack upon the Congress. It is also proved by certain documents in our possession that they have spent public funds in the attempt to dismember our territory by raising Kurdistan into revolt.... The nation demands that immediate steps shall be taken for the pursuit of this gang of traitors; that they shall be severely punished, and that a new Government shall be formed that will be composed of men of honour. The nation also declares that henceforth all communication and relations with the Government shall be broken off.

From A Speech Delivered by Mustafa Kemal Atatürk, 1927

September 11

The situation here is somewhat complicated. The Wali has produced an Iradeh from the Sultan ordering him to raise a body of Kurdish sowars in whom he can have confidence, and march against Mustapha Kemal at Sivas. He is particularly advised that having reached Sivas and liquidated the Unionist organization, he should lose no time in getting rid of the Kurds, and replace them by a Turkish militia.... The Kurds, who are really only out for their own aims, see no reason why they should march to Sivas when they can attack the Turks a few hours away at Malatia. This is, of course, only common sense, but it does not greatly appeal to the Wali who dreads seeing the control of the situation passing into the hands of Kurds, which is likely to occur if they capture Malatia, the centre of a big Kurdish district.

September 12

The Wali has finally made up his mind that a Kurdish tribal attack on Malatia is open to too many risks, and he has therefore decided to disperse the tribal gatherings as soon as possible. The Kurdish chiefs are on the whole relieved. The war has given them a very healthy respect for the power and long arm of the C.U.P. [Turkish Committee of Union and Progress]. The tribesmen, on the contrary, seem genuinely disappointed. The entire lack of any semblance of unity or common purpose between the Kurds must always lend to prevent any real national combination against the Government....

Colonel Bell, the D.C.P.O., Northern Area, arrived at Malatia in the afternoon, and sent me a letter asking me to come in and see him.

September 13

Colonel Bell had, with some difficulty ... negotiated a safe conduct for me to visit the town for one night. I rode in with a couple of armed Kurds. As the result of a full discussion we agreed that it would be impossible for me to continue my tour in the teeth of the armed opposition of the rebel Government, and that therefore the only course left was to return to Aleppo forthwith.

Diary of Major Noel on Special Duty in Kurdistan, 1919
Oriental and India Office Collections, The British Library, London
L/P+S/10/818

Percival Richards/Courtesy Richard Hesketh

The caravan sheltering from rifle fire

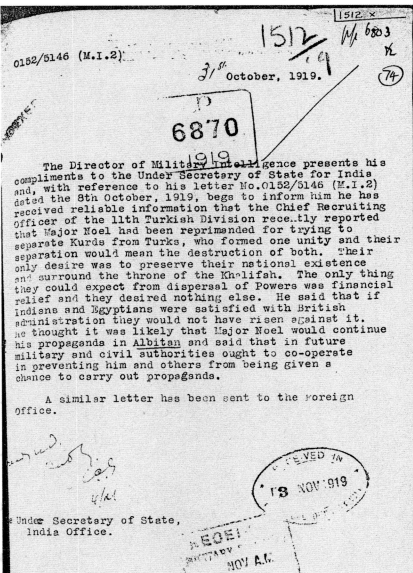

September 18

The European traveller who passes through the country in a motor, who is invariably accompanied by an Armenian or Turkish interpreter, who gains his impressions from seeing the 10% of the population who dwell in the towns where the C.U.P. organization is still all powerful, and where he is the guest of a carefully selected C.U.P. notable or the American missionaries—what can such a traveller know of the Kurds? . . .

That some Kurds massacred Armenians is, of course, only too well-known, but if we consider that the established Government of the country, a Government which has temporal as well as spiritual authority, expressly ordained that the murder and pillage of Armenians was not only lawful but was even a sacred duty, is it to be wondered at that from a primitive and ignorant community like the Kurds, many members should be found who were ready to profit by this state of affairs?

If the police in any big town in Europe were to be withdrawn, would there not be a crop of excesses? . . .

It will be found that the Kurds most implicated in the massacres were the townsmen, who from long contact with the Turks had acquired all the bad habits and characteristics of the Stamboul Effendi. Such men have lost their sense of Kurdish nationality; they are in the swim of the C.U.P. current, and dread a change which might interfere with their present sources of graft. It is this type of Kurd who is produced by the Turk for the edification of chance European visitors.

Both the Armenian and the Turk are against the Kurd for the same reason, namely, that a recognition of the Kurd as a people would interfere with their individual claims to sovereignty.

Diary of Major Noel on Special Duty in Kurdistan, 1919
Oriental and India Office Collections, The British Library, London
L/P+S/10/818

An Armenian refugee woman whom we picked up on the road. And brought into Urfah with us. She spoke very well of the Kurds who had protected her little son (in the picture) through the last massacre

The Armenians relied on the sympathy of Europe, the Turks on the overwhelming majority of the Moslem population. The Kurd was looked upon by both sides as nothing more than a pawn in the game. —Major Noel

From British Secretary of State
To British Civil Commissioner, Baghdad

November 22, 1919

Kurdistan must be left to its own devices, and the practical question is how this can be done consistently with peace and security on the Mesopotamian frontier. We are advised by Noel that there are three essential conditions: (1) that Turkish authority should be excluded from Kurdistan; (2) that Kurdistan should not be partitioned; (3) that the frontier should follow as nearly as possible the ethnological line between Kurds and Arabs. Noel's view is that Kurds, if left to themselves, will be strongly pro-British and will need no encouragement or assistance from us to keep the Turks out. He further holds that the partitioning of the country by attachment of the richest part of it, viz., Southern Kurdistan to Mesopotamia, would afford opportunity for anti-British Nationalist agitation which would result in revival of Turkish influence and consequent insecurity on our borders, possibly reacting on the Persian road.... As regards Kurdistan itself, it is thought that it may still be practicable to encourage the formation of a federation of autonomous States as discussed with you, who might quarrel among themselves but would not molest Mesopotamian frontiers....

The economic and strategic importance of the Suleimaniyah region and its administrative and economic connection with Baghdad in the past are realised, but it is thought that if political independence of Kurdistan as a whole is recognised, it should be possible to obtain all we want by friendly arrangement with local Sheikhs.

His Majesty's Government would be glad to have suggestions from you for carrying out this policy, or any criticisms.

British Public Record Office, Kew
FO 371/4193/157955

From Mr. Ryan
To the British Foreign Office

November 27, 1919

I had a long conversation on the 19th November with the [Turkish] Minister for Foreign Affairs which presented certain points of interest.... I told Reshid Pasha that I wished to tell him something regarding our attitude towards the Kurds, as to which there had been some misunderstanding since Major Noel's visit to Malatia.... Soon after the armistice, I said, the High Commissioner had been approached by all sorts of groups, among them the Kurdish club.... I said it was true that the Kurdish question was of great interest to His Majesty's Government and was the object of close study.... Whatever else happened, we had a future in Mesopotamia, in the northern portion of which pure Arab gradually merged into pure Kurd.

Major Noel was a specialist in Kurds, and like other specialists, he had personal sympathies with the people he knew all about. His mission has been, however, as I had already said, one of enquiry, not of propaganda. He had express instructions to be impartial, and had sought to be impartial. The only reason why His Majesty's government had encouraged the Bedrkhans to accompany him was the hope that their influence could be used to promote peace and quietness in a troubled region during the transition period....

My object in making this statement was to make it clear that any action taken by us from time to time on behalf of individual Kurds was not to be taken as meaning that we were running Kurds, either as nationalists or as possible elements in a combine against the present Government or the national movement.... I was careful to avoid saying anything which might suggest that His Majesty's Government would decide against Kurdish separatist aspirations, and I distinguished clearly between the present and the future.

British Public Record Office, Kew
FO 371/4193/E163681

*Nasir Effendi (Dragoman)
with Izzet Eddin and followers
a nice lot of cutthroat*

Abdul Rezouk effendi

Percival Richards/Courtesy Richard Hesketh

British Occupation of Mesopotamia and the Creation of Iraq

British Indian troops had occupied Mesopotamia (the former Ottoman provinces of Basra, Baghdad, and part of Mosul) in the last year of the First World War. The opinion of British officialdom on the most appropriate future status of Kurdistan was divided. The idea of a semi-independent Kurdish buffer state between Arab Mesopotamia and a much-reduced Turkey was contemplated and initially had some staunch supporters, besides equally staunch opponents. The British authorities in Mesopotamia established relations with the major Kurdish chieftains in the region, and delegated considerable powers to some of them. The most important of them was Shaikh Mahmud Barzinji, head of the most powerful family of religious leaders in southern Kurdistan, who in 1918 was appointed governor of the Sulaimania region.

Shaikh Mahmud had a different conception of the nature of his office than the British high commissioner in Baghdad had, and he set up his own, traditional-style administration. By early 1919 he had declared himself the ruler (hukmdar) of all of Kurdistan and offered armed resistance when the British decided to cut him down to size. The appointment of the strong-willed Major E. B. Soane as the political officer beside him further strained the shaikh's relations with the British. Soane, who more than a decade earlier had lived in the area disguised as a Persian, was distinctly unsympathetic to the shaikh, unlike his predecessor Noel, who had been an enthusiast for Kurdish independence. The shaikh was declared a rebel, his army defeated, and he himself exiled to India in mid-1919. Three years later the shaikh was brought back to what by then had become the kingdom of Iraq. He found a political environment that had changed considerably.

The idea of an independent Kurdistan, still mentioned as a possibility in the 1920 Treaty of Sèvres, became increasingly unrealistic as the Kemalist movement in Anatolia gained strength. The Kemalists' aim was to keep all Turkish- and Kurdish-inhabited territory together—including the parts that were under British control. Their call for common action of Muslims against the Christian powers that were dividing up the Ottoman Empire found many sympathetic ears in southern Kurdistan too. In 1921 Kemalist units, aided by Kurdish tribesmen, brought parts of central Kurdistan under control and advanced toward Sulaimania. The British were determined not to give up southern Kurdistan (the former Ottoman province of Mosul) to the Kemalists. They wished to incorporate it with southern Mesopotamia into the new state of Iraq, which was to remain under British mandate while its political institutions were being developed. Judging monarchy a more appropriate form than a republic, and not finding local persons fit to become king, the British government invited Amir Faisal from Syria and crowned him king. (Faisal, the son of Mecca's ruler Amir Husain, had allied himself with the British during the war and had conquered Syria, but because of an earlier agreement, the British had to cede Syria to the French.)

Fearing that direct government by an Arab king might antagonize the Kurds and drive them toward the Kemalists, the British favored indirect rule for the Kurdish region. Since none enjoyed wider authority among the Kurds than Shaikh Mahmud (although his authority was by no means uncontested), it was decided to invite him back from exile to become the governor of Sulaimania. The shaikh's return created much nationalist fervor in the town.

Independent-minded as ever, the shaikh formed his own government and armed forces, styled himself hukmdar again and then even King of Kurdistan, and addressed King Faisal in letters as an equal. His Kurdish enemies and British officials in the region complained of misrule and corruption. In early 1923 the British dismissed the shaikh again, after which he took to the mountains and waged guerrilla war. Neither the Iraqi army, reinforced by Indian crack troops, nor bombardments by the RAF could force the shaikh's surrender. He held his own in mountain strongholds and controlled much of the countryside until 1927, when he withdrew behind the Persian border. Shaikh Mahmud briefly returned in 1931, once again attempting to set himself up as the local ruler. With tribal support for him waning, the Iraqi army suppressed this final rising without much effort. The shaikh was captured and spent the rest of his life, another quarter century, in enforced residence in Baghdad.

The French and British by 1922 accepted the Kemalists as the only legitimate government of Turkey and in 1923 concluded with them the Treaty of Lausanne, which recognized their territorial gains. Only the former province of Mosul, i.e., southern Kurdistan, remained contested, but it was agreed upon that the League of Nations would, after consulting the population, determine its future status. For a few more years, Kemalists, Kurdish and Arab nationalists, and British officials made efforts to influence the outcome of this popular consultation. In spite of a strong Kurdish nationalist voice, the province was in 1926 definitively added to Iraq. —MvB

THE SPHERE

AN ILLUSTRATED NEWSPAPER FOR THE HOME

With which is incorporated
BLACK & WHITE

Volume LXXVIII. No. 1,027. {REGISTERED AT THE GENERAL POST OFFICE AS A NEWSPAPER} London, September 27, 1919. Price One Shilling.

Copyrighted in the U.S.A

DRAWN BY F. MATANIA

THE EMIR FEISUL AND MR. LLOYD GEORGE IN CONCLAVE AT DOWNING STREET

Emir Feisul, the heir of the King of Hedjaz, visited the Premier at Downing Street on September 19 and conversed with him at length on the question of Syria. The conversation was carried on through the medium of a Foreign Office interpreter. Field-Marshal Lord Allenby and Earl Curzon of Kedleston (Acting Foreign Secretary) were both present at the interview

Shaikh Mahmud (center) with his followers in Sulaimania, ca. 1919

Sir Arnold T. Wilson
British Administrator

The Armistice with Turkey found us once more in occupation of Kirkuk, as well as of Altun Köpri. Arbil was occupied a few days later, in order to furnish essential supplies of grain and fuel. Sulaimani, whither Shaikh Mahmud had long been inviting us, was occupied by Turkish troops. These were withdrawn under the terms of the Armistice and Major Noel was sent to report on the situation there. He arrived in the middle of November and met with an enthusiastic reception. My instructions to him were as follows:

"It should be explained to the tribal chiefs with whom you enter into relations that there is no intention of imposing on them an administration foreign to their habits and desires. Tribal leaders will be encouraged to form a confederation for the settlement of their public affairs under the guidance of the British Political Officers. They will be called upon to continue to pay the taxes legally due from them under Turkish law, modified as may be found necessary, for purposes connected with the maintenance of order and the development of their country."...

Shaikh Mahmud was appointed Governor of the district, and for each of the minor sub-divisions Kurdish officials were appointed to work under the guidance of the British political officers. At the same time, wherever possible, Turkish and Arab officials were at once removed and replaced by natives of Kurdistan, while the Turkish officers and troops in the town were dispatched under escort to Baghdad. Each chief was made responsible to us, generally through Shaikh Mahmud, for the government of his own tribe, and was recognized and paid as a government official. . . .

Our first task was to deal with the want and famine which prevailed in the land. Under the Turkish régime a large part of the town had fallen into ruin, trade had been for long at a complete standstill, and the surrounding country was impoverished and famine-stricken. Foodstuffs and seed-grain were imported and steps were taken to assist a revival of internal trade. The principal public buildings and mosques were repaired and salaries were paid to Kurdish qadhis and other quasi-religious officials. The restoration of order was gratefully welcomed by all but a small minority of tribal leaders and their predatory associates, and it soon seemed clear that the idea of "Kurdistan for the Kurds" under British protection was achieving popularity.

A. T. Wilson, *Mesopotamia 1917–20: A Clash of Loyalties*, 1931

1919

The English in Sulaimania brought in foreigners as janitors, sweepers, cooks. They filled Sulaimania with spies. . . .

A.T. Wilson came to Sulaimania and promised Shaikh Mahmud that the matter of the Kurds would soon be resolved, but after his departure for Baghdad, the English became more aggressive in Sulaimania and controlled affairs completely. They began moving heads of tribes away from Shaikh Mahmud and inciting them to disobey him.

Interview with Ahmed Khwaja, October 1992

In Sulaimania, the alleys, cafés, and markets and the houses of the wealthy persons were buzzing. . . . Little by little, sugar and tea and white flour were brought from the warehouses of Kirkuk and Baghdad to be distributed among the poor and the officials. . . . Noel brought a lot of rupies and banknotes and Turkish lire and poured them into Sulaimania, and without hesitation, spread them on the heads of the tribes and the men of the "hokemdar." . . . In those days, servants were given salaries. After the severe hunger and our living in rags . . . at least it made us forget the memory of . . . the starving people in the mosques, close to dying, and the alleys of yesterday. It made us forget these images and gave us new hope.

Interview with Rafiq Helmi, M. R. Hawar, *The Leader Sheik Mehmood and Southern State of Kurdistan*, Vol. I, 1990

Elementary school teachers, 1921

Unknown/Courtesy Ahmed Khwaja

Shaikh Mahmud with horsemen

A. T. Wilson/Royal Geographical Society, London

The coat of arms designed by Shaikh Mahmud for his government (L-R): A stalk of wheat; a mulberry leaf; a stalk of barley

Ahmed Khwaja, *Çîm Dî (What I Saw)*, 1970

Shaikh Mahmud, hukmdar of southern Kurdistan, in his official uniform as the naqib al-ashraf, *head of the descendants of the Prophet, with Sardar Rashid*

Unknown/
Courtesy Rafiq Studio

Shaikh Mahmud
Kurdish Leader

Responding to the instructions he had received from A. T. Wilson in November 1918, Major Noel arranged a big meeting where all the religious dignitaries, merchants, heads of tribes, and others were present. Noel, as the representative of the British state, read a long speech in Persian. He said in his speech that Shaikh Mahmud had been appointed by the High Commissioner of Britain in Iraq as the "hokemdar" of Kurdistan. And that evening, at Shaikh Mahmud's house, all the important men came together and elected Shaikh Mahmud. Ahmed Aghia Kirkuklizada and I participated. . . . Every month, 15,000 rupies were allocated for the hokemdar, and, as some of the British claimed, Shaikh Mahmud was made the representative of the British forces in Kurdistan. . . . Most of the Shaikh's relatives, and many others, had some job or salary.

Interview with Rafiq Helmi, M. R. Hawar, *The Leader Sheik Mehmood and Southern State of Kurdistan*, Vol. I, 1990

Shaikh Mahmud and Sardar Rashid, governor of Sina and a member of a noble clan from Bukan in Persian Kurdistan

When my father was appointed, the word "hokemdar" had not been heard among us. Sometimes the word was explained as "king." And people thought that the office created in Sulaimania was a Kurdish ministry inside a great Kurdish state and that later other positions and offices like it would follow. . . .

Major Noel said something whose meaning was not clear to us. But we were afraid that asking for a fuller explanation might cause disagreement between some of the tribal heads who were present at the talks. At that time, we didn't want to go into the details of the things that Major Noel didn't explain completely. This was, in fact, a very big mistake on our part. It was careless of us to not ask more. We should have asked for everything to be explained to us.

Interview with Shaikh Raouf, son of Shaikh Mahmud, M. R. Hawar,
The Leader Sheik Mehmood and Southern State of Kurdistan, Vol. I, 1990

Hokemdar's Order

May 22, 1919

Under the order and the command of the General Hokemdar of Kurdistan, Mahmud the son of Said, it has been decided that the Kurdish army should resort to arms against the injustice and deception of the Kurdish people by the British, who broke their promises and denied the Kurds their rights.

May 21, 1919, is the first day of the Kurdish revolution against Great Britain.

Mahmud, the Hokemdar and General Commander

M. R. Hawar, *The Leader Sheik Mehmood and Southern State of Kurdistan*, Vol. I, 1990

A. T. Wilson's airplane in Sulaimania

A. T. Wilson/Royal Geographical Society, London

I visited Sulaimani by air to meet a number of leading Kurdish chiefs. Long conversations followed with Shaikh Mahmud, and with a few of the leaders. . . . Some chiefs were in favour of, others against, an effective British administration in Kurdistan; some insisted that Kurdistan must be under London, not Baghdad; a few told me in secret that they would never accept Shaikh Mahmud as leader, but they could suggest no alternative. . . .

Shaikh Mahmud . . . was given a letter stating that any Kurdish tribe from the Greater Zab to the Diyala (other than those in Persian Territory), who of their own free will accepted the leadership of Shaikh Mahmud, would be allowed to do so, and that the latter would have our moral support in controlling the above areas on behalf of the British Government, whose orders he undertook to obey. The tribes and townspeople in the Kifri and Kirkuk divisions were not willing to come under Shaikh Mahmud, and the latter agreed not to insist on their inclusion.

Shaikh Mahmud was, however, in no way satisfied: he claimed that he had a mandate from all the Kurds of the Mosul wilayat and many in Persia and elsewhere to represent to us their desire to form a unitary autonomous State of which he was to be the head under British protection. The possibility clearly deserved the closest consideration, for if feasible it promised greatly to simplify the task of forming an Arab State from the rest of three wilayats. . . .

Shaikh Mahmud secretly raised a force of some 300 picked men from the Kurdish tribes on the Persian side of the frontier over whom we had no sort of control.

This force, having assembled across the border, suddenly attacked the town. The local levies put up a brave fight but were defeated and routed, and Shaikh Mahmud became master of the situation. The British officers . . . were captured and imprisoned, the Treasury was seized, and Shaikh Mahmud declared himself chief ruler of all Kurdistan. He raised his own flag, issued his own postage stamps, and

*Shaikh Mahmud's
supporters on horseback*
Unknown/Courtesy Rafiq Studio

British training of Kurdish police, Sulaimania, ca. 1920   Lynette Soane/Courtesy Dara Attar

appointed his own retainers to take control of every district. The telegraph line to Kirkuk had been deliberately cut on the morning of the attack on Sulaimani. . . . I at once flew up myself to see what was going on, and saw the six British officers on the roof of their temporary prison in Sulaimani.

This 'regrettable incident' confirmed the now general belief of the inhabitants of Southern Kurdistan that we were no longer able to control events; the rebellion spread across into Persian territory, and several tribes arose against the Persian Government, proclaiming themselves partisans of Shaikh Mahmud and of his scheme for a united free Kurdistan. Shaikh Mahmud was not far wrong when he announced to his followers that our troops had left Kurdistan; but the deductions he made from our dispositions were erroneous. The Commander-in-Chief realized that the impression of British helplessness must be removed forthwith. General Fraser, then commanding the 18th Division at Mosul, was directed to assemble at Kirkuk a 'South Kurdistan Force'

consisting of two Brigades of infantry with cavalry and armoured cars, and to advance at the earliest date possible. . . .

On 17th June, in sweltering heat, General Fraser commenced his advance against Shaikh Mahmud, who was holding the Darband-i-Baziyan pass, in the Qara Dagh range, twelve miles east of Chamchamal.

The next morning, before daybreak, our troops started to scale the almost perpendicular heights of the Qara Dagh, and were practically on the top when at early dawn the guns opened on the pass. The Kurds, expecting a frontal attack in the Turkish style up the roads, were paralysed to find themselves attacked from above and surrounded. . . .

By dawn, the whole pass was in our hands, Shaikh Mahmud and his brother wounded and prisoners, and the whole of this force killed, captured, or dispersed. Forty-eight of the enemy lay dead on the ground and well over 100 were captured, a considerable achievement against mountaineers.

A. T. Wilson, *Mesopotamia 1917–20: A Clash of Loyalties*, 1931

MESOPOTAMIA

MESOPOTAMIA.

THE TRUTH ABOUT THE CAMPAIGN.

WASTE OF LIFE AND MONEY

"We are to-day not far from a disaster."

By EX.-LIEUT.-COL. T. E. LAWRENCE
(Fellow of All Souls College, Oxford).

Mr. Lawrence, whose organisation and direction of the Hedjaz against the Turks was one of the outstanding romances of the war, has written this article at our request in order that the public may be fully informed of our Mesopotamian commitments.

The people of England have been led in Mesopotamia into a trap from which it will be hard to escape with dignity and honour. They have been tricked into it by a steady withholding of information. The Bagdad communiqués are belated, insincere, incomplete. Things have been far worse than we have been told, our administration more bloody and inefficient than the public knows. It is a disgrace to our imperial record, and may soon be too inflamed for any ordinary cure. We are to-day not far from a disaster.

The sins of commission are those of the British civil authorities in Mesopotamia (especially of three "colonels") who were given a free hand by London. They are controlled from no Department of State, but from the empty space which divides the Foreign Office from the India Office. They availed themselves of the necessary discretion of war-time to carry over their dangerous independence into times of peace. They contest every suggestion of real self-government sent them from home. A recent proclamation about autonomy circulated with unction from Bagdad was drafted and published out there in a hurry, to forestall a more liberal statement in preparation in London. "Self-determination papers" favourable to England were extorted in Mesopotamia in 1919 by official pressure, by aeroplane demonstrations, by deportations to India.

Cabinet's Responsibility.

The Cabinet cannot disclaim all responsibility. They receive little more news than the public: they should have insisted on more, and better. They have sent draft after draft of reinforcements, without enquiry. When conditions became too bad to endure longer, they decided to send out as High Commissioner the original author of the present system, with a conciliatory message to the Arabs that his heart and policy have completely changed.

Yet our published policy has not changed, and does not need changing. It is that there has been a deplorable contrast between our profession and our practice. We said we went to Mesopotamia to defeat Turkey. We said we stayed to deliver the Arabs from the oppression of the Turkish Government, and to make available for the world its resources of corn and oil. We spent nearly a million men and nearly a thousand million of money to these ends. This year we are spending ninety-two thousand men and fifty millions of money on the same objects.

Worse than Turks.

Our government is worse than the old Turkish system. They kept fourteen thousand local conscripts embodied, and killed

(1919)
THE NOTORIOUS SHAIKH MAHMOUD (X) (A PRISONER) GUARDED BY INDIAN TROOPS. TAKEN AFTER HIS CAPTURE during THE REBELLION IN KURDISTAN, SENTENCED TO DEATH THEN COMMUTED TO 20 YEARS SERVED 2½ YEARS THEN RELEASED

GHURKAS on patrol during the rebellion of Shaikh Mahmud. Bazian Pass

The Times, London
August 22, 1920

Handwritten captions and photographs by Lynette Soane/Courtesy Sheri Laizer

The next six weeks were spent in exacting punishment from the rebellious chiefs, small columns penetrating every mountain fastness. By the first week in August, order had been fully re-established, and General Fraser withdrew after restoring to the Civil Administration full control of the country, leaving a temporary garrison at Sulaimani and establishing the head-quarters of a reduced force at Kirkuk. Thus ended a brilliant little operation, which, despite preliminary reverses, showed that Indian troops, some of which . . . had never before been in action, were more than a match for the Kurds. . . .

Shaikh Mahmud was brought to Baghdad, where he soon recovered from his wounds. He was in due course brought with his associate Shaikh Gharib before a military court-martial, tried for rebellion, and sentenced to death. The Commander-in-Chief . . . commuted the sentence to a long term of imprisonment. . . .

Though I sympathized with the feeling which inspired this act of clemency, I opposed it officially on the ground that so long as Shaikh Mahmud was alive his adherents in Southern Kurdistan would live in the hope, and his enemies in the fear, of his eventual return, and that his death would contribute more than any other single factor to the restoration of tranquillity. I had seen him in hospital when, with a magnificent gesture, he denied the competence of any Military Court to try him, and recited to me President Wilson's twelfth point, and the Anglo-French Declaration of 8th November 1918, a translation of which in Kurdish, written on the fly-leaves of a Qur'an, was strapped like a talisman to his arm. Some years later he was pardoned and allowed to return from exile. He has been a source of anxiety and expense to the Governments of Persia and Iraq ever since.

A. T. Wilson, *Mesopotamia 1917–20: A Clash of Loyalties*, 1931

MESOPOTAMIA

Major Soane . . . went to the house of Osman Pasha, the father of Tahir Beg. He became his servant and remained in his employment six or seven months. He called himself Ghulam Husain. This Ghulam Husain, who was Major Soane, worked very well at his duties as servant. Tahir Beg also, on account of his good service, treated him with the greatest respect and liked him. . . .

From certain peculiarities of the behaviour of this Ghulam Husain Tahir Beg conceived some doubts; for he observed that his manners were not like those of other servants, so polite and conscientious was he. . . .

One day when they were talking there slipped from the tongue of Ghulam Husain (Major Soane) instead of the word *na*, the word *new*—no. Tahir Beg was puzzled at this and concluded that this man named Ghulam Husain was English, because the word *new*—no is the English for *na*.

C. J. Edmonds, "Soane at Halabja: An Echo," *Journal of the Royal Central Asian Society*, Vol. 23, October 1936

Major Ely Bannister Soane
British Traveler and Political Administrator

Funds certainly were scarce; I could not afford to travel as a European usually does, with servants, paying double for everything and occupying the best quarters everywhere. If I went I must don a fez and pass as a native of the East, must buy my own food, and do my own haggling, must do all those things which no European could or would ever think of doing. In Persia I had had experience of life in disguise as a Persian, and this would be an easier task for I was a stranger among strangers, and any difference in our ways and habits would be put down to that fact. There was a certain attraction, too, in going unattended by anyone, knowing practically no Turkish nor Arabic, across Syria and down the Tigris to Kurdistan. Once there I should be more at home, for I knew two or three dialects and Persian perfectly, which would enable me to pass as a Persian among the Kurds, and to hide ignorance of that habit and custom which are the rule of life in the East. As to Muhammadan observances, I had in Persia learned all that, and as a Shi'a could say my prayers, and dispute the Qur'an with the best of them. . . .

I found myself at Halabja, a place unique in Turkish Kurdistan, in being the residence of such powerful Kurdish people as Uthman Pasha, Lady Adela, Tahir Beg, and Majid Beg, and in being absolutely in the possession of the three huge mansions in which they lived.

The morning after my arrival broke to the sound of clinking tea-glasses outside the door of my room, and opening it I was confronted by a couple of retainers bearing the apparatus of tea "à la persane," a big brass samovar, a basin to wash saucers and glasses, and the little waisted Persian tea-glasses and china saucers themselves.

The bedding was rolled up and carried away, and hot sweet tea served, three glasses being the orthodox number. During the space between the glasses, one smoked, and a decent interval was allowed to elapse between their presentation. The ceremony over, the paraphernalia was carried away, and the day being officially commenced, I set out to see Lady Adela. . . .

Her servants were all Persian subjects, and in Halabja she instituted in her new houses a little colony of Persian Kurds, and opened her doors to all travellers from and to that country, and kept continual communications with Sina, five days' journey away. . . .

Gradually the official power came into her hands. Uthman Pasha was often called away to attend to affairs. . . . Lady Adela built a new prison, and instituted a court of justice of which she was president, and so consolidated her own power, that the Pasha, when he was at Halabja, spent his time smoking a water pipe, building new baths, and carrying out local improvements, while his wife ruled. . . .

In the manner of Kurdistan, this was a private interview, so I found no more than twelve servant retainers, and armed men standing at the door. The room was . . . carpeted with fine Sina rugs, and at the far

Adela Khanum, ca. 1919

Lynette Soane/Courtesy Sheri Laizer

She was of great service to the British during the occupation (Lynette Soane)

Princess Adela Khanum (K.B)

of Halabja Khan Bahadar S. Kurdistan

my dear Kurdish friend

& ruler of Halabja

now L. h - Z.

end stood a huge brass bedstead piled high with feather quilts. Before and upon it sat the Lady Adela herself, smoking a cigarette. The first glance told her pure Kurdish origin. A narrow, oval face, rather large mouth, small black and shining eyes, a narrow, slightly aquiline hooked nose, were the signs of it; and her thinness in perfect keeping with the habit of the Kurdish form, which never grows fat. . . .

Her head-dress was that of the Persian Kurds, a skull-cap smothered with rings of gold coins lying one over the other, and bound round with silk handkerchiefs of Yezd and Kashan. On each side [of] the forehead hung the typical fringe of straight hair from the temples to the cheek, below the ear, and concealing it by a curtain of hair, the locks called "agarija," in the tongue of southern Kurdistan. The back hair, plaited, was concealed under the silk handkerchief that hangs from the head-dress. Every garment was silk, from the long open coat, to the baggy trousers. Her feet were bare, and dyed with henna, and upon ankle and wrist were heavy gold circlets of Persian make. Upon her hands she wore seventeen rings, heavily jewelled, and round her neck was a necklace of large pearls, alternating with the gold fishes

that are the indispensable ornament of the Persian Kurd, and of many of the Persians themselves.

A woman fanned her, while another held cigarettes ready, and a maid waited with sherbet and rose-water. As I entered, Lady Adela smiled and motioned me to a seat beside her on the mattress, and gave me the old-fashioned Kurd greeting: "Wa khair hatin, wa ban i cho, ahwalakitan khassa shala." ("You are welcome; your service is upon my eyes; your health is good, please God.") . . .

Her tones were peculiar, not those of a woman, and though not deep, were clear and decisive, and abrupt. Persian she understood perfectly, though a little shy of speaking it before one whom she only knew as a Persian. . . .

For an hour or more the interview lasted, then she rose and earnestly desired to know if I was quite comfortable, gave orders for new carpets and better bedding for me, and then retired, and for the first time spoke Persian as a farewell, bidding me return to the official "Divan," which she held every afternoon.

E. B. Soane, *To Mesopotamia and Kurdistan, in Disguise*, 1912

MESOPOTAMIA

Dearest,

The political officers and myself are at present living in the Khanum's house, and having a pretty good time. The Lady herself is about sixty-five years of age. But she dyes her hair and paints and powders her face, and on the whole, tries to play the giddy young thing. However she must be very strong willed, because her tribe (before the coming of the British) were nothing but highway robbers, and yet she had 'em in the palm of her hand to do just what she liked with—some woman! . . .

Within a radius of say, a hundred miles each way, the political and myself are absolutely the only two Englishmen to be found. The population is Kurdish, and they have no written language, so we have to rely on what we can pick up. . . . We live just absolutely the same as the Kurds (they live extraordinarily well by the way) and rather like it. . . .

The job is no sinecure, as the population is almost wholly nomad (like me) and it is no easy thing to keep them in order and make them pay their taxes and things. We have a force of gendarmerie recruited from amongst the tribes to keep law and order, and very stout fellows the gendarmes are (set a thief to catch a thief is the British Policy).

Letter from Percival Richards
to his wife, December 20, 1919
Courtesy Richard Hesketh

Dear respected and faithful friend,

You left and broke both our circle and our heart. Only God knows how much sorrow has come into my heart because of the departure of you dear; especially so, because I did not know how far you've gotten. When your letter arrived from Bombay, how happy I became. May you be happy because you made our day. You had kindly asked about me. Fortunately, there is no grief except for the sorrow of you being away. I hope that soon in utmost health and joy you will return to your country, see your friends and be gratified. God willing, hasten your return so that I may once more be happy seeing you. Let me know how you are. Waiting to hear from you, dear.

Wife of Othman Pasha

Seal given by the British reads
"Khan Bahadur Adela"
Letter from Adela Khanum to Lynette
Soane, Major E. B. Soane's wife, 1920,
translated by Amir Hassanpour
Courtesy Sheri Laizer

*Adela Khanum (Lynette Soane is seated to
her left) surrounded by her family, 1920*

Percival Richards/
Courtesy Richard Hesketh

ELY (in centre) AND SOME OF HIS STAFF   KURDISTAN 1920

THOSE WITH CROSSES SINCE

DEAD

ELY (DIED AT SEA 1923

CAPT. FITZGIBBON MURDERED

IN KURDISTAN 1921

CAPT. BOND MURDERED

1922

CAPT. MAKANT MURDERED
                        1922
CAPT. WRIGHT

KILLED NORTH AFRICA

1925.

CAPTAIN LEES GUARD ON A
MOUNTAIN SIDE

SELF. PRINCESS ADELA. ELY, CAPT. LEES & AHMAD BEG
TAKEN AT HALABJA   KURDISTAN SEPT. 1919

Handwritten captions and photographs by Lynette Soane/Courtesy Sheri Laizer

Major Soane came as an Oriental and stayed in the area. He had contacts with a lot of the tribal heads in the area, such as the Jaf and the Pishdar. At that time, it was not Iraq but Mesopotamia. There were three vilayets—Basra, Baghdad, and Mosul, the Kurdish vilayet. Shaikh Mahmud rose up for the rights of the Kurds, but international policy did not allow for this at the time, and the British brought Major Soane back. Major Soane was a political advisor to Shaikh Mahmud, but secretly he was contacting the heads of the tribes in Kurdistan and organizing them against him.

The day Major Soane came back, Shaikh Mahmud went to receive him. From the moment they met, Shaikh Mahmud realized, from the way Soane shook his hand, that he was coming to demolish Shaikh Mahmud's government.

The division of Kurdistan didn't start then. It started when Sykes and Picot sat at the table and divided the country in 1916. The British planned through the Orientalists how to create problems if anything endangered the division they had decided on.

Interview with Shaikh Salar Hafid, Shaikh Mahmud's grandson, living in Iraq, May 1993

MESOPOTAMIA

Treaty of Sèvres, 1920

Article 62

A Commission sitting at Constantinople and composed of three members appointed by the British, French and Italian Governments respectively shall draft within six months from the coming into force of the present Treaty a scheme of local autonomy for the predominantly Kurdish areas lying east of the Euphrates, south of the southern boundary of Armenia as it may hereafter be determined, and north of the frontier of Turkey with Syria and Mesopotamia. . . .

Article 63

The Turkish Government hereby agrees to accept and execute the decisions of both the Commissions mentioned in Article 62 within three months from their communication to the said Government.

Article 64

If within one year from the coming into force of the present Treaty the Kurdish peoples within the areas defined in Article 62 shall address themselves to the Council of the League of Nations in such a manner as to show that a majority of the population of these areas desires independence from Turkey, and if the Council then considers that it should be granted to them, Turkey hereby agrees to execute such a recommendation, and to renounce all rights and title over these areas. . . . If and when such renunciation takes place, no objection will be raised by the principal Allied Powers to the voluntary adhesion to such an independent Kurdish State of the Kurds inhabiting that part of Kurdistan which has hitherto been included in the Mosul vilayet.

From J. C. Hurewitz, *Diplomacy in the Near and Middle East*, 1956

This photograph was made by a local professional photographer. The Cairo Conference lasted for ten days. It is said that Churchill was thrown by his camel and hurt his hand but rode back to Cairo with Lawrence.

Delegates from the Cairo Conference on a visit to the pyramids; Gertrude Bell (center), Winston Churchill (left of Bell); T. E. Lawrence in front of sphinx, March 20, 1921

G. M. Georgoulas/Gertrude Bell Archive, University of Newcastle-Upon-Tyne

From Earl Curzon [Secretary of State for Foreign Affairs] To Admiral Sir J. de Robeck

Constantinople, March 26, 1920

The policy at which we are aiming in the Peace Treaty, as far as it has gone, with regard to Kurdistan is neither a single protectorate for England or France, nor a divided protectorate, nor a group of States under European protection, but an autonomous Kurdistan, severed from Turkey, and not even under Turkish suzerainty. . . .

Do you recommend invitation to come to London being given to Kurdish spokesmen? . . .

Question is one of urgency, and decision cannot be indefinitely delayed.

In attempted settlement of East, there might be considerable advantage if England were known to be author of such a programme.

British Public Record Office, Kew
FO 371/5219/E1776

Gertrude Bell to Sir Hugh Bell

Baghdad, September 5, 1920

The tribes don't want to form part of a unified state; the towns can't do without it. How are we going to support and protect the elements of stability and at the same time conform to the just demand for economy from home? For you can't have a central government if no one will pay taxes and the bulk of the population won't pay taxes unless they are constrained to do so. Nor will they preserve a sufficient amount of order to permit of trade. . . .

We are now in the middle of a full-blown Jihad, that is to say we have against us the fiercest prejudices of a people in a primeval state of civilisation. Which means that it's no longer a question of reason. And it has on its side the tendency to anarchy which is all over the world, I think, the salient result of the war. When one considers it, it's very comprehensible that the thinking people should revolt at an organisation of the universe which could produce anything so destructive to civilization as the war. . . . The credit of European civilisation is gone. Over and over again people have said to me that it has been a shock and a surprise to them to see Europe relapse into barbarism.

Lady Bell, *The Letters of Gertrude Bell*, 1927

Cairo Conference

Fourth Meeting of the Political Committee, March 15, 1921
Present: The Rt. Hon. Winston Spencer Churchill, P.C., M.P. Chairman; Sir Percy Cox, G.C.I.E., K.C.S.I.; Miss Gertrude Bell, C.B.E.; Colonel T. E. Lawrence; Major H. W. Young, D.S.O.; Major Noel, Consultative Member; Major R. D. Badcock, M.C., Secretary

The Committee proceeded to discuss the questions of Kurdistan.

The position was reviewed in the light of the revision of the Treaty of Sèvres, and it was suggested that the southern Kurds should not be included under the Government of Iraq. Sir Percy Cox stated that he had already intimated to his Council of State that during the year within which Kurdistan had the right under the treaty to opt for independence he would deal with Kurdish districts himself, and that at the end of that period the position would have to be reconsidered in the light of future developments. He had already received a protest from the Council against this decision. The area in which the Kurds were predominant was in the divisions of Kirkuk and Sulimanieh and certain districts north of Mosul. . . . Cox was of opinion that these divisions formed an integral part of Iraq, whilst economically they should undoubtedly belong to that country. He agreed with Miss Bell that the people of Kirkuk would wish to take part in the forthcoming election, and that their representatives should sit in the Iraq Parliament. He doubted whether the people of Sulimanieh would hold the same view. . . .

Major Young . . . suggested that it might be preferable not to delay, but to set up a Kurdish State which would be directly under the control of the High Commissioner, and would not be a part of, or responsible to, the Iraq Government. . . . Major Noel stated that . . . now that the British forces were evacuating this area, he considered that the Turks might attempt to detach Sulimanieh from the zone of our influence. . . . He considered that British policy demanded the setting up of a Kurdish buffer State which could be used to counterbalance any strong anti-British movement which might occur in Mesopotamia. He suggested that if there were no customs barrier between the two countries, the Kurds should be given a fair portion of the revenue. . . .

In reply to a question by the Chairman, Colonel Lawrence stated that it was his opinion that the Kurds should not be placed under an Arab Government, although he fully realised that the latter would endeavour to arrange this. . . .

Miss Bell . . . suggested that the whole position should be left for a further period of about six months, after which she was of the opinion that the Kurds would be anxious to join the Iraq Government. . . .

The Chairman . . . put forward that it might be possible to subsidise a Kurdish chief and his more influential subordinates and to grant provisional trading facilities in consideration of an agreement that they would prevent the Turks from carrying out a policy in that area adverse to British interests in Iraq. Even if the Kurds wished to join in the elections, he anticipated difficulty if they were included in Iraq. A Sherif, whose breeding and family history probably led him to hold views on the Divine Right of Kings, might, while outwardly accepting constitutional procedure and forming a Parliament, at the same time despise democratic and constitutional methods. If this were so, it might well be that, with the power of an Arab army behind him, he would ignore Kurdish sentiment and oppress the Kurdish minority. British policy would, on the other hand, be well secured by a friendly buffer State between Iraq and the Turks. . . .

The Chairman agreed with Major Young that it might be possible to form something in the nature of a frontier force of Kurds, under the command of British officers.

British Public Record Office
FO 371/6343/E 8001

FEISAL'S CORONATION.

BRITISH GARRISON IN IRAK TO BE REDUCED.

As already announced in *The Times*, the Emir Feisal will be crowned King of Irak at Baghdad to-day.

An announcement issued last night by the Colonial Office said :—

The referendum designed to ascertain the wishes of the people of Irak with reference to the candidature of the Emir Feisal for the rulership of the new State to be set up under the mandate accepted by the British Government having resulted in an overwhelming vote in his favour, the resolution of the Provisional Council of State that Feisal should be chosen King has been confirmed.

The authorities in Irak are fully satisfied with the political situation there, which will enable the progressive reduction of British troops to proceed with greater expedition than was anticipated. The recent disturbance engineered by Turkish Nationalists in Rowanduz, which is a purely Kurdish area over 50 miles outside the boundaries of Irak proper, is merely local, and has had no effect upon the Arab population over which the Emir Feisal will rule, and the dispatch of a small column to Erbil is a measure of precaution for the preservation of order in this district, which contains both Kurdish and Arab elements.

. The Emir Feisal is the third son of the King of the Hejaz, and will be remembered as the leader of the Sherifian army which co-operated brilliantly with Lord Allenby; the conquest of Palestine and Syria. Lat Feisal was at the head of the Arab Government established at Damascus; he also attended the Peace Conference at Paris as the representative of his father. Disagreement with the French followed, and Feisal was compelled to quit Syria. He came to Palestine and subsequently spent some months in London. Meanwhile a provisional Arab Government had been set up in Mesopotamia by the British, and influential Arabs in that country invited Feisal to become a candidate for the throne. Mr. Churchill, as Colonial Secretary, stated last month that the Emir had been informed that he was at liberty to go to Mesopotamia, and if chosen as their ruler by the people would receive the support of the British Government. The Emir reached Basra on June 24, and has received the support of all the Arab notables of Irak.

The Times, London, August 23, 1921

From Secretary of State for the Colonies, W. Churchill To High Commissioner of Mesopotamia, Sir P. Cox

June 13, 1921

Let me have your views on possibility of our making more capital out of Kurdish nationalism and its potential hostility to Turkish nationalism. I still favour policy contemplated at Cairo of setting up Kurdish buffer between Arabs and Turks and I consider that we ought not to be deflected from this policy either through Arab pressure or for any other cause. I am asking Foreign Office to repeat this telegram to Constantinople.

British Public Record Office, Kew
FO 371/6346/13827

From W. Churchill To Sir P. Cox

June 24, 1921

I decided to obtain the expert advice of Soane and Longrigg thus benefiting by their presence in this country.... The criterion for deciding the boundary line between the areas controlled respectively by yourself and the Mesopotamian Government should rather be the ethnological limit of purely Arab areas than that of purely Kurdish areas. The towns of Erbil, Kifri, and Kirkuk are in no sense Arab though not purely Kurdish, and I am advised that the political situation is likely to be easier on the withdrawal of the British garrisons if they are replaced by units under British officers than by the Arab Army. This appears to me to be sound policy from our point of view also. We are proposing to give the Mesopotamian Government a very free hand and it is in my opinion undesirable that their influence should extend into non-Arab areas. By our position as mandatory power we are committed to defending them from hostile attack and it should not be difficult to convince them that in order to do this effectively we contemplate the creation of a frontier force under British officers in the areas through which alone hostile aggression is likely to materialise.... This frontier force must consist of Turcomans, Kurds, and Assyrians and in my opinion it would be undesirable to station these permanently in posts administered by the Arab Government of Mesopotamia. The assumption of authority by Feisal will provide an excellent opportunity of defining our policy.

British Public Record Office, Kew
FO 371/6346/E7435

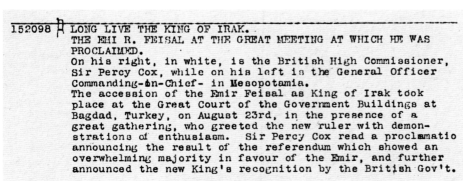

```
152098  LONG LIVE THE KING OF IRAK.
        THE EMIR. FEISAL AT THE GREAT MEETING AT WHICH HE WAS
        PROCLAIMED.
        On his right, in white, is the British High Commissioner,
        Sir Percy Cox, while on his left is the General Officer
        Commanding-in-Chief- in Mesopotamia.
        The accession of the Emir Feisal as King of Irak took
        place at the Great Court of the Government Buildings at
        Bagdad, Turkey, on August 23rd, in the presence of a
        great gathering, who greeted the new ruler with demon-
        strations of enthusiasm. Sir Percy Cox read a proclamatio
        announcing the result of the referendum which showed an
        overwhelming majority in favour of the Emir, and further
        announced the new King's recognition by the British Gov't.
                        OCTOBER 20, 1921
```

Gertrude Bell to Sir Hugh Bell

Baghdad, August 28, 1921

We have had a terrific week but we've got our King crowned and Sir Percy and I agree that we're now half seas over. . . . The enthronement took place at 6 a.m. on Tuesday, admirably arranged. A dais about 2ft. 6in. high was set up in the middle of the big Sarai courtyard; behind it are the quarters Faisal is occupying, the big Government reception rooms; in front were seated in blocks, English, Arab Officials, townsmen, Ministers, local deputations, to the number of 1,500. . . .

Saiyid Hussain stood up and read Sir Percy's proclamation in which he announced that Faisal had been elected King by 96 per cent. of the people of Mesopotamia, long live the King! With that we stood up and saluted him. The national flag was broken on the flagstaff by his side and the band played "God save the King"—they have no national anthem yet. . . .

Sir Percy had been unwell but on the day of the Coronation he began to recover and is now quite fit again, so I who had kept all people off him for a week quietly arranged for the deputations to pay their respects to him. . . . The Kurds came last and stayed longest. The Mayor . . . said that they hadn't had an opportunity to discuss with Sir Percy the future of Kurdistan, what did I think about it? I said that my opinion was that the districts they came from were economically dependent on Mosul and always would be however many Kurdistans were created. They agreed but, they must have Kurdish officials. I said I saw no difficulty there. And the children must be taught in Kurdish schools. I pointed out that there would be some difficulty about that as there wasn't a single school book—nor any other—written in Kurdish. This gave them pain and after consideration they said they thought the teaching might as well be in Arabic, but what about local administrative autonomy. . . . I said "Have you talked it over with Saiyidna Faisal—our Lord Faisal?" "No," they said. "Well you had better go and do it at once," I suggested. "Shall I make an appointment for you?" "Yes," they said. So I telephoned to Rustam Haidar and made an appointment for yesterday afternoon—I'm longing to hear from Faisal what came of it. Fun isn't it? . . . Faisal . . . asked me to tea.

Lady Bell, *The Letters of Gertrude Bell*, Vol. II, 1927

From Sir P. Cox
To W. Churchill

September 20, 1921

King Feisal said as he was still not very clear as to real wishes and policy of His Majesty's Government he was in difficulty as to what line to take. . . . He asked me to tell him frankly what we wanted. . . . In reply I said that at Cairo Conference there was strong belief in some quarters that Kurdish districts of Iraq would as a whole object to coming directly under a benignant government at Baghdad and would claim or at any rate welcome local autonomy and administration by Kurdish officials under direct British supervision exercised through High Commissioner. On the whole I said this idea was favoured by His Majesty's Government. . . .

But I said that . . . I believed it was not object of His Majesty's Government to see these Kurdish districts cut out of Iraq and my own view was that all the time they were governed by Kurdish officials under British supervision and preferably administered by High Commissioner in consultation with Iraq Government the British Government would prefer that these districts remained an integral part of Iraq rather than that they should secede to northern Kurds.

British Public Record Office, Kew
FO 371/6347/E12182

Secret Intelligence Report from Secretariat of H.E. the High Commissioner for Iraq

Baghdad, October 1, 1922

Shaikh Mahmud . . . arrived in Baghdad on September 13 . . . and had an interview with King Faisal on September 16. . . . The King informed the Shaikh that his view as regards Sulaimani had undergone considerable modification. He no longer thought that the province should come under the throne of the Iraq, but he was convinced that the interests of the two were the same—Sulaimani could not live without a close agreement with Iraq and, for the Iraq, Sulaimani was a bulwark against Turkish aggression. He was therefore prepared to give to Shaikh Mahmud every assistance that he was in a position to extend.

British Public Record Office, Kew
FO 371/7835/E12542

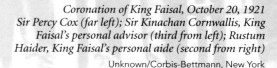

Coronation of King Faisal, October 20, 1921
Sir Percy Cox (far left); Sir Kinachan Cornwallis, King Faisal's personal advisor (third from left); Rustum Haider, King Faisal's personal aide (second from right)

Unknown/Corbis-Bettmann, New York

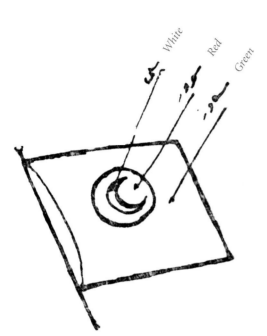

White Red Green

The flag of Kurdistan, which was made upon the order of Shaikh Mahmud and replaced the British flag. Azad Najib hoisted it.

Ahmed Khwaja, Çîm Dî
(What I Saw), 1970

Ahmed Khwaja

Ahmed Khwaja
Kurdish Fighter

We Kurds are famous for being hospitable. After the Ottomans left Kurdistan the British came here to Kifri, so Shaikh Mahmud sent a letter to the General . . . saying, "We are Kurds and we have guns. If you are going to give us what we are entitled to, if you accord us our right, we are going to be friends. If not, we have guns and we are going to fight for it." . . . When the British received their letter, they said, we will send someone to talk with you, so Major Noel came. When he came, he gave us a lot of hope and he said, "You are going to receive your independence. You will have your own country and of course, Shaikh Mahmud is going to be your leader." So we all applauded him happily and someone who was blind said, "Don't believe it, they are not trustworthy."

We were very nice towards the British, we did everything for them. When Major Soane came from Chemchemal there was no road, so Kurdish laborers made a road so that he could travel by his own car

and they did this without wages, so that Soane could reach Sulaimaniya. We were taking British personnel, soldiers, on our shoulders so that they could pass from here to there, or wherever they wanted to go, and even Shaikh Mahmud invited them to his house often and made celebrations for them.

But all we got from Britain was that they gave Kirkuk and its oil to Iraq and they created a single large nation named Iraq from the south and the north. So we got almost none of the things which they promised—independence, Kirkuk, Kurdistan. But we had been convinced that we were going to get what they had said, because they were British and we took them at their word on British honour. . . . The independence which we had didn't last for more than three months.

Interview with Ahmed Khwaja, supporter of Shaikh Mahmud,
from "Birds of Death," Wall-to-Wall TV, 1992

The purpose of this newspaper is to serve the people, and it is the duty of every Kurd to read it and buy it. It is well known that if a nation has no newspaper, nobody will know the mind, the opinions, or the imagination of the people, and the nation itself will not understand its own affairs and will remain without standing among nations. . . . Thus, for victory of the nation of Kurdistan, interest should be taken in this newspaper because it is a national newspaper and an interpreter of the opinions and the servant of the Kurdish nation.

Ali Kemal, editorial (right) in *Bangi Kurdistan (Call of Kurdistan)*, Kurdish national weekly newspaper published in Sulaimania, August 2, 1922, translated by Amir Hassanpour

Secret Intelligence Report From Secretariat of H.E. the High Commissioner for Iraq

Baghdad, October 15, 1922

Major Noel . . . reported that Shaikh Mahmud on arrival at Sulaimani, on September 30, had been given an overwhelming reception by his adherents, the national flag and national badge being everywhere in evidence. The Shaikh made a public address in which his reference to His Majesty's Government was all that could be desired. He is, however, aghast at the greed of his supporters and hampered by the activity and strength of Turkish propaganda which takes the line of trying to persuade him that he is being used merely as a cat's paw by the British.

British Public Record Office, Kew
FO 371/7835/E12542

مقصد لم غزنته یه چونکه رهبری و خذمت بو قوم کردانه له سر همو کوردیك لازمه ام غزنته یه بخوی نیتهوه وه به دل کوبی لی بکری ۰

معلومه که بچ قومیك غزنته یکی نبی نه کس له فکر و خیالی او قومهو نه او نجم کار و باری خوی تی ده کا و او وقته له ناو قومان دنیا بی نام و نیشان دهمینیته وه ۰

بناءً علیه بو سرفرزی ملت کردستان له بیش همو شتیكا لازمه و غبت به غزنته یه بدری ۰

چونکه غزنته یکی ملی و ترجمان افکار و خادم قوم کردانه ۰

The First Division of the National Army takes oath to serve the Kurdish nation, July 11, 1922, in front of the flag of the government of Shaikh Mahmud

Unknown/Courtesy Rafiq Studio

Mahmud Efendi
Kurdish Photographer

My father told me that during the First World War, the Ottomans took him as a soldier. When the Ottomans were defeated, the British Army arrested the officers and built a big camp for them. The British Army offered them different kinds of jobs, and my father chose to learn photography. When the prisoners were released, they returned to their countries.

My father and another man bought a camera and started working in Baghdad as photographers. Then a Jewish man convinced them to sell him the camera and they sold it to him. My father came back to Sulaimania and opened his own photography studio. During 1919 and the early 1920s my father worked there as a photographer.

Interview with Rafiq, son of Mahmud Efendi, April 1993

Shaikh Letif, son of Shaikh Mahmud

Photographer's stamp reads
"Studio Rafiq, Sulaimania"

Shaikh Mahmud with two of his sons, Shaikh Raouf (left) and Baba Ali

Shaikh Abdul Kadir, brother of Shaikh Mahmud

Mahmud Efendi/Courtesy Rafiq Studio

Shaikh Mahmud with gunners

Stamp: *"Government of Southern Kurdistan,"* used for tax records or to buy and sell properties
Ahmed Khwaja, *Çîm Dî (What I Saw)*, 1970

The British military . . . released Shaikh Mahmud and made him leader of Kurdistan. In this way he would defend, for example, Mosul, on behalf of Iraq. He refused to fight with any country's army—Iran, Iraq, Turkey—unless they made Kurdistan independent. . . .

Shaikh Mahmud asked for Kirkuk and they said, "Sorry, it's Iraq's."

Shaikh Mahmud said, "If we have Kirkuk we will do anything for Britain and will even write in English and our children will study in English at school." . . .

The Kurdish people received a warning that Shaikh Mahmud should go to Kirkuk or Baghdad and that if he didn't, they would bomb. . . . Shaikh Mahmud remained in Sulaimania on the 26th, 27th, and 28th when the planes started bombing.

Interview with Ahmed Khwaja, from "Birds of Death," Wall-to-Wall TV, 1992

Shaikh Mahmud may have been perfectly sincere when, before leaving Baghdad, he gave the assurance that he would confine his activities to the liwa of Sulaimani; but the tumultuous welcome in the station yard at Kingirban and the intoxicating air of Kurdistan as he rode across country in easy stages to his capital had quickly wiped out any memory of the limits placed upon him. . . . Very soon I received complaints from the Talabani Shaikhs and others that on his way Mahmud had pressed them to sign a memorial demanding inclusion in a Kurdish state under himself. He reached Sulaimani on the 30th and was greeted as Hukemdar or Ruler of Independent Kurdistan; the local press emphasized that Noel . . . was in fact nothing more than . . . a sort of Consul to serve as a go-between with the High Commissioner. On the 10th October a rescript 'given in Sulaimani the capital of Kurdistan' announced the formation of a 'Cabinet Kurdistan' with eight members. In November the Ruler assumed the title of King. . . .

At Kifri I learned that Christmas Day had been selected for the bombing of Mahmud. The greatest secrecy was being maintained. . . . Two machines were lost. . . . One or two other machines had to turn back owing to engine trouble, and in the end only about half the scheduled number of bombs was dropped; Kinkead was however able to claim a direct hit on Mahmud's front door.

That night 'the Political' and the R.A.F. combined for a fancy-dress Christmas dinner at the airfield mess, which lasted till three in the morning.

C. J. Edmonds, *Kurds, Turks and Arabs*, 1957

1922

Townspeople of Sulaimania

Mahmud Efendi/Courtesy Rafiq Studio

Gertrude Bell to Percy Cox

Baghdad, March 3, 1923
To be quite frank with you Percy (This is in answer to a question you addressed to me some weeks ago) our Kurdish policy has been what I can best designate as opportunistic. . . . Yet we were debarred from seeking a more hopeful course by undertakings which never have been and never will be confirmed. My own view was that since they were obviously tosh it would have been better to face the fact and try steadily to undermine them and this I would have done by allowing Faisal to try his hand while we looked the other way. For I believe that however much we know about the East, what we never can know is the effect orientals will have on one another if you leave them to themselves. . . .

I told you, I think, my impression of Sheikh Mahmud when I saw him here: he is a savage bundle of nerves, timid and suspicious as a wild animal and controlled by no more brain than is possessed by his counterparts in the jungle.

I am wondering how much harm they've done to Sulaimani which they bombed today. There was nothing else for it; we haven't troops enough to sit and wait while S.M. made a tribal raid on Kirkuk; we had to forestall him. I hope we've succeeded, and I think it is very possible that we have, but it has been a detestable business.

Lady Bell, *The Letters of Gertrude Bell*, Vol. II, 1927

اعلان رسمي

قرارمان دا كه لەم روژانه دا قوويكي عسكريه بنيرينه سلماني بو تنظيم أدارهٔ مملكت وترتيب امور قضا ونواحي. أشرآف مملكت ، روسای عشائر ، مأمورين حكومتٌ ، دليكي حافه وصادق دخالت وتسليم به قوميندان أو عسكره بين، كه اكا به سليماني بر / :

خبر دارتان كه بن آى خلفينه كه أكر ابو ه مخالفت ومقابله عسكركه نكه ت او ان به هيچ كوه جي دخلي ايوه نا كه ن وضربان لي نادهن وهيج ادينيكتان بي ناكه يه ن . نقط أر كسانه كه مقابله بكه ن عسكبر تعقيب وتأديب اوان

داكزر بر سرلم ابطالمله به زمان نامه و دشمنانه مقابله عسكركه مان بكه ن وبه نك بو عسكره وطياره بهاو يزن أوسا مسؤليت كوره أكه ويته سراوكسانه كه مسبب بن وعسكر دست ده كات به تعقيب وتأديبيان .

باش قوميندان قوات نفوائيه وعساكر بريه اردوى برطانياى كوره له عراقداه ه آى روايبل مارشال ، فريق أول اردوى هوائى

Leaflet air-dropped over Sulaimania by RAF

Official RAF Notice

We have decided to send within the next few days a military force to Sulaimania for reorganizing the administration of the Division and restoring order to the affairs of the surrounding districts. Notables, tribal chieftains, civil servants . . . and police officials are assured [that no harm will come to them] if they sincerely surrender themselves to the commander of the forces arriving in Sulaimania.

We inform you, o people, that if you do not put up resistance to the soldiers they will not interfere with your lives and not do you any harm. But those who oppose the soldiers will be pursued and punished.

If in spite of this warning there are people who engage in hostilities and shoot at our troops or airplanes, they will be held responsible for the consequences of their acts. The soldiers will pursue and punish them.

The Commander-in-Chief of the Air and Land Forces of the British Army in Iraq, Lieutenant General I. R. Marshall, Air Force

Leaflet from M. R. Hawar,
The Leader Sheik Mehmood and Southern State of Kurdistan, Vol. II, 1991,
translated by Mawlan Brahim

Unknown/Hulton Deutsch Archive, London

SULAIMANIYAH

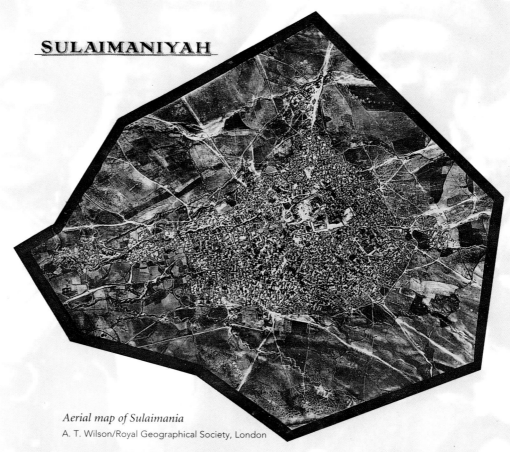

Aerial map of Sulaimania
A. T. Wilson/Royal Geographical Society, London

Beer drinking contest among bombers squadron, Mosul Unknown/Hulton Deutsch Archive, London

You have a booze-up with the opposing rugby team and then you get on the field and you tear each other to pieces and then you go and have dinner with them afterwards. . . . I was in the RAF. I had a job to do. My loyalty was to my commanding officer, who gave me my orders. If the Kurds hadn't learned by our example to behave themselves in a civilized way, then we had to spank their bottoms. And this was done by bombs and guns. And you may take it from me that they were shooting back.

Interview with RAF Wing Commander Gale, 30 Squadron, from "Birds of Death," Wall-to-Wall TV, 1992

COPY.

AIR MINISTRY
OPERATIONS LIBRARY
RECORD COPY.

Air Headquarters,
British Forces in Iraq.
Baghdad.

Reference:-
Air/519/226.

19th, May 1924.

SECRET.

To:-

Chief Equipment Officer, Air Headquarters.
Principal Medical Officer, Air Headquarters.
Air Staff "Signals", Air Headquarters.
Officer Commanding,
        No. 6 (Army Co-operation) Squadron, Mosul.
Officer Commanding,
        No. 8 (Bombing) Squadron, Hinaidi.
Officer Commanding,
        No.30 (Bombing) Squadron, Kirkuk.
Officer Commanding,
        No.45 (Bombing) Squadron, Hinaidi.
Officer Commanding,
        No.55 (Bombing) Squadron, Hinaidi.
Officer Commanding,
        No.70 (Bombing) Squadron, Hinaidi.
Armoured Car Wing Headquarters, Southgate.
Officer Commanding,
        No. 4 Armoured Car Company, Hinaidi.
Officer Commanding,
        No. 6 Armoured Car Company, Kirkuk.
Wing Commander W.H. Primrose, D.F.C.

OPERATION ORDER No. 12.

General.

        Conditions in the Sulaimaniyah area continue to be unsatisfactory.

        Shaikh Mahmud persists in his disobedience of Government orders, and is enlisting armed forces without authority, and using them for illegal taxation.

        The people of Sulaimaniyah have been notified by proclamation that, as a result of the above, the position held by Shaikh Mahmud and his forces will be bombed between the 26th and 31st May; those who wish may leave and retire to places of safety during the above period.

Intention.

        Intensive bombing of Sulaimaniyah will be carried out for two days commencing on May 27th, at 0530 hours local.

        The objective is the well-defined area in the

-2-

centre of the town. This has been marked on a photograph copies of which will be issued to Officers Commanding Squadrons.

        It is desired to inflict material damage as distinct from casualties to the inhabitants.

Operations.   (1) Command.

        (a) Operations will be controlled by Wing Commander Primrose, D.F.C., with Headquarters at Kirkuk which will open with effect from 0500 hours on May 27th.
             Flying Officer Davidson of Air Headquarters will be attached as Staff Officer.

        (b) All communications will be addressed "Sulops Kirkuk".

        (c) The functions of Officer Commanding Troops Kirkuk will be carried out as heretofore.

        (d) Units at Kingerban including Armoured Car Section will be under the orders of Officer Commanding, No. 45 Squadron.

        (e) In the event of weather conditions interfering with the programme laid down herein, Officer Commanding Sulops will re-allot periods as necessary.

        (2) Strength and location of forces.

        The following units will be employed from bases as shown:-

Unit.	Strength.	Base.
No. 6 Squadron.	1 flight.	Kirkuk.
No. 8 Squadron.	2 Flights.	Kirkuk.
No. 30 Squadron.	1 Squadron	Kirkuk.
No. 45 Squadron reinforced by No. 70 Squadron.	2 Flights.	Kingerban.
No. 55 Squadron.	1 flight.	Kingerban.
No. 6 Armoured Car Company.	1 Company, less 1 section at Kingerban.	
No. 4 Armoured Car Company.	1 section	Kirkuk.

        (3) Allotment of periods over targets.

        (a) Periods over the target are allotted as indicated in paragraph 4, all times are local and all watches will be synchronised from the

Bomb blasts Siranurq, 1924

Results

With regard to results obtained in Iraq by bombing practice and night work. I do not think anyone who has watched the improvement in bombing can fail to appreciate the fact that whereas a year ago we largely relied on noisy inaccuracy and moral effect, we now cause real casualties, and material damage that produce a real, as opposed to a purely moral effect.

Where the Arab and Kurd had just begun to realise that if they could stand a little noise, they could stand bombing, and still argue; they now know what real bombing means, in casualties and damage; they now know that within 45 minutes a full sized village . . . can be practically wiped out and a third of its inhabitants killed or injured by four or five machines which offer them no real target, no opportunity for glory as warriors, no effective means of escape, and little chance for retaliation or loot such as an infantry column would afford them in producing a similar result.

Night bombing is necessary to avoid a safe period intervening between daylight operations, when they return to inspect damage, eat, sleep, evacuate personnel and material, and graze their herds.

British Public Record Office, Kew
AIR 5/338/19244

BOMBS AND TAXES.

How does the average Briton, large-hearted and not small-minded, charitable, sensitive, compassionate, readily moved by any appeal on behalf of the helpless, almost foolishly fond of animals, feel when he reads that members of the British Air Force have carried out highly successful bombing expeditions in Mesopotamia against certain tribes which have declined to pay taxes to King Feisul?

There are many points of view from which the matter might be discussed. Many contend that we have neither interest nor right to interfere with the affairs of the inhabitants of this remote and very unpleasant part of the world. Others object that we are bound alike by honour and by definite obligation to uphold the Government of King Feisul, and that, moreover, regard for the most substantial British interests coincides with the duty of safeguarding that potentate.

It is not necessary for the present purpose to discuss these questions. How far we are bound, how far we are practically interested, what amount of the British taxpayers' money a British Government is justified in spending for either purpose—these are matters for Ministers and Parliament to decide. But on the one simple question of the methods of terrorism adopted against Mesopotamia tribesmen who decline to recognise Feisul's authority or to pay his taxes the British public has an immediate right to be heard, and even a duty to make itself heard.

There is no special vileness in the objection to pay taxes. Everybody dislike paying taxes. Very few even of our enlightened citizens would pay taxes if they could avoid doing so. It is only because the Inland Revenue service is in the highest degree both pervasive and persuasive that taxes are paid with relatively so little trouble. If the majority of us enjoyed the advantages of the remoter Iraq tribesmen, the revenue returns would undoubtedly suffer. Why, then, should we cast a stone—or, rather, a bomb—at these people? Who are we to concur in the "final notice" taking the form of "aerial action continued without intermission for twenty-four hours"?

If it were a question of putting down slavery, dacoity, cannibalism, or of suppressing some dangerous movement aimed at the Pax Britannica in the East, bombing by British aeroplanes might be justified, horrible as such a form of warfare must always be. But in this case justification is hard to discover. We have, as citizens of the British Empire, no serious quarrel with these people. We have, as trustees of the general welfare of humanity, no title to treat them as if they were enemies of the human race. They are probably not very lovable specimens—given, no doubt, to homicide, turbulence, ways that are dark and tricks that are vain. But the specific crime for which they are bombed—the crime of not paying taxes to a ruler either unrecognised or very reluctantly acknowledged—is not, we think, one which the average conscience of this country will declare meritorious of punishment so drastic.

It is really a very serious matter from every point of view. The em-

The Evening Standard, London
January 30, 1924

From the Secretary of State for the Colonies
To the High Commissioner of Iraq

January 31, 1924

Adverse comment has been aroused by accounts of recent air operations on Euphrates which have appeared in press here during last few days. . . . Accounts of these incidents produce unfortunate impression here especially when accompanied by the heavy casualties inflicted on the 30th November, and will not easily be explained or defended in Parliament by me. . . . I would ask you in particular to consider afresh the possibilities of adopting some alternative policy by which actual resort to bomb-dropping would be avoided.

British Public Record Office
CO 730/64/4566

Two Kurdish officers with British bomb

Yahya Efendi/
Courtesy Drakshad Jalal Ahmed

Three planes came the first time and each one dropped a bomb the size of a roll of hard sugar. The next time, they dropped very heavy bombs, and I remember the houses destroyed. Some people were killed in the second bombing, but in the third bombing, many people were killed.

I remember I went to see one of the women, and her hands were cut, and her fingers were not there. Her feet were also cut and her baby was torn, but still she was not dead. I stayed there with her until she died.

During the fourth bombing, I was in the street when the planes came. A piece of wall fell on top of me, and I was pinned under the wall, and a bone in my back was broken. Since then, I have had a limp.

During the fifth bombing, the British dropped papers announcing the bombing. So Shaikh Mahmud and all the people deserted the town. Those people who backed Shaikh Mahmud didn't dare go back to the city. We lived outside in the villages. I lived with my father in a village close by and did not come back to Sulaimania for one year.

When we came back, out of ten houses, nine were damaged. Not a single shop remained in the market. All were burned.

Interview with Shaikh Fatulla Shaikh Rashid,
living in Sulaimania, October 1992

Bombed homes in Sulaimania

It is a commonplace here that aircraft achieve their result by their effect on morale, and by the material damage they do, and by the interference they cause to the daily routine of life and not through the infliction of casualties. The casualties inflicted have been most remarkably small.

Report by air officer commanding Iraq, 1922
British Public Record Office
CO 730/64

"These men were officers of Shaikh Mahmud. The photograph is by Yahya Efendi, who was a spy for the British. No one had a camera at that time except him. The British army gave him that camera."   —*Shaikh Fatulla Shaikh Rashid*

Yahya Efendi/Courtesy Rafiq Studio

Kurdistan
33. Sheikh Mahmud's shelter.

Postcard

Unknown/Courtesy Badr Al Haji

Bangi Haq [The Call of the Truth] is victorious and will not be destroyed by artillery and bombs.

A political, social, and literary official newspaper issued from the high command of Kurdistan. Its purpose and hope is to achieve the rights of the Kurds.

1. Five months ago, in the name of all of Southern Kurdistan, the formation of the Kurdish government began, and we entered into elaborate negotiations with the British officials and councils. The creation of the Sulaimania government brought peace and security. The English began making excuses (against the interests of this government) and broke their promises. . . . Eventually, without any reason and any need, the people of Sulaimania were threatened by warplanes . . . but the nobles, of their own free will, chose me as their president and king. . . . The English threatened the people of Sulaimania with warplanes to drive me out. . . . This brutality against the people will not pass unpunished, and the civilized world and humanity will hold them accountable.

2. . . . For the safety of the people and the houses and the children of Sulaimania city, I left temporarily. . . .

3. . . . The officers and the persons who didn't leave Sulaimania until March 11 and joined us then will be spared punishment, and I will forgive them. . . . Until we enter Sulaimania victorious, anybody who accepts any assignment for the benefit of the English is an accomplice to the corruption, and his punishment will be execution according to the decision of the council of the people.

Front page of the Kurdish newspaper *Bangi Haq*, one of three
issues printed in the cave of Jasunu, southeast of Sulaimania;
M. R. Hawar, *The Leader Sheik Mehmood
and Southern State of Kurdistan*, Vol. I, 1990

Report by the Air Officer Commanding Iraq Command on the Operations in Southern Kurdistan against Shaikh Mahmud, October 1930–May 1931

The overwhelming ambition and instability of character of Shaikh Mahmud proved too strong for the pledge which he had given, and early in September, 1930, it became known that he was collecting an armed tribal force on the Persian border, evidently with subversive intentions. . . . Though he received warning letters on September 10th from both the High Commissioner and the Minister of the Interior, he crossed from Persia into Iraq on September 17th. Proof was thus given, if further proof were needed, that nothing less than the death or capture of this firebrand would leave the field clear for a peaceful solution of the problem of Southern Kurdistan.

The greater part of the country in which the operations took place is exceptionally difficult both for troops and for aircraft. . . . The rocks, scrub and trees gave ample cover for the enemy from air observation, and the long hours of low flying which were consequently necessary put a severe strain on the flying personnel. Shaikh Mahmud knew every inch of the country and had many years' experience of guerrilla warfare in these mountains. . . . No ordinary military force had by itself any chance of catching Shaikh Mahmud so long as he remained among the hills he knew so well.

It now seemed to me that . . . the Iraqi Army . . . should be given the opportunity of working without British control or support and of operating in the field entirely under the command and control of its own officers. . . . We were within two years of the termination of the mandate, and the Iraqi Government had never yet undertaken the control of its own military operations.

Royal Air Force Museum Archive, London
020264

1930–31

It is said that Shaikh Mahmud has repeatedly broken his promises, that he is cruel and tyrannical, that he is selfish and ambitious, and that he is nothing better than an outlaw bandit. But the defence has really a stronger case. His broken pledges were mostly given in duress and his faults are in the main the negative aspects of his positive qualities. His tyranny is the will of a tyrant, but it is mellowed by the generosity of a prince. If he is cruel, where are the witnesses? ... His ambition and his pride cannot be denied, but they are for his nation and not for himself alone, and many another has been as proud and as ambitious as he and thought none the worse of. An outlaw brigand, let that be granted, so were Garibaldi and Mustapha Kemal. But when all has been said on both sides, perhaps the wisest judgment is that his greatest fault is that he was born a century too late.

Captain Vyvyan Holt, Oriental secretary to the high commissioner for Iraq, "Report on the Operations in Southern Kurdistan Against Shaikh Mahmud, October 1930– May 1931," British Crown Copyright, Royal Air Force Museum Archive 020264

Dead Kurds being brought into Sul after the Penjwin scrap against Shaikh Mahmud

Colonel Lyon/Courtesy Dara Attar

SHEIKH MAHMUD'S SURRENDER

AGREEMENT WITH IRAQI GOVERNMENT

FROM OUR CORRESPONDENT

BAGHDAD, MAY 20

The following details of the arrest of Sheikh Mahmud, the Kurdish rebel leader, have been gathered from unofficial sources :—

Persian military forces had been concentrated near the Persian frontier village of Piran, where Sheikh Mahmud had taken refuge, and proclaimed their intention of ejecting him from Persian territory on May 14. Iraqi forces had planned a simultaneous attack on the Iraqi side of the frontier if the Sheikh attempted to cross.

On May 12 Sheikh Mahmud, having requested a conference in Iraqi territory, was granted safe-conduct, and rode from Piran to Penjwin, where he was met by the Mutasarrif and Captain Holt, Oriental Secretary to the High Commissioner. He was told that he must surrender unconditionally, but that the safety of himself and his family would be guaranteed. He said that he would probably accept the offer, but asked to be allowed to return across the Persian frontier to make arrangements with his followers and family.

Nothing more was heard from him on May 13, and the Persian and Iraqi forces continued their preparations for a joint attack on the following day. On the morning of May 14 troops on both sides of the frontier were ready to move when an urgent message reached the officer commanding the Iraqi forces that Sheikh Mahmud had ridden into Penjwin in the middle of the night and was sound asleep in a mud hut. After a conference he unconditionally agreed to the Iraqi Government's terms, but asked that no Iraqi Army escort should accompany him to Sulaimani town. In view of his record, however, an escort was deemed necessary. On the approach of a detachment of Iraqi cavalry, who escorted him part of the way to Sulaimani, Sheikh Mahmud burst into tears and implored the guard to shoot him, apparently considering a march across the mountains under an Iraqi Army escort an ineffaceable affront to his dignity.

During the march to Sulaimani the captive received everywhere the greatest commisseration from all, and the inhabitants of Sulaimani turned out to greet him and kiss hands. He was immediately transferred to the aeroplane, accompanied by Captain Gowan, the administrative inspector of Sulaimani, and was flown to Baghdad, whence, after the briefest of halts, the flight was continued to Ur of the Chaldees. The whole journey of 600 miles from Penjwin was accomplished in one day.

Sheikh Mahmud's surrender may have substantial results on the pacification of Southern Kurdistan. It means the end, probably for a period of years, of organized resistance to the Iraqi Government. It is improbable, at all events in the lifetime of the present generation and administration, that Iraqi Government will ever be really popular in Kurdistan, but the sober elements in the Kurdish population realize that there will be less injustice for the common people under the rule of Baghdad than could ever have been expected had Sheikh Mahmud's rebellion succeeded.

The Times, London, May 21, 1931

MESOPOTAMIA

Resistance to Centralization in Iran

In the early years of the twentieth century, Iran—or Persia, as the country was then known abroad—went through its first modern revolution, which in 1906 gave it a constitution and a parliament. Internal power struggles kept central authority weak, however, and it was perpetually challenged by warlords and tribal leaders in the periphery, especially on the Ottoman and Russian frontiers. The most unruly of the Kurdish tribes were the Shikak, who inhabited the mountains west of Lake Urmia. Their paramount chieftain, Jafar Agha, had long successfully resisted the government's efforts to impose its authority in his region. The provincial government finally got rid of him in 1905 by inviting him to Tabriz for a supposed reconciliation and then having him killed—a ruse to which more Kurdish leaders were to fall victim in this century. Jafar's younger brother Ismail, nicknamed Simko, soon took his place as the leading frontier warlord of northwestern Iran.

Simko rose to prominence in a time of revolution and war, when various armed forces were fighting one another in northwestern Iran. The city of Tabriz was a stronghold of the constitutional movement, and in the years following 1906 it consistently came out in support of democracy and the constitution. The countryside, and especially the Kurdish districts, showed little interest or sympathy for the movement and its leaders, while the nearby northern neighbor, Russia, considered the constitutional movement as a threat to itself. Ottoman troops occupied parts of the region in 1906 and stayed there until they were pushed back by Russian armies that intervened in 1911 against the constitutional revolutionaries of Tabriz. Soon after the outbreak of the First World War in 1914, the Nestorian Christians of Hakkari fled the Ottoman Empire to the relative safety of Urmia, where there already was a Nestorian community and where the Russians extended them protection. In the wake of their own revolution, the Russian troops left Iran, leaving a power vacuum that Simko attempted to fill.

The Nestorians, whom the British were trying to weld into an anti-Ottoman fighting force, apparently intended to carve out an independent state for themselves in the Urmia region. This brought them into a direct conflict of interest with Simko, who by then combined his role as a traditional warlord with Kurdish nationalist aspirations, and successfully united numerous tribes under his command. In the last year of the war, the Nestorians' religious and political leader, Mar Shimun, arranged a meeting with Simko for negotiations on cooperation against the Ottomans and Persians. Intensely distrusting the Nestorians' plans, Simko set up an ambush and killed Mar Shimun and most of his retinue.

A coup d'état in Tehran in 1921 brought the Cossack officer Reza Khan to power as the army commander and minister of war. He rapidly consolidated his power, reorganized the army, and set up a powerful central administration. Contenders were eliminated, tribal and regional rebellions suppressed, frontier warlords reduced. Simko, who on several occasions since the war had repelled the poorly trained Iranian forces that had been sent against him, reached the widest extent of his powers in the spring and summer of 1922. A newly strengthened and reorganized army delivered him a decisive defeat in August of the same year, however, and Simko fled across the border, into Iraq. After vain attempts to organize support from nationalist Kurds in Iraq and Turkey, he accepted an Iranian amnesty in 1924 but not much later made an abortive attempt to regain his former regional power. Defeated once again, he settled in Iraq until the Iranian government lured him back in 1930 with a promise of a governorship and had him killed in an ambush.

By 1925 Reza Khan had crushed all tribal revolts and warlords on the periphery and broken the opposition to his rule in the center. He had reduced the weak last shah of the Qajar dynasty to insignificance. And when toward the end of 1925 parliament abolished the Qajar dynasty, he crowned himself shah, adopting the name of Pahlavi for his dynasty. He carried through a program of authoritarian modernizing reform not unlike that in Mustafa Kemal's Turkey. The measures that most affected the Kurds were the forced settlement of nomadic tribes, a policy that began in the 1930s, and the banishing of leading families, away from their tribes and other dependents. Both policies were meant to incorporate the tribes into the Iranian nation (and to facilitate policing them). Although they caused considerable social disruption, they were only partially successful and had not reached their objectives by the time Reza Shah was removed from power in 1941.

—*MvB*

Map of the Kurdish tribes in Iran
Reproduced in Hassan Arfa, *The Kurds,* 1966

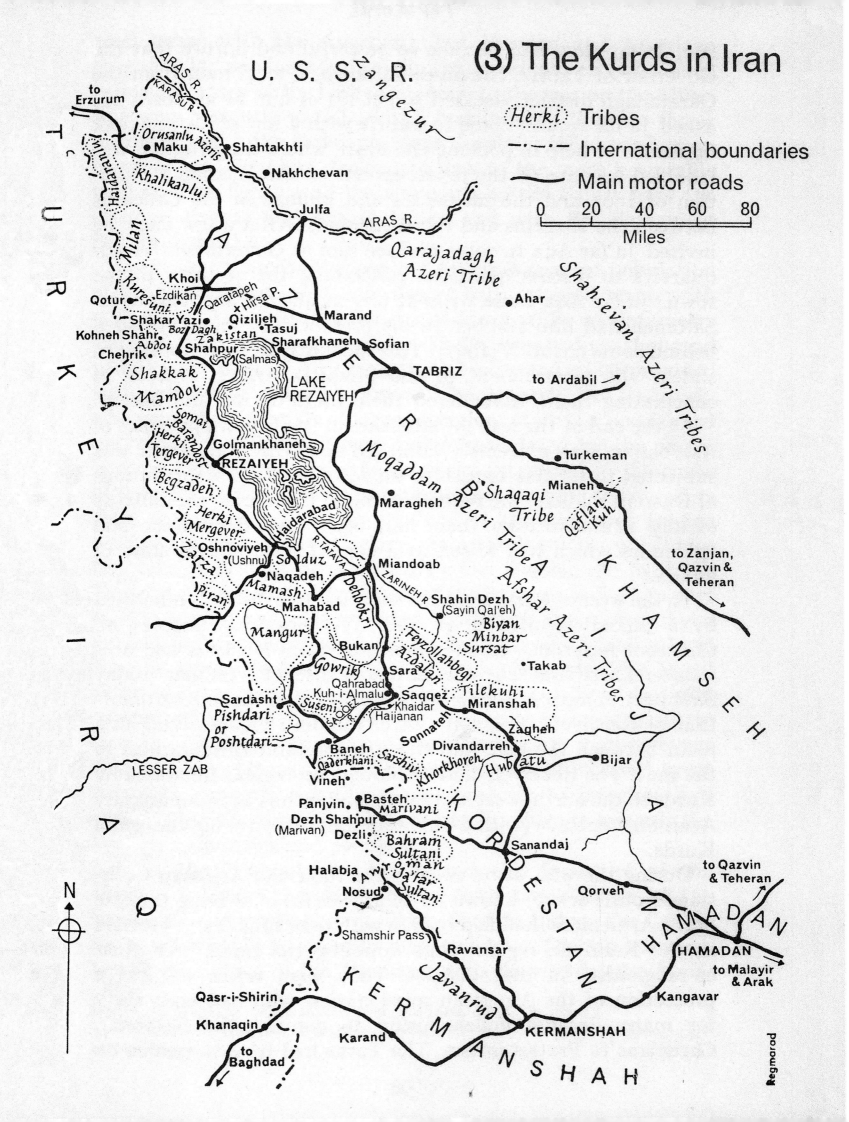

(3) The Kurds in Iran

Herki Tribes
–·–·– International boundaries
——— Main motor roads

0   20   40   60   80
Miles

U. S. S. R.

Zangezur

ARAS R.

to Erzurum

KARASUR

Orusanlu *Azeris*
Maku
Shahtakhti
Nakhchevan
Julfa
ARAS R.

Haidaranlu
Khalikanlu

Milan

TURKEY

Qarajadagh Azeri Tribe

Ahar

Shahsevan Azeri Tribes

to Ardabil

Khoi
Qaratapeh
Hirsa P.
Marand
Kuresuni
Qotur
Ezdikan
Qiziljeh
Shakar Yazi
Boz Dagh
Tasuj
Kohneh Shahr
Zakistan
Sharafkhaneh
Sofian
TABRIZ
Abdoi
Shahpur
Chehrik
(Salmas)

Shakkak
Mamdoi

LAKE REZAIYEH

Turkeman
Mianeh
Shaqaqi Tribe
Qaflan Kuh

Somai
Baranduz
Herki Tergever

Golmankhaneh
REZAIYEH

Maragheh

Moqaddam Azeri Tribe

Begzadeh

Herki Mergever
Zarza
Oshnoviyeh
(Ushnu)
Solduz
Haidarabad

R. TATAVA

Miandoab

Afshar Azeri Tribes

KHAMSEH

to Zanjan, Qazvin & Teheran

Naqadeh
Mamash
Piran

ZARINEH R.
Shahin Dezh
(Sayin Qal'eh)
Biyan
Minbar
Sursat

Mahabad

Takab

Mangur

Dehbokri

Bukan
Feyzollahbegi

Gowrik
Sara
Azdalan

Qahrabad
Kuh-i-Almalu
Saqqez
Tilekuhi
Miranshah

Sardasht
Suseni
R. OTZ
Khaidar
Haijanan
Zagheh

Pishdari or Poshtdari

Sonnateh

Divandarreh
Bijar

Baneh
Qaderkhani
Sarshiv
Khorkhoreh
Hubatu

LESSER ZAB

Vineh

Panjvin
Basteh
Marivani
Dezh Shahpur
(Marivan)
Dezli

Bahram Sultani
oman
Ja'far Sultan

KORDESTAN

Sanandaj

to Qazvin & Teheran

Halabja
Awr
Nosud

Qorveh

HAMADAN

Shamshir Pass

Ravansar

Javanrud

HAMADAN

to Malayir & Arak

N

IRAQ

Qasr-i-Shirin
Khanaqin
Karand

KERMANSHAH

Kangavar

KERMANSHAH

to Baghdad

Regmarad

Farmanfarma
Iranian General and Governor

The Ottoman forces were still in Iranian territory and the Kurds were engaged in cruelty around Urmia. Eqbal al-Saltaneh [Khan of Maku] was still in mutiny and many of his Kurds had poured into the villages of Khoy and all the time were looting another village. Ismail Agha, or as the Kurds call him Simko, had also mutinied and was raiding the region around Salmas. . . . Farmanfarma left Tabriz for Saujbulaq, and when he reached Miyanduab, he sent a group of cavalry in advance and the next day on the first or second of January rode towards there [Saujbulaq] with the remainder of the forces. The people of the city who were in their heart pro-Iranian, went to welcome them and engaged in much merrymaking and thus the city was captured again [1907]. But Muhammad Fariq Pasha, the Ottoman commander, was stationed a few farsakhs [each farsakh is about 6 kilometers] from the city and was constantly inciting the Kurds into revolt.

Ahmad Kasravi, Iranian nationalist and historian,
Tarikh-e Mashrute-ye Iran (The History of Iranian Constitutionalism), 1965

At that time Kurdistan was very dangerous, and the government was trying desperately to deal with the issue of centralization. By the 1850s, the borders of Iran were kind of set, and within these borders there was the issue of some minority disturbances.

The government of Iran was never able to subjugate the Kurds. They were nomadic, they would disappear behind mountains. Farmanfarma was sent to Kurdistan, as the young general, the rising star of the Qajars, to crush a rebellion. But he could not do anything. He got beaten continuously, and at some point he decided politically that he could not go back to the capital from his first major commission and say he'd lost. So he proposed a marriage to a Kurdish chieftain's daughter. Her name is Mah Beguim. She had two famous brothers—Fada Khan and Majid Khan. I don't know who her father was, but they were from Mahabad [Saujbulaq].

The marriage occurred, she was taken to Tabriz as his wife, and from that marriage there was one daughter. He then left to go back to Tehran, leaving her in Tabriz (his first wife is still in Tehran). Farmanfarma's half-sister, Khanoum Jan, ended up overseeing this young Kurdish woman, who, from all of that I have heard, was intensely unhappy with him and with life in a city. She was totally tribal; suddenly from a tribe where she was on a horse and with guns, she was told, "Now you're going to wear a veil and you can't come out of this house"—all these restrictions were put on her. She wrote her brothers who then came at night to abduct their sister. They scaled the walls, jumped into the palace, and took their sister back to Kurdistan, but they left her daughter in Tabriz. She was my grandmother.

My grandmother grew up with this notion that her mother was incredibly wild—savage—that she could not play the piano and only wanted to ride horses. For me what is obvious about this photograph is that Farmanfarma has a connection to the Kurds here. Otherwise you would never get him sitting on a carpet on a chair with that many Kurds standing behind him in total obedience. He's definitely old enough that at this point my grandmother is alive. It's the groom coming home. On another level—in that he was the governor of Kurdistan a few times in his life—this could possibly be "Here comes the governor back from the capital" or "this is our new governor," but he is one of us.

Interview with Nasser Ahari, Iranian architect living in the U.S., May 1996

Farmanfarma with a group of Kurds from Saujbulaq

1907

Jafar Agha
Kurdish Leader, Brother of Simko

Jaffer Agha, chief of the Kurds of Chari, a district of Salmas, about fifty miles north-west of Urmia . . . had been contumacious towards the Government, and resisted a small expedition sent to punish him for his misdeeds, which were many, but recently found it expedient to offer his submission. He was thereupon invited to come to Tabriz to cement the reconciliation under a solemn safe-conduct, and he made his appearance during this summer, accompanied by sixteen retainers. For two or three weeks he was hospitably entertained, and all went merry as a marriage-bell until the day came when he was to bid his official farewell to Nizam es Sultaneh. I was sitting quietly at home late in the afternoon of this day when I heard a burst of rifle-fire from the direction of the Government House, followed by a series of shots, which continued for ten minutes or a quarter of an hour, and then gradually died away in the distance. . . . It transpired that Nizam es Sultaneh and the higher officials had assembled in the reception-room on the first floor to receive the farewell greetings of Jaffer Agha, and that the latter was introduced alone into the anteroom and told to wait a moment. To him appeared an officer told off for the purpose, who discharged a revolver into the chieftain's body, while others performed the same kind office for two of his bodyguard who remained outside in the corridor. The three corpses were then thrown down into the court below. . . .

The authorities made as much capital as they could out of the three corpses, having them dragged in triumph through the streets and then hung by the heels, like carcasses in a butcher's shop, from a first-floor balcony overlooking a public square. . . .

The horrible treachery of the thing provoked little or no criticism. It was the time-honoured way of dealing with Kurds, and, in view of the impotence of the Government, practically the only way. The folly of the Kurds in letting themselves be entrapped time after time in this manner is almost unbelievable, but they never seemed to gain wisdom from experience.

A. C. Wratislaw, *A Consul in the East*, 1924

Jafar Agha Unknown/Courtesy Memo Yetkin

Unknown/Statens Ethnografiska Museum, Stockholm

Ismail Agha, "Simko"
Kurdish Leader

I am aware that my reputation is one of treachery and deceit in dealing with Governments and I therefore address you who have standing and credit in the eyes of the British Government upon the following matter: My recent actions and all my actions have no hostile intention with regard to the British Government. On the contrary I have a sincere desire to be on friendly terms with that Government. For this reason I request you to approach the officials of that Government on my behalf for the purpose of arranging some mutual understanding. For this object I am prepared to come south as far as Ushnu, for the sake of meeting any representative sent by the Government to discuss matters.

I would prefer that an English official be sent, but in the event of this being impossible, a man who is trusted by the Government, is capable and can read and write.

I am willing to abide by any orders given by the Government, but am chiefly anxious to establish relations with said Government, there being many points that could be effectively and to both parties advantageously settled by means of well designed understanding between the two parties.

I request that secrecy may be afforded to this communication.

Appeal by Simko cited in British secret memorandum
No. C/63 by the assistant political officer in Rania,
to the political officer in Sulaimania, July 20, 1921
British Public Record Office, Kew
FO 371/6347/138842

Simko, "Hero of Kurdistan"　　　　　　Unknown/Courtesy Karim Zand

There is no remaining Power now except that of the British Government. The Bolsheviks have shot their bolt and gone away. Persia, as a Power, does not exist. The Turks are represented by Mustafa Kemal and not more than 20,000 men round Angora, and in this quarter there is no stability.

—Simko

The chief Simko, or Ismael Agha, is the most picturesque character. His name is true to form, for he has been an outlaw, has played fast and loose with the Russians, Persians, Assyrians, Armenians, and British, according to the exigencies and shifts of his border region, and somehow kept on top. . . .

He is a natural leader. To look at him is to recognize a man of force and resource. . . . In conversation he is magnetic, genial, witty, shrewd, suave or brutally frank, and always playing a game. One feels that all the time. He is playing a game and enjoying it hugely. He is the typical romantic border desperado, carving out a career with his wits and rifles, and playing with men and lives—a bad game but the only game he knows, the only game that seems possible to him where political changes are the rule. . . .

What he wanted was justice for the murder of his brother, or, rather, revenge. . . . Would not the great American consul see to it that he had satisfaction? He then swung off into a wilder plea, a plea for his people, a plea which, with all the villainy and mixed motives behind it, had a genuine note. It was an appeal to the three great nations— England, France and America. . . .

"Here I am," he said in his inimitable way, with his flashing eyes, "living at the top of my mountain, my people eating grass (this was literally true of some tribes, who were starving) and no one about us but the false Russians, the false Turks and the false Persians. How can my voice reach Paris? You must carry my appeal. We need help and we look especially to America."

H. Mackensen, "A Remarkable Rescue," *The Kurdistan Missionary,* June 1920

Simitko (Kurd rebel) flanked by Russian consul and Zakaria Nazarbegic

"Regarding the Russian consul seen in this group picture taken with my grandfather, Simitko and his body guards, I can't exactly say what the occasion might have been."
—Takush Ohanian Aftandilian

Hovsep Hovsepian/Courtesy Takush Ohanian Aftandilian/Project SAVE

Maybe coincidently the Russian consul was in my grandfather's house when Simitko came to visit. Perhaps my grandfather wanted them to meet. I was told that Simitko, the Kurdish rebel, took refuge in my grandfather's house with his entourage, as shown in the picture, in Tabriz and escaped to safety from there.

My grandfather owned two villages in Kurdistan—Dar-achegh and Dar-aghezi—near the town of Soujbulagh. He would give the villagers the land rent and tax free to cultivate, and they would bring his share of the harvest profits each year. I remember having heard that they would bring gold coins to him—it was such a rich village.

Due to his knowledge of economics, accounting, and languages (Armenian, Russian, Persian, Turkish, and some Kurdish) my grandfather served as liaison in the Ministry of Commerce. In order not to risk the Armenian community's reputation with the government, my grandfather, Zakaria Nazarbekov, secretly gave refuge to Simitko and, being a humanitarian and a gentleman, he hid Simitko in his own home.

Interview and letter from Takush Aftandilian, granddaughter of
Zakaria Nazarbekov, living in the U.S., September 1996

The Simko episode may be considered as the first attempt by the Kurds in Iran to create an independent or autonomous region, but the chief actor, Simko, had neither the desire nor the ability to create a state in the modern sense of the word, with an administrative organization.
—Hassan Arfa

In the summer of 1921, a detachment of gendarmerie . . . was sent from Teheran to Tabriz to reinforce the local forces. . . . I was then in command of one of the squadrons sent from Teheran. In September, I was sent with my squadron and a mounted machine-gun section to reinforce a detachment of eight hundred men holding the Mahabad region south of Lake Rezaiyeh. When I arrived in Miandoab, I learned that this detachment had received a surprise attack from some four thousand Kurds under Simko and been utterly defeated, losing more than four hundred killed, all prisoners being shot by Simko and his followers. . . .

In November, I tried a surprise attack with my squadron on the Kurdish village of Ezdikan, possession of which would have opened to us the way towards the plain of Salmas, but a local Azeri landlord, in whose village I had been stationed and who was to act as my guide in this operation, deserted us in the middle of our night march. He fled towards the Kurds and alerted them, with the result that instead of surprising them, I was surprised myself. . . . I was forced to retreat, leaving forty killed and nine prisoners in the hands of the Kurds. These men were brought before Simko, who asked the N.C.O. [non-commissioned officer] to explain to him the mechanism of one of the machine-guns they had captured. The man began to explain, then suddenly turned the gun on Simko who, bouncing from his seat, seized the man's hands, assuring him that he now understood perfectly how to work the gun. The man's daring so pleased Simko that he released him and his comrades, making each of them a present of a gold Turkish lira.

Hassan Arfa, Persian general, The Kurds, 1966

Simko's fighters
Unknown/Courtesy Azad Mukriyani

Simko with his son, Khosro   Unknown/Courtesy Azad Mukriyani

Report on the Operations in Azerbaijan against Ismail Agha (Simko), Undertaken by the Persian Government

August 5–28, 1922

By the end of July, Simko controlled all Persian territory west of Lake Urmia from Khoi in the north to Sainkaleh and Sakiz in the south. His movement thus began to assume serious proportions and he became a real danger to the State. The seriousness of the situation was fully realised by the War Minister, Reza Khan, who made up his mind to take steps to crush Simko. . . .

It is interesting to note that the Turks, from whom the Persian Government feared Simko might get assistance, have rendered no help to the latter. On the contrary, the Turks have promised to arrest Simko should he cross the frontier into Turkey, and to hand him back to the Persian authorities for punishment. Latest information states that Simko has crossed the frontier and that the Turks are making efforts to round him up. . . .

This successful campaign against Simko has greatly strengthened Reza Khan's position, and he remains more than ever the outstanding figure in the country. The morale of the army, which had suffered from the reverses at Simko's hands in the spring and early summer, is now excellent.

Lieutenant Colonel M. Saunders, military attaché
British Public Record Office, Kew
FO 371/7835/E12242

From the High Commissioner for Iraq
To the Secretary of State for the Colonies

November 2, 1922

I have received very friendly messages from Simko who has arrived unexpectedly in a village north of Arbil. He asks to be allowed to come to Arbil for an interview.

It will be difficult and in view of effect on Kurdish nationalists dangerous to take active steps to turn him out and he might be useful to us apart from the difficulty of Persian sensibilities. Do you think that our relations with Persia make it obligatory that I should refuse to have anything to do with him.

British Public Record Office, Kew
FO 371/7835/E12056

From Sir P. Loraine (Tehran)
To Foreign Office

November 8, 1922

Persian Government has made no secret of its communications with Kemalists in order to secure capture and surrender of Simko. . . . If we give Simko any countenance, I do not see how we can disprove inevitable assertion that we are allowing him to use Mesopotamia as a base for organizing a further revolt amongst Persian Kurds; also he may actually do it. Moreover, after consulting Sir P. Cox in Baghdad last year, I assured Persian Government that we were disinterested in the fate of Simko and should regret it if that assurance since repeated were belied. . . . If our authorities back Simko, my relations with Minister of War will be seriously affected and I beg His Majesty's Government to reflect earnestly on the effects here.

British Public Record Office, Kew
FO 371/7835/E12399

429

Simko

PERSIA.

POLITICAL

Decypher.   Sir P. Loraine (Teheran)
                        November 29th, 1922.

        D. 5.35.p.m. November 29th, 1922.

        R. 8.30.a.m. November 30th, 1922.

No. 429.

In order to forestall Persian representations and unnecessary agitation when news of Simko's whereabouts reached Teheran from other sources, I acquainted Prime Minister privately with his arrival in a portion of Irak not under direct control of Irak government with his desire to establish relations with British authorities and with instructions sent to High Commissioner, see your telegram No. 286.

His Highness expressed extreme gratitude for this communication and hoped that we shall take into account anxiety of Persian government to have him arrested and promptly handed over to them should he come within reach of British authorities.

I suggest replying that he has not come under control of our authorities, that should he do so Sir P. Cox would exact binding guarantees against any renewal of his operations against Persia, but that in absence of any treaty relations between Persia and Irak there are no grounds on which Irak government could legally surrender a political refugee.   But I await your instructions

                                        as

British Public Record Office, Kew
FO 371/7835/E13446

Simko in Sulaimania

I was instructed to go out to see Simko. Accordingly on the 4th November, I flew to Koi . . . and on the 5th to Arbil. . . . I motored out to the rendezvous at the Gerdi village of Bahirka ten miles on the road to Dêra. Simko was accompanied by his brother Ahmad, two or three minor relatives, and about twenty retainers. The Aghas were dressed in smart uniforms of British-Army serge, Russian top-boots, and the high cylindrical felt hats of the Shikak completely hidden by the turban of silk handkerchiefs wound tightly round; the jackets were double-breasted with stand-up collars and full skirts of cavalry type, the breeches might have been cut in Savile Row. . . .

His attitude was much the same as Saiyid Taha's: he had no particular feeling of resentment towards the Persians—he had given as good as he had received—but he wanted to get even with the Turks, who had made a pretense of backing him and had then turned upon him; he was astonished that we should be so careful of the susceptibilities of the Persians, since they were known to be co-operating all along the border with the Turks who had turned us out of Ruwandiz and Ranya and were still openly warring against us. He had come in the hope of finding us ready to champion the cause of Kurdish freedom against two governments hostile to us; if he was wrong he had no wish to demand asylum but would make his way back to his tribes and do his best alone.

During this interview I had an interesting demonstration of the reason why it is always so easy to get wind of any Kurdish tribal intrigue. The meeting was held behind closed doors in the guest-room of our host, Jemil Agha Gerdi. From time to time his coffee-man would come in to distribute coffee in the Arab fashion, which demands two or three rounds on each occasion; after each round he would loll nonchalantly against the doorpost, and the assembled Kurds seemed to be quite unaware that he was listening carefully to everything that was being said. It fell to me or Lyon to turn him out or stop the conversation whenever the precaution seemed necessary.

C. J. Edmonds, *Kurds, Turks and Arabs*, 1957

This is a picture of Begzade, Debokri, Mangur, and Mamash, who are Kurds from Mukryan, together with Amir Abdullah Khan Tahmasebi.

The flag is dedicated to the Mukryan Kurds by the Persian War Ministry and the Iranian Supreme Commander. The text reads: "From his Highness the War Minister and Supreme Commander, this flag is granted to the Kurds of Soujbulagh Mukri because of their devotion."

I am positive the "devotion" of these chieftains is their participation in the Persian Army's drive against Simko's rebellion.

Diagram and letter from Hassan Ghazi, Kurdish intellectual living in Sweden, 1994

In Mahabad an old son of Ali Agha Amir Aliyar, a well-known feudal lord of the Dehbokri of Bokan, recognized the picture. I wrote his descriptions on the back of the picture which I enclose in this letter. . . . This picture was taken in 1921 in front of a coffee shop in the village of Darman, near Mahabad, where Mokri armed tribes were returning from Saghez ana Baneh.

These people were sent to Baneh to fight against Hama Rashid and his Pishdar followers.

Letter from A. Zhîyan, Kurdish scholar living in Spain, 1994

A former minister of war, General Abdollah Khan Amir Tahmaspi, was sent from Teheran to negotiate with the Kurdish chiefs with the object of bringing them over to the side of the Central Government. Being an able negotiator, he succeeded in convincing several of them to join the Government forces against the few remaining rebels.

Hassan Arfa, The Kurds, 1966

Photograph by Giw Mukriyani
Handwritten notes by Hassan Ghazi, 1994

PERSIA 4

"MUKRI AND SHAKAK TRIBES TAKE OATH OF ALLEGIENCE TO NEW SHAH OF PERSIA

PHOTO SHOWS: Members of the Mukri and Shakak tribes who have pledged allegiance to the new Shah with whom they have entered into close alliance like their forefathers who always proved loyal to the country and fought Russia and Turkey in many battles. Modern Mukri have proved once more their power by subduing other Kurdish tribes who refused to pay taxes to the new Government. This picture shows a visiting Persian general from Teheran who is being received cordially by the tribes.
890R960   PERSIA 4

Distribution caption attached to photograph

Underwood and Underwood Collection
Corbis-Bettmann, New York

MAHMOUD AGHA ÊLKHANÎ ZĀDA. (DÊBOKRI)
(COUSIN OF AMIR ASʿAD)

MOʿMIN BAG OF YAKSHAWA
(ONE OF THE CHEIFTAIN OF
BEGZADA FAIZULLABAĢÎ TRIBE)

HAJI KĀKĀ AGHA

My grandfather Ali Agha Aliyar died before I was born. They tell me he was a very strong personality, a dominant presence. Apparently the Iranian government gathered the tribal chieftains—they were courting them, giving them prominence. They gave my grandfather a title, along with some others so that they wouldn't revolt. In the 1920s and 1930s the shah wanted the Kurds to change and not wear their Kurdish dress. My grandfather was not a Kurdish nationalist, but was well respected by Kurds who were, because of his independent stance vis-à-vis the Iranian government. He refused to give up his Kurdish dress, and was the only chieftain who did so. He didn't want the government to tell him what to do, even though he was a conservative.

Interview with Awat Aliyar,
Kurdish medical physicist
living in the U.S., March 1997

IBRAHIM AGHA
QĀRĀMĀNÎ
DEBOKRI CLAN

QARANI AGHA
MĀMASH
(SUPREME CHEIFTAIN
OF MĀMASH TRIBE)

ALI AGHA
ALIYAR (AMIR ASʿAD)
DÊBOKRI CHEIFTAIN

AMIR ABDULLA KHAN
TAHMASEBI
(PERSIAN COMMANDER)

Giw Mukriyani

Kurdish Photographer

My father worked from 1925 to 1977 as a photographer for two reasons: first, to make money to publish his newspapers—Zari Kermanji, Runaki, Hataw, etc.—and secondly, to record Kurdish cultural life and prominent Kurdish poets and writers by photographing. Most of the women in Arbil had their photographs taken in my father's shop because he was trusted. Photography was cheap, so many people visited twice a year.

In Arbil, the Revolutionary Command council decided in 1974 that all the photographs were to be gathered up and destroyed, as they were cultural products. According to this decision no cultural works were permitted in private houses. I bought an enlarger and copied all the photographs in case the originals were destroyed or decomposed when I buried them underground. Where and how I hid them is a matter I cannot tell. I beg your pardon, but it is a secret matter.

Interview with Azad Mukriyani, son of Giw Mukriyani, living in northern Iraq, by Mawlan Brahim,1994

Said Hussein Huzni Mukriyani, brother of Giw

Sayed Heusni [Huzni Mukriyani] is not merely an historian, he is also the local journalist and newspaper proprietor. There is a brass notice on his door which reads, Zari Kermanji (The Cry of the Kurdish) which is the name of his paper. . . . His type is set by hand. From the oak of the mountain-side he cuts small blocks of wood. He planes them smooth and true and upon them he etches the illustrations for his paper. He inks his plates, turns the primitive printing press, then sets and binds his sheets together to form the monthly magazine. A copy goes to the High Commissioner and another to the League of Nations at Geneva. The Cry of the Kurdish is called a 'monthly' magazine, but often enough the little paper is suppressed on account of its Kurdish sentiments which are not always approved of by the Government at Baghdad.

A. M. Hamilton, *Road Through Kurdistan*, 1937

Wedding in Mahabad

1920s

108

Courtesy Azad Mukriyani

Left: Shaikh Abdullah Geilani, grandson of Shaikh Ubaidullah; right: Shaikh Alaaldin Kamali Zadeh, with his son

Gharani, head of the Mamash tribe, with his son Ali, who later became a member of parliament under the shah

Unidentified

Unidentified

Forces of Simko

Augusta Gudhart

American Missionary

I remember hearing the hoofbeats of galloping riders on the cobbles before the gate, and wondering at what minute they would be upon us. It was not long. I heard a wild bombardment, and before the door could be opened, it was smashed in, and several Kurds were in our compound, with guns pointed and knives drawn, shouting, 'Ashirat, ashirat,' and 'pul—zer' (money, give).

They rushed through all the rooms, smashing furniture, breaking open cupboards, ripping up the carpets, carrying out everything that pleased their fancy and loading their horses. I tried to remonstrate with them, hoping that the magical word, 'Americans,' would stop them; but it only increased their madness. In a few minutes they were gone, and in a few more minutes another party was in. When they saw that everything of value had been taken, they took my clothes from me. When I resisted, they beat me with their muskets, until I fell down half senseless. . . .

When I recovered from my daze, Javahir threw one of her garments around me—they had spared her, not thinking her clothes worth while. . . . The firing had now ceased, comparatively, but when I looked out of the gate, I saw the street jammed with Kurdish horsemen. . . . Wriggling between pawing and neighing horses, and crouching along the wall, we finally reached the other gate. The Kurds were so busy that they apparently did not notice us. . . .

In a sort of maidan, or open space, on the outskirts of the city, there is a small hill and from where we were, we could see that here the Kurdish chief had made his headquarters. Here his share of the booty was being piled up. Once upon a time I had met Simitko, when he was not so war-mad. Then, in his smooth French, he had asked us to establish a mission among his people, that they might be educated and learn the ways of civilization. He had expressed a great admiration for Americans. Now, with this recollection in mind, we determined to take a dangerous and hazardous step—to go to the chief himself and demand his protection. If he refused, we should probably be carried off to the seraglio of some of his lieutenants; if he granted his protection, it would be no certain safety; for Oriental minds are capricious at best; but if we did not go, we should probably meet a terrible fate. . . .

As we mounted to the top of the hill, and the opposite slope appeared before us with the river flowing at its foot, we saw the captured Persian garrison being led forth in small parties, and shot down by machine-gun fire. All of them were stripped to the waist and barefoot. Some were made to crouch on the ground, while the rapid fire raked them over. Others were made to stand in rows and sing the 'Moharram,' or national song of Persia. As they sang, the machine gun swept them down like some invisible scythe. . . .

Just then, Simitko emerged from his tent. It seemed an age before he spoke. Would it be life or death? He said a few words to us, regretting what we had seen, and declaring that it was war. My heart uttered a prayer of thanks when he ordered some of his soldiers to take us back and give us aid. . . .

Every Persian found in the city had been killed; the dead of the garrison, unburied, lying there in heaps on the river slope, numbered about seven hundred according to a count made by my gateman, while in the streets lay the dead bodies of men and horses on which the dogs came and fed. Women had been violated, and children had been left fatherless and hungry. Every house, whether Kurdish or Persian, had been sacked and looted. . . .

I now had the task of looking after some thirty-odd wounded Kurds, and we were treated with outward respect. A bevy of guards did duty at our gate, but we were virtually prisoners. . . .

I went to the chief for the last time, for permission to leave the city. . . . For four days we plodded over the plains and hills of the desert country north of Souj-Boulagh. . . . The fourth day we reached Bokhan, a village of some importance, from which there was a postal service to Tabriz. . . . A number of the village elders came to us with a present of some thirty-five tumans, which they had collected for the khanums—holding them out with both hands as a mark of respect. . . . The simple cordiality of these people did much to restore our disturbed outlook on life, and when, ten days later, we were bundled into the conveyance that had arrived to take us on to Tabriz, there was some sweetness mixed with the gall.

Augusta Gudhart, "The Blood of the Martyrs,"
The Atlantic Monthly, Vol. 130, July 1922

1922

Kurdistan Missionary

"Go ye into all the world, and preach the gospel of the whole creation!" Mark 16: 15.

| Volume 15. | MINNEAPOLIS, MINN., OCTOBER, 1923. | No. 10. |

Kisbogh, Agh Bogh   Miss Gudhart   Ali Agh

Songi Ali Bogh   Sultan Salari Agh

Two Servants kneeling in back

Some of the Kurds, who accompanied Miss Gudhart back to Soujbulak.

Martha Dahl
American Nurse and Missionary

May 11, 1925 . . . Arrived Saturday, May 9th. Just nine weeks since I left Chicago. After staying three days in Tabriz we started out in a carriage again. The roads were better on this side of Tabriz and the country beautiful. . . . The second day out we saw Lake Urumia. Shall never forget the sunset that night as I stood looking at it from the roof of the caravansary and then later that wonderful bright moonlight. As we came we saw many Kurds. Those who have tried to describe the Kurds to me have done a poor job of it. I had never hoped to find that they were such an interesting looking people, so very different from any people I had seen. Their costume is very picturesque and even though they were all decorated with guns and long knives in the belt I did not feel the least fear. . . . The people here are afraid that we have come to make them Christians. Many stay away from the hospital for that reason. I just wish our many people at home who refuse to support our work could just see these splendid looking men. I think they would be convinced that here is a people, who would become a world power for God in the Mohammedan world if they were won for Christ. . . . The number of patients is increasing each month and when we have our new hospital we hope to do great things.

May 31, 1925 . . . I . . . feel very much at home. I am so glad to be here, feel it is where the Lord wants me and I am so happy. I just love these people and I am longing for the day when I shall be able to speak their language so I can do something for them.

All Aboard for Kurdistan!

Dr. H. Schalk and party sailed first part of September.
Mrs. Anna Bachimont appeals to us in behalf of the Kurds.
Miss Gudhart already is in Soujbulak, others may be there.
Dr. Mustafa Kasi joins our forces.
Pastor Otto Becker calls to us across the ocean.

September . . . . nds are cabled to National Ba . . . .

To secure . . . . stors and none af them capital . . . . sum of $2,495.

DEAR RE . . . . uine joy of this occasion by co . . . . fund. Make it five or more if . . . . beral giver.

Send your . . . .

Mis . . . . owa.

Mr. and M . . . . this fall. Miss Martha Dahl, R. N., is ready to go at any time. Still others are waiting for the opportunity to go. Many applications can not be accepted for lack of funds.

In Christ's Name we ask of you to help. Bring the Gospel to the waiting Kurds.

Martha Dahl with neighbor in Mahabad, 1955

Minutes for the Executive Committee

1. The Ex. Committee received with deep regret a report concerning an unfortunate affair between Miss Dahl and a native married man.
2. While we do not absolve Miss Dahl, we can not refrain from expressing our sorrow that the mistake was made of sending her on a trip covering some three months in the company of an inexperienced youth and an immature maid, and this so soon after her very serious illness. And we emphatically advise against such a procedure in the future.
3. We feel that the best course, if it can be done without serious detriment to the Kingdom of the Lord Christ, would be for Miss Dahl to be forgiven and continued in her present relationship and work. This, however, to be conditioned by Miss Dahl's clearly recognizing the wrong of such an affair and finally and completely severing all questionable relationships with the man in question.

"Minutes of the Committee of the Whole for the Members of the Executive Committee," 1926
Courtesy Region 3 Archives,
Lutheran Orient Mission, St. Paul

June 21, 1925 . . . I have already spent six weeks at Soujbulak. . . . I give anesthetics for operations and most of the rest of the time I spend in studying the language and helping with sewing for the hospital. . . . It is getting hot here now and we will soon be going to the mountain for a month till the worst heat is over. We are waiting for the chief commander of the Persian army, who is visiting all the cities. Grand and great preparations are being made. The streets have been kept clean for a week and are very nicely decorated with flags and carpets. We have been busy making Persian flags, too, and my American flag is up for the first time.

April 1926 . . . Shortly after Christmas we received a letter from the governor of Sardosh that they needed a nurse. As there were not many to choose from I had to be the one to go. . . . The governor sent seven horses, two soldiers and three servants to get me. Besides I had Mirsa Hussin and a girl along. . . .

Nearing the village where we were to stop for the night the soldier rode ahead to announce our coming, then came back to meet us. . . . The lady of the village soon came to bid us welcome. She was very eager to let us know that her husband owned the village, 15 horses, how many servants she had and what a big lady she was. . . .

Some other women came looking in through the open door, when I greeted them they all came in and were very anxious to talk. Mirsa Hussin and the girl I have with me both talk a little English so with their help I could talk a little to them. One question that so often is put to me, "Where is your husband?" When they are told that I am not married they look at me rather astounded. They do not see how that can be. Here when a girl is ten years old they begin to look for a husband for her. . . .

Many sick people have come to me during these days as there is no doctor here. Besides I am studying languages with Mirsa Hussin, so the days go so fast. This is such a beautiful place with these wonderful snow mountains. Dear people at home, help us with your prayers and your money that our motto "Kurdistan for Christ" will soon be realized.

Yours in the Master's Service,
Martha Dahl

From *The Kurdistan Missionary*, May 1925, August 1925, and April 1926
Courtesy Region 3 Archives, Lutheran Orient Mission, St. Paul

Inset, left: *Martha Dahl on her way to Kurdistan*
Unknown/Courtesy Cyrus Habibi
Background, left: The Kurdistan Missionary, Lutheran
Orient Mission, Vol. 15, No. 10, October 1923

Martha Dahl in Kurdish dress   Unknown/Courtesy Cyrus Habibi

Kurdish horsemen lead Turcomans during the coronation ceremonies for Reza Shah

WATCH YOUR CREDIT..................
FL111135   " P & A PHOTOS"
(PHOTO SHOWS WILD KURDISH HORSEMEN SALUTING
            NEW SHAH OF PERSIA.)

FORMER SOLDIER CROWNS HIMSELF SHAH OF PERSIA

RIZA KHAN, A FORMER SOLDIER, WHO BECAME PREMI
AND THEN SEIZED THE THRONE FROM THE WEAK RULE
WHO SPENT HIS TIME AND MONEY IN FRANCE, CROWN
HIMSELF SHAH OF PERSIA, A FEW DAYS AGO, WITH
GREAT ORIENTAL SPLENDOR, SELDOM SEEN IN THAT
COUNTRY. THIS EXCLUSIVE PHOTO TAKEN AT THE
ACTUAL CORONATION CEREMONIES SHOWS A PART OF
THE PERSIANS——— THE WILD KURDISH HORSEMEN
SALUTE THEIR NEW RULER.
(SFM-B-5-22-26)

The majority of the tribal chieftains collaborated with the central government at that time. The only one who didn't was Simko.

Simko went to meet Reza Shah with 700 horsemen. . . . Simko took out his pistol and cocked the trigger. There was a skirmish between two horses, my grandfather's horse and the horse of the commander of the cavalry, who hit the other horse with the butt of his gun. Because of this, the rest of the group started to skirmish. The situation became very tense, and Simko began to wonder if these things happened in order to sabotage his plan. Simko divided the group and then Reza Shah's entourage came—in four or five automobiles.

Reza Shah didn't have any sophisticated security with him when he found out that he had been trapped in some way. But Simko felt that because of the disunity, he could not implement his plan to kill Reza Shah at that time. Reza Shah had a gun and didn't get out of his automobile. He opened the door and Simko went forward and welcomed him, shaking hands. Reza Shah said, "Simko, you look so young. I have heard about you for a long time." At the same time, he tried to keep his mask to prove that he was not frightened. He asked Simko if he could write. Simko said no, but Reza Khan told him that he spoke Persian very well. When Reza Shah left, Simko became angry and said, "You forced me to bow my head to Reza Shah when I was planning to eliminate him."

Interview with Sannar Mamedi, living in Sweden, October 1993

1926

Simko was trying to negotiate with the Iranian government to get more land. . . . On our way to negotiate with the government in Zaneda, one of our cars broke down in Naqadah, and we were forced to head back. While returning, people told us there was an ambush, but Simko was not afraid. . . .

Before we reached Ushnaviah, someone shot at us. There were Kurds from the other tribe of Zerdah, but they were with the government. . . . One of Simko's men was killed by a bullet. A second man's arm was broken. Then I saw a bullet hit Simko's leg, and he fell down. But I did not see him die. . . .

The next day, they called the shaikh I was traveling with to identify Simko's body. They asked him if the man they killed was Simko. The shaikh was afraid and said, "Yes, it is Simko." I tried to tell them that it was not Simko, so the shaikh started hitting me. I knew it wasn't Simko because Simko was injured and fled to another tribe who was loyal to him, and I think he died with them.

I am suspicious of this photograph because it doesn't look like Simko, who had two pistols, long boots, a skirt. The dead man is not wearing these things. They took him and arrested him and claimed this man to be Simko. But I say no, this is not Simko.

Interview with Muhammed Ali Kamal, Kurd living in northern Iraq, May 1993

END OF SIMKO THE KURD

(FROM OUR CORRESPONDENT)
TEHERAN, JULY 21

The Persian War Office reports the defeat and death of the notorious Shakak Kurdish brigand chief, Simko, who caused great trouble in Persian Kurdistan in 1922, and after that marauded in the Turkish and Iraqi sections of Kurdistan.

✱✱ Simko, who was a fierce and handsome young man, first became notorious by ill-treating American missionaries at Suj Bulak (Persia) in October, 1921, when he shot a number of Persian gendarmes who had surrendered to him. His mountain castle of Shehr-ich, above Urumiyah, was captured by Persian troops in August, 1922, after a troublesome campaign, and Simko, with part of his "tail," had to escape across the frontier into Turkish territory.

The Times, London, July 22, 1930

Iranian soldier with body said to be Simko's. Translation of writing on the photograph:
"Your valiant blood was shed by a villain. Your Kurdish youths will take revenge."

Unknown/Courtesy Rafiq Studio

Rebellions in Turkey

Appealing to a common Muslim identity and to the need to defend Muslim territory against local and foreign Christians, the Kemalist movement found considerable support among the Kurds. Only in a few places were there stirrings, inspired either by loyalty to the sultan's government in Istanbul or by nationalist aspirations. They were easily suppressed. The leaders of the Istanbul-based Kurdish association either left the country or accommodated themselves to the reality of a Kemalist victory. Some of them later appeared in French-controlled Syria and made efforts at a Kurdish revival through their exile organization, the "Kurdish League" Khoybun (established in 1927).

The victory of the Kemalists over the Armenians and Greeks in 1922 forced the Entente powers (Britain, France, Italy, and Greece) to renegotiate the terms of the peace agreement. The Treaty of Lausanne (1923) recognized the Kemalists' gains and no longer mentioned the possibility of an Armenian or a Kurdish state on former Ottoman soil. The borders of the new Turkey, as agreed upon in Lausanne, corresponded almost exactly with the Kemalists' original ambitions—with the exception of the southeast, where the status of the former Ottoman province of Mosul with its Kurdish majority (and large oil deposits) remained unresolved. Its future was to be decided after a consultation with the population under the auspices of the League of Nations. The Turkish commander for the southeast, Özdemir, made energetic efforts to win the Kurds of Mosul over to the Kemalist side, but the repression of Kurdish culture in Turkey proper gradually alienated them. In 1926 the province was incorporated into the kingdom of Iraq.

Mustafa Kemal, determined to turn Turkey into a modern, western-ized country, embarked upon a series of radical reforms. The aboli-tion of such traditional Muslim institutions as the Caliphate, the religious courts, and traditional religious schools—all in 1924—not only caused disaffection in conservative religious circles but also rep-resented a break with the period when Muslim identity and common Muslim interests had united the Kemalist movement. Turkish nationalism, which was promoted as the unifying force that should replace Islam, obviously did not hold the same appeal for the Kurds.

In 1925 the first large Kurdish rebellion against the new regime broke out. Preparations for such an uprising had been made by an under-ground organization of Kurdish military officers and nationalist intellectuals, but the actual leadership fell to the charismatic leader of a Sufi order, Shaikh Said. The uprising has often been described as a conservative religious reaction to the government's modernizing policies; there was, however, an undeniably Kurdish nationalist dimension to it. Severe reprisals were taken against the rebels but also against leading Kurdish personalities who had not been involved.

The Shaikh Said rebellion provided the government with the pretext for banning the entire political opposition, establishing an authori-tarian, centralist regime, and speeding up reform from above. In order to bring in the new, progressive society that the Kemalists were striving for, all symbols of the old order—especially those of traditional Islam and ethnic cultures—had to be destroyed. Sufi orders were banned; traditional Muslim or tribal headgear and robes had to be replaced by Western-style hats and jackets; the Arabic script was replaced by the Latin alphabet and its use became a punishable offense.

The Shaikh Said rebellion was followed by a rebellion centered on Mount Ararat, in 1928–30. Local tribesmen provided the main fight-ing force, but individuals and small groups came from all over north-ern Kurdistan to join them. This uprising was better organized than the first, due to the firm leadership of Ihsan Nuri, a Kurdish military officer who had also taken part in the preparations for the Shaikh Said uprising. The organization Khoybun played an active part in this uprising, taking care of logistics and international contacts. Khoybun had good relations with Armenians, which proved especially useful.

The government used great military force in putting down these and the rebellions that followed. Numerous community leaders, and later entire tribes, were deported to other parts of the country. The gov-ernment decided that assimilation of the Kurds to Turkish culture would be the best way of preventing future separatism, favoring forced resettlement over compulsory education. In 1927, a resettle-ment law was passed that provided for the deportation of Kurds to regions where Turkish culture was dominant and for the settlement of Turks in the more fertile Kurdish areas. Although the law was only partly translated into practice, the numbers of those deported was probably many tens of thousands.

The last great rebellion took place in Dersim, an inaccessible, moun-tainous region that had never before been pacified. Its population, adherents of the heterodox Kizilbash or Alevi sect, was organized in small tribes that often were at odds with one another and had a long tradition of resisting external authority. In the government's view it exemplified the "feudal" forces of reaction that stood in the way of Turkey's march to homogeneous nationhood. In the mid-1930s, the government concentrated its "modernizing" and "civilizing" efforts on this last bastion of tribal order. Minor acts of resistance, coordi-nated by the poet Alişêr and the religious leader Seyid Riza, provided the excuse for heavy-handed military operations in 1937 and 1938. Villages were torched, thousands of people killed. Not even the tribes that had welcomed the government were spared reprisals. A large proportion of the survivors were deported to western Turkey.

After the pacification of Dersim, Turkey appeared to have solved its Kurdish problem. Ever more Kurds were speaking Turkish and hid their Kurdish identity or parroted the official doctrine that they were in fact Turks by origin. Only those who had gone into exile could openly represent Kurdish interests. Syria had become the center for Kurdish nationalists from Turkey, and Khoybun, in which the brothers Celadet and Kamuran Bedirkhan played central roles, their chief mouthpiece. Their political activities were, after the Ararat rebellion, marginal; the French authorities, wishing to maintain good relations with Turkey, did not allow them to play a significant part. Their cul-tural activities, however, made a lasting impact. Through publishing books and journals, they developed northern Kurdish as a written language and laid the foundations for a Kurdish cultural renaissance that was to take place half a century later.   —MvB

Turkish military map of Shaikh Said operation, 1925
Türkiye Cumhuriyetinde Ayaklanmalar (1924–1938), 1972

Şehsait Harekâtı
Başlangıç durumu

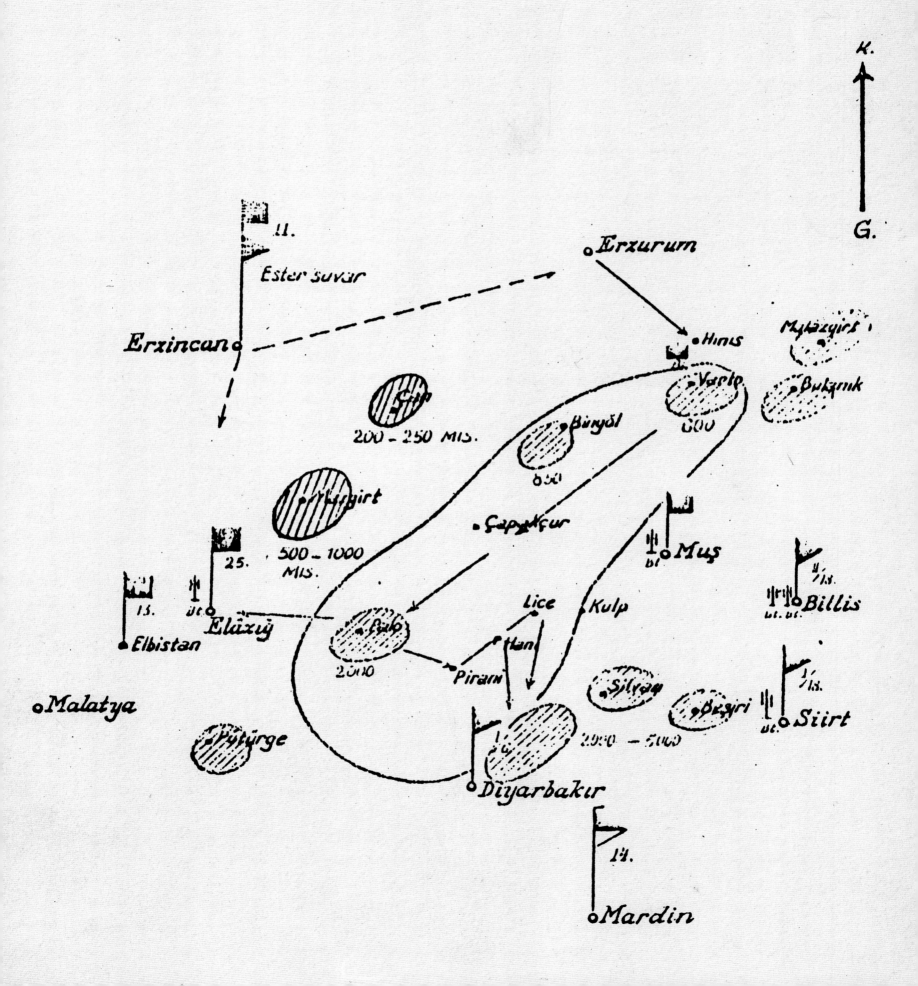

Kurdish Declaration to Kemalist Government, Ankara

November 15, 1920

1. The Ankara government should state whether or not it accepted officially the promise of Kurdish autonomy as agreed to by the sultan's government in Istanbul.
2. It should answer the people of Dersim as soon as possible as to the views of Mustafa Kemal's government concerning an autonomous administration of Kurdistan.
3. All of the Kurdish prisoners in jail at Elaziz, Malatya, Sivas, and Erzincan should be freed.
4. Administrative officials of the Turkish government should be withdrawn from the areas with a Kurdish majority.
5. The military detachments that are reported to be sent to the district of Kocgiri should at once be withdrawn.

M. Nuri Dersimi, *Kürdistan Tarihinde Dersim*
(Dersim in the History of Kurdistan), 1952

British Secretary's Notes of an Allied Conference Held in Lord Curzon's Room at the Foreign Office, London S.W., on Saturday, February 26, 1921, at 11 A.M.

Bekir Sami Bey [minister for foreign affairs] replied that as he had already had the honour to tell the Supreme Council, the populations of Kurdistan possessed complete representation in the Grand National Assembly....

It was true that after the Armistice a few Kurds had asked for the separation of their country from Turkey . . . one of whom was Cherif Pasha. This committee had asked for the independence of Kurdistan, but its members in no way represented the population for whom they claimed to speak, and [he] suggested that they were actuated by personal rather than national motives....

Lord Curzon then referred to Bekir Sami statement that the Ottoman Government would grant autonomy in the vilayets where the Kurdish population was predominant, and enquired what exactly he meant by this autonomy.

Bekir Sami Bey replied that this autonomy . . . meant that the vilayets were allowed to decide their own budget and generally manage their own internal affairs. The system contemplated was, in fact, one of administrative decentralisation.

In reply to a further question from Lord Curzon, who indicated that this autonomy really amounted to little more than what was known in England as local self-government, and that no real concession was being made to the Kurds as Kurds, Bekir Sami Bey protested that the Kurds did not desire any such concession; all they want was to live together with the Turks like brothers, as they had lived for centuries; there was no greater difference between the Kurds and the Turks than between an Englishman and a Scotchman.

British Documents on Atatürk, Vol. 3, January–September 1921, 1979

Background: *Mustafa Kemal, among the Kurdish leaders in 1920*

Unknown/From *The Turkish Crime of Our Century*

Mustafa Kemal and Diyap Aga, the Kurdish representative to the Grand National Assembly, from Dersim

Unknown/Courtesy *Aydınlık* newspaper

General meetings were being held in the Dervish lodge. . . . Mustafa Kemal Pasha ordered my arrest. . . . I was put in a private room. On 20 December, 1920, I petitioned the local government, saying that I wanted to be with the other prisoners. A chain was tied to my feet. In recreation breaks, the only way I could enjoy walking around was by putting this long chain around my neck.

Since the prison was connected to the governor's house, I could see from the windows that I was being saluted by the people. All the prisoners in the prison were Kurds.

M. Nuri Dersimi, *Hatiratim*
(My Memories), 1992

The Kurdish revolt for which we have been working these two years past is about to break out. The areas which are to rise simultaneously are, DERSIM, DIARBEKIR, BITLIS, VAN, whose population totals five to six millions. These people have throughout the past year refused to pay taxes to the Turks and are only waiting for the presence of myself the representative of the Badr Khan race to unite. We are heart and soul pro-British. We want a British mandate and if Britain will assist us we on our part will be her buffer state between her Iraq and her enemies in Russia and in Turkey. We will co-operate with the Armenians and with other Christian communities.

The help that we want immediately is firstly, the presence of a very few keen British Officers, such as Major Noel, who will accept Kurdish dress and come with us and report to His Majesty's Government whether my promised revolution is a genuine thing or not. Secondly, at least two mountain guns, a few machine guns, five thousand rifles and some ammunition.

Note from Khalil Badr Khan, member of the Kurdish Club,
to Percy Cox, high commissioner for Iraq, October 28, 1921
British Public Record Office, Kew
CO 730/6/16

To Mr. Shuckburgh, Colonial Office,
Middle East Department
From Colonel Meinsertzhagen [Military Intelligence]

November 9, 1921

Our policy in Iraq is based on a friendly Turkey. Here we have a proposal based on making her our eternal enemy. So far our hands are clean. Let us continue in this state.

The stirring up of revolt is seldom justified, even in war, and invariably reacts on the party behind the scenes. This is apparent throughout history. I have little confidence that the Kurds are a homogeneous nationality. Noel would doubtless have us believe it, but Noel is one of the General Gordon Type, a fanatical enthusiast, who is capable of leading the Empire to disaster in order to fulfill his own dreams.

I strongly advocate protesting in the strongest terms against such a proposal, even as an alternative to direct action between Feisal and Angora. It is really no alternative and would merely exasperate the Turks at a moment when our policy is to rely on their friendship. All recent telegrams show that though the French have scored a temporary success with Kemal at our expense, the Turk has by no means lost his respect for us. If we forfeit this last vestige of hope, we shall sink in the eyes of the Middle East to the same level as the Latin Races. God forbid such degradation.

British Public Record Office, Kew
CO/730/6/55824

Background: Leaders of the Koçgiri revolt in prison. Above, L-R: Kimil Aziz, Mahmed Ali, and Nuri Dersimi, Divrigi village, Sivas region, 1921

Unknown/Courtesy Mehmet Bayrak

121

Lord Curzon's Speech at Lausanne

January 23, 1923

The whole of our information shows that the Kurds with their own independent history, customs, manners, and character, ought to be an autonomous race. One of the objects and, indeed, one of the partial results of our administration has been the setting up of a system of local autonomy with local administration and local schools, where an attempt is made to teach the written Kurdish language. Why should these people in this condition be taken and handed over to Angora? Why should there be a plebiscite of this people? Angora asks for a plebiscite: the Kurds have never asked for it; poor fellows, they do not know what it means. . . . Further, the whole of the economic connections of this Kurdish country are with Baghdad and not with the north. What justification is there for cutting this economic connection? . . .

It is supposed and alleged that the attitude of the British Government in regard to the retention of Mosul is affected by the question of oil. The question of the oil of the Mosul Vilayet has nothing to do with my argument. I have presented the British case on its own merits and quite independently of any natural resources that may be in the country. I do not know how much oil there may be in the neighbourhood of Mosul or whether it can be worked at a profit or whether it may turn out after all to be a fraud. During the time I have been connected with the foreign affairs of my country I have never spoken with or interviewed an oil magnate. I have never spoken or negotiated with a single concessionaire or would-be concessionaire for Mosul oil or any other oil. I do not think that every one in this room can say the same.

British Public Record Office
CO 370/46/4849

The Illustrated London News,
January 13, 1923

A "BONE OF CONTENTION" BETWEEN TURKS AND ALLIES A

PHOTOGRAPHS BY CAPTAIN V

SHOWING TYPICAL INHABITANTS, WITH DISTINCTIVE COSTUME AND HEADGEAR: ONE OF THE PRINCIPAL STREETS IN MOSUL.

WHERE CARCASES MAY BE KEPT HANGING FOR DAYS, SUBJECT TO THE ATTENTIONS OF FLIES: A BUTCHER'S SHOP IN MOSUL.

SHOWING THE LEANING TOWER (IN THE EXTREME RIGHT BACKGROUND) AND A NATIVE GRAVEYARD (BEYOND THE HORSE-LINES IN FOREGROUND): A VIEW OF MOSUL.

FORMERLY UNDER TURKISH RULE, BUT INCLUDED IN Y THE MANDATE FOR MESOPOTAMIA: MOSUL, ON THE TIGR

THE LIGHTER SIDE OF THE ARAB TEMPERAMENT: MOSUL CHILDREN AND OTHERS ON SWINGS AND PRIMITIVE "GREAT WHEELS": FLIMSY STRUCTURES WHICH OFTEN COLLAPSE AMID SHRIEKS OF LAUGHTER.

WHERE DESERT NOMADS ASSEMBLE TO BARTER AND OBTAIN PROVISIONS: A BUSY CORNER OF THE MOSUL MARKET.

Mosul, which lies on the Tigris, near the site of ancient Nineveh, some 270 miles north-west of Baghdad, has become a bone of contention between the Turks and the Allies at the Lausanne Conference. The town was occupied by the British in November 1918, and when the Mandate for Mesopotamia was granted by the League of Nations to Great Britain, Mosul, which had previously been under Turkish rule, was incorporated in the new Arab state of Irak. The Turks, encouraged by the Russian Bolshevists, have continually protested against this arrangement, and have demanded the retrocession of Mosul to themselves. During the Lausanne Conference they have spread reports of discontent among the inhabitants of the town and of an imminent rising. A rumour from Angora that aeroplane hangars at Mosul had been burnt by rebels was denied by the Colonial Office. There is no railway to Mosul, the line from Baghdad ending 70 miles

THE LAUSANNE CONFERENCE : MOSUL, THE ANCIENT NINEVEH.

USBAND AND C. E. BARON.

SHOWING THE PRIMITIVE CHARACTER OF THE STREETS AND BUILDINGS IN MOSUL, AND TYPES OF PEOPLE : AN OPEN-AIR BAZAAR.

FROM 80 TO 100 FEET HIGH, AND 12 TO 20 FEET THICK : RUINS OF THE MASSIVE NORTH WALL OF MOSUL, WITH A TOWER.

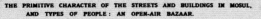

W ARAB STATE OF IRAK SINCE BRITAIN ACCEPTED
PANORAMIC VIEW OF THE FAMOUS OIL CENTRE.

SHOWING THE MOHAMMEDAN SCHOOL, WITH CHILDREN IN THE OUTER COURT (IN THE LEFT FOREGROUND) : A GENERAL VIEW OF MOSUL FROM BRIGADE HEADQUARTERS.

WHERE THE "MILKMAN" BRINGS ROUND HIS COW TO BE MILKED FOR EACH CUSTOMER : SERVING A CUP.

NOT A LARGE ELEMENT IN THE POPULATION OF MOSUL, WHICH CONSISTS MAINLY OF KURDS AND ARABS WITH A SPRINKLING OF TURKS : A GROUP OF CHALDEANS WITH THEIR DONKEYS.

away, at Shergat. The rest of the journey is done by motor-car. The population of Mosul is about 70,000, mostly Kurds and Arabs, with only a small proportion of Turks, about one-twelfth of the whole. Mosul is an important oil centre. The Germans found oil there and in Mesopotamia in 1904, and tried to get a concession. They reported to Berlin that the prospects were good, and to Turkey that they were bad : but the Turks heard of the Berlin report, and negotiations lapsed. In 1908 British inquiries were made, and just before the war the Turkish Petroleum Company was formed, by British and German interests. After the war, the German interests were transferred to the French under the San Remo Agreement, and subsequently American interests were also admitted. At Lausanne recently, replying to criticisms, Lord Curzon stated that complete accord prevails between the British and American interests at Mosul.

At to-day's session of the Commission Ismet Pasha [Turkish prime minister and the chief of the delegation] ... quoted the "Encyclopaedia Britannica" in support of the argument that the Kurds were Turks except for their language. Eighty-five percent of the population, he said, were Kurds and Turks.

Ismet Pasha next brought forward historic arguments, quoting ancient history, and declaring that, geographically and climatically, Mosul was Anatolia. The same applied economically. The Kurds were always united with the Turks. They had representatives in the Angora Parliament who could not see their brethren separated from Turkey. The population of the Vilayet had resisted British occupation, and only a minority voted, under pressure, for King Feisal.

In regard to the suggestion of Kurdish autonomy, Ismet Pasha said the Kurds always enjoyed full citizenship under Turkish rule and that not a single Kurd would change their status.

The Times, London, January 24, 1923

Kurdistan. When an educated person pronounces this word he doesn't mean only the area of Sulaimani, but a broad, geographical region, and he thinks of the many and united Kurdish people. The natural frontiers of this country ... are clear. ... As the population of Mosul is Kurdish, why should the recovery or retention of this wilayet be demanded by outside peoples? The Turks, Arabs, and Assyrians base their claims on the presence of a small number of their people. ... The demand we make of the Lausanne Conference is not the protection of a minority. It is the vindication of the right to live of a great independent people with a country of its own.

Editorial by Muhammed Nuri, *Rhozh-i Kurdistan (Sun of Kurdistan)*, weekly Kurdish newspaper published in Sulaimania, No. 6, December 12, 1922, translated by Mawlan Brahim

TURKEY

As a result of a thousand years of common religion, common history, and common geography Turks and Kurds are connected both materially and spiritually. Today they are facing common enemies and common dangers. They can avoid these dangers only by a common effort. Therefore, we can definitely say that it is a religious and political obligation for both nations to love each other. A Turk who does not love Kurds is not a Turk and a Kurd who does not love Turks is not a Kurd.

Ziya Gökalp, June 5, 1922, quoted in Rohat Alakom, *Ziya Gökalp'in Çilesi Kürtler*, 1992

We are frankly Nationalist . . . and Nationalism is our only factor of cohesion. Before the Turkish majority other elements have no kind of influence. At any price, we must turkify the inhabitants of our land, and we will annihilate those who oppose Turks or 'le turquisme.'

Ismet Inönü to the Turkish Congress of the Turk Ojaghi (clubs for the propagation of Turkish culture),
as cited by Sir Lindsay to Mr. Austen Chamberlain, Constantinople, May 4, 1925
British Public Record Office, Kew
FO371/10863/E2634

Proclamation to the Kurdish Tribes
To Rasul Agha, Chief of the Dizai Tribe

June 26, 1922
Dear Chieftain,
There is not a single Mohammedan who has not so far realized how great and serious was the calamity which befell our country in the Great War and also during the period which has elapsed since the Armistice. There is not a single Mohammedan who does not understand the real and true purpose of the British, which has caused the occupation of Holy Stambul the seat of the Caliphate, by elements hostile to Islam; . . . and finally, to sow hostility and dissent among the Mussalman population, and to break them finally, created the present objectionable situation in south Kurdistan.

There is not a single soul who does not understand the spirit of the Government of Faisal, a despicable instrument in the hands of the British. But this deplorable situation has affected the Honour of God, and therefore He, in order to prove the Miracles of the Prophet, who said in the holy words of the Koran that Islam would live until the Day of Resurrection, has thrown into the battlefield one Mustafa Kemal to remove the enemy occupation from Ottoman territories and save them from desecration and turning out the foreigners who were in occupation of an important part of our country and, thank God, the country is regaining its independence.

For this reason the government was unable to render any important assistance in south Kurdistan and in the Mosul vilayet. Now, thank God, we have come into this region in order to break the legs of the foreign forces ruling here and to save our Holy Country. With the mercy of God, we shall begin shortly to organize the people for a general movement. . . .

Euz Demir, commander of the al Jazirah,
and Iraq Organization and General Movement

British Public Record Office, Kew
CO 730/32

Origin of Kurdish Independence Party and
Reason for Its Formation

November 8, 1924
Informants state that the society is a secret one and therefore the names of officials are not broadcasted, as would be the case in a Government Administration. The Kurdish Independence Party originated in Erzerum three years ago, its object being to throw off the yoke of Turkish rule and improve the development of Kurdistan, which was being held in check by the barbarous conduct of the Turks. In order to appreciate the situation, which gave rise to this movement, it is necessary to relate a few of the more outstanding outrages to which their race as a whole was subjected. These may be summed up briefly as follows:

1. Turkish language only was allowed in courts. This afforded an opportunity of misinterpretation and misrepresentation of the case.
2. The Turks forbade the institution of primary schools. . . . They refused to allow the Kurds to learn their own language, and, since the Kurds did not wish to learn Turkish, education became practically non-existent. . . . In addition they closed down pious institutions—the only source of education left to the Kurds.
3. Kurds could expect no justice except through bribery.
4. In order to prevent unity amongst the Kurds, the Turks made a point of setting one tribe against another.
5. Taxes, for which no benefit was ever derived, had frequently to be paid more than once a year.
6. The Turks attempted to exterminate the Kurdish race by:
   a. Deporting all the more enlightened Kurds and replacing them by Turkish refugees from outside, in order to create a Turkish majority.
   b. Omitting the word *Kurdistan* from all their educational books.
   c. Ordering all Kurdish Government officials to accept Turkish nationality.
   d. Giving Turkish names to Kurdish mountains. . . .
7. The election of Deputies to the Turkish National Assembly was not made by one free vote of one people, but by order and appointments from the Central Government.

Internal report sent from S.S.O. Baghdad to Air Staff Intelligence, Baghdad
British Public Record Office, Kew
AIR 23/411/NO1/1929

[W]e made use of all circumstances only from one point of view, which consisted therein: to raise this nation to that plane where it is justified in standing in the civilized world, to stabilise the Turkish Republic more and more on steadfast foundations . . . and in addition to destroy the spirit of despotism for ever. . . .

Turkish Youth! your primary duty is ever to preserve and defend the National independence, the Turkish Republic. . . .

The strength that you will need for this is mighty in the noble blood which flows in your veins.

A Speech Delivered by Mustafa Kemal Atatürk, 1927

A

SPEECH

delivered by

MUSTAFA KEMAL ATATÜRK

THE KURDISH REVOLT.

INSURGENT GAINS.

ABDUL HAMID'S SON AS KING.

(FROM OUR OWN CORRESPONDENT.)

CONSTANTINOPLE, FEB. 25.

The insurgent Kurds were reported yesterday to have occupied Kharput and Diarbekir el Azir and to have overrun Dersim and part of Mamuret. The insurgents have proclaimed one of Abdul Hamid's sons as King of Kurdistan. A state of siege has been proclaimed in Malatia, to the west of the Euphrates. Turkish airmen are bombing the insurgents, but pending the arrival of adequate forces no serious engagement is to be expected for a few days.

The Ghazi Pasha, Marshal Fevzi Pasha, the Chief of the General Staff, and General Kiazim Pasha, a former Minister

for Defence, were present at a protracted meeting of the Cabinet, and the plan for the military campaign is said to be now completed.

At yesterday's meeting of the Popular Party no material new facts appear to have been brought to light. Fethi Bey, the Prime Minister, announced that fresh legislation would be introduced for treating as high treason the publishing of a newspaper or the making of a speech in which religion is used as a means for exciting popular sentiment, but he rejected the proposal to proclaim martial law in Constantinople. General Ismet Pasha was among those who spoke in support of the Government.

There is a general expectation that once the troops are in a position to attack the insurgents will soon be forced to surrender. But the period after the revolt has been stifled will be a very hard test for the Government. The universal tendency here is to impute the revolt to British instigation, and one newspaper this morning refuses to see the slightest trace of the existence of any Kurdish national movement either among the ignorant mountaineers or those educated Kurds who have given proofs of their attachment to Turkey, and therefore it ascribes the rebellion to ignorance and blind fanaticism, which must be annihilated at whatever sacrifice.

The Times, London, February 26, 1925

Right: British Public Record Office, Kew
FO 371/10867/E1360
Background: The Times, London,
February 25, 1925

1925

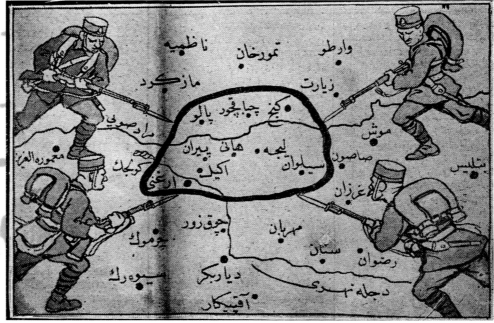

Turkish soldiers encircle Piran, Egil, Hani, Lice, Silvan, Palu, Bingol, and Genc, published in Cumhuriyet, *a Turkish newspaper*

Cumhuriyet, March 30, 1925

10

E
121
E 1360
7 MAR 1925

1925   TURKEY

Registry Number E 1360/1091/44.

FROM
Foreign Office
Memorandum.
(Mr. Morgan).

Dated 4th Mar. 1925.
Received in Registry 7th Mar. 1925.

E: Turkey.

Last Paper.

E 1335

References.

(Print.)

(How disposed of.)

*Oft Mr Lindsay
(from Mr Oliphant)
March 14*

Kurdish revolt.

Discusses possibilities of rising having been engineered by Angora with objects of (1) successful rebels crossing frontier to free their brothers in Mosul and then surrendering whole territory to Turkey; (2) taking successful rising in Turkey as pretext for Kurds in Irak proclaiming union with Turkish Kurds, all ultimately submitting to Angora; or (3) using as pretext for concentrating troops on Irak frontier.

(Minutes)

Turkey will certainly do all in her power to crush any movement tending to create an independent Kurdistan. The Turanian ideas of the Committee of Union & Progress are still prevalent in Turkish governing circles. Turkey wishes to extend her influence towards & be in close relations with Central Asian Moslems and the rise of any buffer state in Eastern Asia Minor would be an obstacle to the plan & will certainly be crushed

James Morgan
9. 3. 25.

It is certainly desirable that we should be

Diary of Events at Mezreh (Mamouret-el-Aziz)
(From a letter written by a European inhabitant of the town)

March 24 . . . *Towards sunset sound of guns and firing of rifles and machine guns. The Vali in a car escorted by 25 mounted gendarmes fled.*

Soon afterwards 300 Kurds entered the town and proceeded to sack; first the Government House, and then the Department of Justice. They then opened the prison, and the prisoners showed the Kurds the houses of the officers and rich men so that the first could be made prisoners and the houses of the latter looted. In this looting the porters and wood-choppers of the town, mostly Kurds, also joined.

March 26 . . . *During the day, the notables of the town tried to organise a militia amongst the population, but there was not much enthusiasm, for although most of the population was armed as it always is, they did not like to show their arms for fear of being disarmed by the rebels. However, one Hassim Bey an officer of the army managed to get some courage into the people and they eventually attacked the rebels; drove them out of the town leaving 50 dead; there were an equal number of casualties amongst the population.*

March 28 . . . *The Government at Angora sent its congratulations to the people and announced the early arrival of troops. Telegraphic communication which had been interrupted was reopened; but all telegrams were censored and letters had to be posted open.*

British intelligence report
British Public Record Office
FO 371/10837/E2359

"*Our planes are above the heads of the rebels*" (top text)
"*The rebels are scattered by our bombs*" (bottom text)

Cumhuriyet, March 30,1925

Since the government will not be able to admit its negligence, the explanation that the revolt was due to foreign intrigue and the forces of reaction will serve very well for dissemination through the medium of the press, of public speeches, etc. And by these means we can smother or threaten all the centers of reaction and paralyse the intrigues both of the opposition and of the foreigner.

British summary of Turkish press, March 2, 1925
British Public Record Office

"*The Turk is a naked sword: Whoever crosses with him is cut apart*"

Cumhuriyet, April 18, 1925

From Mr. Lindsay, British Ambassador to Turkey

Constantinople, April 22, 1925
The few remaining rebel centres appear to have been captured.

The extreme severity of the Turkish measures of repression may temporarily break the spirit of rebellion, but will probably produce a good deal of future hostility to Turkish rule on the part of the remaining Turkish Kurds, and this may eventually complicate the situation on the Irak frontier.

END OF KURDISH RISING.

SUDDEN COLLAPSE.

(FROM OUR OWN CORRESPONDENT.)

CONSTANTINOPLE, APRIL 16.

With the capture of Sheikh Said [reported in *The Times* yesterday], together with nine other tribal chieftains and a body of 25 followers, the Kurdish rebellion is declared to have completely collapsed militarily, and no further *communiqué* will be issued. The Kurds, left without leaders, are submitting *en masse*.

Sheikh Said, who has been taken to Varto, is reported to have been found in possession of important papers referring to the revolt and of a large sum of money in gold. Günj was recaptured by the

Government on Sunday and a regular administration has been restored throughout the disaffected area. The reorganization of the administration was again discussed at a meeting of the Cabinet yesterday, presided over by Mustapha Kemal Pasha, and it is expected that reforms will be announced very shortly.

The sudden collapse of the rebellion is the more welcome since it was unexpected, and justifies the employment of comparatively large forces and the policy of encirclement.

The *Tanin* received this morning an order not to appear to-morrow. The reason for the suppression of the journal is unknown, and such action appears strange at this juncture, since for several weeks past nothing has been written in it of current politics.

The Times, London, April 17, 1925

E 161

E 3020
25 MAY 1925

1925   TURKEY.

Political events in Turkey.
Refers to Constantinople despatch No.322 of 22nd April, (E 2497/1091/44).
Comments on accusation framed against Hussein Jahid Bey, as result of which he has been banished for life to Chorum, village in interior. Besides these proceedings Angora Independence Tribunal has been dealing with many other cases and effect has been strongly deterrent. Diabekir tribunal, dealing with person implicated in Kurdish rebellion has been even more extreme. Result of repressive measures is that government's position is stronger, and that progressive Party is silent and its growth arrested.

Registry Number: E 3020/194/44
FROM Mr. Lindsay (Constantinople)
No. 356
Dated 20th May 1925
Received in Registry 25th May 1925
1: Turkey

Last Paper. E 2634
References.

(Print.) Turkey (Without enclosure)
(How disposed of.)

(Action completed.)
(Index.)

Next Paper. E 4850.

(Minutes)

The King
Cabinet
Dominions

The last attempt at maintaining any illusion of democracy in Turkey has now been abandoned, and a kind of "cheka" (on Russian lines system of government by terror) appears to be in process of ~~opposition on the contrary~~ creation.

The democratic experiment was never genuine, and from our point of view it will probably be easier to deal with a

a strong tyranny. But it is a depressing prospect for any one who may have believed in the future of the Turks.
G. W. Rendel.
26. v. 25.

Capital punishment for dissolving or obstructing the Assembly is a ... in parliamentary

"The steel fist of the Republic is crushing the rebels"   Cumhuriyet, April 12, 1925

From Strategic Services Office, Baghdad
To Air Staff (Intelligence) Air Headquarters

May 22, 1925

The following report . . . has been received from a well known Kurd, whose political views are decidedly patriotic and anti-Kemalist. . . .

Causes leading up to the rebellion

The Kemalist programme . . . commenced a campaign of forcibly 'turcosizing' all weaker powers within their reach and not only seizing the property of but also massacring non-moslems. Amongst those against whom this policy was directed were the Kurds. . . . All moral relations with the Turks having thus been utterly broken, the Kurds demanded either a national independence or special racial privileges. To secure these demands they started secretly to request the assistance of neighbouring countries through the medium of their newly formed Kurdish Society, but soon realising the hopelessness of this quest they fell back on the one hope left to them, that of revolution, which they commenced in the winter of 1924. . . .

Turkish propaganda

In order that such Turks as were discontented with the Angora Government should not support the Kurdish movement, thousands of pamphlets and hundreds of reliable agents were despatched into the districts for the purpose of spreading the propaganda that the Kurdish insurrection was the outcome of British money, which was also being used for recruiting Armenians and Assyrians, the great enemies of Turkey, to unite with the Kurds against the Turks and so place obstacles in the way of the restoration of Mosul to its rightful owners. In addition the British with their money were aiming at creating an Assyrian and Armenian state in Eastern Anatolia in order to weaken the Turkish Republic—a fact which showed how the Kurds were being deceived by the British.

From Mr. Lindsay, British Ambassador to Turkey
To Mr. Austin Chamberlain, British Foreign Minister

Constantinople, June 2, 1925

I have the honour to report that the Independence Tribunals continue their activities uninterruptedly at Angora and at Diarbekir. . . .

It is impossible to report these trials to you in any detail. Though the accounts, especially those from the Diarbekir Tribunal, take up a good deal of space in the papers, they are too obviously garbled to allow of any reliance being placed on them and too fragmentary to enable a reader to get any connected idea of what passes. Judging, however, from what is printed in the papers, one or two general impressions do stand out:

a. The papers represent Sheikh Said as an uncouth, semi-idiotic individual, worthy only of ridicule. His reported utterances are almost all those of a simple man, acting under a strong religious impulse. He had seen Islam menaced by the attitude of the Government, and, of course, it had been his duty to rise and fight.

b. The accused are brought before the court in batches, five or six at a time, even twenty or thirty. They seem almost invariably to indulge in violent recriminations against each other, each one seeking to show that he was forced to take up arms by the violence of some other, on whom alone the blame must lie. These mutual accusations must be an unedifying spectacle; they excite the hilarity of the court, and render it an easy task to find verdicts of guilty.

c. Curiously little has transpired or been allowed to transpire as to any British instigation of or participation in the Kurdish movement. . . . It is said that Sheikh Said hoped, after taking Diarbekir, to get into touch with the British authorities via Gezireh. This is about all the mention made of British activity reported so far in the newspaper accounts.

"An iron ring tightens itself around the rebels between Genc and Çapakçur"   Cumhuriyet, April 12, 1925

Some time ago, I saw an advertisement in a Turkish journal . . . and at the bottom it said that some photographs of Shaikh Said were also going to be put on sale at that auction in Istanbul. . . . I thought, if these photographs cannot be bought by a Kurd, then someone else will buy them and they will be lost to the Kurds. . . .

At the auction, the sale of these photographs brought the case of Khalid Beg Jibri to my mind. In one of his stories, Demir Ozlu writes that after Khalid Beg was hung, his sword and a few other belongings of his were sold at an auction. As Ozlu asks himself, who knows where Khalid Beg's sword and clothes are now?

On the back of these photographs of the 1925 uprising, someone had written a few notes about these pictures in Turkish. . . . From these notes it is clear that the pictures were taken by Turkish officers at the time of the uprising. As far as I know, only two of them were published in Turkish newspapers in 1925, and the others have never been published.

M. Malmîsanij, *CIRA*, a Kurdish journal
published in Sweden, December 1995

*Shaikh Said and his collaborators
captured by the commanders
of the 12th Division of the Turkish
army and Ismail Hakki Bey, the governor
of Genc (standing behind wearing a fez)*

Unknown/Courtesy Said Aydogmus and M. Malmîsanij

Shaikh Said being brought to the gallows   Unknown/Deng-Azadi, Istanbul

Repression of the Kurdish Revolt

Notwithstanding the very savage methods of repression used by the Turks, the revolt is still smouldering in certain more inaccessible areas. . . .

Also the temper of the Kurdish population in a number of districts had not been absolutely broken, for Kurds, Nestorians and Arabs were meditating continuing to harry the Turks, who had not succeeded in completely disarming them. . . .

Situation in Diarbekir

In the town the situation is catastrophic. The military administration is tyrannical and all-powerful. No assemblage, even of women and children, is permitted in the streets and open squares. All the Turkish schools, with the exception of the High School, have been closed, as the elementary schools have been under the direction of the hodjas.

The bazaar is empty, the shops are closed and the villagers from the surrounding districts will not bring their produce into the town.

The military secret intelligence system, staffed from Angora, makes daily arrests and the prisons are full. Apart from the well-known executions of the leaders of the Kurdish revolt, there have been hung at one place of execution just outside the town 215 Kurds and 50 Turks. More than 300 hodjas and petty sheikhs have disappeared, leaving no trace.

Many villages in the immediate vicinity have been razed to the ground and the crops over large areas have been either burnt or trampled down. The result is that the main preoccupation and difficulty of the military authorities is the question of supplying the troops from which they depend almost entirely upon local requisitioning. The possession of a well-stocked barn or a flourishing crop is sufficient ground for a denunciation and the summary execution of the owner on suspicion of complicity with the rebels.

British Public Record Office, Kew
AIR 23/237

1925

Cumhuriyet archive

Verdict
Court of Independence

You have all acted in behalf of one cause—the establishment of an independent Kurdistan. Some of you have done so by mobilizing a group for your personal interests, some of you have been guided by the provocation of foreigners or by political greed. In bringing about the general revolt you have been contemplating and planning for years, you have brought devastation to the region. Your revolt was quickly put down by determined, decisive action on the part of the Republican government and by the lethal blows struck by the Republican army, and now you are gathered together here to answer to justice.

Everyone should know that the government of the young Republic will not tolerate reactionary agitation or any kind of other accursed activities and that its firm measures will leave no place for this sort of rebellious movement. The poor people of this region, who have for centuries been exploited and oppressed by shaikhs, aghas, and begs, will be liberated from your evil agitation and, guided by our Republic that promises them progress and happiness, they will henceforth live in prosperity and happiness. You will pay with your lives, by hanging from the gallows of justice, for the blood that you have shed and the families that you have destroyed. This is the verdict in accordance with the stern but just laws of the Republic. . . . Send away the convicts.

From the verdict of Mazhar Müfit Kansu, judge of the Diyarbakır Independence Tribunal, sentencing Shaikh Said and forty-five associates to death, quoted in *Genelkurmay Belgelerinde Kürt Isyanları*, Vol.1, 1992, translated by Martin van Bruinessen

THE EXECUTION OF SHEIKH SAID.

(FROM OUR OWN CORRESPONDENT.)

CONSTANTINOPLE, JUNE 30.

The special correspondent of the *Aksham* at Diarbekir sends a long account of the final scenes at the execution of Sheikh Said, the Dervish leader of the recent insurrection in Turkish Kurdistan, and his companions. Much of the report is marked by a blood-thirsty gloating, and it contains accounts of conversations between the condemned men and the onlookers, including even a member of the Tribunal of Independence, which are astonishing, according to Western ideas and undesirable to reproduce. The last remark ascribed to Sheikh Said has a certain interest. In reply to questions by the Army Commander, General Mursel Pasha, as to who was the greatest enemy of Turkey, the Sheikh is alleged to have answered simply, "The British."

The Times, London, July 1, 1925

Left: *"The traitors who caused the bloodshed of innocent Turks, penetrating Elaziz, have paid with their lives on the gallows near the military base. We show our readers the real face of the revolt"*

Vakit (Time), Turkish newspaper, June 7, 1925
Courtesy M. Malmîsanij

From H. Dobbs, High Commissioner for Iraq

Angora, November 22, 1926

Tewfik [Rushdi, Minister of Foreign Affairs] drove me in his car to the house of the President, to whom he introduced me. The President spoke in Turkish and I spoke in French, Tewfik acting as interpreter. . . . The President seemed to be in a most friendly mood, and frequently smiled in a very attractive way. . . . It was all very well to talk of self-determination and the rights of minorities, but these must be subordinated to the rights of existing nations. The Kurds would for many generations be incapable of self-government. . . . The fault of the East, he said, was its belief in theory and its divorcement from fact. The Turkish Empire had been ruined by its fantastic belief that it could combine all Moslem peoples in one great pan-Islamic union. This had aroused the suspicion of other Powers. In order to avoid a repetition of this absurdity he had abolished the Khalifate.

I replied that his Excellency would learn the attitude of Great Britain from the lips of the British Ambassador, but that so far as my personal sentiments were concerned, I had always been deeply distressed at the interruption of the ancient friendship between Turkey and Great Britain, and had rejoiced at the recent signs of its re-establishment. I should seize every opportunity in my capacity as High Commissioner for Iraq of consolidating that friendship.

After some further complimentary phrases, I took my leave.

British Public Record Office, Kew
FO 371/11557/E6677

From Sir George Clerk
To Sir Austen Chamberlain

Angora, November 24, 1926

Sir Henry Dobbs's visit to Angora was most successful. The Turks were genuinely glad to get into personal relations with him, and showed their satisfaction to the best of their ability, while his tact and frankness not only made an excellent impression, but established a friendly basis on which the future relations of Iraq and Turkey, which by force of circumstances are bound to be complicated and occasionally difficult, may, it is to be hoped, be discussed with goodwill on both sides.

British Public Record Office, Kew
FO 371/11557/E6677

Notes on Conversation with Tewfik Rushdi Bey,
Turkish Minister of Foreign Affairs

A propos of the abolition of the Khalifate, which he had been discussing, Tewfik Rushdi said that the Turkish Government had come to the conclusion that the Kurds could never be assimilated and must be expelled. Modern Turkey was founded on hecatombs of dead and must continue to be ruthless. She had got rid of the Greeks and the Armenians and her next move would be to get rid of the Kurds. This was necessary not only because of their hopeless mentality but because, after the Mediterranean and Black Sea coast lands, the Eastern parts of Anatolia were the most fertile and were needed for the settlement of the Turks. Moreover it would never be safe to leave Kurds in the frontier tracts. Turkey must have there people on whom she could depend. They hoped that the greater number of the Kurds when expelled would go to Persia. Some no doubt would go to Russia, Iraq and Syria. In any case Turkey would never take them back. I asked him whether he did not think it would be very difficult to carry out the programme and whether it would not keep the Turkish frontiers disturbed. He said no. They reckoned that there were only 500,000 Kurds left in Turkey and these could be dealt with easily. In any case they were determined to see this policy through. (His figures are of course grossly underestimated. The number of Kurds in Turkey must be at least 1½ million.)

H. Dobbs, November 29, 1926

British Public Record Office, Kew
FO 371/11557/E7086

Hasan Hayri
Kurdish Parliamentarian

Hasan Hayri was from Dersim, and when the Turkish delegation was in Lausanne in 1923, the delegates from other countries said, "There is a Kurdish population in Kurdistan, in the east of Turkey. If we sign the agreement, what will happen to them?" And Ismet Pasha, the chief of the Turkish delegation, said, "The Turkish government of Turkey is not only the government of Turkey. It is a Turkish and Kurdish government. And the Kurdish and Turkish people have decided to live together, so it is no problem." But he had to prove that this was the case. He told Kemal Pasha to do something in Ankara to show that the Kurdish people were with the Turkish people.

Kemal Pasha took this man, Hasan Hayri, and told him that the next day he must wear Kurdish national clothes and come with him to parliament to show everybody and show the journalists from other countries that the government of Turkey accepted the Kurdish peoples' existence and their traditions and their clothes and culture. And the next day, Hasan Hayri arrived in Kurdish clothes and he spoke in the parliament about how the Kurdish and Turkish people had decided to live together, and how the Kurdish people didn't want to secede. And then Pasha asked him, "Please write a telegram and send it to Lausanne with the same thoughts you expressed in the parliament." So Ismet Pasha showed the telegram to the other delegates from the European nations. And they said okay, and they signed the agreement together, and after a while Hasan Hayri was arrested and sent to a special court in Turkey called the Independence Court.

There were no jurists, just members of parliament and members of Kemal Pasha's party. And they said, "You are a Kurdish nationalist. You want to separate Turkey and build an independent Kurdish republic." He said, "No. No. You know who I am. I am Hasan Hayri. I talked in the parliament. I sent a telegram to Lausanne, so how can you say to me 'You are a Kurdish separatist?'" They replied, "We know that one day you wore national Kurdish clothes and in these clothes you went to the Turkish parliament, so you are a Kurdish separatist."

He was condemned to death. And when they took him to the gallows and asked him for his last words, he said, "I want my grave to be in a place where the Kurds can walk by and spit on me because of my betrayal of them."

Interview with Mehmed Emin Bozarslan,
Kurdish writer living in Sweden, October 1993

Right: *Studio portrait of Hasan Hayri*

Unknown/Florence Billings Collection, Smith College

Leila Bedirkhan
Kurdish Dancer

I'm not Persian . . . I'm a Kurd. My grandfather was the crown prince of Kurdistan, which is on the frontier between Persia, Turkey and Syria.

But since the Turkish conquest, the independent princes in our family have become spread over a wide area. I was born in Turkey, in Constantinople. When I was very young, I left for Egypt with my mother and spent my childhood there. I only came to Europe after the war, to study in Switzerland.

I've always loved dancing. In Egypt, when I was a child, I learned it through instinct, by watching the common women dancing.

I don't learn my dances. I dance instinctively using very stylized popular themes. I also invent dances. . . . As you can see, they have no specific origin. . . . I don't use my legs much when I'm dancing; I mainly use my arms and my body.

Helene Bory, "The Kurdish Princess Leila Bedirkhan Talks to Us About Her Dances and Women of the Orient," *Paris Midi,* December 16, 1932

Dancing was just a pastime for me when I was a child, something I enjoyed doing—in the same way others learn to play the piano or to do embroidery (which I also learned to do, by the way). When, after the tragic death of my father, the Emir, I fled from my revolt-stricken country, dancing became my very reason for living, my life's aim. I traveled through Austria, Germany, and Switzerland; after some early performances in most of the large cities in these countries, I settled in Paris where, after two recitals, I decided to spend a year researching the religious rites of ancient Persia, Egyptian Mazdeism [Zoroastrism], Indian, and Oriental sacred dances.

Comedia, December 9, 1930

Right: *"Kurdistan Princess Reveals Harem Dances!"*

TEATRO ALLA SCALA - LEILA BEDERKHAN
(Regina di Saba) NEL BALLO *"Belkis,,*

FOT. M. CAMUZZI
DELLA S. A. CRIMELLA

Princess Leila performing at La Scala Theater

M. Camuzzi/Kurdish Institute of Paris

WATCH. YOUR CREDIT.......
FL 12376'   "P & A PHOTOS"
(PHOTO SHOWS PRINCESS LEILA)

KURDISTAN PRINCESS REVEALS HAREM DANCES!

    PRINCESS LEILA, DAUGHTER OF THE LAST
EMIR OF KURDISTAN, WHO WAS INITIATED INTO THE
SEXRED SACRED DANCES OF THE HAREM, IS RE-
VEALING THEIR MYSTERIES AND IS NOW DANCING
PUBLICLY. IN A PARIS THEATRE. SHE RECENTLY
PAID A VISIT TO LONDON. PHOTO SHOWS PRINCESS
LEILA WEARING ONE OF THE DRESSES SPECIALLY
MADE FOR HER BY PAUL POIRET, THE DESIGNER.
        (B NY 12-31-26)

"Standing and staring—a common diversion throughout the Near East."

"For sounds, smells, costumes, and foods, Kharput's Bazaar is peculiar."

"'Doorstep Babies': What with marching armies, deportations, and wholesale migration, due to famine and changing frontiers, old-established communities have been dispersed and families scattered far and wide, especially since the World War. Babies in this Kharput nursery are the children of Armenian mothers, though their fathers were Kurds."

Melville Chater
American Photographer and Writer

An American missionary who had spent most of his life in the country . . . shook his head when I proposed a trip into the Dersim region. "They're 'half devil and half child,'" he told me. "Though they're supposed to have been under Turkish rule for the last four centuries, they still refuse to pay taxes and still live in clans, which are generally fighting each other when they're not fighting the government. . . .

"Scattered throughout the Near East, about half of them are orthodox Mohammedans. The remainder are called Kizilbash—that is, Redhead—because they wear red turbans. They profess an extraordinary mixture of Mohammedanism, nature worship, and Christianity. . . .

"Sometimes I've stayed overnight with Kurds. The family, my horse, and I all dined on the same dish—cracked barley. Though the law of hospitality protects you while under their roof, they consider it perfectly honorable to attack you, once you're outside their front gate. No; the Kurds are better off your visiting list.". . . However, as it chanced, some of us were destined to put them on our visiting list before long.

I occupied the cot nearest the sole access to our veranda, and, notwithstanding the Kurds' sacred law of hospitality, I privately determined to stay awake. It was hard work, and I was just dozing off when I heard certain suspicious rustlings that brought me to my feet. Again the rooftops were full of Kurds—crouching, mysteriously whispering figures. I was just beginning to wonder if they were there to witness a massacre of Americans, when the moon's pale disk freed itself from among the hills and swam into full view. Simultaneously the Kurds arose, making low bows and salaaming profoundly to the risen planet; then they descended their stone stairways and disappeared within the doors for the night. What I had witnessed was a religious rite—one of the pagan practices of this strange people. . . .

The Kizilbash goes in for all sorts of things, from primitive forms of baptism and communion to a belief in guardian angels and a veneration of the sun and moon. . . .

Our Kizilbash hosts were up and at their tasks before the stars paled. . . . As the sun rose, each man, woman, and child turned eastward, bowing to it a polite good-morning, then resumed the day's routine. We Americans crawled lamely out of bed, washed at the public fountain, then visited some of the surrounding houses. . . .

The Kurdish woman, with her slit skirt, which reveals the Turkey-red trousers, tight at the ankle—with her chin-muffling burnoose, and the broad sash, tightly drawn so as to accentuate her body's mold—could give Fifth Avenue or Rue de Rivoli lessons in coquettish dressmaking. . . .

In order to lighten the motor truck, three of us hired donkeys from the murshid, the price including two donkey-persuaders—a pair of small boys—who would accompany us to Malatia. I was preparing to cut a stick from an adjoining tree, when horrified shrieks arose from the women, and the murshid bustled up to inform me that this was a sacred tree, not to be touched, much less cut. He then made the tree a profound obeisance of apology, and we rode off, stared at to the last by the assembled women, several of whom now wore newly acquired ornaments consisting of American salt-spoons, string-suspended about their necks. The Kurds are, indeed, very deft "borrowers."

Melville Chater, "The Kizilbash Clans of Kurdistan,"
National Geographic, October 1928

Right: *"Pranky fate! One woman she garbs in tatters, another in all the glories of a fashion show. This Kurdish country woman, despite rags and poverty, clings to her yashmak, symbol of woman's seclusion in the Moslem world; but now modern women of the Moslem cities are putting aside the veil."*

Melville Chater (left), Donald Horsford (right), *National Geographic*, October 1928

FLAG OF KURDISTAN

Kurds Demand an International Inquiry

In the name of the Kurdish people, and of civilization, The Hoyboon, the Government of Kurdistan, invites the Governments of the United States, Great Britain, France, Italy, indeed, all the civilized governments, to take the initiative to create an International Commission, which shall investigate the campaign of atrocities which Kemalist Turkey has been perpetrating in Kurdistan since 1925. The findings of the Commission could well determine the merits of the Kurdish case, as those of the professions and pretensions of the so-called Kemalist republic.

Kurdistan Proclaims Her Independence

In October, 1927, Kurdish leaders of diverse political faiths and affiliations met in Convention, without Kurdistan, to elaborate a National Pact, and to take necessary steps to realize their national aims. This convention unanimously (a) created The Hoyboon, the supreme national organ, or the Kurdish Government, and, (b) clothed that Government with full and exclusive national and international powers.

The Hoyboon, thereupon, proclaimed, on October 28, 1927, the independence of Kurdistan, as laid down in the Sèvres Treaty; designated Kurd Ava, at Egri Dagh, as the provisional capital of Kurdistan, and, by resolution, expressed the friendly sentiments of the Kurdish people for Persia, Armenia, Iraq, and Syria, and their determination to wage relentless war against the Turks—until they had abandoned, in perpetuity, the Kurdish soil, now under their grip.

The war between Turk and Kurd is going on—and will go on—until the objective of the Kurd has been attained. . . .

Kurdish-Armenian Relations

The first task of The Hoyboon, following its creation, was an effort toward a final reconciliation, and if possible, cooperation with the Armenians.

I write upon Kurdish-Armenian relations with a mingled feeling of regret and of gratitude. That, through the sinister influence of the Turk and the ignorance of the Kurd, the Armenian, in certain localities and at certain periods, has suffered is a cause for deep regret. That we have already buried the past is cause for congratulation and gratitude. . . .

Prince Süreya Bedr Khan, *The Case of Kurdistan Against Turkey,* 1928

BY AUTHORITY OF

HOYBOON

SUPREME COUNCIL OF THE KURDISH GOVERNMENT

KURD AND TURK.

THE FIGHTING IN KURDISTAN.

(FROM A CORRESPONDENT.)

Though three years have passed since the Turkish Army broke the back of Sheikh Said's revolt against the religious or, as his followers would have said, the irreligious reforms of the new Turks, Kurdistan is not yet pacified.

The severity with which the rebellion was suppressed angered or alarmed chiefs who had not joined the Sheikh, and in the autumn of 1925 Turkish columns were engaged with rebellious clans in the Mardin-Midiat region and in the border territory north of Mosul. There were good reasons for the Turks to be enraged with the Kurds, who had destroyed the fiction of Turco-Kurdish friendship and solidarity which was to have served as propaganda at Geneva when the Mosul question was discussed : the Kurdish chieftains instinctively felt that the new

Turkey would do what the old Turkey had only threatened and would compel them and their tribes to pay taxes, give conscripts, and in general settle down to the normal life of Turkish peasants, looking to the Governor and the gendarme rather than to the Aga and the Pir.

The operations of 1925 were successful, but a number of Kurds and their leaders were able to escape, the Goyan into Iraq, some of the Midiat people into French Syria. In 1926 came more fighting, accompanied by executions, village burnings, and the deportation of Kurdish notables, with their families who were set down at Adana or Sinope. There were three centres of resistance—the Dersim, with its heretical Zaza-speaking inhabitants ; the Nisibin area, in the Central Taurus ; and the mountain region about Lake Van. Nisibin was pacified first, and Hadjo, the chief rebel, escaped into French territory. In spite of numerous executions the Dersim remained defiant. The Jalali and Haideranli rose in the Bayazid region and cut up a Turkish battalion. Troops from Erzerum came up and restored the situation. A number of Kurds—some reports speak of 150 notable families—were deported to Western Anatolia. Many died on the way, and some of the better looking women are said to have disappeared. A large number of the rebels escaped with their families into Persia.

Last year there was more fighting. In February Salih Izzet Bey with about 4,000 regulars and gendarmerie defeated the Kotch-Ushagh clan in the Dersim. Later in the year the Sassun and Bohtan tribes in the Bitlis province were attacked and are said to have been subdued. On the Persian border there was a " small war." The " Monarchists," or " reactionary conspirators " of the Turkish Press, whose raids into Turkish territory caused an extremely acid interchange of notes between Angora and Teheran, were Haideranli and other Kurd runaways, and though the Persians profess to have moved them away from the border it is unlikely that they will be surrendered. The Shah's Government had its own views as to how the Turco-Persian frontier should be drawn in 1918, and the Pahlevi Monarch may take the same view as his Kajar predecessors.

Meanwhile the Turks seem disposed to modify their Kurdish policy, at least locally. Kurd refugees in Iraq, Syria, Persia, and Soviet Transcaucasia are a bad advertisement, and there are signs that the Turkish Govern-

The Times, London
April 7, 1928

Kamuran, Süreya, and Celadet Ali Bedirkhan

Yado Agha and Ado Agha, leaders of the Harput front, with followers behind them

Ihsan Nuri
Kurdish Military Officer

Ihsan Nuri Bey is reported to be in Iran, and in touch with the Russians; he would be a likely choice as leader of a Kurdish revolt in the Ararat mountains adjoining Azerbaijan when climactic conditions become favorable in the spring.

Born at Bitlis in 1892, Ihsan Nuri Bey left the Istanbul Military College in 1910, and served in the Turkish army throughout the first World War.... He instigated the last Kurdish rebellion in 1924, when two battalions of the Second Division mutinied at Beit al-Sha'ab. The rising was crushed, but Ihsan Nuri is said to have escaped to Baghdad, where he published an anti-Turkish pamphlet advocating an independent Kurdistan. After another abortive rebellion against the Turks in 1925, Ihsan fled to Iran, where it is believed he remained under police surveillance.

Unsigned, February 15, 1946
Strategic Services Unit, A 66354,
Persian Gulf Collection, The National
Security Archive, Washington, D.C.

Ihsan Nuri Pasha (fourth from left); Xalis Beg, chief of the Sipki tribe (second from left); Ferzende Beg Heseni, leader of Hesenan tribe, commander of the army (third from right); Ehmede Haci Bro, Kurdish officer (far right)

Unknown/Courtesy Munzur Çem

Yashar Khanum was my grandfather's sister. I asked her niece—my aunt—what she remembers about her and she said:

"I corresponded with my uncle, Ihsan Nuri, though I was not smart enough to keep his letters. Years later I found his book, The History of the Kurds, and I saw that he was regarded as a hero. In one of the rebellions in the east, he and his troops came up against the Republican Army, and after fighting for some time, he took shelter in Iran. He sent one of his men to Turkey to your grandfather, a military physician, who was in Denizli. The man told your grandfather that Ihsan Nuri had sent for his wife. Your grandfather was very, very furious. And your great-grandmother said, 'Over my dead body, I wouldn't give my daughter to that traitor.' After a while, they realized that they should ask this question to Yashar Khanum. And Yashar Khanum said, 'I want to go to my husband.' So despite all the pressure your grandfather put on her, she left, and she never talked to her brother again. After a very difficult trip with a Turkish soldier of Ihsan Nuri's as an escort she reached the Iranian border, and Yashar Khanum was handed over to Ihsan Nuri at the border. After that, Ihsan Nuri was officially banned from returning to Turkey. He was classified as a traitor, so he could never come back. Neither could Yashar Khanum. Ihsan Nuri went to Kurdish meetings in Europe, but he always traveled via Soviet airlines. The Shah of Iran gave them a house in Tehran and a summer house in Rezaieh and paid his salary and travel expenses."

Interview with Kumru Toktamis,
Turkish sociologist living in the U.S., August 1994

THE KURDISH RISING

(FROM OUR OWN CORRESPONDENT)
CONSTANTINOPLE, JULY 21

It is reported that a clan of Kizil Bashes and other clans in the northern part of Turkish Kurdistan have joined the insurgents.

It appears that another former Turkish officer, in addition to Major Mahmud, Captain Ihsan Nuri Bey, is acting as one of the Kurdish leaders. The organization and discipline of the insurgents are reported to be good. They are wearing armlets of red, green, and white, and on their caps is an emblem representing Mount Ararat. General Salih Pasha, the Turkish commander, has established his headquarters at Bayezid, but there is no news of how the fighting is progressing round Mount Ararat.

The Times, London, July 22, 1930

Right: *Ihsan Nuri Pasha and his wife, Yashar Khanum*
Unknown/The Kurdish Institute of Paris

1927

"The wife of a Kurdish chief taken prisoner is obliged to disclose the general headquarters of the rebels."
—Jean Weinberg

The commander of the Mount Ararat movement was Ehsam Noory Bey [Ihsan Nuri], once a colonel in the Turkish army, and later the right hand of Sheikh Sayid whose son was then being tried at Angora; but the hero of the region was a wild and gallant freebooter called Ibrahim Agha Hiske Tello, instigator and leader of all the most daring raids, a ubiquitous and altogether amazing personage, capable, apparently, of fighting personally and simultaneously on three different fronts. . . .

His fame had already passed into song, and encouraged by his shouted name, women would take up the rifles dropped by the wounded. Fighting side by side with their men, they seemed to enjoy the sport, for they returned to their villages, blood-stained and smiling with the boast, "We are not afraid of our enemies. When we see them coming, we laugh, for how can an army reach us here?"

It is true that their houses, stone-built and mud-faced out of the mountainside, are plastered on almost invisible ledges, or within fissures that look like shadows. It seemed then that unless the whole mountain were blown up, it would be impossible to dislodge its gallant defenders, but the Turks are as good fighters as the Kurds, whom they outnumbered ten to one. They were backed by every device of modern warfare, including planes, tanks and heavy artillery. The weight of metal poured into the mountain during the subsequent weeks was an earnest of Turkey's determination to 'finish with the accursed race.' . . .

Ignored by the whole civilized world, isolated from their fellow Kurds and, towards the end, deprived of munitions and food, they fought doggedly and hopelessly for a freedom which was theirs long before they raided Xenophon and his retreating ten thousand, and which they maintained as an inalienable right. But from the beginning they were doomed. Like the Riff and like Jebel Druse, Mount Ararat succumbed to the 'forces of civilization.'

Rosita Forbes, *Conflict: Angora to Afghanistan*, 1931

To The Right Honourable Arthur Henderson, M.P. [British Member of Parliament], From British Embassy, Constantinople

July 16, 1930

The following information given to me by Mrs. McGrath, better known perhaps as Rosita Forbes, who passed through here on Friday last on her way from Aleppo to London, is of some interest. . . .

Hearing of the trouble on the Turkish frontier and of an opportunity to go there, her journalistic instincts led her to make the attempt. . . . She went on horseback and was among the Kurds for eleven days. . . . Mrs. McGrath spent three days at villages on Ararat, where she photographed one of the wrecked Turkish aeroplanes. (She did not see the unfortunate occupants whom the Kurds had killed and then stretched on poles with a placard announcing that that was the treatment awaiting every Turkish aviator.). . .

Throughout her journey on the frontier Mrs. McGrath saw no signs of any Turkish officials or soldiers and heard very little of fighting. She was quite definite on the subject of Persian assistance to the rebels, as witness her Kurdish guide's meeting with the General at Tabriz, and she knew for a fact that ammunition and supplies were regularly crossing the frontier from Persia.

I imagine that Mrs. McGrath's guide took good care to keep well clear of any Turkish troops. Still, she certainly risked both her personal safety in that wild country and the chance of an 'incident' between Turkey and ourselves though I hope that her confidence will be respected, for otherwise the intermediaries who, certainly for cash but also in good faith, arranged her journey will pay a heavy penalty. For this reason she told me that she would be unable to make use of her experience in the English press.

I have sent a copy of this despatch to His Majesty's Minister at Tehran and the Acting High Commissioner at Bagdad.

I have the honour to be, with the highest respect,
Sir, Your most obedient, humble Servant,
George R. Clerk [Ambassador to the Turkish Republic]

British Public Record Office
FO 371/14580/E3897

MOUNT ARARAT KURDS BEATEN

(FROM OUR OWN CORRESPONDENT)

CONSTANTINOPLE, Sept. 15

The Government has published a laconic *communiqué* to the effect that military operations against the Kurds in Mount Ararat have ended, and that complete success attended the Turkish forces. In some quarters, however, it is believed that many Kurdish insurgents escaped into Persia.

The Times, London, September 16, 1930

A group of Kurdish prisoners

Jean Weinberg/National Archives, Washington, D.C.

> *Language is one of the essential characteristics of a nation. Those who belong to the Turkish nation ought, above all and absolutely, to speak Turkish. . . . Those people who speak another language could, in a difficult situation, collaborate and take action against us with other people who speak other languages.*

Mustafa Kemal "Atatürk," quoted in *Cumhuriyet*, February 14, 1931

Proposal for the Punitive Campaign in Pülümür
(To Take Place October 8–November 14, 1930)

During my inspection tour of the province of Erzincan I concluded that it is necessary to punish the villages of Aşkirik, Gürk, Dağbey and Haryi. These villages . . . which due to the insufficient force of the provincial gendarmerie have not been seriously chastised, have through their mischief a highly negative impact on the Turkish people and incite the surrounding Kurdish villages to banditry. Therefore the provincial administration should send these villages a notice telling them to pay taxes and accept conscription and to surrender their arms. If this does not produce the desired effect, it is in my opinion appropriate to despatch an air force unit to Erzincan to have these villages destroyed, in order to effect the other Kurdish villages in this region, which all behave very insolently, and thus to establish government authority.

In the central district of Erzincan live 10,000 Kurds. Using the (common) Alevi religion, they make efforts to kurdicize the existing Turkish villages and to spread the Kurdish language. There is reason to worry that in a few years time Kurdishness will flood the entire province of Erzincan. Believing that Alevism is an expression of Kurdishness, several villages that are Turkish by custom but Alevi by religion have given up their mother tongue and now speak Kurdish. It is necessary to keep a close check on the villages of Rusaray, Mitini, Şıncığı, Kürtkendi and Kelarik, which are in the forefront of these efforts and which are hotbeds of all sorts of mischief. Some of the villagers will need to be deported to Thrace, and some of the tribal chieftains of this district will have to be secured by keeping them in enforced residence in the city under police supervision. There is a need for fundamental measures to prevent the Turkish Alevi villages from speaking Kurdish and to allow the Turkish language to spread throughout the district.

It is known that certain government officials in this province belong to the Kurdish race. Thus, for instance, it has come to pass that the coroner of Erzincan, Şevki Efendi of Pülümür, gives political protection to the Kurds and that at night Kurds gather in his house. This man needs, by whatever means, to be removed from the province, and the same treatment is due to other officials like him.

The most urgently needed measure regarding the present problem that I am bringing to your attention is that the Kurdish villages mentioned in the first paragraph above be severely punished and that officials who are with certainty known to be Kurdish be as soon as possible removed from their positions.

Report by General Fevzi Çakmak, chief of Turkey's general staff, to the prime minister and the minister of the interior, on an inspection tour of Kurdish districts in the wake of the suppression of the Ararat rebellion, dated September 18, 1930 *Genelkurmay Belgelerinde Kürt Isyanları (Kurdish Rebellions in Documents of the General Staff)*, Vol. 2, 1992, translated by Martin van Bruinessen

TURKEY

Mr. Morgan to Sir John Simon

Constantinople, October 24, 1934
The Kurds of Dersim, a wild and mountainous region lying between Erzincan and Elaziz (Harput), well to the west of the other Kurdish districts in Turkey, have been well behaved in recent years and took no part in the series of Kurdish risings which began with Sheikh Said's revolt in 1925. They have thus so far escaped the heavy hand of the republic, whose principles they have, it may be assumed, hitherto completely failed to assimilate.

British Public Record Office, Kew
FO 371/17967/E6663

Leaflet Distributed by the Fourth Inspector General During the Second Tunceli Pacification Operation

As you see you are surrounded by our soldiers. Our planes are also flying over your heads and see what you are doing. You were misled by a few fools. You abandoned your homes and your fields, and in fear, distress, hardship and pain you carried your hungry, tired women, children and animals into dark and stuffy caves. Diseases will soon spread as a result of heat and hunger. Our soldiers have conquered your mountains, penetrated everywhere and are about to enter into your final sanctuaries. Yet the state does not hurt her children. Even when she punishes those who disobey, her heart breaks for them.

Quoted in Türkiye Cumhuriyetinde Ayaklanmalar
(The Uprisings in the Republic of Turkey), 1924–1938

Alîşêr and his wife, Zêrifa, in the mountains   Unknown/Deng-Azadi, Istanbul

It is a rifle. It is my rifle. Oh yes, it is my rifle. My rifle is big. Your rifle is big. The barrel of the rifle. We do not have bread. Our house is big. Zin and Feremez. It is summer. It is an ox. It is a cow. It is a goat. They are two children. There is no fruit. We have bread. It is expensive. Yes, he is my father. He is my friend. Temo is your friend. Today there are no fruits but we have bread. Come here. The barrel of the rifle is long. We see the cock and the trigger of the rifle. Today. It is bright today. In my house there are two children. She is our daughter.
HEY, IT'S A RIFLE. IT'S HEAVY.

Kamuran Ali Bedirkhan, Elfabeya Min (My Alphabet Book), 1938,
translated by Martin van Bruinessen/Courtesy Mirella Galietti

My heart, let us travel in the Dersim mountains.
How beautiful is this country, Dersim.
Look at the grape gardens of Sultan Dagi.
All the lovely flowers of Dersim.
How many kings have ruled the world,
Yet to take Dersim confounds them,
They are hurled away.
The arms of holy Dersim are still perfect.
It is a country of lions that the foxes cannot enter,
It is a secret of reality that the mind cannot understand,
It is Kurdistan's rose that the oppressors cannot pluck.
The road to Dersim is closed to them.
Let them disturb the country of Kurdistan,
Fervent Dersim will come to the rescue quick as lightning,
Its floods destroying all.
There are many heroes and they bear swords
And their power reaches all of Kurdistan
And the seven countries cower.
This is the gift of God: that Dersim's back is strong.

Poem by Alîşêr, collected by Munzur Çem, for "Halk Türkülerinde
Dersim Isyani (The Dersim Revolt in Folksongs)," Dengê Komkar,
Kurdish monthly magazine published in Germany, Nos. 93–98, 1987

1937

146

Leaders of the Hormek tribe of Dersim: Karerli Mehmet Efendi (left) and Bertal Yurtsever (right), with Dogan Dede, an Alevi priest from Malatia

Unknown/Courtesy Nuri Medyali

During the 1938 Dersim massacre, Yurtsever and fifty members of his family were killed by Turkish military. They had been promised deportation to western Turkey. Instead, all of them, including women, three of whom were pregnant, children, and old men, were shot to death, and then gasoline was poured on their bodies. They were burned to ashes twelve miles from their village, Ciwraq. My mother and everyone else who lived in the village told me this.

When the military came to Dersim, they spoke to my grandfather, who pointed at a goat and told them that the military was treating them like animals. My grandfather was a businessman, an educated person, and a leader of his tribe. He and his tribe did nothing against the government. They even carried barley and wood for the animals of the military before the uprising, but the government didn't care. They wanted to eliminate tribal leaders who could be a potential threat. Regardless of whom they sided with, most of them were killed.

Interview with Nuri Medyali, Kurdish businessman living in the U.S., September 1994

One afternoon, a soldier came to the house of one of our neighbors with the excuse that he wanted water. He told the people there not to believe the soldiers, that they were going to massacre us. A villager named Babaye Kuyas went to talk to the headman. But the village headman, who trusted in his friendship with the commander of the troops, did not listen to him. He told the villagers to be reasonable, that we didn't have problems with the government, that we hadn't done anything wrong, so the soldiers didn't have any reason to kill us. Next day, they gathered all of us and made us walk outside our village. After a while we saw that they had set our village on fire.

We had to climb a hill. Two old villagers, Xido the hunchback and Ele, could not walk. The soldiers took them out of the group and killed them with a rifle butt as we watched. In the meantime, a Kurdish soldier from Diyarbakır came closer to the group and said, "They will kill you all. Run." But because he didn't want the other soldiers to understand him, he said these things as if he were singing a Kurdish song. Many did not notice.

Interview with Xece by Munzer Çem, Kurdish writer living in Sweden, summer 1976

The Times, London,
June 16, 1937

KURDS WHO OBJECT TO EDUCATION

A REVOLT SUPPRESSED BY TROOPS

FROM OUR OWN CORRESPONDENT

ISTANBUL, JUNE 15

In his address to the Kamutay yesterday the Prime Minister, General Inönü, referred to recent disturbances among Kurds in the Dersim, about which no official announcement had previously been made. He explained that they had been due to the hostility of the local population towards the introduction of compulsory education and other reforms and had become sufficiently serious to make it necessary for the Government to send troops to the affected area. During the operations the Army and gendarmerie had lost 13 killed and 18 wounded, but the situation was now well in hand.

During the Dersim operations Sabiha Gökchen, one of the Ataturk's adopted daughters, who had volunteered for service in the Turkish Flying Corps, so distinguished herself that she has been awarded the Flying Medal set with brilliants. This, the highest honour which can be won for aviation in Turkey, is rarely awarded.

Sabiha Gökchen is 22 years of age and holds a Turkish military pilot's certificate. She is stated to have shown the greatest bravery and resource throughout the operations, and to have dropped the final bomb which virtually put an end to the insurrection.

The armed resistance of the Dersim people was suppressed by the summer of 1938. We began to consider returning. We were told that a census would be taken, that we would receive identity cards and then we would be released. The soldiers constantly assured us and told us not to worry. Only some families were going to be sent into exile and the rest were going to be released. But some of the captives from different regions were telling horrible stories. It was difficult to believe the soldiers. They brought us to an abyss by the river. Then we were sure we were going to be killed. My hands were tied to the hands of another young guy. I tried to free myself. My father noticed what I was doing, and told me to jump into the river as soon as they started shooting at us and swim. Then the soldiers were ordered to fire. The sound of the machine guns was mixed with the screams of people. I released my hands and at that moment my father must have been shot; his blood was all over my face. He had stood up in front of me and sheltered me. I was not hit. I turned and jumped into the river. When I came to the surface, there were bullets all around me. I swam underwater as much as possible. Then I hid under some bushes; the soldiers couldn't find me. Whoever they could find that day they killed.

Interview with Usê, a Kurd from Dersim, by Munzur Çem, summer 1977

No.405.
(340/26/37)   E 3819
                 8 JUL 1937

British Embassy,
Istanbul.
3rd July, 1937.

Sir,

I have the honour, with reference to Mr. Morgan's despatch No.361 of the 17th June, to inform you that, according to a telegram received from His Majesty's Consul at Trebizond on the 28th June, the rising in the Dersim area appears now to have been effectively quelled.

2.   Mr. Matthews learns from a reliable source that the last body of rebels, numbering between 500 and 600 men, surrendered to the authorities on or about the 24th June. The losses sustained by the Government troops are believed not to have been heavy, but there are said to have been considerable losses among the gendarmerie and in the Air arm, which played an important part in suppressing the rising. Great enthusiasm was manifested in the Turkish press when it was reported that Sabiha Gökçen, one of Atatürk's adopted daughters and a notable aviatrix, had successfully bombarded one of the rebel strongholds.

3.   Mr Matthews is informed that martial law is in force in the disaffected areas, although postal and telegraphic communications are maintained. It is stated that many of the leading rebels who have surrendered are to be hanged.

4.   The British Pro-Consul at Mersin also reports that local opinion is unanimous in regarding the rising

as ...

The Right Honourable

Anthony Eden, M.C., M.P.,

etc.,   etc.,   etc.

British Public Record Office, Kew
FO371/20864/E3819

as having been stamped out, and that most of the rebel leaders have surrendered. One of the chief leaders, Seyid Riza, is apparently still at large.

5.   The Istanbul press has published details of the programme of reforms to be instituted in the Dersim area. These include the construction of roads, bridges, schools and barracks, as well as the establishment of gendarmerie posts. It is apparently proposed to introduce the banking system, and Mr.Catton has learnt that the İş Bank will shortly open several new branches in the Dersim region. It is also stated in the press that the feudal system will be abolished and that the chief Kurdish leaders will be transported to other and distant parts of Turkey.

I have the honour to be, with the highest respect,

Sir,

Your most obedient,

humble Servant,

"It's incredible how many Turkish soldiers are standing behind one Kurd sitting."
—Memo Yetkin, Kurdish publisher living in Sweden

I knew a person who was from my area who studied in Istanbul in the 1960s. He met an elderly retired army officer, and they gradually became very close. In the course of their discussions, the officer asked my friend where he was from. When he said he was Kurdish, the officer said he had been in the Kurdish area on assignment and started to describe the things he had witnessed in Dersim. Because my friend was an intellectual he asked in detail about the experiences that the man had had in the area. Normally, in a society like Turkey's, one doesn't have the time to sit and listen to the history of old people. But this interest on my friend's part was taken positively by the man, and he opened up. And they became very intimate. He told my friend about working for the military intelligence in Dersim and that he had taken some pictures. He had given the pictures to the archives office, but he also had some in his personal possession. . . .

One day, in the evening, he invited my friend to his house, and after dinner and some drinks, he showed him the pictures, which impressed my friend considerably. He watched very closely to see where the officer put them back on the shelves. While the officer was out, he took a chance and stole the pictures. From that day on, he did his utmost not to run across him.

In 1968, we had a group called the Association of Students from the Town of Agri, and we planned to distribute a paper. This friend of mine said that he had some very interesting pictures and that if we dared to publish them he was ready to give them to us. We didn't dare to publish them at that time, but because he was a very close friend of mine, he gave me copies. I have kept them since then.

In those days, we didn't know much about Dersim or the history of the Kurdish movement. We were very eager to know more from whoever had some relationship to Kurdish history.

Interview with Reso Zilan, Kurdish scholar living in Sweden, September 1993

Photographs taken by a Turkish military officer, Dersim

Unknown/Courtesy Reso Zilan

Seyid Riza

Kurdish Leader

For years the Turkish government has attempted to assimilate the Kurdish people and with this objective has been oppressing them, forbidding them to read newspapers and publications in the Kurdish language, persecuting those who speak their mother tongue, organizing forced and systematic migrations from the fertile lands of Kurdistan to the uncultivated lands of Anatolia, where these migrants perished in large numbers....

Three million Kurds live in their country and ask only to live in peace and freedom while keeping their race, language, traditions, culture, and civilization.

Through my voice they ask your Excellency to let the Kurdish people benefit from the high moral influence of your government and to bring an end to this cruel injustice.

I have the honor, Mr. Minister, to ask you to receive my highest considerations.

Generalissimo Seyid Riza of Dersim

Letter to the Turkish Ministry of Foreign Affairs, July 30, 1937
British Public Record Office
FO 371/20864/E5529

Seyid Riza with Turkish military officers   Unknown/Deng-Azadi, Istanbul

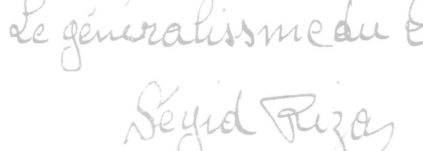

Dersim operation   Unknown/*Aydınlık* archive, Istanbul

In 1937, when the Turkish army attacked Dersim I was fourteen years old. We heard that my grandfather had been arrested and hanged in Elazığ with a group of other people. Among them was the youngest son of my grandfather. He had been wounded when fighter planes bombed my grandfather's mansion. A member of my family, who was a collaborator, handed him over to the soldiers who took him to the hospital for treatment. On the day they hanged my grandfather, they hanged him as well, by his father's side.

In 1938, soldiers unexpectedly proceeded toward the inner lands of Dersim. This was a surprise for those tribes that had not stood on the side of my grandfather, because they had made a deal with the commander of the military troops in 1937; according to the deal there should not have been any military operation. But the army did not respect their agreement.

One member of my family, Rehber Kop, who frequently had dealings with the government, had firsthand responsibility in the defeat of the Dersim people. He decided that he wanted to move to western Turkey. He had made a lot of money in his dealings with the state and was sure he was going to be given a nice piece of land in return for his services. He was proud of his connections. He took fourteen other members of the family with him. On their way to military headquarters he was shot by two military officers, then the others were killed. When we heard that, we realized that anyone could be killed. We ran and took shelter in the woods, but they found us and sent us into exile.

Interview with Ali Riza Polat, grandson of Seyid Riza from Dersim, living in Turkey (killed by unknown gunmen in 1983), by Munzur Çem, summer 1977

The director of General Security said . . . "The Dersim operation is over. Six thousand white-pants-easterners have arrived in Elazığ. They will ask Atatürk for amnesty for Seyid Riza. We should not let them meet Atatürk.". . .

I went to see the prosecutor. I explained to him the state of affairs. He told me that . . . since the courts were closed on Saturdays it was impossible to come to a verdict during the holidays. And he added: "I cannot influence the court." Yet we wanted the verdict before Atatürk's arrival to have the issue of Seyid Riza closed by that time. . . .

I said, "If you can work overtime at the end of the day, why can't you work overtime before the beginning of the working day? We'll open the court right before dawn following Sunday midnight." The judge said, "There won't be electricity at that time." We had a solution for that too. The prison would be lighted with car lights.

We fetched Seyid Riza. He sat in the car between me and Police Director Ibrahim. . . . He understood when he saw the gallows. He turned to me and said, "You are going to hang me. You came all the way from Ankara to hang me." We looked at each other. For the first time I was facing a man who was about to be executed. He smiled. . . .

Atatürk . . . showed me a photograph. Seyid Riza was hanging from the gallows. . . . Atatürk did not like this kind of thing. And he was a democrat. I destroyed the negatives and the prints. . . . I went to see Atatürk and said to him, "I followed your orders." "Have you destroyed them all?" "Yes, sir. I only kept two of them. . . . If you allow me, I will give one to your Highness and keep the other one for myself."

Ihsan Sabri Caglayangil,
former Turkish minister of affairs,
Anılarım (My Memories), 1990,
translated by Kumru Toktamis

Background: *Seyid Riza*

Courtesy Mustafa Düzgün

When I was seventeen or eighteen years old, I decided to write about the Dersim revolt because the revolt happened in my region, but I didn't have a clear plan. Then around the middle of 1970, I think the Turkish writer Barbaros Baykara's novels Dersim 1937 *and* Tunceli 1938 *were published. I read them and became very sad and angry, because they were totally wrong. It looked like an army report. . . . I decided to write the Dersim revolt as a novel. . . .*

Throughout my research, I kept two thoughts in mind: (a) I knew if people didn't trust me, they wouldn't talk to me. If the army or police knew what was happening, it could be risky for them. Therefore, it was important to have contact with their relatives, friends, etc. before visiting them. For example, Seyid Riza's grandchild Ali Riza helped me a lot. (b) It was possible to get wrong information from people. I found that people didn't like to tell about certain events. They didn't like to talk about the mistakes or bad deeds of their friends and relatives. They didn't want to talk about rapes and so on. Therefore, I asked different people about the same event.

When I decided to write my novel, Gülümse Ey Dersim *(Smile Dersim), I planned it as four volumes. The war between the Turkish army and the Kurdish Qozan tribe who lived around Ali Bogazi (Ali Valley) in southwest Dersim, would be the first volume. During the military coup in 1980, the Turkish security forces found it during a search and confiscated it. They confiscated nearly four hundred pages of the third and fourth volumes with many other documents as well. I had copies of a large part of the second and third volumes, but I didn't have copies of the first volume. . . . I couldn't publish the volume that was about the 1926 revolt because I couldn't collect enough information about it again.*

Letter from Munzur Çem,
September 1994

Under the Iraqi Monarchy

During the brief period when it might have mattered, the Kurds of southern Kurdistan were insufficiently united to press for independence or other collective rights. By 1921 British policy-makers had decided that the province of Mosul was to be part of the new Iraq. The chief reason was the presence of oil deposits in this province (in the Kirkuk district). Before the war, the Anglo-Persian Oil Company had already held about half the shares of the concession holder, the Turkish Petroleum Company, while Shell and German capital each held another quarter. In 1919, when France and Britain divided up the Arab lands, the expropriated German share was given to France in exchange for its consenting to British control over Mosul. Angry at being cut out, Washington put heavy pressure on London and had part of Anglo-Persian's shares surrendered to American companies in 1922. The possibility that Mosul province might have to be ceded to Turkey was no longer seriously considered. Even before the Mosul dispute was officially settled, the British pressured King Faisal to grant the international consortium (which was soon to be renamed the Iraq Petroleum Company) a highly favorable concession until the end of the century. Exploitation soon began, and in 1927 the first gusher was struck.

The League of Nations recommended in December 1925 that Mosul be included in Iraq, on condition that its non-Arab character be recognized, the status of the Kurdish language protected, and teachers and officials recruited among the local population. Britain's mandate was to be extended to safeguard the orderly integration of Mosul into Iraq. Kurds had hoped for more, and were disappointed with the League for not endorsing autonomy (which had in 1922 explicitly been promised them by the British government). Arab nationalists resented both the mandate and the League's conditions, which would weaken their hold of the state. King Faisal and his government were aware that Iraq would only achieve complete independence if they complied to a certain degree with the League's wishes, but they were under constant pressure from Arab nationalist circles. In 1932 the mandate formally ended, and Iraq became a member of the League of Nations.

The Iraqi government was dominated by Sunni Muslim Arabs, who constituted a minority in the country. The south was mostly inhabited by Shiite Arabs, the north by Kurds. Shiite Muslims in fact constituted over half the population of Iraq; most of them were Arabs but there were also Shiite Kurds and Turcomans. Baghdad had a large Jewish community, whose presence there dated back to the Babylonian period; numerous smaller Jewish communities were scattered across Kurdistan. In addition to significant Christian minorities (Nestorian and Chaldaean Assyrians, as well as Armenians) there were furthermore a host of syncretic religious communities, such as the Yezidis and the Kakai in Kurdistan. Under King Faisal a certain measure of equilibrium was maintained, and the minorities were to some extent represented in the administration and the army. But after the king's death in 1933, the balance was lost. His son Ghazi won the sympathy of Arab nationalists by brutally repressing a revolt by the Nestorian Assyrians, another nation to whom the British had once promised a state of their own. In the following years the army put down rebellions by Shiite tribes in the south and Yezidis in the north.

Kurdish nationalist sentiment, which flourished in the towns and cities, was not allowed political expression, but it was kept alive in various associations of urban intellectuals. It also contributed to a revival of Kurdish literature and other cultural activities. Among the Kurdish tribes, which had been accustomed to only minimal government interference in their affairs, the efforts by the central government to bring the entire region under effective control led to new rebellions. Perhaps the most remarkable of the Kurdish rebel chieftains was the eccentric religious leader Shaikh Ahmad of Barzan, whose district was repeatedly up in arms against the government as well as hostile neighboring tribes. In 1932 bombardments by the RAF destroyed over half the houses in his district and forced the Barzanis to the mountains. The shaikh himself reached the Turkish border, where Turkish troops took him prisoner and hanged a number of his men. The shaikh's younger brother, Mulla Mustafa, held out in the mountains for another year but finally surrendered. Shaikh Ahmad then also returned to Iraq and swore loyalty to the king; the brothers were not allowed to return to Barzan but were were forced to live in internal exile, first in the south, then in Sulaimania.

Active cooperation between such independent-minded tribal chieftains and urban Kurdish nationalists was not to emerge until later. Educated Kurds tended to dismiss the tribal chieftains as embarrassing remnants of a feudal past, for whom there should not be a leading role in the future. Chiefs such as Shaikh Ahmad, for their part, had more parochial interests at heart than Kurdish nationhood; their problems were at least as much with neighboring chieftains as with the distant government. It was geopolitical developments unfolding in the wider environment that gave them roles to play in the Kurdish national movement.

—*MvB*

This country cannot live unless it gives all Iraqi elements their rights. . . . The fate of Turkey should be a lesson to us and we should not revert to the policy formerly pursued by the Ottoman Government. We should give the Kurds their rights. Their officials should be from among them: their tongue should be their official language and their children should learn their own tongue in the schools.

Abdal Muhsinal Sa'dun, Iraqi prime minister,
to the Iraqi Chamber of Deputies, January 21, 1926
British Public Record Office, Kew
FO 371/11460/E1878

Student elections in Arbil

Unknown/Courtesy Azad Mukriyani

Memorandum on Administration of Kurdish Districts in Irak

February 24, 1926

There are twenty-five schools in the Kurdish districts. Five of these are Christian, the language in use being Chaldean and Arabic. In sixteen of the remainder the language of instruction is Kurdish. . . .

It must be remembered that before the war Kurdish was not used as a means of written communication, either private or official. A fair number of poetical works in Kurdish were in existence, but the development of the written language as a means of communication is entirely due to the efforts of British officials. . . . Sulaimaniya has for some years possessed a Kurdish newspaper, and the use of written Kurdish for both private and official communications has been general for some time. The work begun by the Government of occupation is being loyally carried on by the Irak government. Two Kurdish news-sheets are published in Bagdad, and everything possible is being done, not only to permit, but actively to encourage, the free use of the Kurdish language. . . .

King Faisal said—"Among the first duties of every real Iraki will be to encourage his brother, the Iraki Kurd, to cling to his nationality and to join him under the Irak flag—common emblem of their country for the material and intellectual happiness of all. They will be, by their union and co-operation, active members in the prosperity of a common home. I also have no doubt that every true Iraki is imbued with this same feeling towards all the racial elements in his country."

Letter from His Majesty's Government to the Secretary General
of the League of Nations/British Public Record Office, Kew
FO 371/11460/E1878

To the President of the League of Nations

March 21, 1931

Your Highness, it is an honor to bring to you the complaint and cry of a nation which is under your protection and authority....

The Kurds think that you are their protectors.... Until now, we have been demanding our rights in your name....

We don't wish to be the ruler and the oppressor of any nation. We have no intention of taking the lands of others. But we will not allow ourselves to be ruled and commanded by others. We want only to rule and to command and to reside over ourselves. We believe that millions of people sacrificed their lives for the sake of their rights, rights that your honorable League upheld for the Kurds and see as just....

Forgive me, but I ... assure you that ... these revolutions and uprisings were all results of bad faith, and unjust acts and goals of the administrators of Iraq.... No relations remain between us and the monarchical government of Iraq because England and Iraq... have ended the mandate in a treaty between themselves. Resolving our case is logical and necessary and your honorable League must in the order of things, return to the decision of 1920, which you approved. We ask that you accept our respects.

Shaikh Mahmud, In the name of the population of southern Kurdistan, quoted in Basile Nikitine, *Les Kurdes: Étude Sociologique et Historique*, 1956

Postcard sent to Ibrahim Ahmed from Kurdish pen pal in 1931
Unknown/Courtesy Ibrahim Ahmed

Source of intrigue! League of dissimulation!
Is this how you give the rights of minority peoples?
Workshop of corruption! League of sufferings!
"A club in the hands of Mr. Henderson!"

Salam Ahmad 'Azabani, "Bo Komeli Eqwam" (To the League of Nations), poem regarding Mr. Henderson, British prime minister, September 1931, quoted in Amir Hassanpour, *Nationalism and Language in Kurdistan*, 1992

Iraq Becomes a Nation

Twelve Years of British Stewardship Comes to an End at the Beginning of October

By the end of this month, or at any rate in the first days of October, Iraq will have been elected a member of the League of Nations and the British mandatory regime in that country will have come to an end.

To the mass of the British people this consummation seems to have been too long in materializing. For the opinion, derived in the main from the "popular" Press, still prevails that in Mesopotamia we have spent millions of pounds and have sacrificed hundreds of lives—and all to no purpose. The feeling is that we ought to have concentrated on interests nearer to the heart of the Empire and to have evacuated Iraq once we had beaten the Ottoman Empire there, years and years ago. Such critics of British policy in Iraq have, however, never suggested exactly when we ought to have scuttled out of Iraq, nor have they reflected on the important consequences which such an evacuation would most surely have entailed. It was enough for them, and it has always been enough, for they chose not to fortify their sentiments with study of the facts, that British money was being spent on a country outside the British Empire, and that, of all places, in the "swamps and deserts" of Iraq. . . .

Primarily this decision of the League of Nations, which, of course, is acting upon the recommendation of Great Britain, the Mandatory Power, to accept Iraq as a member of the League, is important to this country because it implies that Great Britain's twelve years' stewardship in Iraq is terminated. . . .

The essence of this mandatory system is for civilized Powers to lead peoples that have not reached the stage of being able to govern themselves to such a plane of development as will enable the League, which in the first place granted the mandates, ultimately to pronounce that such backward peoples are now able "to stand alone under the strenuous conditions of the modern world."

How our Expeditionary Force to Mesopotamia (which, in addition to securing a strategic object, also had the aim of making safe the oilfields of Southern Persia for the Navy) was drawn, or rather had to fight, ever northwards into Iraq, is a matter of history. The Armistice arrived with the greater part of the more civilized Arab territories of the Ottoman Empire in Allied hands. . . .

At the moment all looks well on the whole for Iraq. With all her neighbours she has signed, or is shortly to sign, Treaties of Friendship. . . . [T]his complete change in the atmosphere of foreign relations is something of which King Feisal and his Ministers have a right to be proud. Nor has less success attended the difficult problem of oil concessions in the country. Two large concessions have been awarded, first to the Iraq Petroleum Company, and secondly to the British Oil Development Company. The I.P.C., as it is generally known, is now in process of laying down its long pipe line from the oil fields to Mediterranean ports in Palestine and Syria respectively.

The future of Iraq holds problems which she has yet to solve; most urgent, perhaps, is the problem of her Kurdish population in the north. Properly handled, this is by no means insoluble, and if, by an increasing process of autonomy, Kurdish mistrust of the Arab is softened, there should be a magnificent future for this northern vilayet, which contains the most varied soil in Iraq.

Great Britain, it may be argued, has generally satisfied the dictates of honour, has secured her prestige in the Middle East, and has adequately safeguarded her Imperial strategical interests.

Kenneth Williams, *The Sphere*, October 1, 1932
Courtesy *The Illustrated London News* Picture Library

Primitive installation for the purification of crude oil, outskirts of Kirkuk, Iraq, 1930

1930

Kamil Chadirji/Courtesy Rifat Chadirji

IRAQ

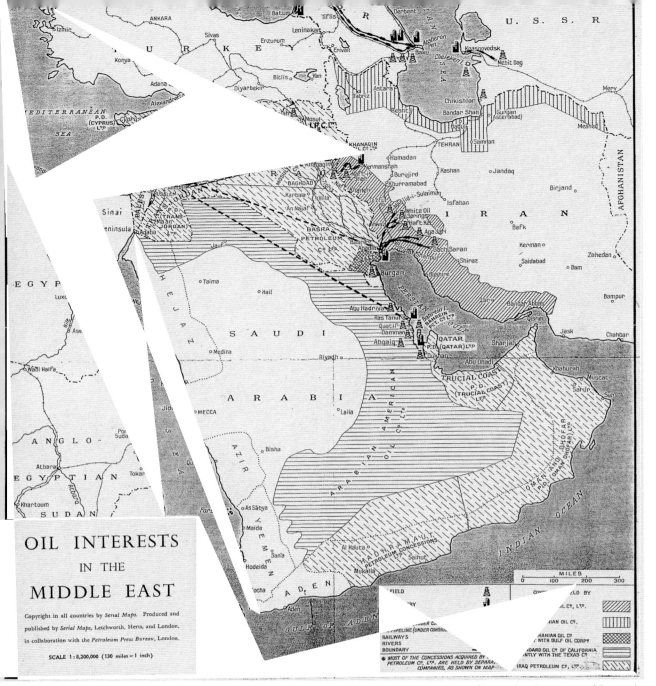

OIL INTERESTS
IN THE
MIDDLE EAST

Copyright in all countries by *Serial Maps*. Produced and published by *Serial Maps*, Letchworth, Herts. and London, in collaboration with the *Petroleum Press Bureau*, London.

SCALE 1 : 8,200,000 (130 miles = 1 inch)

Courtesy University of Birmingham Department of Geography

Black Gold Spurts Up from Noah's Ark

How Yankee Skill Laid $50,000,000 Pipe-Line Over Iraq's Ancient Sand

The other day the shade of Noah and his Ark hovered over a curious meeting on the sands of the romantic Kingdom of Iraq.

A group, composed of brilliantly uniformed officials and well-dressed businessmen, had gathered for the formal opening of the great $50,000,000 oil pipe-line connecting Iraq wells with the Mediterranean. Present were Sir John Cadman, tycoon of the British-owned Anglo-Persian Oil company; agents of Sir Henry Deterding, Napoleon of the Shell Oil Company, of Andrew Mellon (Gulf Oil) and of John D. Rockefeller (Standard Oil); bewhiskered Paul Bastide, representing French interest, and, last but not least, King Ghazi, of Iraq. . . .

Colonel Lawrence wrote, "In October 1913, when England launched the Queen Elizabeth, first of the cruisers to burn oil, I knew then that it was up to me to concern myself with the supply of oil for my country and not with archaeology." Lawrence knit the sheikhs together into a splendid shock force for the British Empire and its oil. But to give them a ruler and a kingdom was left to a no less extraordinary actor in this drama. Actress, one should say, for it was none other than Miss Gertrude Bell, of London.

This young girl, homely, dour and academic, seemed the most unlikely person to charm the rebellious souls of the Arabian tribesmen. But the sheikhs were responsive to any pale-faced female and when she talked their language and showed un-feminine courage, they capitulated.

Frank C. Hanighen for King Features Syndicate, February 23, 1935/ FDR Library, Hyde Park

A river of crude oil, result of an uncontrolled gusher

Oil well on fire, Kirkuk District
Eric Matson/Library of Congress, Washington, D.C.

Right: Courtesy *The Illustrated London News* Picture Library

1932–35

Volume CXXXI No. 1717

The SPHERE, December 17, 1932

THE SPHERE

With which
is incorporated
"BLACK & WHITE"

The Empire's Illustrated Weekly

London, December 17, 1932

LIQUID MILLIONS
GUSHING to the SKY

An Oil-well in Kirkuk, Iraq, Spouting Its Priceless
Liquid in a Solid Column from the Ground

Iraq, now a member of the League of Nations, is a country with great potentialities. She has oil as well as other minerals. The latest fields to be tapped are those of Kirkuk, lying some eighty-five miles south-west of Mosul. Several wells have been sunk and "corked" pending the completion of the pipe-line by which the oil will be carried to Haifa, on the Palestine coast, for distribution to the world. The pipe-line is destined to cross 600 miles of desert. It is the Iraqi oil which has, to a great extent, and coupled with the wane of British prestige in Persia, precipitated the present crisis with the Anglo-Persian Oil Company, an article on whose history appears on p. 462

IRAQ

Postage—Inland, 1½d.; Canada and Newfoundland, 1½d.; Foreign, 2½d.

Freya Stark

British Traveler and Journalist

Baghdad, October 1929 . . . The people here are of all fascinating sorts—the beautiful ones being Kurds. Never have I seen more fine-looking men, so agile and strong with legs bare to the thigh and red turbans, and long hair under, and a wild aquiline handsomeness that is quite intoxicating and I only wish I could paint it.

London, September 2, 1930 . . . Today I saw Miss Farquharson and heard about the Arab League—and was joined by Mrs. Soane, the widow of the Kurdistan traveller (and a very unreliable little woman it seemed to me), but a godsend for she will give me all the Kurdish introductions I need.

Baghdad, December 16, 1931 . . . They are having a little war in Kurdistan: it has been a secret for some time so I did not write, though Mrs. Chapman told me about it. The Sheikh of Barzan, near Suleimania, got the Iraqi vanguard, killed some, captured twenty-nine, and prevented the bombing of villagers by tying the prisoners on the roof.

IRAQ'S "LITTLE WAR"

OFFICIAL RETICENCE IN BAGHDAD

FROM OUR CORRESPONDENT
BAGHDAD, APRIL 5

The progress of the Iraqi Army's campaign against Sheikh Ahmad of Barzan and his Kurds, due to the Government's determination to establish civil administration in that part of the country which in the past has been, as it explained in the announcement issued a fortnight ago, "deprived of the advantages of settled government," is quite unknown to the public.

The attitude of the Royal Air Force may be summed up as: "This is not our war. We are merely coöperating with the Iraqi Army, on which rests all responsibility for issuing *communiqués.* We can say nothing about it." The Iraqi Ministry of Defence seems to consider that the less said about the campaign the better, lest the publication of Iraqi casualty lists should encourage the insurgent Kurds.

The result of this reticence is that Baghdad is completely ignorant of what is happening in the Kurdish mountains 300 miles away. The necessity for giving British taxpayers some information about the little war, in which British *personnel* and machines are engaged, appears to have dawned on nobody.

I gather that the Kurds are adopting guerrilla tactics and are sniping and trying to cut off transport convoys. The Government's declared intention is to open up the country by building motor-roads and pacify it by constructing police posts. Meantime wounded Iraqis are being conveyed in British aeroplanes from the theatre of war to Baghdad hospitals. Up to the present the death of the sergeant-pilot, which was reported yesterday, and the wounding of his observer are the only British casualties

The Times, London, April 6, 1932

Baghdad, April 10, 1932 . . . I have been hearing about the Kurds and the war: it is always very sad to see the tribal life being pressed out of existence, though I see that it has to be. But this 'civilising' is a dreary job. . . .

Mr. Hamilton came to lunch and told me all about the Kurdish affair. It appears they had an awful smash up—two battalions involved in the mountains, cut off from their fodder, food, ammunition, over 1,000 horses, all their baggage, all of which Sheikh Ahmed's people carried off. General R.R., who is supposed to advise, but does not get his advice taken till all is in the soup, rushed up with a small force to try and extricate, and then got his wound in the foot—and very nearly got cut off with the force to be rescued, for they were all surrounded and only disentangled by some very strenuous bombing by the R.A.F. So now they are where they were before except that the Kurds have lashings of stores and ammunition. This is rather sad for the first effort of Iraq to manage the Kurds on her own: I suppose it will be kept from the League of Nations, or 'arranged' at any rate. . . . Mr. Hamilton is very pro-Kurd—a nice young man, who says he hasn't talked to anyone as interesting as me for years (because I hardly spoke at all), and wants me to go up and stay with him and explore Kurdistan.

May 27, 1932 . . . Well now I have just been doing some real journalism. We have this war going on and nothing but the meagrest news, and The Times in London clamouring to hear about it. My editor unable to get them to allow him to write anything (or hear anything for the matter of that). I had a happy thought and suggested going up into the enemy country and getting news there, but Mr. Cameron was not bold enough for this and said if I went it must be officially: so I asked the A.V.M., and of course could get nothing satisfactory, and went to Vyvyan [Holt] who said it was a 'monstrous' idea. But then he suggested I might get leave to look at all the despatches and get an article that way, and that is what I have now got leave to do. The A.V.M. most kind; will let me copy the maps and get the news, and may even get some photos taken of the actual fighting area, and says he will give me the bits of 'local colour' himself. To get firsthand help from the British Commander of Operations is no bad start for a journalist, is it?

Lucy Moorehead, *Freya Stark: Letters*, 1975

WARFARE IN

THE MINISTER OF DEFENCE, Ja'afar Pasha, on a visit to the troops. With him are two officers of the British Mission, Major P. W. Clark, R.E. and Major E. G. Warren, Northamptonshire Regt.

THE KURDISTAN MOUNTAINS: A REBEL SHEIKH

ON THE BANKS OF THE RU KUCHUK.—Iraqi troops waiting to cross over the Ru Kuchuk near its junction with the Greater Zab. This was accomplished on native rafts made of inflated skins. This column working from the south captured the Sheikh's deserted capital, the village of Barzan.

FLYING OVER KURDISTAN.—The part that the R.A.F. is taking in the operations of the Iraqi Government against the rebel Sheikh Ahmed is described on page 13. This photograph shows the dangerous character of the country for airmen. (R.A.F. Official.)

KURDISTAN VILLAGE.—The larger photograph is a R.A.F. official picture of a typical village in the Barzan country. The subjects of the rebel Sheikh live in these rough stone houses with flat roofs of mud and brushwood. In summer they move with their flocks and tents higher up the mountains. The smaller picture is of Iraqi troops on a raft.

DR. BARNARDO'S

Baghdad, July 7, 1932 . . . Such a hectic *time getting the second article off for* The Times. *Meanwhile, comments on the last article are pouring in—Times, Manchester Guardian, a furious letter (which I rather agree with) on behalf of the poor Kurds. It feels very funny reading it and thinking that I set the ball going.* —Freya Stark

IRAQ

Rowanduz Road over the bridge of Gali Ali Beg Valley, northern Iraq

Studio Iskan/Courtesy Ali Rowanduzi

A. M. Hamilton
British Engineer

The Director called for a large map and began to explain the task that the department had undertaken, and I heard for the first time the full story of the Rowanduz road-project. . . .

'You'll find,' said the Director, 'that road construction up here in Kurdistan . . . will mean cutting a track out of the solid rock of the mountain-side and you'll need steel bridges of fairly long span to cross the rivers. The work will take longer and cost a great deal more, but once done it should be of lasting and permanent benefit to the people.'

When I asked why this road was being constructed, he replied: 'There are two reasons, trade and administration. You know that all great nations, past and present, have found roads essential for maintaining law and order. Once highways have penetrated a region the wildest people are pretty sure to become peaceful simply by copying civilized modes of life. Moreover, empires that rely purely on military conquest usually fail to hold their people together for long.' . . .

The matter had been discussed with the Shah of Persia who had been convinced eventually that the road had no motive other than trade and the tranquillization of the Kurdish tribes—a problem of as much importance to the Persians as to the Arabs. . . . When the Rowanduz road first began to penetrate the mountains, the question . . . was how would the lawless tribesmen behave towards the road-engineer and his unarmed working parties. Doubtless they knew that the building of the

road meant the end of their ancient independence. It may be remarked here that the road-line was admittedly not the best one from a purely engineering point of view, but would hither and thither through the territory so as to pass near or through the villages of the most dangerous men, in the hope that contact with civilization might persuade them to become more peaceful. . . .

Ismail Beg was quite the most influential man in Rowanduz. For several years he has been the local deputy to the Iraq Parliament. . . . He, more than any Kurd, had used his great influence to convince his people of the benefit to them of this road that was to penetrate their land. He said that until roads were built throughout the mountains, Kurdistan would never prosper. . . . He was one of the many Kurds who were greatly disappointed that our Mandate was not to be continued for the twenty-five-year period we had originally suggested. . . .

'Little by little we shall get what we need in Kurdistan if only you British will help,' he would say. . . . 'Kurdistan should be to the Middle East as Switzerland is to Europe, a small but inviolable neutral State. . . . Where are the roads and the railways in Turkish Kurdistan? Why are there destitute Kurdish refugees coming from Turkey pleading for help? . . . The condition of affairs is no better in the Persian part of our land. There the Kurds are forced to wear strange new hats—as if that in itself would make them loyal Persians! There has been a war over those same hats. . . .

1932

Rashid Beg's car, Khoshnaw tribe

Unknown/Courtesy Giw Mukriyani

'You have told us often enough that your road would bring trade, and we believed you. But what are the first articles of commerce that we see upon it? A marching army of many battalions of Arab soldiers, an endless string of lorries bringing ammunition and airplane bombs, armoured cars with machine-guns. Strange merchandise indeed! . . .'

'Official reports say that Sheikh Ahmad is an obstructionist to the government and that he attacked other tribes. Hence the Iraq Army had to be sent,' I interjected. . . .

(He drew several sheets of paper from his pocket.) 'We need hospitals and schools and schemes of afforestation, and improved breeds of sheep and goats so that we may sell more meat and wool. Electricity should be supplied from our rivers and waterfalls. Improvements are needed in our dyeing and weaving, so that we could compete with the Persians in carpet-making. . . .

'Of course, we can't get all this at once, but the large revenue Iraq gets from the oil-fields might be used to help us instead of being spent on waging wars in these mountains and making the Kurds bitter and hostile. Remember the oil-fields are in Kurdistan, so we have some right to ask for benefits from the revenue they earn. Yet all we seem to derive from our oil are bullets and bombs.'

I broke in again, 'First of all there must be peace, and to this end the R.A.F. must support the Iraq Government if need be. Anyway the bombing of Sheikh Ahmad was very humane. His men were told by loudspeakers on the aeroplanes that if they submitted and gave up their chief they would be pardoned, and the villagers were warned by the leaflets that were dropped before the bombing began, so that the women and children should have time to escape. . . .'

[Ismail Beg replied], 'Ask your airmen if Sheikh Ahmad's followers ran away before bombs or machine-gun bullets. As for the leaflets, could one single man be found to read them in those illiterate villages? In any case if the crops are all burnt by incendiary bombs it means starvation and famine when winter comes, which is worse than a quick death in a fight. . . .

'You surely must have heard from your men what the interpreter who spoke so loudly from the aeroplane loudspeakers really said. This was his message of goodwill. It began with the sacred lines from the Koran that are known to all Mohammedans.

' "Bismillahi 'rrhmani 'rrahim," it commenced—"In the name of God, the compassionate, the merciful, we are going to drop bombs upon you," so said the voice from Heaven!'

A. M. Hamilton, *Road Through Kurdistan*, 1937

Background: *The new road up Spilik Pass*
A. M. Hamilton

SOME DO'S AND DON'T'S TO BE TAKEN SERIOUSLY

KEEP YOUR DIGNITY - AND RESPECT THE IRAQI'S DIGNITY TOO.

* DON'T SLAP HIM ON THE BACK.

* DON'T WRESTLE WITH HIM OR STRIKE HIM.

* DON'T CALL HIM A "DOG" UNDER ANY CIRCUMSTANCES.

* DON'T REFER TO THE PEOPLE AS "NATIVES."

TRY TO UNDERSTAND AND FOLLOW THE CUSTOMS OF IRAQ.

SEEK THE FRIENDSHIP AND HELP OF THE PEOPLE.

LEARN TO BARGAIN IN THE ORIENTAL SHOPS.

* BEFORE YOU HIRE A SERVICE OR BUY GOODS, SETTLE ON
  THE PRICE.

ALWAYS ACCEPT COFFEE OR TEA WHEN YOU ARE OFFERED IT.

IF YOU DRINK ANYTHING ALCOHOLIC, DO IT WHERE THE MUSLIMS
        CAN'T SEE YOU.

REMEMBER THE FEAR OF THE "EVIL EYE".

* DON'T STARE AT ANYONE.

* DON'T POINT YOUR CAMERA IN HIS FACE.

ALWAYS RESPECT THE WOMEN.

* DON'T STARE AT THEM.

* DON'T FOLLOW THEM.

* DON'T SPEAK TO THEM.

KEEP AWAY FROM MOSQUES.

Memorandum on Near East, August 22, 1942
Courtesy FDR Library, Hyde Park

Henry Field
American Anthropologist

The Field Museum Anthropological Expedition to the Near East, sponsored by Marshall Field, has concluded its work for 1934, consisting of an anthropometric survey of the native population of Iraq, and similar studies in Persia and the Caucasus region of the U.S.S.R.

The leader of the expedition, Henry Field, assistant curator of physical anthropology, has returned to his post in the museum, ready to begin the task of assembling and studying the data collected, which has for its purpose an attempt to solve certain racial problems.

One of the objectives is to determine the relationship of the peoples of the Near East, both those of to-day and their ancient ancestors, to the modern and ancient peoples of Africa, Europe and Asia. This is a question of great scientific importance into which no satisfactory research has previously been made.

The work of the expedition covered a period of ten months, during which 17,000 miles were traveled, and 3,000 persons were submitted to studies, consisting of anthropometric measurements and observations, the taking of front and profile photographs, hair samples, blood samples, and other data pertinent to tracing racial origins.

Observations were made upon selected subjects from each of the important racial groups. Of special interest in Iraq were the Kurds, fierce-looking mountain tribesmen, of whom 750 submitted to the anthropologists' calipers and cameras, and the Yezidis, fanatical devil-worshippers, 300 of whom cooperated by acting as scientific specimens.

Science, Vol. 81, No. 2093, February 8, 1935/Courtesy The Field Museum, Chicago

1934

The little village of Sandur, Iraq, is composed of fifty Jewish and ten Muslim families, all living in houses of simple construction. The flat roofs are supported by poles

Jews of Sandur, adhering to the Mosaic Law, must marry within the village; marriages between first cousins being sanctioned, a pure racial type is preserved and accentuated

In the synagogue, where large pillars and vaulted roof indicate early Christian construction, the high priest displays the embossed "sofartorah" containing the sacred texts

The herding of domesticated animals and the primitive cultivation of rock-strewn hillsides, together with some trading in neighboring villages, support this small community

FIELD MUSEUM OF NATURAL HISTORY

Asia magazine, Vol. 36, 1937
Neg. #A113277C/Courtesy The Field Museum, Chicago

The Jews of Sandur

There is little question that the Jews of Kurdistan, in northern Iraq, reached Mesopotamia at an early date. . . . Some miles to the north of Mosul, near the road from Dohuk to Amadia, lies the little village of Sandur. . . . This village is one of the few examples where Jews of an ancient community at a long-established site have practiced agriculture for many generations. . . .

The headman of the village gave us some information regarding the history of the Jews of Sandur. According to their oral tradition Sennacherib took some pagans from Sandur to Jerusalem and returned with Jews to fill their place. Kurdish tribesmen have on two occasions, the last being in 1904, forced them to leave their mountain retreat and seek refuge with friendly Kurdish Aghas in Dohuk. The general unrest caused by political, religious and economic agitations engendered a feeling of insecurity among this small group of Jews, and no month passed without a minor raid for food, clothing or sheep by some local Kurdish tribe. . . .

The headman of Sandur in 1934 said that their greatest desire was to sell their village and move to Palestine where they believed that they could live in peace for many generations to come—a statement which can only lead to uneasy reflection at the present time.

Henry Field, *Asia* magazine,
Vol. 36, October 1937

*Background: Chicago Evening
American*, April 9, 1929, neg. #A113276C
Courtesy The Field Museum, Chicago

IRAQ

The time was 1934. The place, Aqra in Kurdistan. It had been a long, hot day and I had spent it measuring and photographing Kurds for one of my six volumes on the Anthropology of Iraq. They had been reluctant to take off their white turbans in front of others, especially a Christian, but the Agha had ordered fifty of them to submit to my calipers and camera.

An aged Kurd sat throughout the morning and afternoon sessions, chain-smoking from the basket of extra long native cigarettes provided by the foreigner. No words came from the blue smoke clouds until I began to wrap up the anthropometer and spreading calipers.

Then he told me his name was Achmed and muttered something in Kermanji Kurdish. Showket, my photographer-interpreter, smiled as he translated, "I do not know why you are measuring my friends. I am told you are writing a book. That is incredible. There is only one book in the world—The Koran. Anyhow, I think you are extremely stupid. I see you measuring each left ear. Since the ears must be of real interest to you, why don't you go around the corner to the prison? There are thirty Kurds in there, all of whom will be hanged three days from now. Cut off their ears. They won't need them after dawn on Thursday. What you're doing I call stupid.". . .

That night at dinner I told the story to the Agha who replied, "None of this is true. Those men are sheep stealers and will be punished, but not by death. You were talking to the village idiot!"

A Kurd entered and spoke to Showket who whispered to me that the high ranking personage sent a message that he was not accustomed to wait for anyone. I was intrigued by this communication, so, excusing myself, I followed Showket to the room where an impressive and commanding figure, undoubtedly a Kurdish Chieftain, was waiting.

Stepping forward with my right hand over my heart, I greeted him in Arabic. He glared fiercely as he said, also in Arabic, "And unto you Peace. I am Sheikh Mahmud." Before me stood a Kurdish brigand on whose head the British Government had put a price of $25,000—dead or alive.

To cover my surprise, I replied that I came from Chicago where we had our own Brigand Chiefs. He smiled as he shook hands. Seated in native chairs with Showket as interpreter, Sheikh Mahmud talked volubly in Kurdish. He had risked coming to Aqra to ask me to intercede on his behalf with our Great Sheikh (F.D.R.) in Washington. . . . Showket told him I would carry his message to the Department of State but I could not promise favorable action. This seemed to content him.

Henry Field, *Arabian Desert Tales*, 1976

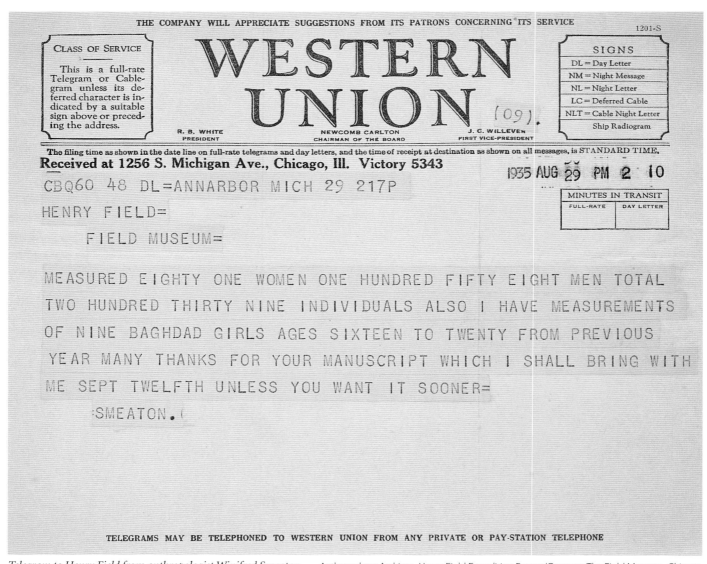

Telegram to Henry Field from anthropologist Winifred Smeaton   Anthropology Archives, Henry Field Expedition Papers/Courtesy The Field Museum, Chicago

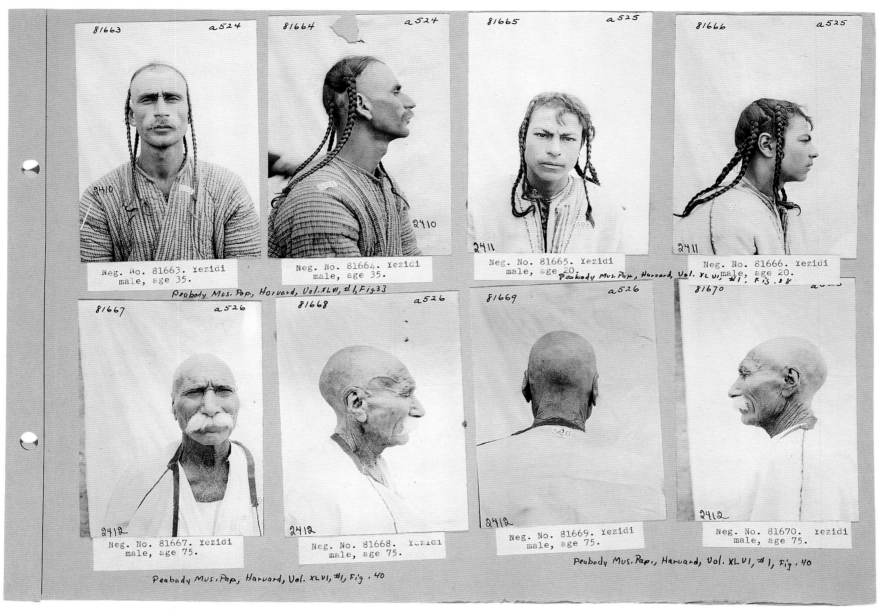

81663 a524 — 2410 — Neg. No. 81663. Yezidi male, age 35.

81664 a524 — 2410 — Neg. No. 81664. Yezidi male, age 35.

81665 a525 — 2411 — Neg. No. 81665. Yezidi male, age 20.

81666 a525 — 2411 — Neg. No. 81666. Yezidi male, age 20.

Peabody Mus. Pap., Harvard, Vol. XLVI, #1, Fig 33

Peabody Mus. Pap., Harvard, Vol. XLVI, #1, Fig. 38

81667 a526 — 2412 — Neg. No. 81667. Yezidi male, age 75.

81668 a526 — 2412 — Neg. No. 81668. Yezidi male, age 75.

81669 a526 — 2412 — Neg. No. 81669. Yezidi male, age 75.

81670 a52? — 2412 — Neg. No. 81670. Yezidi male, age 75.

Peabody Mus. Pap., Harvard, Vol. XLVI, #1, Fig. 40

Peabody Mus. Pap., Harvard, Vol. XLVI, #1, Fig. 40

Page from Henry Field's Album #139, photographs by Richard A. Martin

Anthropology Archives/Courtesy The Field Museum, Chicago

On June 13, 1934, before 8 A.M., I measured thirty-four Yezidis from the Sheikhan district and one from Jebel Sinjar, who happened to be visiting there. . . . The head form reveals considerable variation because of the use of the cradleboard. The cradle where the child is tied down is used east of Mosul by Yezidis, Arabs, and Kurds. The child can move his head only from side to side and should he or she prefer to be on one side more than the other, asymmetrical occipital flattening will result and be apparent all through life.

Henry Field, *The Anthropology of Iraq*, XLVI, No. 1, 1951

On the road which leads to Syria our party passed several Yezidi villages, including El Khan, Sheikh Khanis, and Tell Yusifka, whose inhabitants gazed at us inhospitably. Turning off the main track we approached the village of Jeddala, in which live many of the leaders of this curious faith. We were received with some apprehension by the elders, particularly when the scientific instruments were taken from the cars and preparations begun to measure and photograph the men who were standing nearby. As usual, considerable interest was displayed in the cameras and in the head callipers. . . .

The first subject, a young man, stepped forward with considerable mistrust. As he took off his white headdress his beautifully plaited locks hung in four braids down to his shoulders. Every eye was riveted on the youth and with a few reassuring words in Arabic whispered in his ear, I began to measure his head, an operation to which he submitted with characteristic stoicism. When the performance was concluded several of the older men came forward to ask him if he felt any the worse for his experience, the psychological moment for us to reward him with a silver coin.

Henry Field and J. B. Glubb, "The Yezidis, Sulubba, and Other Tribes of Iraq and Adjacent Regions," *General Series in Anthropology*, No. 10, 1943

IRAQ

Miss Winifred Smeaton, who is now in Baghdad, studied in the Department of Anthropology during the summer of 1932, and is now qualified to do anthropometric work. Her presence in Baghdad offers a unique opportunity for an unusual piece of work to be done, as she could measure and study the women of various groups (to whom I would have no access) while I am working with the men.

Plan for Field Museum Expedition to Near East, 1934 (Report Submitted for Dr. Laufer's Approval), Anthropology Archives, Henry Field Expedition Papers, The Field Museum, Chicago

Notes on Personnel

Miss Winifred Smeaton . . . measured 500 women (Shammar, Yezidis, Jews, Kurds, Assyrians, Marsh Arabs) as well as assisted me with several large groups of Kurds. These data will prove of great scientific value since measurements on women in Iraq is so extremely difficult. The condition of heat and dirt combined with crowds of children, etc. made her work done under far from ideal conditions. . . .

S. Y. Showket accompanied me during 1928, and in this part of the world I consider it essential to have an Iraqi accompany the expedition. Mr. Showket is a professional photographer from Basra who speaks Arabic, Kurdish, Turkish, Chaldean and English, and knows how to handle people whether it be government authorities or subjects to be measured. His help proved invaluable.

1934 Expedition Report, Henry Field Papers, The Field Museum, Chicago

Page from Henry Field's Album #139 Photographs by Richard A. Martin Anthropology Archives/ Courtesy The Field Museum, Chicago

Neg. No. 84373. Kurd female, age 47. Kurdestan, Iraq.

Neg. No. 84335. Kurd fe age 40. Kurdestan, Iraq.

g. No. 84331. Kurd female, ge 30. urdestan, Iraq.

Neg. No. 84332. Krud femal age 27. K,,rdestan, Iraq.

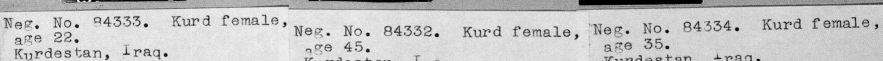

le,Neg. No. 84342. Kurd female,
age 50.
Kurdestan, Iraq.

Neg. No. 84372. Kurd female,
age 38.
Kurdestan, Iraq.

Neg. No. 84331. Kurd female,
age 45.
Kurdestan, Iraq.

Neg. No. 84333. Kurd female,
age 22.
Kurdestan, Iraq.

Neg. No. 84332. Kurd female,
age 45.
Kurdestan, Iraq.

Neg. No. 84334. Kurd female,
age 35.
Kurdestan, Iraq.

Shaikh Abdul Kadir and Hapsa Khan

Lotte Errell
German Photographer

Hafza Chan [Hapsa Khan] is the woman "whose husband gets up when she enters the room," people say, talking about her. She is the best known and most famous woman in Kurdistan of to-day. . . .

She used to ride over the country only accompanied by her servants to inspect the lands. . . .

Later she married the member of a revolutionary family, Sheikh Kader, the brother of Sheikh Mahmud. . . . Hafza Chan was the first woman in Suleimania to understand that only education could help women to get their freedom. When she herself was young it was "impossible" for a girl to go to school. Girls had to stay at home and to learn cooking and housekeeping, to serve the husband and the family, to go round visiting other women and chat.

Hafza Chan was educated of course in the same manner and only a long time after she had grown up, even after she was married, did she start "to go school." She gave an excellent example to all her friends and she tried to help them to get some education. . . . Every afternoon she receives in her courtyard all the women who want to learn by her wisdom and who want to discuss problems of the day with her. They live separated in the house but are often quite powerful as far as their husband and family is concerned.

Lotte Errell, text accompanying
photographs upon distribution
Courtesy Museum Folkwang, Essen

Right: *Hapsa Khan*
Lotte Errell/Museum Folkwang

Hapsa Khan's father was a respected man in Sulaimania, and all the intellectuals of the community gathered at his house to talk, to read poetry, to discuss the community. . . . He only had two daughters, no sons. After her father died, Hapsa Khan didn't want to close this house just because there wasn't a man, so she sat in her father's place. She said, "There is no difference between men and women so . . . I am going to continue. . . ."

Her visitors were writers, artists, men of high rank. Some people were angered from a religious point of view that she was imitating a man, but she did not stop. . . . Shaikh Mahmud himself said that if she had been a man, she would have been a strong challenge.

Interview with Drakshan Jalal Ahmad Hafid,
niece of Shaikh Mahmud, living in Iraq, 1992

1930s

Lecture Given to the Royal Central Asian Society
April 3, 1935
by Mrs. Lindfield Soane

Baghdad has changed a great deal. . . . Very few British officials are left, and most of them were uncertain as to whether their contracts would be renewed. An Iraqi official told me that they did not need them any more as they were now quite capable of governing themselves! All English signs had been replaced by Arabic, and it was most difficult to find one's way about. I believe one is allowed to have a sign outside a shop in English, but the tax is so heavy that they avoid it. . . .

I went from Baghdad by train to Kirkuk, leaving one evening at 6 p.m., arriving next morning at 7 a.m. I must admit that it did not hold the fascination or the hair-raising adventures which I experienced on my previous visits just after the war, when one travelled a great deal on horseback, and the tracks on the huge mountains were barely two feet wide; one slip of your horse's hoofs and you would be dashed thousands of feet below. I used to shut my eyes and trust to my surefooted friend. I was a mere girl at the time. The Kurds were a novelty to me, and I a greater novelty to them, as I was the first European woman to travel in many parts of the country. There were hardly any roads, and relics of the war served as landmarks. I used to cross rivers on inflated pigskins— too terrified to cross on my horse's back. I can well remember shepherds leaving their flocks and running for their lives at the approach of a "Henry Ford." I think they thought it some prehistoric monster. Now the Kurds are moving with the times, and one can travel by car over a large part of the country—that is if you keep to the main roads. . . . They have no fear of aeroplanes, as they have been bombed frequently enough to know how to escape injury and consequently to disregard them. When they hear of an attack the villages near the supposed operations are deserted, and all cattle and belongings concealed in the hills. Their villages, which are mostly composed of mud-houses, matter nothing to them, and not infrequently when there is time they actually remove the beams forming the roofs and bury or take them away. When trouble is over, all that remains to be done is to return with flocks, herds, goods, chattels and roof beams, reroof the small houses and resume life where it left off. . . .

On the way back via Damascus Sheikh Mahmud was waiting at Ramadi to see me; although he was a political prisoner he was allowed to wander about the grounds. We talked for an hour, and any ill-feeling I may have had towards him in the past seemed to vanish. There was something rather refined about his features, so unlike his portraits, and under his childlike expression one could read the disappointment of a man that had been beaten. It was hard to imagine that this was the same Sheikh Mahmud who had given the British as well as the Iraq Government a very anxious time. He is now in Baghdad, and not allowed to go to Kurdistan.

Lynette Lindfield Soane, "A Recent Journey in Kurdistan,"
in the *Journal of the Royal Central Asian Society*, Vol. XXII, July 1935

"The pride of Kurdistan, the first thrashing machine." —Lotte Errell

"Kurdistan changing to modern times and modern methods! The first thrashing machine of American origin." —Lotte Errell

Kurdish nomad

Lotte Errell/Museum Folkwang, Essen

Background map from Lynette Lindfield Soane,
"A Recent Journey In Kurdistan," 1935

Celebration of the independence of Kurdistan:
(left to right) Ahmed Kafash, a Kurdish officer;
Karim Nazemi, with the flag of Kurdistan;
Mohammad Firuzi, a Kurdish officer

THE KURDISH REPUBLIC OF MAHABAD

A Kurdish State

On August 25, 1941, the British and Russians simultaneously attacked Iran and forced Reza Shah, who had shown strong pro-German sympathies, to abdicate in favor of his son Mohammad Reza. For the rest of the war, the northern part of Iran remained occupied by Russian troops, the southern part by British, leaving a central neutral zone. Meanwhile, the Tehran government's control of this central area, which included most of Kurdistan, was considerably weakened. Tribal chieftains and big landlords, banished from the region under Reza Shah, were allowed to return to Kurdistan, where they attempted to reassert their powers. At the same time, young educated urban Kurds in Mahabad, who were in contact with Kurdish nationalists in Iraq, established an underground association, the Komalay Jiyanewey Kurd (also briefly known as Komala or JK), which was both nationalist and socially radical. The balance between the various forces was held by urban notables such as the Qazi family of Mahabad, who carefully maintained relations with both the central government and the Russians in Azerbaijan, and de facto performed many of the functions of a local government.

Developments were speeded up by the end of the war. Russia, which for some time had been reluctant to evacuate northern Iran, supported the left-wing Democratic Party of Azerbaijan when it took power in this northwestern province and established an autonomous government in December 1945. The Kurds did not need much encouragement to establish their own autonomous government. The Komala had been persuaded to accept the leadership of Qazi Mohammad, the strongest personality in Mahabad, and to merge into a broader-based mass party, the Democratic Party of Kurdistan (KDP). On January 22, 1946, Qazi Mohammad proclaimed the Republic of Kurdistan. Kurdish replaced Persian as the official language.

The Kurdish republic comprised only the northern part of Persian Kurdistan, the wider Mahabad region; the Tehran government maintained a hold on the districts further south. The army of the Republic, consisting of local tribesmen, was reinforced by several thousand experienced fighters from Iraq led by Mulla Mustafa Barzani and his brother Shaikh Ahmad, who took refuge in Iran in September 1945 following the suppression of their latest uprising. Mulla Mustafa had in 1943 defiantly returned to Barzan from his internal exile in Sulaimania and defeated the army unit sent to capture him. Alternately negotiating and fighting, the Barzanis held their own until the end of the war, when a new government offensive expelled them from their strongholds. Besides the Barzanis, there were other Iraqi Kurds who crossed the border and played minor parts in the republic. These included some smaller groups of tribesmen and, more significantly, a few Kurdish officers of the Iraqi armed forces, who had earlier acted as go-betweens in negotiations between the Barzanis and the government and some of whom had been active in nationalist circles. The latter's political and military experience gave them considerable influence in Mahabad.

In April 1946, after the Soviet Union had been granted important oil concessions, Russian troops began evacuating Iran. Soviet advisors urged the Azerbaijani and Kurdish republics to negotiate a settlement with the Tehran government. While showing military muscle, Qazi Mohammad attempted to gain a degree of autonomy for the entire Kurdish region. These efforts dragged on for months but came to nothing. Meanwhile, the republic was weakened by a border conflict with Azerbaijan and by growing internal dissensions. The urban nationalists who were most strongly represented in the political leadership disliked and deeply distrusted the tribal chieftains, but the defense of the republic depended on tribal forces. Toward the end of the summer, several tribal chieftains either completely deserted or negotiated their own private settlement. When the Iranian army finally marched on Mahabad in December, it took the city without battle. Qazi Mohammad and two relatives, who had surrendered, were court-martialed and hanged. Mulla Mustafa Barzani and his forces returned to Iraq, whence they fought their way through Turkey and northern Iran to the Soviet Union, where they were to live as refugees for more than a decade. Kurdish culture, which had briefly flourished in Mahabad, was suppressed again in Iran.   —MvB

Chapter VI

PLATE XVI

← 4½" →

26 of Azar
Dec 17, 1945.
Iranian Flag replaced by ~~changed for~~ Kurdish
flag at Mahabad Justice Department

Archibald Roosevelt

American Intelligence Officer

Before fate was to unveil the path of my future career . . . there was a special facet of my role in the opening battle of the Cold War in Iran that came to a tragic conclusion during my last days in Tehran. This was my involvement with the Kurds, which began during the latter part of my assignment to Baghdad. . . . The story of the Soviet-backed Kurdish Republic of Mahabad is a fascinating footnote in history of which I was virtually the sole American observer on the scene.

Archibald Roosevelt, *For Lust of Knowing*, 1988

1931—British want to settle Assyrians in Barzan—Barzanis refuse. Iraqi govt. fights them—Barzanis to Turkey. . . . Barzan region has 25,000 people, 350 villages. . . . Few sheep, fewer cattle—mostly goats. Few horses—more mules + donkeys bec. of the mts. People brave, lying forbidden to each other—only to foreigners for own benefit. Naqshibandi Sunnis. Keep law of Zakat [Islamic alms tax]. Love marriages—woman must love man. . . . Death for adultery. Don't like govts.

Mulla [Mustapha Barzani] reaches Barzan with 3 Barzanis. Mulla well built, middle statue [stature], swarthy, big eyes, meeting eyebrows. Knows Persian, Arabic—some Turk and Eng. Now 43 yrs old. When arrived Barzan made overtures to govt. Wrote them: To Barzan not to rebel but only to live quietly with family. Govt orders security forces to pursue, sends family—still in Sul [Sulaimania]—to Hilla. So Mulla gets ready, composes old tribal hatreds, tries to show tribesmen life + death question. Hewa [Kurdish Hope Party] + other nationalists support, present grievances to Brit and Iraqi govts and British get worried. Send note to Iraq govt to change Kurd policy + to Mulla: The rebellion must be stopped or Mulla to be considered enemy of UN.

From handwritten notes, Archibald Roosevelt Papers,
Manuscript Division, Library of Congress, Washington, D.C.

May 25, 1945

During recent months, a Kurdish independence movement . . . has come out a little into the open in the area around Mahabad. It is called Komala, meaning, "masses," "populace," or "gathering."

Komala has been secretly in existence for about 18 months. Its origin has not been definitely established as Russian but it has had positive support of two or more Russian agents. . . . Old Simko's (Isma'il Agha) son is said to be positively numbered among the Komala chieftains. . . .

Komala is trying to organize Mahabad as its Iranian Kurdish center. There it is said to have the tacit blessing of Mohammed Qazi, undisputed lord of the city. The Russians . . . have been playing up to the Qazi, supplying him with plenty of sugar and tea and cloth and there is a reasonable suspicion that part of their good will has been purchased with ammunition also. However, the Qazi's participation in Komala so far has been of a more or less passive nature. . . .

Komala's chief interest seems to be in setting up an independent Kurdish state to be composed of Turkish, Iranian and Iraq Kurdistan. To achieve this purpose it is expected that there will be fighting. To this end Kurds throughout the Iranian area at least are arming and organizing their own "militia." . . .

Komala has a newspaper *Kelavizho* published in Mukri Kurdish in the Arabic alphabet. Copies of it are distributed more or less secretly and are scarce. The place of printing, source of paper and supplies etc., are still a well guarded secret but it is reasonably supposed that it is printed in Mahabad. . . .

It is also reported that Komala has a flag of Kurdish Independence. However, source knows of no one who has seen or can describe it.

Archibald Roosevelt Papers, Manuscript Division,
Library of Congress, Washington, D.C.

Barzani (seated third from left) and his men in Shaqlawa, Iraq

Mulla Mustafa Barzani
Kurdish Leader

August 16, 1945

The Mulla Mustafa has been attempting to set up a sort of illegal government of his own in Kurdistan, and has taken the tribal affairs of surrounding territories into his own hands. . . .

The Mulla is thought by a number of sources to have so built up his position during the past year and a half as to be able to count on considerably more tribal support than in 1943. The nucleus of his force consists of the Barzani, the Zibari, and part of the Doski tribes. . . . It is safe to say at least that he will get no support from the settled and more prosperous tribes in the Sulaimania region. . . .

Few would deny that the Barzani revolt is a tempest in a teapot. It has, however, a certain significance as another manifestation of the unsatisfactory situation of the Kurds. It is inevitable, however, that the young educated Kurds will play an increasingly greater role as the importance of the tribes gradually diminishes, and that the former can more truly be called nationalists than outlaw bands such as that of Mulla Mustafa. If the time ever comes for both these young Kurds and the hitherto isolated tribes to unite, they may be a formidable force in the Middle East, provided they can get some support from one of the Great Powers. It is becoming clear to many Kurds that there is only one Great Power likely to support them, the Soviet Union, and more and more Kurds are envisaging the creation of a Kurdish Soviet Republic. The Russians cannot be unaware of the possibilities of this situation, and if they are not exploiting these at present, there is no reason to suppose that the future will not bring a greater manifestation of interest on the part of the Soviet Union.

September 5, 1945

Some time in 1944 . . . the Regent voiced to the British Embassy the opinion held by most intelligent Iraqis, that the British had one policy for the Arabs and another for the Kurds, and asked the British to change this policy. The British, for reasons of their own . . . decided henceforward to support the government in controlling the Kurds.

In accordance with this new policy, British advisors and area liaison officers who had shown sympathy for the Kurds were systematically removed, and replaced by others whose careers made it probable that their sympathies would be with the Arabs. . . .

As a result of this policy, the Kurds who had come to like and trust the replaced British officers, all of whom knew Kurdish, found themselves now with no other contacts with the British but officers who had no understanding of their problems and did not even know their language. Hence, the Kurds lost confidence in the British and could no longer be so easily controlled.

Eventually the Mulla Mustafa began taking steps without reference to the wishes of the British political officers, and the Embassy evidently decided that he would have to be suppressed before his unpunished disregard of authority won him more adherents.

After the final break between the Mulla Mustafa and the government, the British ordered all area liaison officers and political advisors out of the area. . . . The ostensible reason is to avoid losing British officers to a stray Kurd bullet—but the real reason is political: the British Embassy does not wish to give the Iraqis a chance to say that the British are interested in the affair, are in favor of the Kurds, or are up to some nefarious trick.

As a result of the shake-up in personnel, and restrictions on movement of the remainder, the British are comparatively poorly informed as to what is going on in Kurdistan.

Archibald Roosevelt Papers, Manuscript Division,
Library of Congress, Washington D.C.

IRAQ

RUSSIA ASKS UNO DELAY UNTIL APRIL 10;
U.S. ACTS TO PUT IRAN FIRST ON AGENDA;
KURDISH TRIBES RISE AGAINST TEHERAN

NORTH IRAN TENSE

Government Planes Sent to Help Army Quell Disorder Near Iraq

WIDER UPRISINGS FEARED

Three Garrisons Attacked— Tie-Up With Insurgents in Azerbaijan Implied

By GENE CURRIVAN
By Wireless to THE NEW YORK TIMES.

TEHERAN, Iran, March 20—An uprising among the Kurds in northwestern Iran, which has been in the incipient stage for the past week but virtually overlooked because of the country's multiple troubles, has reached a stage where intervention of the Iranian Air Force has become necessary. A squadron of small bombers has been sent up north and will go into action as soon as the weather permits.

The present disorder is confined mostly to a province in Kurdistan on the Iraqi border just below Turkey, but it is feared the Kurds of Iran, Iraq and Turkey eventually may join to try to re-establish ancient Kurdistan as an independent country. This has been their fond hope for centuries.

3,000 Kurds in Action

The current move apparently is intended to gain control of north-western Iran from the Kurdistan province clear up to the Turkish-Russian borders. This is the western side of Azerbaijan Province, but it is predominantly Kurdish.

It is understood that the Kurds have about 3,000 mounted tribesmen in action at scattered points.

TRIBESMEN MARCH IN A CRITICAL AREA

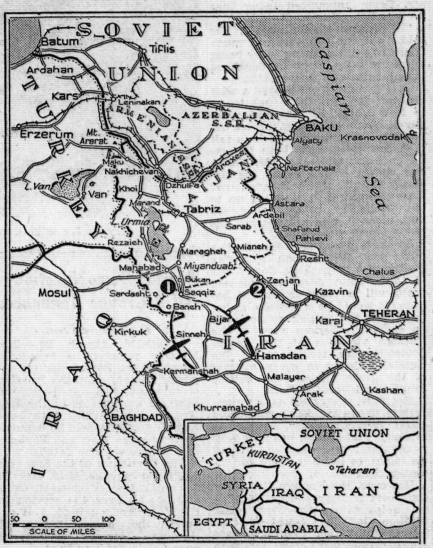

March 21, 1946

Kurdish warriors have attacked Iranian garrisons at Saqqiz (1), at Sardasht, to the west, and at Baneh, to the southwest. Iranian planes are poised at Hamadan and Kermanshah ready to attack the tribesmen. Saqqiz, a center of the disturbance, is just south of Bukan, where a Russian column was reported recently. Kurdistan, home of the tribes, lies in Turkey, Iraq and Iran, as shown on the inset. Near Zenjan (2) loyal natives of the region joined the fight against the separatists of Azerbaijan.

NO HALT IS LIKELY

Security Council to Meet Monday—Russia's Plan Needs Seven Votes

IRAN SEES PRESSURE MOVE

Envoy Denies Soviet Assertion in Postponement Plea That Negotiations Continue

Statements by Gromyko and Stettinius are on Page 2.

By HAROLD B. HINTON
Special to THE NEW YORK TIMES.

WASHINGTON, March 20—The Soviet Union requested today that the meeting of the United Nations Security Council, scheduled for Hunter College next Monday, be postponed until April 10, on the ground that direct negotiations are still continuing with the Iranian Government, which has certified a dispute to the Council. Trygve Lie, Secretary General of the United Nations Organization, communicated the Soviet request to all Council members but took no steps to defer Monday's gathering, which he expects to convene at 2:30 P. M.

At the same time as he announced the Soviet move Mr. Lie made public a letter from Edward R. Stettinius Jr., United States permanent representative on the Council, serving notice that he would move on Monday that the formal complaint by Iran be placed at the head of the Council's agenda and that progress reports on direct negotiations be required of both Governments immediately.

Deferred Consideration Before

At the meeting in London last

Soviet Weather Contact Cut;
U. S. Siberia Stations Closed

By SIDNEY SHALETT

Qazi Mohammad (center), and Mulla Mustafa (below), on the day the Republic was proclaimed at Chwar Chira Circle, January 22, 1946 (the Second of Rebandan, 1324)

Unknown/Courtesy William Eagleton

Tribes of Kurds in Revolt in Iran

There is no evidence to prove that the Russians engineered the latest revolt but few doubt that they would have given the necessary encouragement. . . . There are four tribal leaders behind the revolt. Two are brothers from Iraq, Ahmed Barzani and Mullah Mustafa Barzani, and two are Iranians, Hama Raschid Khan Banehi and Gahza Mohammed [Qazi Mohammad]. All have taken active parts in previous uprisings and are well known in this part of the world.

They depend almost entirely on tribal cavalry and are not equipped, so far as is known, with artillery. Their principal weapons are modern rifles and machine guns. Theirs is mountain guerrilla warfare, and the effectiveness of an air attack may not be all that could be desired.

The Kurds' military strategy is to select one main target, hit it hard, and then, if unsuccessful, scatter into mountain passes. There are seldom large troop concentrations that could be bombed.

General staff officials here admit that this revolt is important but are not unduly concerned and appear confident that it can be nipped.

The New York Times, March 21, 1946

Qazi Mohammad with Mulla Mustafa Barzani during the Mahabad Republic

Unknown/KDP Archive, Salahaddin

IRAN

PLATE XIX ✓ ✓ ✓ (Chapter VIII)

The Cabinet and other officials Mahabad February 1946

Seated: Qazi Muhammad

Original photograph used for preparation of the book The Kurdish Republic of 1946, *1963*

Unknown/Courtesy William Eagleton

Qazi Mohammad
Kurdish Leader in Iran

Question: *In Tehran, they say the Kurds under your leadership want separation and independence of Kurdistan. Is this true?*
Qazi: *No, it is not true, because we want the Iranian government to implement the constitution and we want to live autonomously under the Iranian flag.*
Question: *How long have you been autonomous?*
Qazi: *We have had internal autonomy for four years.*
Question: *How do you administer your autonomy?*
Qazi: *A while ago in this region we held an election among the high representatives of the Kurdish people who were gathered in Mahabad to choose a board of nine members, led by me, with whom we are able to manage our autonomy.*
Question: *In Tehran, they say that you have sent some people to Baku [in Soviet Azerbaijan] and they brought back a printing press and arms. Is it true that you formed a Communist Party?*
Qazi: *These stories are fabricated by the military authorities and are not true. We have bought paper and a printing press in Tabriz and you can find out about the location where we bought them. The formation of a Communist Party is a lie. Here in Kurdistan, and according to the constitution of Iran, people have full freedom of their opinions. We have an open party, which is the Kurdistan Democratic Party.*
Question: *Is it possible to explain the aims of the Kurdistan Democratic Party?*
Qazi: *Yes, I'll tell you briefly about the platform of the Kurdistan*

Democratic Party. (1) The Kurdish nation in Iran should be free in administering and conducting its own affairs in its territory and live freely within the borders of the Iranian state. (2) [Kurds] should be able to study in their language in Kurdistan, and correspondence in government offices should be in Kurdish. (3) As the [Iranian] constitution stipulates, the provincial and district councils of Kurdistan should be established immediately, to supervise and manage all social and governmental affairs. (4) Government officials should be from the people of the area and there should be a compromise, according to law, between the peasants and landlords so that the future of both sides will be secured. (5) The Kurdistan Democratic Party should strive for the fraternal and egalitarian coexistence of all the people of Iran.
Question: *Does the Kurdistan Democratic Party have relations with the non-Iranian Kurds? Do you want the unity of all Kurds?*
Qazi: *No, not at all.*
Question: *During the elections the Democratic Party of Azerbaijan allowed women the right to vote. Have you done this?*
Qazi: *Although I regard this act by the Azerbaijanis as a good thing, I must tell you that we have not achieved such a success.*
Question: *Is there a "Komala" in Kurdistan?*
Qazi: *"Komala" means party and there is no such thing in Iran. There is a party by this name in Iraq, which has no connection with us.*

Interview with Qazi Mohammad, *Kurdistan* (Kurdish newspaper published every other day in Mahabad), January 13, 1946, translated by Amir Hassanpour

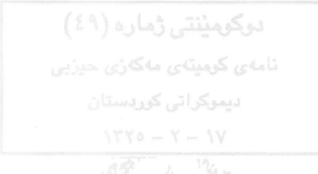

Appeal to the United Nations

There is little chance that any strong backing for an independent Kurdistan will be found in the United Nations. Such a state would have to be formed by taking large areas out of three sovereign states, Turkey, Iran and Iraq. It would absorb some of the chrome lands of Turkey. . . . It would include the British-controlled oil wells of the Mosul and Kirkuk districts in Iraq. If it should be established, it would offer no promise of internal stability or permanence. For the Kurds have never been a unified people. They have no national tradition, no background of unity and no experience of self-rule. But even though the idea of a unified Kurdish state is completely unfeasible, the Kurdish movement for *Khoiboun* is the most dangerous of all the troubles which now beset the Middle East—because of the support which it has from Soviet Russia. Even if a limited Kurdish region were to be set up as an independent unit in Iran alone, the situation would be bad. The Kurdish tribes of Turkey, numerically the largest group, could almost certainly become involved in the independence movement. In that case, the Turks would go to war to maintain the unity of the state which they have knit together with so much self-sacrifice and expenditure of blood. . . .

All of the Kurds have grievances against the states of which they are now subjects. Grievances, ammunition and a fighting people—this is the explosive combination with which the Soviet Union is playing the hoary tsarist game of expansion.

William Linn Westermann, "Kurdish Independence," *Foreign Affairs*, July 1946

Teachers and staff of the education office of Mahabad, 1946

Unknown/Courtesy Rafiq Studio

2

Interview with Qazi Muhammad

Shortly after the usual dismal breakfast of cold soft-boiled eggs (too soft), fly-infested honey and bread flaps, filthy buffalo butter and tea (way overstrength), we were conducted to Qazi Mohamed's office. This is situated in party headquarters, a white building on the main square formerly occupied by the Russians, and still plastered inside with Russian propaganda pictures and outside with huge paintings of Soviet decorations--hardly a suitable ...ing for the capitol of a free people.

...tered into Qazi's office, we found him sitting behind his desk, a short, dignified looking man in an old Persian army private's coat, with sparse whiskers spread over his pale, ascetic face. He suffers from a serious stomach complaint, and eats little except mast (curdled milk) and milk products, and has not been able to get his ailment diagnosed and treated. After receiving us, he read a brief prepared speech to us in Persian, in a distinct, slow, quiet voice, occasionally flushing a glance at us with his rather mystical eyes. The speech was concerned with the oppression suffered by the Kurds, their national aspirations, and the necessity for freedom-loving peoples, and especially the United States, to help them attain their liberty and human rights in accordance with the principals on which the war was fought.

I answered that the United States had always stood for the liberty and free enjoyment of human rights of all peoples, and hoped that this ideal would one day be attained throughout the world; that we were in Kurdistan to look into the situation of the Kurds and report it to our government, and we hoped very much that this situation was improving, and that the Kurds were not merely exchanging one tyranny for another. Qazi said that all were free in the area controlled by him to say and write what they pleased. I said I had been gratified to note that whereas in Democrat Azerbaijan the people were allowed to listen only to the Tabriz and Moscow radios, I had heard in Mahabad the previous night both London and Ankara broadcast on the streets. This pleased him very much, and he said that the situation in Tabriz was entirely different from that of Mahabad. He was la... pleased, however, at my account of the Maghadah incident, and I also remarked that I had been shocked to find his building plastered with Soviet propaganda, though he did not offer any explanation.

Although evasive about the Soviets, he did remark very pointedly that the Kurds were compelled to accept help from anyone who would give it to them, but would not accept domination by anyone. He said that the Kurds had presented a petition asking for rectification of their grievances to the Big Three at a European conference (Potsdam?) but that Britain and the United States had ignored them. He asked why, in view of the principles of the Atlantic Charter, did the United States persist in ignoring the Kurds? The Kurds, he insisted, all look to the United States, the most advanced nation of the world, to help them overcome their backwardness. "If only instead of sending 30,000 soldiers to Iran you had sent 100 teachers!" But instead of helping the Kurds, he remarked that the U.S. is helping their enemies, such as the Turks, by giving them arms and equipment to use in subduing them.

He expressed bitter hatred of the British, who he said had long been the enemies of the Kurds. He mentioned specific grievances against the British--the turning over of Kurdish rebels against the Turks who had fled to Syria and Iraq to the Turkish Government; the crushing of Sheikh Mahmud and of Mulla Mustafa's Barzanis; and their alleged instigation of Kurdish tribes in Iraq, allegedly massed near the border, against the Mahabad government.

For the French, however, he had high praise, for their encouragement of Kurdish nationalism in Syria. They had, he said, let the Kurds make radio broadcasts and conduct schools in their own tongue, but now the Arab Government was taking away these rights and subjecting the Kurds to oppression. He said that the French were creating some sort of school in France for the Kurds, in connection with which Dr. Kamuran Bedirkhan of Syria and 'Ali Kamal of 'Iraq were going or had gone to France. He might add here that Napoleon Jackel, French Agence France-Presse correspondent, known to us here as a Communist or fellow-traveler, made a trip to Mahabad some weeks ago and was evidently lionized. Kurds there expressed their satisfaction with a number of French newspaper articles recently appearing on the Kurds, which were possibly written by this man, and it sounds as if the French had done a little propaganda work in the area.

E/a Tehran, Iran

23 Sept 1946

Page 5

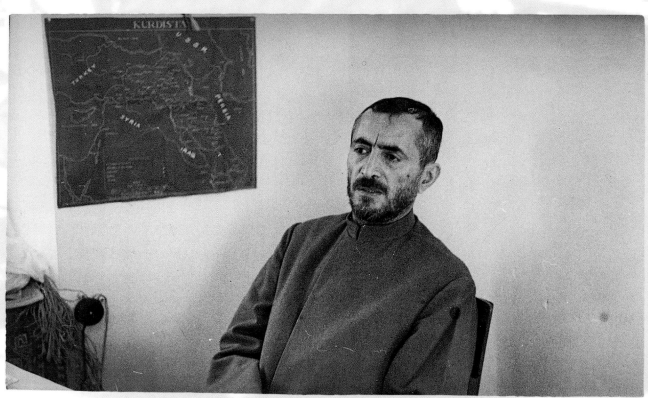

This picture of our father must have been taken around the First World War [before the October Revolution of 1917]. At that time, our family was leading the Kurds in our area against the Russians. We lost more than 80 men and many of our clan were sent to Siberia. My father fought against the Russian czars to defend our name and our city of Soujbulagh [Mahabad]. He took some prisoners of war, and it was from them that he learned the Russian language.

Letter and background from Ali Ghazi, son of Qazi Mohammad, living in Germany, March 1995

Qazi Mohammad in his office in Mahabad with map of Kurdistan behind him, 1946   Archibald Roosevelt/Library of Congress, Washington, D.C.

To His Excellency, the Great Leader of the Kurdistan Republic

Enemy Tricks and Disapproving the Withdrawal of Our Troops

The reports for May 26th [1946] have been submitted to the Ministry of War [referred] under the dispatch No. 338. But since Mr. Karimi is leaving to see you and to report the results of the negotiations, I have to tell you my firm views. I have no hope that the enemy pursues a true goal of friendship and agreement; [rather they] waste our time. If the enemy's pretext is to secure supplies and sustenance for their forces in Baneh, Mirade and Saqqiz, I assure you that their supplies are fully secured. They can administer comfortably with the reserves they have. And if it is just a pretext to remove the hold of our forces over the region [where] their forces [are situated], we definitely cannot retreat even one hand-span, and evacuate these areas [for them] which we have taken by force of our weapons. But if the Iranian government wants to reconcile and come to agreement, I guarantee that there will be no advances or attacks from the side of [our] Democrat forces until the end of negotiations. That is why I found it necessary on this occasion to report to you my administrative and military opinion. It is very difficult for us to retreat and I wait to receive your orders.

[Hama Rashid,] commander of the forces of Bukan and Sara Region, Mahabad

Document (right) published in Mahmud Mulla Izzat, *The Democratic Republic of Kurdistan*, 1992, translated by Hassan Ghazi

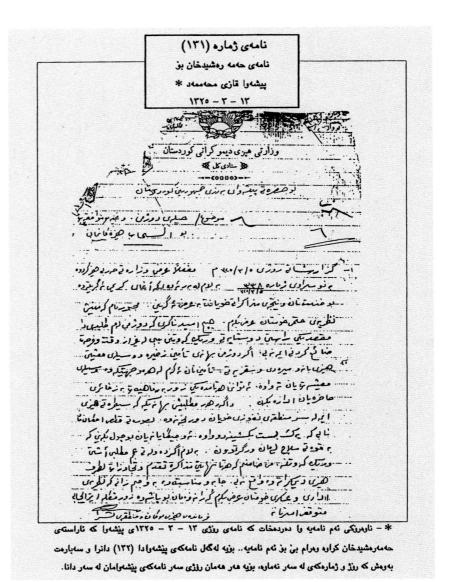

In Mahabad

Archibald Roosevelt/Library of Congress, Washington, D.C.

Hama Rashid was a powerful khan whose villages were situated on both sides of the Iran-Iraq border. He revolted against the Iranian government in the early 1940s and in 1946 joined the Kurdish Republic with two hundred horsemen. He was assigned by Qazi Mohammad to be commander of the Bukan area, where his forces faced Iranian army positions in Saqqiz. Hama Rashid left his position a few months before the fall of the Republic, taking all of the official correspondence with him from Mahabad, and settled back on his land across the border.

I was sent by Ali Abdulla, then governor of Sulaimania, to talk to him about land reform in his region in 1973. I informed him that I was doing research on the history of the Republic and asked if he would share the documents with me. They were kept out of sight in sacks in a barn. He gave me all the documents. By mere chance, they survived the wars that raged in 1974 and I was able to get them out of Kurdistan in 1985.

Interview with Mahmud Mulla Izzat, Kurdish scholar living in Sweden, October 1993

1946

Kurdish poets Hajar (left) and Hêmen (right)
with Qazi Mohammad in Mahabad

Unknown/Courtesy Chris Kutschera

Mahabad Central Committee

June 3, 1946
Your honour, Commander of Bukan and
Sara Region [Hama Rashid],
In response to letter #471, May 31, [19]46

Even the most minor action right now
must be in accord with the international situation, especially our cause, which is a
major one.

That is why we are forced to choose peaceful means as much as possible. We cannot
take another path. The delay is for this reason;
otherwise I would act more quickly than you.

On the one hand I am happy that your
wife and family have arrived and been rescued safely, but on the other hand I am sad
[to ask] when will the Kurds be owners of
their own land. May God have mercy.

Qazi Mohammad

Document published in Mahmud Mulla Izzat,
The Democratic Republic of Kurdistan, 1992,
translated by Hassan Ghazi

KURD CHIEF SEIZED BY IRANIAN TROOPS

Teheran Says Surrender Spells End of His Dissident Regime —Two Towns Taken

TEHERAN, Iran, Dec. 15 (Æ)—
An Iranian Army communiqué announced today that Ghazi Mohammed, head of the so-called Kurdish
Republic, had surrendered to Central Government troops after
heavy fighting in which additional
parts of Azerbaijan Province were
brought under Government control.

The announcement said his surrender apparently spelled the end
of the "republic," which had ruled
parts of western Azerbaijan
under a truce with the Tabriz
regime of Jaafar Pishevari. The
Pishevari forces had yielded to the
Central Government.

The Army disclosed that the
southwestern Azerbaijanian city of
Miyanduab, a key city of the Kurdish area, had capitulated yesterday
following a battle in which severe
casualties were inflicted on a force
of 1,000 irregulars. Miyanduab is
eighty miles south of Tabriz.

After the battle Ghazi Mohammed pledged his support of the
Central Government of Premier
Ahmad Ghavam, and the Government troops were "welcomed," the
communiqué said.

Miyanduab and other Azerbaijanian towns occupied by Government troops in their march through
the semi-autonomous Province to
police forthcoming national elec-

Young ones! **Peshmerga!** *Brave ones! Fearless ones!*
You pick up the sword and we sharpen the pen!
With God's help we will take out of the hands of foreigners
The clean Kurdish homeland, and we will eliminate
*   all the pain of the Kurds.*
I congratulate you and say, God grant long life
O Kurdish president and respected leader.

Poem by Hêmen, recited in the Feasts of Celebration of the Independence of Kurdistan,
reprinted in *Kurdistan*, No. 15, February 16, 1946, translated by Amir Hassanpour

The New York Times,
December 16, 1946

IRAN

TURKEY

U.S.S.R.

June 15
June 10
MAKU
June 9
June 3
JULFA
MARAND
QOTUR
KHOI
SHAPUR
TABRIZ
Somai
Valley
May 29
LAKE REZAIEH (URMIA)
REZAIEH
Tergawar
Valley
MARAGHEH
May 27, 1947
Dalanpar
Mt.
Mergawar
Valley
Kalashin
Pass
USHNAVIEH
NAQADEH
MIANDOAB
BARZAN
KHELAN
MAHABAD
RUWANDUZ
IRAQ
SARDASHT

The Kurdish Republic
of 1946

Motor Roads

Retreat route of the
Barzanis to the U.S.S.R.

1947

At first he did not wonder aloud why I was concerned about the Qazis since they had collaborated with the Soviets. I said that they were essentially nationalists doing what they could for the betterment of their people, and the Soviets were the only ones interested in helping them, that we would, in effect, be a party to their execution, and in fact be blamed by the Kurds, which would be viewed with horror by Kurdish nationalists. He asked me what he should do about it, and I suggested that he ask the Shah to instruct Razmara to bring the Qazis to Tehran for a fair and open trial.

The Ambassador asked and got an immediate appointment with the Shah. George [Allen] began by expressing a hope for the amelioration of tribal problems, including those of the Kurds; he then went on to say that while the Qazis had collaborated with the Soviets, they had done a lot for education—and the Shah interrupted him.

"Are you afraid I'm going to have them shot?" he asked with a smile. "If so, you can set your mind at rest. I am not."

The next day the Qazis had been hanged at dawn, "after the approval of his Imperial Majesty, the Shahinshah."

One has to conclude that the Shah may have sent out the order as soon as our Ambassador had closed the door behind him.

Handwritten notes by Archibald Roosevelt for memoir, *For Lust of Knowing*, 1988/Archibald Roosevelt Papers, Manuscript Division, Library of Congress, Washington, D.C.

Background: Map from William Eagleton, *The Kurdish Republic of 1946*, 1963

BARZANI TRIBE IN RUSSIA

Fugitives From Iraq Battled Armies of Three Countries

TEHERAN, June 19 (AP)—The Iranian War Ministry said tonight that the Barzani tribesmen who battled armies of three countries in a 200-mile trek from their home in the Iraqi mountains had reached Russian territory.

The tribesmen had been chased out of Iraq for banditry. They crossed into Turkey, then went to Iran, where they engaged Iranian Army forces in the northwest corner of Iran within sight of the Turkish and Russian borders.

A War Ministry official said the band, estimated at 600 to 1,000 men, crossed the Araxis River five miles east of a point where the borders of the three countries meet. The tribesmen apparently swam the river and left much of their arms, equipment and pack animals behind, the official said.

The New York Times,
June 20, 1947

»قاضی محمد«

Qazi Mohammad on the gallows, March 31, 1947   Unknown/Courtesy Martin van Bruinessen

*In Mahabad and elsewhere
hasty efforts were made
by Kurdish officials to destroy
all records, documents,
and photographs. At the
same time, individuals and
families removed all traces
of their involvement in
the Kurdish movement by
burning letters, commissions,
and photographs of
themselves, Qazi Mohammed
and Stalin.*

William Eagleton,
The Kurdish Republic of 1946, 1963

*These photographs were all
clandestinely slipped
to me by people who were
trying to help me write
something. But nobody
talked openly about the days
of Mahabad, publicly.
All my investigations and
interviews were done behind
closed doors.*

Interview with William Eagleton
by Laura Hubber, November 1995

189

UNEASY COEXISTENCE

The road from Naqadeh to Mahabad
William Eagleton

Order Restored in Iraq

Mulla Mustafa Barzani's rebellion of 1943–45 and the events in Iran fanned nationalist feelings among the Iraqi Kurds, especially in the Sulaimania region. There were, by the mid-1940s, a number of small but devoted nationalist associations with an educated urban membership. These ranged ideologically from the conservative and rather pro-British (Hiwa) to the left-leaning or Marxist (Rizgari Kurd). At this time Kurds were still well represented in the middle and higher echelons of the Iraqi army and government. While most were Iraqi patriots, some officers were clandestinely affiliated with Hiwa. In 1944, some Kurdish army officers served as intermediaries between the Barzanis and the government, thereby attempting to give this local rebellion with its limited aims a truly national dimension. The following year, when the Barzani brothers with their thousands of followers took refuge in Iran, these Kurdish officers also crossed the border.

Communications between the Iranian and Iraqi parts of Kurdistan have always been more frequent and easy than with the Turkish part. Simko had twice sought refuge in Iraq, and so had later Kurdish chieftains from Iran when persecuted by Reza Shah's army. Shaikh Mahmud had had Iranian Kurds among his fighters, and had himself, together with his faithful followers, taken refuge in Iran in the late 1920s. Kurdish leaders, both tribal and urban, were well aware of conditions in Iranian Kurdistan following the British and Russian invasion. The virtual disappearance of central authority across the border raised hopes of uniting the Iranian and Iraqi parts of Kurdistan as a self-ruling entity, if necessary under some form of international mandate. When the Mahabad Republic was established, it had the warm sympathy and loyalties of all Iraqi Kurdish nationalists.

The fact that the Soviet authorities openly supported the Mahabad Republic strengthened pro-Soviet sympathies among Iraqi Kurdish intellectuals (and may also have had the effect of alienating conservatives from Kurdish nationalism). Radical left organizations grew at the expense of the conservative Hiwa, and the Iraqi Communist Party had a disproportionate number of Kurdish members—especially in Sulaimania. In the government view, Kurdish nationalism became directly associated with the Soviet threat, which led to a wave of arrests of suspected radicals.

In mid-1946, Mulla Mustafa Barzani, whose prestige among Iraqi Kurds had further risen because of his role in the Mahabad Republic, was instrumental in forging the first alliance of urban nationalists and Kurdish chieftains in Iraq and having them jointly establish a new party, the Kurdistan Democratic Party (KDP), modeled on Mahabad's ruling party. (Barzani himself did not come to play an active leading role in this party until his return to Iraq in 1958. Following the defeat of the Mahabad Republic, he only briefly crossed into Iraq, on the first leg of a long march through Turkey and again from Iran to the Soviet Republic of Azerbaijan.)

The fall of the Mahabad Republic signaled a sea change in the Iraqi government's dealings with Kurds. Four Kurdish officers who had taken part in Mahabad were arrested upon their return to Iraq and hanged. Recruitment of Kurds into the army officer corps also stopped around this time.

Although the KDP was initially dominated by conservative tribal chiefs and landlords, it also suffered government repression. In the early 1950s, leadership of the party was taken over by radicals, the most prominent of whom was the poet and lawyer Ibrahim Ahmed—which made it even more suspect in government eyes. The KDP never became a mass party. Whereas radical intellectuals such as Ibrahim Ahmed became the chief ideologists of Kurdish nationalism, it was traditional leaders like Shaikh Mahmud, who spent his last years in enforced exile in Baghdad, and Mulla Mustafa Barzani, in his distant Soviet exile, who became its most powerful and emotive symbols. Life found its orderly daily course, but under the surface there remained the expectation that one day these leaders would return—to be buried in Sulaimania like Shaikh Mahmud, or to lead a new movement, as Mulla Mustafa was to do.

In the early 1950s, a significant demographic change took place: the considerable Jewish community of Kurdistan almost entirely emigrated to the new state of Israel, as most Iraqi Jews did. There had been some emigration to Palestine before, but the establishment of Israel and the strong anti-Zionist response in most Arab states speeded up this process. There appears not to have been any anti-Semitic agitation in Kurdistan, however. The relationship between the Kurds and the Jews of Kurdistan had been generally good, though not equal. It is perhaps significant that many of the Jewish merchants of Baghdad who departed for Israel left their businesses in the hands of the Shiite Kurds (Feylis), whom they had preferably employed as their assistants. The Kurdistani Jewish community in Israel has maintained strong emotional ties with its region of origin.   —*MvB*

Abdul Waheb Muhammed Ali Rowanduzi
in prison in Mosul, 1948
Unknown/Courtesy Ali Rowanduzi

Background: *"We demand the release of all patriots and general amnesty for the Barzanis"*
Demonstration in Baghdad, 1948
Rafiq

Ibrahim Ahmed (right) and Jalil Hushyar, both members of the KDP, in Abu Ghraib Central Prison, Baghdad, 1950

Unknown/Courtesy Ibrahim Ahmed

The Iraqi government forbade possession of typewriters. You could not even use a typewriter unless you had permission from the Home Secretary. We had a typewriter but we didn't have permission.

When Nail Haji Isa, the number-two intelligence man, suddenly came to Sulaimania, a friend who had borrowed our typewriter abruptly returned it to my home. Nobody wanted to be found with such a thing. Another friend warned me that my name was on a list and that my house would be searched.

I checked to see that there were no incriminating patriotic papers or letters lying about that could be considered dangerous, and we hid the typewriter at the bottom of a huge garbage bin and heaped it full of litter.

The search was thorough, but they found nothing except a copy of one of the legal newspapers of the time. In this paper there was a letter to the editor concerning a Kurdish issue. The police took the paper as evidence of my interest in the subject. A spy went to search further in the cellar. While he was there he probed the garbage bin with a stick. The stick struck the typewriter on the bottom. As they were leaving, he said to me quietly: "Tell them to change the place of the typewriter."

You see, he was a spy for the government against Communists, not against Kurds, being Kurdish himself.

Interview with Ibrahim Ahmed, Kurdish writer and KDP secretary, by Sheri Laizer, September 1994

1948

194

Caption reads: "Commemoration of the martyrs for the independence of Kurdistan"
Four Iraqi Kurdish officers (L-R): Muhammad Qudsi [son of Mahmud Efendi], Khairullah Abdulkarim, Mustafa Khoshnaw, and Izzat Abdulaziz, all of whom fought with Barzani in Mahabad and were executed on June 19, 1947, upon their return to Iraq, after being promised amnesty

Testimony of Our Martyrs

Last words of the four Kurdish officers executed in Baghdad, June 16–19, 1947

Izzat Abdulaziz:
The tree of liberty will be watered by my blood and that of my comrades. I am hopeful that it will bloom soon and provide liberty and happiness to the homeland. Kill the imperialists and their despicable helpers.

Muhammad Qudsi:
I have been nourished by my mother with love for the homeland. This rope, a so-called symbol of punishment, that has fallen to me as the price of my attachment to the homeland is very dear to me. It is the rope that will carve my name into the hearts of my compatriots and the memory of my nation, who have me, instead of father and mother. Death is a great honor under these circumstances. As for you, executioners, don't enjoy yourselves too much, because tomorrow you will be crushed by shame and disgrace.

Mustafa Khoshnaw:
Executioners, tell your masters that my blood will be avenged. I do not fear your potency; it is that power which will elevate me to a Martyred Hero of Kurdistan. . . . I leave three young children behind me—they will learn that I died for the homeland, and I hope once grown up they will be inspired in their life by my example.

Khairullah Abdulkarim:
My mother was from Mosul and my father was a Kurd. I was left by them when I was very young. I fought with my uncles for the liberation of the homeland and for freedom for the Kurds. In doing so, I followed my heart, and I hope to have shown myself worthy of the memory of my father and deserving of my homeland. Death to our enemies, and long live Kurdistan!

Bulletin Mensuel du Centre d'Études Kurds, No. 4, 1949, translated by Stuart Alexander

IRAQ

I was born in a village called Sandur near the Turkish border. The two things that characterized this particular village were that all the people were Jewish and all of them were farmers. The thing that stood out the most was that the synagogue was in the center of the village. It was very large and built of stone, unlike the other mud-brick buildings. Most of the people were completely uneducated except those who acquired education through the synagogue itself.

The relationship between the Jews in my village and the Muslims in the neighboring villages was excellent, but there was a great change in the early 1940s. The Arabs had developed a strong relationship with the Nazis, and that had its effect on the relationship between the Jews and Muslims in Kurdistan.

Since all the people in the village were religious, when it was announced that the state of Israel was established, there was an almost spontaneous decision by all of the people in the village to leave. That's why the village was emptied of all its inhabitants.

We were taken by truck to Baghdad. Before allowing us to get on the planes, the Iraqi authorities checked that we had nothing except the clothing on our backs. We lived in refugee camps, and as the years passed, we dispersed to different places throughout Israel.

To go from an Eastern country with a primitive society to one that was more westernized was a tremendous cultural change. We had to go through a change of a thousand years in two or three years.

Interview with Yacov Yacov, Kurdish Jew living in Israel, May 1994

Passport of Haviva Zaken, born in 1922 in Zakho, northern Iraq
Courtesy Moti Zaken

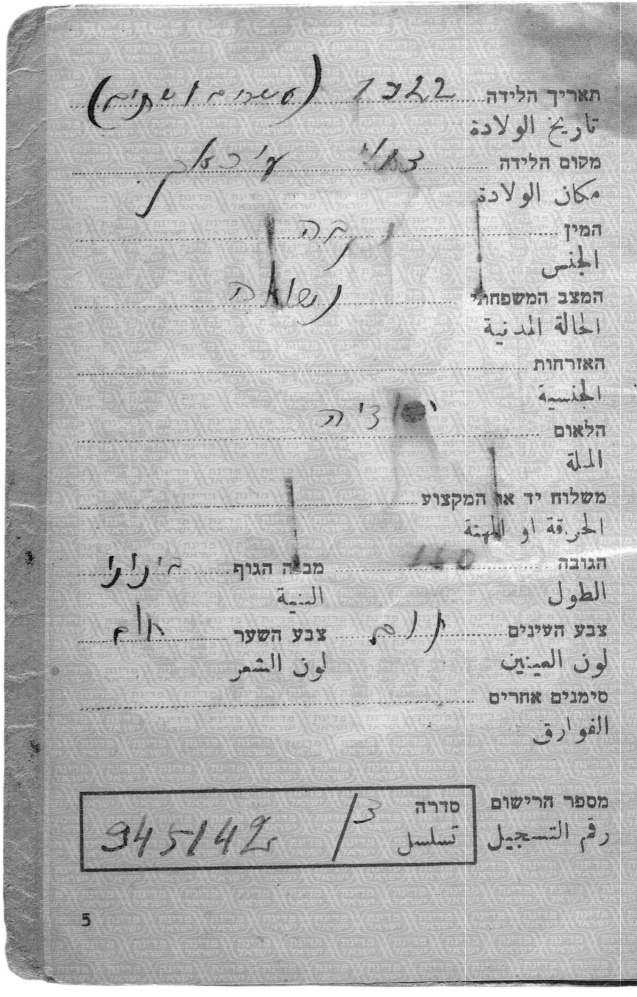

A family of new arrivals from Kurdistan at reception ceremony, Lydda airfield (now Ben-Gurion Airport), Tel Aviv, Israel

F. Schlesinger/Central Zionist
Archives, Jerusalem

Ralph Solecki
American Anthropologist

The Kurds had no idea what I was doing, only that I was digging for something which I said was prehistoric. And that sort of satisfied them. I don't think that they had any sense of a great history. I impressed on them that the things being excavated were before their lifetimes and nothing to do with the Kurds, so they didn't mind. It wasn't "Haram"—forbidden. They didn't give me any inkling of curiosity except for one or two people and one of them was my foreman, who was very observant, and he could see that the artifacts found in one site could be comparable to artifacts from the other. He began to understand something about the archaeology of the area, at least in the cave and the village site. If he were in Western culture he would be sitting where I am, professor or engineer or something. He was a Barzani. "Barzani" means that he was in the thick of everything, as opposed to the Shirvani, who lived across the mountain and were not as aggressive as the Barzanis.

The evening we arrived there were gunshots, and a wheat field across the river went up in flames. The Kurds on our side of the river were the enemies of the Kurds on the opposite side. They had nothing to do with each other except fight.

I knew that there were all kinds of outside problems, but I didn't want to pry too much because that would mark me down as a kind of spy. And since the government representative was there too, I couldn't compromise him. So it was a case of keeping your nose clean.

Most people had never seen an American. They thought that I was English, and I wasn't going to disabuse them. They regarded me as kind of a curiosity—my shoes, my boots, my trousers, the hat I wore, and so on.

The cave was a convenient place to dump their cleanings from the sheep corral. Instead of trekking it all to the front of the cave, they simply walked over to the side of the excavation and dumped it. I think we had something like five meters of refuse to clean out at the beginning of the season. It was some small trouble, but with manpower, since I didn't have to shovel it out myself, I didn't mind.

I knew about Henry Field's work, but he mainly did physical anthropology in Kurdistan. I knew of his interest in the area. We had lots of correspondence back and forth. Actually, I think I must have sparked his interest again. After I found Shanidar Cave, he came back to Iraq and went up to the mountain, and found the Baradost Cave, but he didn't get anything.

Interview with Ralph Solecki, March 1993

Kurdish workmen at site of digging in Shanidar Cave, 250 miles north of Baghdad, believed to have been more or less continuously inhabited for 100,000 years

Ralph Solecki

Page _____ of _____
cp. No. _____
From _____

RESTRICTED
(Classification)

Page ___1___ of _____
Encl. No. ___1___
Desp. No. ___115___
From ___Baghdad___

August 7, 1953

SUBJECT: Trip by PAO Lee Dinsmore, Kirkuk in Northern Liwa, Barzani area.

August 2 to 5, 1953

The single, most striking observation on this short trip into Barzani tribal country was that of the scarcity of population, razed villages and lack of contact with the main lines of communication and commerce. This fact has much to do with the continuing attitudes of separateness and contributes to the conviction on the part of the inhabitants that they are not really a part of the country, Iraq. Very much the same attitude is expressed by government servants in these areas who feel that assignment to a distant Nahia or Qada in the region is akin to banishment. In 1946, after the latest Barzani insurrection, large numbers of these tribesmen and their families left the area and went to Sheikhan in Mosul, Makhmour and Koi Sanjak in Erbil, Iran and to prison or government-supervised exile in the south of Iraq. A group also followed Mulla Mustafa. Recently, the government has released the majority of the group held in detention in the south and some of them have begun to arrive back in their villages in the North. Ahmed Agha, Mulla Mustafa's brother, is one who must stay in Basra and is not allowed to return. They are poor and have little to return to except their mountains, and they are bitter. Several loan officials think that it would be unwise for the government to allow the Aghas to return but that there would be little trouble if they were kept in the south where they have no influence. Hamad Agha el Mergasuri has returned within the past 10 days to the tiny village of Mergasur. There is a police post with 30 men stationed in it but nothing left of the village except three or four widely scattered houses. He expressed himself quite frankly to me as hoping for aid to the Kurds and said that he had no money with which to begin to farm. This "aid" was understood to be that which the government should give. The young Mudir Nahiaa, Faiq Aqrawi, was present and quite obviously reluctant to carry on a lengthy conversation on the subject of the Barzanis and their problems. In another conversation with him, he asked the reporting officer if he knew Awni Youssef, Erbil lawyer. (See report on this man of April 10, 1953.) The Mudir also discouraged our showing some film strips to the police and villagers in the evening. His advice to me was all in the negative whenever the subject of our film van was introduced. It is my opinion that he does not want American films or printed materials in his area. His reference to Awni Youssef is probably enough to

Destroyed Barzan Village, 1955

In the bombed-out house of the shaikhs of Barzan, Iraq, 1955

William Eagleton

Barzan Village no doubt had been burned a number of times, but it must have been completely destroyed when the Mahabad Republic collapsed.

There were those who looked back with nostalgia at the time that Mulla Mustafa was their leader, although he was in the Soviet Union and had virtually no contact with the people in northern Iraq. There were other tribes who always opposed the Barzani. I visited both sides. I made a point of visiting everybody.

I carried a camera around when I took my various trips, and as a way of repaying hospitality I took a lot of pictures and would send them to Kurdish chiefs and their families along with a note. But I was more concerned about the Barzanis than most of the others because the name Mulla Mustafa had considerable resonance at that time. Mohammed Agha Mergasur and his sons were rather sheepish about being photographed in the ruins of the Barzani houses. Nobody would presume to take the place of the shaikhs of Barzan.

Interview with William Eagleton, former American consul in Iran, by Laura Hubber, November 1995

Opposite: Memorandum, Persian Gulf Collection, Aug.–Dec. 1953, The National Security Archive, Washington, D.C.

IRAQ

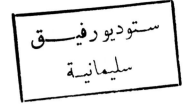

My father had continued to work as a photographer from the early 1920s until 1930. After the establishment of the Iraqi government, there were no officers in that government, so they recruited former Ottoman officers. My father worked in the Iraqi government until 1945–46. When my brother joined Barzani in the early 1940s, the Iraqi government pushed my father out of the army, and he returned to Sulaimania in 1946. [Since] his camera was still left in the shop after sixteen years, he reopened, and my sons and I are still working in that shop.

My father made all his photographs in natural light, without flash. The ceiling and sides of the studio were glass. He made curtains for the ceiling and the sides, and with a wooden stick he would move the curtain where the person was sitting, to control the light. There was no electricity, so they depended on the sun.

I was about fourteen when I started to work with my father. He thought of photography only as a job.

My father did not think that if he took a photograph it would become part of history. He didn't want to work as a political man. He ran the studio because he lived in Sulaimania. My father hated my brother's joining the political parties, working as a politician. My father thought that my brother [Muhammad Qudsi] should work for him in Sulaimania, but instead he went to participate in the Mahabad Republic. When he returned to Iraq he was one of the four officers executed.

Interview with Rafiq, living in northern Iraq, April 1993

Mahmud Efendi/Courtesy Rafiq Studio

Rafiq
Kurdish Photographer

People paid me to make photographs in the studio. But when I went outside to the villages, I made pictures for myself. —*Rafiq*

Sulaimania

Rafiq

The streets of Sulaimania

Rafiq

Each one of us [photographers] worked alone and kept our secrets to ourselves. Nobody was allowed to contact people here. I didn't meet any journalists or photographers. Maybe they came and were with the leaders, but nobody came to me to exchange ideas about photography. —Rafiq

The Monarchy Consolidates in Iran

After the fall of the Mahabad Republic, the Iranian government reestablished firm central control of its Kurdish districts and suppressed all expressions of Kurdish identity. Mohammad Reza Shah, however, was not yet a strong authoritarian ruler, as his father had been. Consequently, political life was more open and freer than it had been in the 1930s, and a wider range of political opinion was tolerated, including both conservative religious and Communist challenges to the legitimacy of Pahlavi rule.

After the experience of Russian and British occupation during the war years, there was a general desire for political and economic independence. The fact that oil, Iran's chief economic resource, was entirely controlled by British companies in exchange for ridiculously low royalties became the most prominent political issue. The National Front, a coalition of pro-democracy and nationalist forces led by the charismatic liberal politician Mohammad Mosaddeq, advocated nationalization of Iran's oil and made a strong showing in the 1950 elections. In 1951 Mosaddeq became prime minister, against the explicit wishes of the shah.

Mosaddeq initiated a series of reform measures—nationalization of Iran's oil, an agrarian reform, and efforts to curtail the shah's powers—that gained him nationwide popularity but that also caused powerful vested interests to unite against him. Although Iran paid the oil companies compensation, the oil companies refused any settlement and with American support organized a worldwide boycott of Iran's oil, causing severe economic problems. The government's agrarian reforms, though moderate, mobilized powerful landed interests as well as much of the religious establishment against it. Mosaddeq's major ally among the clergy went over to the royalist camp in disagreement with some of the reform measures. The relations between the National Front and the Communist Tudeh Party, which could mobilize large masses and could theoretically have been an ally in the confrontation with Britain, landed interests, and the monarchy, always remained cool and informed by mutual suspicion. The military, finally, resented Mosaddeq's attempts to bring it under more effective control. In August 1953, Mosaddeq's government was brought down by a military coup prepared by Britain's MI6 and the CIA; the prime minister's original supporters had become too divided to effectively rally around the government and oppose the coup. In the following years the shah succeeded in effectively establishing himself as the sole ruler, no longer challenged by the military or by civilian politicians.

During the Mosaddeq years the situation in Kurdistan was not much different from that in the rest of the country. The Iranian KDP, which was much weakened since the defeat of the Mahabad Republic, had adopted a left political position and cooperated closely with Iran's Communist Tudeh Party. During the Mosaddeq years it briefly came out into the open again and found it still could mobilize popular support, especially in Mahabad. It was not the only party with popular support among the Kurds, however. The National Front also enjoyed considerable support, especially in the southern Kurdish districts, where the Front had members of leading tribal families in its ranks. The debates on agrarian reform triggered a peasant rebellion in the Bukan area in 1952, where peasants refused to pay the landlords their traditional dues and landlords left the villages in fear. Here, too, the 1953 coup brought the restoration of the established order.

The KDP went underground after the shah's coup and briefly published a clandestine journal. In 1955 several of the top leaders were arrested and sentenced to long prison terms; most of the remaining party leadership fled abroad, to eastern Europe or Iraq. It would be more than two decades before they could return. The party organization was not entirely destroyed, however, and during the 1960s this network was used to channel food, clothes, and other support to the Kurdish guerrilla movement in Iraq.

In the following years, the shah gradually destroyed all social forces that had a power base independent of himself. Tribal chieftains and big landlords initially were co-opted and supported against peasant discontent; later a non-radical land reform completed their transformation into an urban political and business elite, cut loose from their rural and, it was hoped, their ethnic backgrounds.   —*MvB*

Izzat Luhoni in military uniform with Mohammad Amin Beg and Hussein Beg Rustam Sultan, Hawrami tribesmen invited to Tehran to discuss problems with the government, 1948

Mohammad Mokri/Courtesy Izzat Luhoni

عزّت‌شیر   محمد امین ...   شیخ سلام   ۱۳۲۷/۱ در طهران

I went to Mahabad on a hot August day. There was not a cloud in the sky and the sun beat down with fierce intensity. . . .

The streets of Mahabad were practically bare except for grinning boys, ten or twelve years old, who sold sticky, brown-colored candy the size of golf balls, round and bulging with walnuts and covered with flies. A bazaar led off the main street. . . . There were the smells of coffee, candies, roasting ears, leather, spices, lamb on skewers being broiled over charcoal. There was the noise of hammers striking metal. Deep-throated calls of the stall holders filled the compound. . . .

The lot of the average Kurd is misery. . . . He knows practically nothing about modern agriculture. Even if he did, he would not benefit from his knowledge, for most Kurds are serfs working for a khan or some other landlord on shares and perpetually in debt. Qazi Mohammed knew the power of the landowners and the political astuteness needed if real measures of reform were to be realized.

Moreover, if his program of reform were to be popular with the people, he had to remove the suspicion that it was the creature of the godless Soviet regime. . . .

And so Qazi Mohammed put his scholars to work to find in the Koran and in the teachings of the Prophet principles necessary for his reforms. What he would have done, how he would have proceeded to put through a program of reform no one can tell. We only know that his basic political approach was through the Moslem religion. So far as I could learn he had taken but one specific step under the guidance of the Koran. He had banned usury.

That alone gave him great support among the peasants. In Persia the lawful interest rate on agricultural loans is 12 percent. But . . . it is not unusual to find loans to farmers at 40 percent or more. The money lender is usually the landlord. He rents the land on shares that may leave only a fourth or a fifth or even less for the tenant. Once the tenant gets into debt to the landlord he is a perpetual serf. . . . When the landlord is a khan and the tenant a member of the tribe, more considerate terms are apt to be arranged and the tenant not so badly bled. But even legal interest is a heavy cross to impoverished people. . . .

I learned at Mahabad some of the tactics and accomplishments of Qazi Mohammed

Cemetery of Mahabad

and his Democrats. During his year of power many things had happened that stirred the Kurds.

The Kurdish costume, which had been banned by Reza Shah, came back into use. Schools were provided for every child through the sixth grade. Textbooks for the primary schools were printed in Kurdish. A newspaper, a periodical, and two literary magazines were published. A printing press had been supplied by the Soviets.

Qazi Mohammed attached to his staff two young poets—Hazhar and Hieman—who wrote not only of Kurdistan and its glories but of Stalin and the Red Army as well. . . .

There is strong evidence that although Qazi Mohammed used the Soviet power to get his republic established, he planned to develop it along democratic lines. In the latter months of his regime he was in constant touch with the American foreign service in this area, seeking American support and endeavoring to be rid of his dependency on his Soviet sponsors.

But the khans deserted him—not because of his program of reform, but because of his Soviet support. The Kurds have a long memory. . . . They remember Russian troops under the Czar murdering and plundering in Kurdistan and burning whole villages. Their memories of Russians are so poignant that in a Kurdish camp a mother will quiet a crying child by whispering, "Hush or the Russians will hear you."

I forded the river at Mahabad and started out of town to the road that leads down from Maku. . . . A young Kurd and his wife came down the shaded road. He rode a donkey; she walked proudly by his side. We exchanged greetings. . . .

"We are Kurds," he said. "We are making a pilgrimage. We come to pray at the grave of Qazi Mohammed." There was a note of defiance in his voice; and his eyes, as well as the dagger in his belt, conveyed a resolution to meet any challenge to his mission.

The grave of Qazi Mohammed is indeed a shrine; hundreds of Kurds flock there each week to worship. The hanging of this Kurdish hero killed only the man, not the idea of Kurdish independence. His death in fact gave the idea new impetus. In the eyes of the simple peasants who walk hundreds of miles to pay homage to his memory, Qazi Mohammed was a good man who gave his life that their dream might come true.

William O. Douglas, American Supreme Court justice and writer, *Strange Lands and Friendly People*, 1951

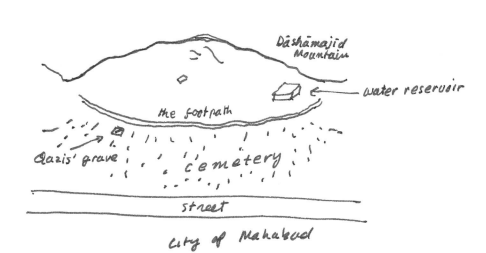

Dāshāmajīd Mountain

water reservoir

the footpath

Qazis' grave

cemetery

street

city of Mahabad

When we got ill (in my childhood), my mother would take us to the Qazis' grave in order to heal; it was a shrine and my mother told us that they were martyrs.

This probably led to the decision of the Iranian government to remove the graves of the three Qazis. They did not say, of course, that they wanted to remove the graves. They called it a "forestation" project or, in Persian, jangal-e masnou'i (artificial forest) at the foot of the mountain where the cemetery lay. Thus, they built a footpath a few meters off the graves and removed many tombstones including those of the Qazis (I do not remember the exact date but it was either in 1959 or 1960).

I took the pictures after the tombstone and bricks had been removed. When taking the pictures, I was cautious to pretend that I was photographing the landscape not the graves. Also, I did not give the film to a local photo shop. It was developed and printed in Tehran.

Pictures and handwritten note by Amir Hassanpour, Kurdish scholar living in Canada, June 1996

Mohammad Mokri
Iranian Ethnographer

When the Democratic Party of Kurdistan was founded, the Russians started intervening in matters. I was against that and I told Qazi Mohammad, "It's none of our business. You're deceived." But he was very ambitious, he and his representatives. He was in Baku and they brought back weapons. I was not happy about that. I sent a telegram to Tehran saying things were not working well. In Tabriz and Mahabad things were bad because the Russians were interfering and soon we were going to lose Azerbaijan and Kurdistan. So I immediately left for Tehran. A month after I left, Qazi declared independence. I stayed in Tehran.

After some time I became director of education for the nomads and tribes of Iran, not only for the Kurds but for all of Iran. I traveled, and took pictures of all the tribes. I went to the regions that one could go to with a Jeep. I traveled to Kurdistan by horse. I had an escort and in that way I visited all the tribes, taking ethnological notes, linguistic notes, notes on their music, their ways of living, their food, their dances, their folkloric songs, their clothing. I published part of my notes and my photographs. However, since it amounts to seven to ten volumes, I haven't yet had the means to publish it all at once. I will publish it little by little every year if I find the means.

I liked photographing things because I wanted my work to be documentary. When I invited about twenty elders from all Kurdistan to my house in Tehran, I let them sing so I was able to record ancient Kurdish music. In the evenings I would take notes, whereas during the day I would visit the people in their houses, in their rooms. I would talk to them about their occupations, to the women about their work.

Interview with Mohammad Mokri,
living in France, June 1994

Salar Zafar and his son, Mohammad Khan, of the Sanjabi tribe

Unknown/Courtesy Mohammad Mokri

"Salar, as an Iranian nationalist, fought against the czar of Russia, the British, and then the Reza Shah monarchy. In 1930 he sought refuge in Russia and disappeared after the deportations under Stalin."

"When I went to visit a tribe, they would meet me. I looked at the way the women covered their heads and wore their hair. In the houses there were no chairs, except in the house of the chief. When I asked someone to bring a chair for her, she was very honored. I didn't want her to become too tired from the sun." —Mohammad Mokri

FOREIGN SERVICE DESPATCH

US OFFICIALS ONLY (Where Indicated)

FROM : AMCONSUL, TABRIZ

DESP. NO. 42

TO : THE DEPARTMENT OF STATE, WASHINGTON.

DATE March 13, 1953

REF : Tabriz Despatch 33, February 8, 1953.

2 For Dept. Use Only m1	ACTION NEA	INFO	DEPT. EUR OLI I IFI TCA UNA
	REC'D APR 1		OTHER

RECD APR 6 1953

Economic Section
Office of Greek, Turkish
and Iranian Affairs

SUBJECT: KURDISTAN: Political Developments During February, 1953.

TABLE OF CONTENTS

SUMMARY

Agrarian unrest is beginning to strain relations between some tribal chiefs and their tenants. Belief that the U.S. is supporting Dr. Mossadegh's land reform program has resulted in some anti-American feeling which is, in turn, severely hampering Point Four operations in the area. Further reports of corruption in the Fourth Army Division have been received. Agitation for Kurdish independence is showing renewed signs of life and some tribal leaders are considering the creation of a "Komela" type separatist organization.

CURRENT POLITICAL ATTITUDES

Kurdish impatience with the Government increased during the month as chances for a settlement of Iran's political and economic difficulties seemed to grow more distant and as internal pressures rose again. Anti-American sentiment became more evident as the United States was credited with backing Dr. Mossadegh's agrarian reform programs.

It had been previously reported that some of the chiefs had shown signs of regarding Kurdish problems as dependent in part upon a settlement of the larger issues of Iranian politics.(1) However, during February, as a successful solution to any of these country-wide problems began to appear more and more remote, there was a corresponding tendency to return to the old slogans of Kurdish nationalism. This showed itself chiefly in discussions of a revival of the "Komela" separatist movement and argument over the advisability of supporting a petition to the United Nations (see below).

---

(1) Tabriz Despatch 33, February 5, 1953.

DECLASSIFIED
E.O. 11652 Sec 3.5
NARA Date 8/15/86
By cml

JDIams:wth
REPORTER

SECRET
Security Information

APR 8 1953

ACTION COPY — DEPARTMENT OF STATE

The action office must return this permanent record copy to DC/R files with an endorsement of action taken.

Peasant with a wooden plow drawn by oxen in the province of Ardelan, between the town of Sanandaj and the border of Iraq

Wolfgang Rodolph

The main mass of the land, as much as 95 per cent of it, belongs to the landlords. . . .
The distribution of the harvest between landlord and peasant . . . is determined firstly
by the nature of the soil and the crops sown there and secondly by the ownership
of the seeds and agricultural implements. . . . If the landlord has provided the
seed, he receives no less than one-half of the harvest from irrigated land, and if he
has provided both seed and implements he receives as much as two-thirds.

O. L. Vil'chevskiy, "Mukrinskiye Kurdy," summarized in *Central Asian Review*, No. 7, 1959

Once more I witnessed the defeat of the most genuine uprising of my people. If I say the most genuine, I believe that I have not made any error, because this uprising had bubbled up among the most toiling classes of Kurdistan and spontaneously. Except for one or two persons, there were, among the peasantry, no representatives of any class or strata of Kurdistan [not] even the petty bourgeoisie. In fact, a large portion of these peasants were faithful members of the Kurdish Democratic Party and devoted allies of the Tudeh Party of Iran. But unfortunately, the Kurdish Democratic Party held up too late and could not lead this genuine uprising adequately. Undoubtedly, had this uprising been led adequately, at this time when reaction [i.e., Iranian regime] was extremely weak, it [the uprising] would have been able to spread all over Kurdistan and would have become the beginning of a revolution that I think would not have taken long [to succeed]. . . .

Regretfully, this excellent opportunity and this good occasion was not utilized. Our own inexperience more than anything else delayed the revolution in Iranian Kurdistan. Other classes and strata of people in Kurdistan did not help the peasant uprising and remained idle.

Hêmen, *Tarîk û Rûn*, translated by Amir Hassanpour in "The Peasant Revolt of Mukri Kurdistan," for the Middle East Studies Association Annual Meeting, November 1989

I wanted to preserve a culture I sensed was vanishing: many dialects, customs, and traditions, many ways of living that were about to disappear. I wanted to record everything in order to keep it because I felt I had a mission, that I could serve in a scientific way before it would be gone.

I recall one time the shah told me, "If the tribes learn how to read and write they will no longer be obedient." I said, "My Majesty, it is necessary because times have changed; the people should no longer be like that." After that, my relationship with the shah changed.

When Mosaddeq returned to power I became an active supporter. We began to do away with all the illegal taxes that the landlords demanded of the peasants. We didn't want the Communists to win over the peasants. Mosaddeq signed a law abolishing all the taxes, and giving the largest percentage of the peasant's produce back to him. In all the Kurdish villages the peasants demanded these changes, and the shah supported the landowners. The center of the revolt was Bukan, near Mahabad.

Interview with Mohammad Mokri, June 1994

Behind the Iron Curtain

By the middle of the twentieth century there were significant Kurdish minorities in the Transcaucasian and Central Asian republics of the Soviet Union, and some of these communities had lived there for centuries. Many of the Kurds in Georgia, Armenia, and Azerbaijan were Yezidis whose ancestors had fled to these regions in the nineteenth century to escape from religious persecution by the Ottoman government and their Sunni Kurdish neighbors. There were also Sunni Kurds in the latter two republics, however, and in fact Kurdish tribes are known to have lived in the region since at least the sixteenth century. Further to the east, there was another Kurdish enclave in Turkmenia, part of a large group of tribes resettled in that region around 1600 to protect Iran's northeastern frontier.

In the early 1920s, one district of Soviet Azerbaijan that was predominantly inhabited by Kurds (positioned between Nagorno-Karabagh and the border of Armenia proper) briefly achieved autonomous status (it was known as "Red Kurdistan"). After a few years, however, it was fully incorporated into Azerbaijan, and the Kurds there have been subject to attempts at assimilation ever since. The numbers of Kurdish speakers recorded in official statistics rapidly declined. In Armenia, the Kurds achieved certain cultural rights; in 1930 a (party-sponsored) newspaper in Kurdish was launched in Yerevan. The paper was closed down in 1937, by which time the Kurds had become suspect in Stalin's eyes. In several waves of deportations in the 1930s and early 1940s, tens of thousands of Kurds were banished from the Transcaucasian republics to Central Asia or Siberia. The deportations hit the Kurds of Azerbaijan especially hard; Azerbaijan's party boss, Bagherov, was notoriously hostile to the Kurds in his republic. In the 1950s some but not all of the deportees were allowed to return. Today there are still considerable Kurdish communities in the Central Asian republics of Kazakhstan and Kyrgyzstan that owe their origins to the Stalinist deportations.

In early 1947 Mulla Mustafa Barzani, with five hundred faithful warriors, marched into Soviet Azerbaijan and requested asylum. From the moment the fall of the Mahabad Republic was imminent, he had made various diplomatic overtures and appealed to Iraq for amnesty, but all his efforts were in vain. Ordinary villagers were allowed to return to Iraq, but he and his closest collaborators were threatened with the death penalty. The Soviet Union was the only alternative left, and there too he was not very welcome. The Barzanis at first stayed together in Baku, Azerbaijan's capital, where their arrival had a galvanizing effect on the remaining Kurds and caused a sudden rise in ethnic awareness. This probably contributed to the Barzanis' being sent, after some time, to Tashkent in Uzbekistan and then dispersed over various republics of the Soviet Union. Many of them were given the opportunity to study, some completing university during these years of exile. Some married Russian or Uzbek women, whom they brought back to Iraqi Kurdistan when they returned in 1958.

As the effects of Stalinism were gradually receding, the Armenian Soviet Republic sponsored a moderate Kurdish cultural revival. The paper *Riya Taze* appeared again; books in Kurdish were published; and the Armenian Academy of Sciences offered courses in Kurdish studies. In the early 1960s Radio Yerevan began broadcasting programs in Kurdish, which could be received in most parts of Kurdistan. The impact of this first Kurdish radio transmission on the self-awareness of the Kurdish populations of Turkey, Iran, and Iraq can hardly be overestimated.   —MvB

Avloyev family, deported under Stalin from a Kurdish village near the Turkish border to Jalalabad, Kyrgyzstan, 1965

Demonstration of Kurds with Barzani, demanding security for the Kurds, Tashkent, Uzbekistan, 1947

The Barzanis in Russia

Barzani says: "We marched for fifty-two days. In the high mountain passes, the late spring snow was six to twelve feet deep. We fought nine encounters, lost four killed and had seven wounded. The four were buried, and the seven we took with us. . . ."

"How did the Russians receive you?" I asked. "How can I say how they received us?" he replied. "They did not receive us. But at least they did not send us back to Iraq. Every government has its laws concerning frontiers and refugees. They accepted us as refugees. They dispersed us in the country. . . .

"We were divided into groups. I went one place. Others went other places. We asked for instruction and were given teachers according to our abilities—whether as carpenters, or mechanics, or in agriculture or some other subject. Some studied geology, some science, some economics. I asked to go to the Academy of Language in Moscow and I was sent to Moscow.

البـارزانـي وعلـى يمينـه عيـسى سـوار وعلـى يسـاره سـعيد احمـد
مـوسـكـو/ ١٩٥٧

Barzani, with Said Ahmed (left) and Isa Swar (right), Moscow, 1957

Unknown/KDP Archive

Unknown/KDP Archive, Salahaddin

Barzanis training in the USSR

Unknown/Courtesy Rojhat Efe

"I spent twelve years in Russia," the General observed. "And I did not become a Communist. . . ."

From other sources I have learned that in fact only a few of the Barzanis were influenced by Communist indoctrination. . . . In talking with many of these men during my travels I gathered that they were grateful to the Russians, who had given them not only a refuge but, in many cases, their first chance to learn a trade and their first formal education. Many of them lived in towns for the first time. But most seemed to have been immunized against political indoctrination by the combination of their religious feeling, national feeling and tribal pride. . . .

Barzani himself was permitted to travel a good deal. During the summers he visited his Kurds—scattered around the Soviet Union. Those who had finished their training worked in factories, a few went on to higher institutions. A few were used in farming or as kolkhoz guards. About eighty got married, mostly to Moslem Turkoman girls, a few to Christian Russians. Some of them later adopted Islam.

Dana Adams Schmidt, *Journey Among Brave Men*, 1964

Nadir K. Nadirov
Kurdish Engineer

During the early years of Soviet rule, the state allowed the Kurdish people to experience a social, cultural, and national revival. At Lachin, the first capital of the district, the Kurdish newspaper Soviet Kurdistan *appeared. In Shusha, the second capital, the district government opened a technical school, regular radio programs appeared, and children studied in their native language. Kurdish textbooks and political and artistic literature flourished as well.*

Under Stalin, this progress came to a halt. In an official about-face, the very word "Kurd" was banned, a distinct Kurdish territory vanished, and the organized assimilation of Kurds accelerated. The census now listed Kurds under the category "other nationalities" as the Soviet government ceased to officially recognize this people.

Nadir K. Nadirov, "A Scattered People Seeks Its Nationhood," *Cultural Survival Quarterly*, Winter 1992

My father died before the [Soviet] deportation from Nakhichevan. My mother came with nine children. In 1933 they gave us a shovel and said build yourselves a home—no one even knew where we were. It was just an empty field and probably didn't have a name. There were no cars, no roads, no planes, no communication—just steppes.

One year later, they came and visited each family in the middle of the night and asked who was the head of the family. My father had already died, so my brother, Abdullah, said he was the oldest son. He was twenty-two years old and had just gotten married. I was five, and the youngest. Abdullah was taken away. My sister lived nearby and her husband was taken too. Neither of them ever returned.

Since the collapse of the Soviet Union, my sister's son has searched to find out where his father was taken. He requested information from the archive and an answer came back. He was taken to prison in 1938 and shot as an enemy of the people—an Iranian spy. He didn't even know where Iran was. He was illiterate. Though my brother disappeared that same night, my search has not turned up any information.

Interview with Nadir K. Nadirov, living in Kazakhstan, January 1996, translated by Anthony Richter

"Our family still lives in the village. The special relocation caused people for decades to fight for their physical survival, so our grandfather struggled so that our family got an education. This is who we've become: (center) Karei Nadirova, grandmother and mother of the fathers of Sadik, Anvar, and Nadir Nadirov; (counterclockwise) Rashid, president 'Pharmacia,' shareholders association of northern Kazakhstan; Zarkal, teacher; Abdullah, teacher; Azim, vice president, oil shareholding company 'Shimkent Nefteorient'; Falok, mother; Nazim, head of Urological Department of Shimkent Regional Hospital; Zarifa, director of kindergarten; Kazim, Ph.D., dean of Kazakhstan's Institute of Chemistry and Technology; and Azo, housing administrator, Shimkent," 1960s.   —Nadir K. Nadirov

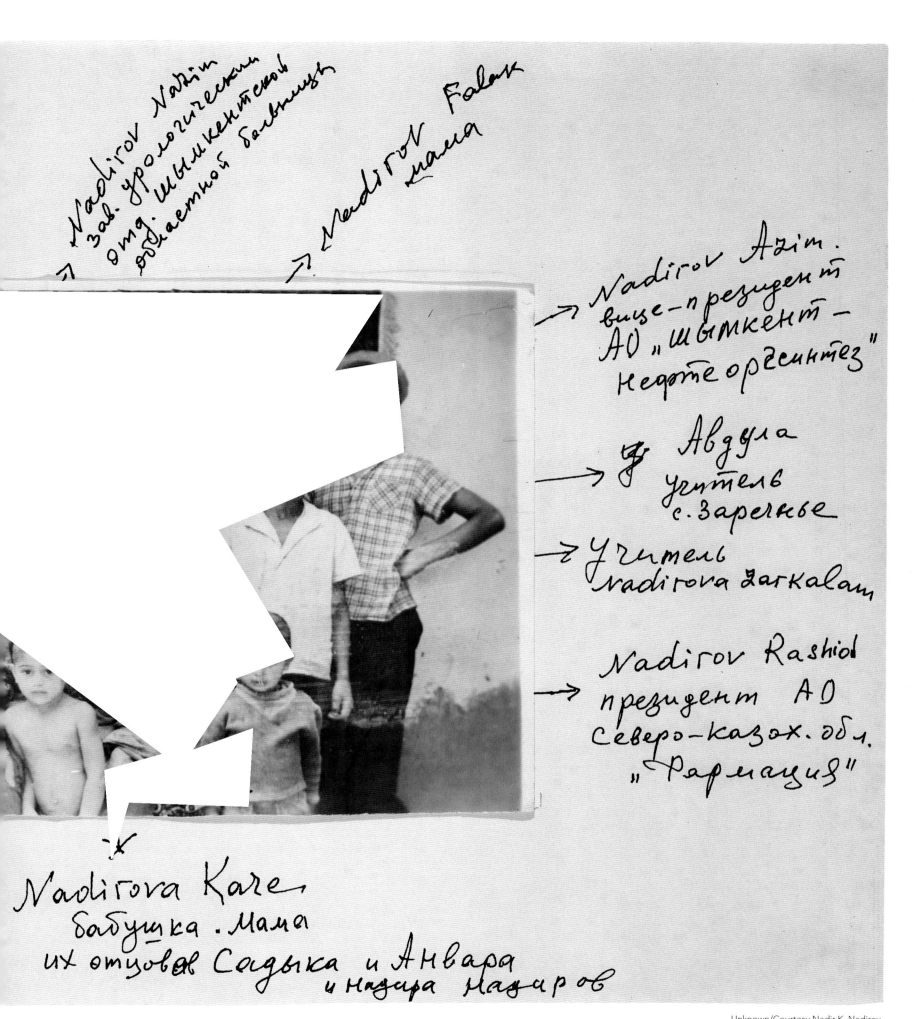

Nadirov Nadir
зав. урологическим
отд. Шымкентской
областной больницы

→ Nadirov Falak
мама

→ Nadirov Azim.
вице-президент
АО „Шымкент-
нефтеоргсинтез"

→ Ÿ Авдула
учитель
с. Заречье

→ Учитель
Nadirova Zarkalam

→ Nadirov Rashid
президент АО
северо-казах. обл.
„Фармация"

Nadirova Kare
бабушка. Мама
их отцов Садыка и Анвара
и Надира Надиров

Arabe Shamo and his eldest daughter, Vera,
Yerevan, Soviet Armenia, 1966

Unknown/
Courtesy Zina Shamilova

Arab Shamilov (Arabe Shamo)

Kurdish Novelist

My father first came to Yerevan for the Communist Party to work in the Yezidi villages. Our shaikhs were against the kolkhoz—collective farms. People had always depended on them for everything and they didn't want their role to be replaced.

My father thought that for the poor people the kolkhoz was a good idea. He opened schools, wrote books for children, began a college, and then started the newspaper Riya Taze. *At that time the Communist Party wanted the Yezidis to become part of the society, to work for socialism. My father wanted his people to become educated and make progress. They had no other road.*

In 1937, during our New Year's celebration, he was at home with his children (from his first wife) in Leningrad, and some men came and showed him their KGB documents. They began to look in his rooms, at his books, and they found a letter from Hanjan, the leader of the CP in Armenia at that time. That letter said that the Kurdish children in secondary schools had no books in their language and that he must write. It said, "You are a member of our group and if you don't write we will bring you back from the Academy."

The KGB people said that Hanjan made a group against Stalin's party and the Soviet Union and that my father was a member. They were suspicious of Hanjan because of his relationship with the dashnaks in America. My father was arrested and did not return for nineteen years. The first five years he was in Leningrad's prison in solitary confinement without a court decision. Then they sent him to Siberia. After ten years in prison, he was under house arrest and allowed to marry. Both of his daughters were from his Russian wife, Manefa.

After Stalin died he was released for rehabilitation. He decided not to go back to Leningrad, but to his people in Yerevan. When he returned he was not involved in politics, just his own writing.

Interview with Zina Shamilova, daughter of Arabe Shamo,
living in Yerevan, Armenia, July 1996

A family listens to Radio Yerevan in Soviet Armenia

Unknown/Courtesy *Riya Taze*, Yerevan

The main policy was the Russification of all other peoples. In 1955 after the death of Stalin, things began to change. Riya Taze reopened. It was really an instrument of the Armenian Communist Party but published in Kurdish. They often clearly told us that it was not a Kurdish newspaper but a paper of the Soviet Union in the Kurdish language. Everything was supplied by the Communist Party and managed by them. Most of the time that meant official articles that the Party gave us. We were not allowed to mention the word "Kurdistan." Everything we wrote we had to first submit in Russian.

Whether it was Georgia or Armenia, it was the boundary with the Western world. The Russians thought that one day these countries would be liberated. In terms of propaganda they wanted to show that everyone was equal. They used propaganda and politics to make the Kurds and Georgians believe that this was the reality.

The radio was an instrument for the foreign policy of the Soviet Union. I know a lot about this because my father was in charge of the radio and my mother was a speaker on the radio. They worked there for twenty-five years. It was very important. It permitted us to preserve our Kurdish songs.

Interview with Temure Xelil, Yezidi journalist
for *Riya Taze*, a Kurdish journal, December 1992

Head of Communist Party having talk with
collective farmers, District Alagas, Jajaris village

Martin Chahbasian/
Riya Taze, Yerevan

Yezidi dancing and singing group, District Talin, Sorik village

Unknown/Courtesy *Riya Taze*

There were no books on the Kurds in Kurdish, but there were many in Russian. Through songs and language we knew that we were different from the Armenians. On paper there was officially no difference, but in reality there were many differences because we didn't have what the Armenians had.

 With the Azerbaijanis, the Kurds were not subjected to forced assimilation. They married amongst each other, and slowly the Kurdish differences disappeared. But the Armenians were trying to assimilate us, and that pushed us to preserve our own traditions. . . . The government saw the Kurds only as shepherds, or cleaners. The papers never made references to the intellectuals or wise Kurds. Even the Kurds were slow in doing this.

Interview with Temure Xelil, Yezidi journalist for *Riya Taze*, December 1992

Collective farmers gather grapes. Instead of 216 tons originally planned for, they have contributed 300 tons. District Hoktemberian, Armavir village

1950s

Martin Chahbasian/*Riya Taze*, Yerevan

One day someone called, "Come, come, come!" And we went to hear what happened. When we got there, we saw he had turned on the radio. He was listening to it very carefully. This was the first radio in the village. Many people came together. But what was happening? It was the Kurdish language on the radio! People looked at each other and said, "Oh, there is Kurdish radio! Look, they are talking Kurdish," and so on. It was Radio Yerevan.

And then people started to listen to Radio Yerevan. Because of the Turkish state's propaganda, many people didn't believe that it was possible to write and read in the Kurdish language and to use it on the radio. Even my father asked, "How is it possible to publish in Kurdish?" I showed him an article in Kurdish and read it for him. Then he believed me.

Interview with Munzur Çem, Kurdish writer living in Sweden, September 1993

SOVIET ARMENIA

Identity Contested in Turkey

In republican Turkey, every citizen was by official definition a Turk. The original view of Turkish national identity, which was formulated by the leading thinker Ziya Gökalp (who himself was probably of Kurdish descent), did not deny the existence of various ethnic groups within the Turkish nation but gave privilege to Turkish culture over other ethnic cultures. Turkishness, in this view, was an identity of choice, and it carried connotations of modernity, progress, and pride in the achievements of the young republic. Mustafa Kemal ended his speech for the tenth anniversary of the republic with the phrase "Happy is he who calls himself a Turk!" These words have been reproduced under millions of Atatürk busts. This slogan soon acquired a darker connotation: It is perceived as an order to renounce identities other than the Turkish one. And indeed there has been little happiness since for those citizens who refused to call themselves Turks.

In the original view, whatever a person's ethnic origins, he or she (for women were also declared equal) could theoretically reach the highest positions in the Turkish state. From early on, however, the government had recourse to forced assimilation, and preferred mass deportations as an effective means of turkification. By the mid-1930s it was forbidden to even mention the words "Kurd" and "Kurdistan." Turkish identity was then no longer a matter of choice; the Kurds were taught that they were Turks even by racial origin, and they had to be referred to as "Mountain Turks." Their language (which is related to Persian) was declared a Turkish dialect with some Persian influence—but speaking it was nonetheless forbidden.

While on one hand, Kurdish ethnic identity was denied and the Kurds were declared to be of Turkish race, on the other, ethnic stereotypes and ethnic prejudice continued to exist. Kurds were frequently the targets of discrimination—which caused many to make even more strenuous efforts to adapt themselves to Turkish culture. Those Kurds who found employment in public service or who were successful entrepreneurs knew better than to put their luck at risk by flaunting their Kurdish backgrounds, and a high proportion of the Kurds who settled in cities became more or less assimilated and came to identify themselves with Turkish culture.

Kurdish identity did not entirely disappear following the suppression of the Kurdish rebellions. There remained the villages, of course, where Kurdish continued to be spoken as a matter of course. In the cities, there remained small circles of self-conscious Kurds, mostly educated members of the traditional aristocracy, who took pride in being Kurds and were concerned with Kurdish culture and with the economic welfare of their fellow Kurds and of "the East" (the current euphemism for Kurdistan in Turkey) in general. The first expressions of a Kurdish awareness, however, were only to take place when the period of high Kemalism was over.

The Turkey of the 1930s was an authoritarian one-party state under a strong leader. Atatürk's death in 1938 did not bring any significant change. His successor, the former general and prime minister Ismet İnönü, who adopted the title "National Chief," embodied more than anyone else the Kemalist state tradition. In the aftermath of World War II (in which Turkey remained neutral), Turkey, under American pressure, changed itself into a multiparty democracy. The first really free elections, in 1950, ended in an overwhelming victory for the Democratic Party, which represented a coalition of interest groups opposed to the Kemalist system. Each province elected its own deputies to parliament, which meant that there were henceforth many deputies of Kurdish origin, who to some extent spoke up for the specific interests of "the East"—though perhaps more for the interests of the landowning class. The Democratic Party regime brought rural economic development and overall economic growth (partly paid for with foreign loans), which resulted in increasing foreign influence, rising inflation, growing inequality, and disaffection among workers, civil servants, and students, conditions that were to lead to the party's fall.

A left-populist military intervention in 1960 brought a new constitution, which paradoxically opened up some freedom of expression—albeit narrowly. In the next few years, Kurdish intellectuals published a number of short-lived journals that focused on the problems of "the East" and occasionally contained a few lines in Kurdish. Although steering clear of explicit nationalism, these journals demonstrated an awareness of the Kurds as a distinct group with distinct interests, which in itself was felt to be a threat to the state. These publications were banned and their editors punished, but new publications kept appearing: a Kurdish dictionary and grammar book, an alphabet book, translations of a sixteenth-century history of the Kurds and a seventeenth-century Kurdish romance. The Turkish sociologist Ismail Beşikçi published studies of contemporary Kurdish society, the first writings in Turkey to openly mention the Kurds and to speak of national oppression.

Meanwhile, Mulla Mustafa Barzani's successful guerrilla struggle in Iraq had a great impact on the Kurds in Turkey, raising their awareness of their own Kurdishness. In 1965, a group of Kurdish notables established the clandestine Democratic Party of Turkish Kurdistan, a sister party of the Iraqi KDP. The party organized supply lines for Barzani and carried out nationalist propaganda, especially among the tribes. Toward the end of the decade it organized a number of mass meetings for "people from the East" where demands for cultural rights and economic development of "the East" were voiced. A radical breakaway section led by "Dr. Şivan" (Sait Kırmızıtoprak) by the end of the decade started preparing for guerrilla war, but its plans were stopped short when Şivan himself was killed in Iraqi Kurdistan in 1971.

Another, independent wing of the Kurdish movement was born from the left-wing politics of the 1960s. The (socialist) Workers' Party of Turkey, established in 1965 by trade union activists, found an unexpected degree of support in some of the Kurdish provinces. In a memorable resolution at its 1970 congress, the party declared that there was a Kurdish people in Turkey, that the region where most of them lived (still called "the East") was seriously underdeveloped, and that this underdevelopment was at least in part due to deliberate government neglect. It called for recognition of the Kurdish language and government efforts to develop the economy of "the East." The emergence of a Kurdish movement, however modest, was one of the chief reasons for another military intervention in 1971.   —MvB

Sait Kırmızıtoprak, one of the "49ers" and a future leader of the KDP, with his sister Fadime and brother-in-law Hıdır in Kütahya, western Turkey, 1958

Courtesy Nuri Medyali

Road to Zakho

When a permit to travel is asked for, the people in Ankara have every chance to investigate and if they feel that one is not a friend they need not give one. But when you do give it to a friend and then treat him like an enemy, you make an enemy of him. —*Freya Stark*

Freya Stark
British Traveler

It was a bad year. Iraq had just been filled with murders. . . . Demonstrations, not too fervent, but obedient, were going on [all] over Turkey. In spite of this, through the efforts of friends both Turkish and English, the authorities came to be persuaded that eccentricity and not crime was the more probable motive of my journey. A few leading questions about Kurds made it clear that I had no political axe to grind in that or any other direction; I handed in a carefully thought-out list of the places I wished to go to; and, in the course of a few days with my permit in my pocket, was flying to Van by Diyarbekr. . . .

The Vali . . . remarked that it was out of the question to take photographs, as the permit I carried expressly forbade them. . . . I explained . . . to the Vali . . . that, as I imagined the clause referred to military matters, I promised to turn my eyes away from every soldier's self, house, or equipment, and furthermore to take no pictures that could possibly do any harm to the prestige of his country abroad. "You can understand," I said, "that I have come all this way only to write a book, and a book without pictures olmaz [cannot happen]."

This is a magic word and, with its opposite olur [can be done], is as important to the Turkish traveller as ever shut and open Sesame were to Ali Baba. . . .

To the Turk it seems that when we photograph the picturesque striped garments of the hills that are still worn, we are deliberately insulting the bureaucracy and ranging ourselves on the side of what they hope may very soon disappear. . . .

The etiquette in Hakkiari is never to mention the existence of the Kurds. This is a pity, since the government's work here with schools and roads and the general progress of modern life is admirable, and it is no small task to bring security into regions that, in the whole course of their history, have never known it. Even forty years ago, it would have been impossible to travel through this country without some special friendship of the tribes; I had tried and failed twenty years ago to do so, when the Herki were going up to their summer pastures near Lake Urmiah from the foothills of Erbil; and now a man with his horse and a mule were going to take me through the very heart of the land

1958

226

The tents of Soma

with no danger at all. "We know all about the Kurds," I kept on repeating to the Vali. "We used to fight a little war with them every summer in Iraq."

In spite of such assurance . . . my attitude towards minorities in general and Kurds in particular might obviously be very easily suspected, and I put this down not to any tactlessness of my own, but to the writing of people before me. The zealous Victorians were always wondering to whom the Turkish empire was to be distributed; the fact that lots of people are now following the same line of thought with the British does nothing to soften the Turkish reaction: the word Armenia was erased from maps and school-books and even Bibles long before Turkey became a republic, and every English man or woman travelling in these far provinces is felt to be a possible champion of any of the unmentionable minorities whose continued existence is so glaringly obvious when one happens to be in their country and unable, because of their language, to make oneself understood.

The Vali, and the older and more experienced officials have learnt to become realists and to take the nomadic lives as a natural phenomenon to be slowly dissipated by the building of roads. But the young memur, ardent from the ghastly nationalisms of the school-room, still has to learn the fundamental equality of men. He spends the early years of his career in the fierce unfriendly fastness of the mountains, feeling as if wild animals were all around him, and yet heroic in his determination to do that and more for his country if the need exists. He can be compared with the young Englishman in the days of our empire sent out to look after secluded places, except for this basic difference that the English Government official nearly always liked the wilder people in his charge.

This, perhaps, I thought, as I lay at rest after lunch with the wall of rock shining beyond the tent's opening in the sun: this perhaps is the answer to the Vali's question 'what is it to be a barbarian?' Is it the not-recognizing of ways other than one's own? The essence of civilization is to respect the variety of life; and how few of us do so?

Freya Stark, *Riding to the Tigris*, 1959

TURKEY

Şahabettin Septioğlu (Agronom)

Ziya Şerefhanoğlu (Lawyer)

Sait Elçi (Accountant)

Muhsin Şavata (Businessman)

Şevket Turan (Military Officer)

"They allowed us to have a camera in jail a couple of days during a holiday and we took a lot of pictures."
—Naci Kutlay

The "49ers" in detention, Orhaniye Military Prison, Istanbul

Unknown/Courtesy Naci Kutlay

Halil Demirel (Forrest Engineer)

A. Efem Dolak (Journalist)

Naci Kutlay
Kurdish Writer

After the Shaikh Said and Dersim uprisings, it was a very oppressive period. . . . It was so bad that people could not even say that they were Kurds. Even four or five people could not come together. But after the Second World War and the beginning of the multiparty system, it was difficult for the leaders of the government to keep the Kurdish people silent. Slowly, people started to talk. . . .

In the mid-1950s, the children of the middle class began to get an education. We were humiliated in society by people calling us Kurds with tails or dirty Kurds, and so on. That pushed us to say, "Well, we are Kurds. Why can't we hear Kurdish on the radio when we can hear French and English?"

Those of us who were going to university organized some folkloric nights. We supported each other. We sang together and talked among ourselves. In the beginning, it was just like that. Nothing else.

When, at the end of the 1950s, the police started to interfere, Kurds started to organize. One of our main objectives was to develop the "Eastern cities." We would come together and speak Kurdish among ourselves—that's how the police came to easily identify us.

We were accused of trying to divide the nation of Turkey (with the support of foreign governments), and of being against its unity and for the formation of a Kurdish state.

They took us to the Ankara police station and then to a military prison in Istanbul. There were forty cells in the prison, and that's why they arrested forty people. Nine of us were not arrested, but we were tried. That's why even though forty people were arrested, they called it the trial of the Forty-niners.

Most of us were university students. A few were doctors, lawyers, educated Kurdish people. Three were workers. One cannot say that we were rightists or leftists. Our common ground was being Kurds.

After a while, it was necessary to try us, to take us to court. The trials took place in Ankara fourteen months after our arrest.

If there isn't torture, prisons are universities. My time in prison enlarged my vision, and it enlarged my world.

Interview with Naci Kutlay, living in Sweden, October 1993

This operation should be used as an argument to obtain economic aid from the U.S. The event should be represented to the American authorities as a "Communist Kurdish movement."

To the relatives of the suspects, the event should be explained as a Communist movement. So far there's no evidence that can be used against the suspects, but with an unexpected raid some evidence may be obtained.

Excerpts of two reports submitted to the Ministry of Interior Affairs, July 31, 1959, summarized in the verdict of the chief of staff military court, dated May 3, 1968
Naci Kutlay, *49'lar dosyasil (The File of the 49)*, 1994

In this book, which I have called The History of Varto and the Eastern Provinces, I shall first of all explain how the Mountain Turk tribes living in our eastern provinces have come to be called "Kurds." I shall relate the situation of our eastern provinces before the Christian era, and the history and real racial origins of these Mountain Turks. I shall explain how and under what sort of pressure these people later brought about the Kurmanji and Zaza languages, how they have lost or damaged their original Turkish language, and how several centuries ago they started thinking of themselves as a different community from the Turks. I shall discuss the evil results of Ottoman policies, feudalism, and the establishment of the Hamidiya regiments. I shall describe the Constitutional period, the First World War, the struggles and other events in the east [of Turkey], and the rebellion of Shaikh Said. . . .

The one and only ideal that motivated me to write this book was [the desire to liberate] these common Turkish and Turkoman tribespeople and these peasant villagers—who in reality are of Turkish blood and of pure Turkish stock—[from] the suffering of speaking these half-baked Kurmanji and Zaza languages. Although all of the Mountain Turks nowadays know that they are of Turkish race, their languages are full of Persian, Arabic, Armenian, and Aramaic words and have thus become unintelligible. These people have not been able to rid themselves of these confused and meaningless languages.

In this work I shall make efforts to enlighten the thought of these compatriots and racial brothers of mine and to offer them much information on their real race and language. . . .

It is the national duty of these brothers of ours, the Mountain Turks, to walk on the path toward national unity and integrity that was opened up by the Great Atatürk, by the National Chief Inönü and the National Republic [of Turkey]. This duty commands us to follow the true path, that of love of the Republic and the fatherland, and to protect national unity and integrity. We are Turks; we shall speak Turkish. For the defense of the Turkish Republic and the Turkish fatherland, we shall plow the land in the plains, and in the mountains fight like maned lions against those who attack our fatherland. We shall live as victors or die as martyrs.

M. Şerif Fırat, The History of Varto and the Eastern Provinces, Institute of Research on Turkish Culture, 1961, translated by Martin van Bruinessen

M. Şerif Fırat

DOĞU İLLERİ VE VARTO TARİHİ

(ETİMOLOJİ · DİN · ETNOGRAFYA · DİL VE ERMENİ MEZALİMİ)

(BEŞİNCİ BASKI)

TÜRK KÜLTÜRÜNÜ ARAŞTIRMA ENSTİTÜSÜ

Cover of The History of Varto and the Eastern Provinces (Etymology, Religion Ethnography, Language and Armenian Atrocities), 5th edition, ca. 1982

The towns in the east are both the doors and the fortresses of our country. If we lose control of the towns in the east, it will not be easy to maintain our position in western Anatolia.

General Gürsel's preface, Doğu Illeri ve Varto Tarihi, 1961

Muzaffer Ilhan Erdost
Turkish Writer and Publisher

I was in the mobile gendarme troop in Şemdinli as a veterinarian. One of the people told me that, without knowing the tribes, I could not understand what happened there. And I asked, "What is the tribe? How can I learn about it?"

I received an invitation from Ahmed Beg, the chief of the tribe, who invited me to have food with him. At first I didn't want to go because I was a populist. I wanted to be with the poor people, not with an agha. But after a while I went. They offered me a meal. I had guards with me, so I asked the agha to give the same food to my guards. He said, "They have their food. Don't interfere." When you go there, if you don't go to the home of the chief of the tribe, you insult him.

I was in Şemdinli at a time of freedom. But even so, I have many examples of the pain those people had. The source of that pain was not only pressure but poverty. People always took part in the uprisings and wars in the region, and they lost their people in those fights. The women could not speak any Turkish and could not read and write. They were very politicized because of their lives.

When I went there, I saw the poverty and the wealth of the people. I felt very warm toward those people in the mountains. "The brotherhood of the Kurds and the Turks" is not a meaningless phrase.

When you go there and ask the people who participated in the uprisings or were witnesses, at first they don't say anything. After a while, they get to know you, and at the same time they ask people whether they should talk to you or not. I stayed there about a year, and after a year, they started to talk to me. After that, I could photograph them.

Interview with Muzaffer Ilhan Erdost, living in Turkey, October 1993

Coming back from hunting baby wild goat in the Narkole Mountains

The Work Is Divided, Women Reproduce

The lineage is carried by the son, not the daughter. It lives by the son's using the rifle and continuing the family in his name. And the woman is either bought or sold. . . .

In the grazing highlands a woman must milk the sheep, process the milk, collect grass, make dried dung for the winter, look after the children, cook, and things like this. However, at the same time the people depend on the land. In the village they have fields of rice, tobacco, and wheat. They seed, water, and work on it so the pigs will not get in their fields. They mow, make bundles, grind, blend, and mix. Who will do this? The man can do these things too. But the man has other things to do. Things like knitting, weaving, plowing the fields, and building the walls. It is most important to get the necessities of the house ready for winter before the roads are obstructed. He will sell his products, carry flour, salt, prepare his gas, oil, sugar, tea. He has social duties. He has weddings and funerals. He has problems, but by coming together the men talk about their problems. If necessary, he'll defend the honor of the community. He'll spend his life on roads that are days away from the town. When he comes back home, he needs somebody who will cook, look after him.

Muzaffer Ilhan Erdost, *Şemdinli Röportaji*, 1993

The bride just before her wedding in the village of Bususin

Muzaffer Ilhan Erdost

*A girl is a child until she's eleven. After this age she becomes a bride
and goes away. She produces children. At a young age she gets tired and
turns into an implement producing income. She wants another
woman to come and take care of everything or to share the weight of
the grazing, the field, the herd, and the house—to lessen her burden.*
  —Muzaffer Ilhan Erdost

Ismail Beşikçi
Turkish Sociologist

My professors told me not to get involved in the Kurdish question because it was dangerous. At the same time they suggested that I read Şerif Fırat's book, The History of Varto and the Eastern Provinces, *which was published to prove that there were no Kurds. I went to the library and tried to learn about the Kurds but all the sources repeated the same thing: Kurds do not exist. The Kurdish language does not exist.*

When I finished my degree, I entered the military service and went to Bitlis province in April 1963. What I first saw in Bitlis were nomadic tribes. A very large group was going to the mountains, to the Mount Nimrod plains. In those days, the state wanted the nomads to stay in their homes, and all this disturbed the nomadic life.

I developed a close relationship with the nomads and villagers and made some observations about the nomads. I asked: What is the religion like in their society? Where do they stop and what do they do when they pass through villages, and what is their relationship with the villagers?

In the spring, there was a struggle between Barzani and the Arabs [in the Iraqi government], and they moved my detachment from Bitlis to Hakkarı province to protect the border. The border divided a village. Part of the village was in Turkey and part was in Iraq. I knew the villagers were crossing the border and getting their supplies from Iraqi Kurdistan, not from Hakkarı. The state rationed salt, flour, and gasoline because they thought that if they gave more, the Kurds would help the struggle in southern Kurdistan. Sometimes I heard villagers say, "We don't have much sugar and tea, but we can find a way to send part of it."

Traveling people carried information; radios in Turkey did not. In Turkey there was no acknowledgment that Kurds lived in other countries, like Iran and Iraq. The villagers around the Hakkarı border knew about the struggle in Iraqi Kurdistan, but the other Kurds in Turkey were not conscious of Kurds living in other countries. There was no public awareness.

I went to Atatürk University as an assistant, and my first work at the university was about the nomads. The university put a great deal of pressure on the people who worked on the Kurdish issue. It was almost forbidden. In 1967, we published some articles in different magazines using the word "Kurds." Then two students and I tried to do fieldwork about smugglers in the border villages. We had to walk from Cizre to Şırnak because the mayor threatened the people if they gave us a car. When we went to the villages, the authorities followed us. After we passed out questionnaires, these questionnaires were stolen from our hotel room. That trip was the first time I faced intense pressure from the government.

In 1971, after the coup, I was arrested and taken to Diyarbakır for trial. It was during those trials that the Kurdish question started to be discussed in greater detail. The prosecutors in Diyarbakır tried to prove that there were no Kurds, and we tried to prove that there were Kurds. I think the Diyarbakır courts were very important in the development of Kurdish consciousness. The state unwillingly provided that opportunity. Prosecutors claimed: There are no Kurds. But one could see that during the trials there were translators. One had to explain that.

Interview with Ismail Beşikçi, living in Turkey, May 1993

"The tent is an essential unit of nomads' housing needs. Nomadic Beritan tribes' tents are made with black goat hair and on average weigh over two hundred pounds. For winter settlements nomads look for a landscape in which they can graze animals. The size of one's herd of sheep is a sign of wealth for nomadic people."
—Ismail Beşikçi

232

The nomadic Alikan tribe starts moving into the highlands towards the end of April. The journey takes place in two stages. At first stage the shepherds move with their herds, at the second stage the people move with their belongings. Everything is loaded on the backs of mules. The belongings of a family of 8–9 people can be carried by 8–10 mules. People usually walk, except the elders and the sick sheep. Newborn lambs are carried by women and children. —Ismail Beşikçi

In this nomadic community boys occupy a higher status in the patriarchal family and there are many instances of masculine authority. Girls are not permitted to have their meals with their fathers. They may eat only left-overs of the males. The nomadic family has nothing like a "family meal." Whoever gets hungry takes some bread and cheese, and eats them in some corner. A meal is served only for the males and their guests. Children and women never join them. Women sit down only after the men have finished eating. Women eat men's left-overs.

Daughters have no inheritance rights. A married daughter may claim absolutely no inheritance. Older brothers are duty-bound to care for their sisters until marriage. Sons inherit the horses, mules, sheep, goats, weapons, trinkets, etc. This not only reinforces male authority within the family, but also prevents outsiders from coming into any property. The father may, while he is still living, distribute his property among his sons. . . . Since daughters have no hereditary rights, they are not entitled to have a trousseau purchased with the "head-price," that is to say, the money paid for the bride by her future husband's family. The bride's father pockets this money. In rare circumstances, a daughter may be given a horse, sheep, or something else as she leaves for her husband's home, but the use of any of these is decided by the husband. . . .

In large nomadic families, the father's authority is supreme. Everyone treats him with the highest respect. Although there may be differing or opposing views about marriage and the sale of the daughters, the father has the final word.

Ismail Beşikçi, *Doguda Degişim ve Yapisal Sorunlar (Social Change and Structural Problems in the East),* 1969

TURKEY

Mehmed Emin Bozarslan

Kurdish Writer

I decided as a Kurdish person and as a Kurdish writer to challenge the undemocratic and inhumane policy of the Turkish state and publish this book. I wrote and published it in 1968 in Istanbul. With the help of my friends I distributed it throughout Kurdistan, Istanbul, and Ankara. It was banned immediately.

When I went to Diyarbakır, they arrested me.

They took me to trial, and the court asked me, "Why did you write this?" I said, "This language is a live language and people are speaking this language, and as a person in this area, I wanted to help people learn to read and write." *But he sent me to prison, and on the paper he signed, he wrote that my crime was to try to divide Turkey. He wrote that I tried to divide Turkey through this book, which is only sixty-four pages. I was in prison for four months. Then they released me, but* Alfabe *was still banned. The trial continued for six years, until 1974.*

This book continues to be banned in Turkey. It was the first Kurdish alphabet book in Latin letters in northern Kurdistan, and it is the only alphabet book in the world that is banned.

Interview with Mehmed Emin Bozarslan, living in Sweden, October 1993

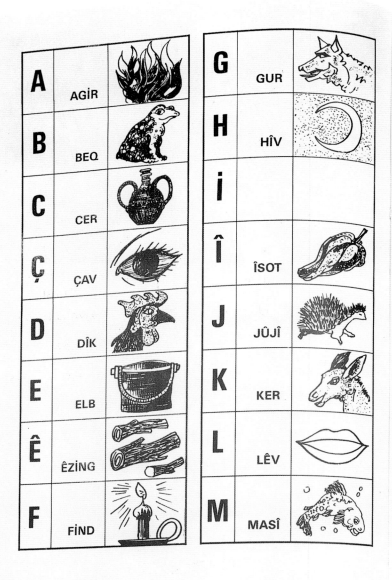

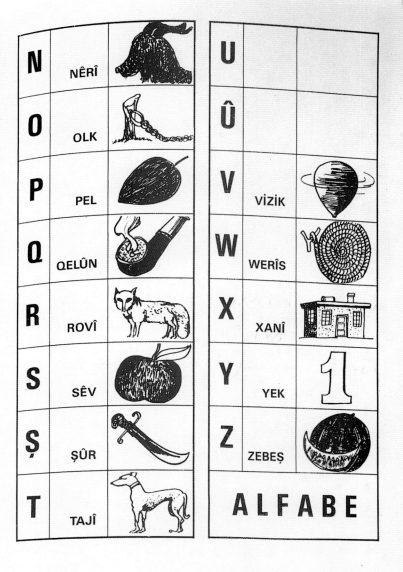

Pages from Alfabe *by Mehmed Emin Bozarslan*

a

Freedom is very good.
Our flag waves.
The earth is revived with water.
The leaves catch fire.
The mill grinds grain.
The water in the vessel is cold.

Azadî gelek xweş e.

Alaya me pêl dide.

Ax bi avê vedijî.

Agir bi pûş ket.

Aş tene dihêre.

Ava cêr sar e.

The earth is generous
Our earth is very generous.
It gives us wheat, it gives us bread.
I give it manure, I give it water.
It gives me work, it gives me bread.

Translated by Martin van Bruinessen

Ax merd e

Axa min gelek merd e.

Genim dide min, nan dide min.

Ez zibil didim'ê, av didim'ê.

Ew ked dide min, dan dide min.

Shepherds, opposite a teahouse, near Erzincan, 1976

The Lycée of Diyarbakır

In the first week that I went to the lycée (in 1976) I got rid of my necktie and adapted myself to the dress style that was in vogue then; henceforth I was a lycée student dressed in a parka coat, boots with laces, a fisher's pullover, and linen trousers. There were only teachers for three of our classes. The students in school were divided into two camps: leftist and lumpen. In our view everyone who was not committed to a political movement was a lumpen proletarian. Seventy percent of the students of our school were sympathizers of specific political organizations. . . .

One day after leaving school I went with my friend Ömer, a classmate from lower secondary, to the DHKD (Revolutionary People's Cultural Association, a left-wing Kurdish club). It was the first time for me but Ömer had gone there a few times before. . . .

It was a stormy period at the Diyarbakır lycée. There was no teaching anymore. Around us arms were fired, there were marches and demonstrations and other actions, and everyone rapidly chose his political affiliation. The organizations that in that period found a broad following among youth in the universities and lycées were democratic mass organizations (i.e., legal associations representing clandestine Kurdish parties). . . .

By the last months of my second year in the lycée I became a proper member of the Revolutionary People's Cultural Association. . . . I had not reached the legal age for membership, so when I signed up I wrote a higher age on the membership form. . . . The first things we learned upon becoming members of the association were the fundamentals of the political movement of which we had become part. If we did not sufficiently understand the meaning of these principles, we learned them by heart. . . . The efforts to raise my political awareness mostly concerned the ideas of other (Kurdish and left) organizations and the fine points that distinguished our own association from the others. . . . Time and again discussions among the young revolved around questions that we were not equipped to debate because we lacked the necessary acquaintance with political theory: "Must Kurds and Turks militate in common organizations or in separate formations?", "Are the dominant relations of production in Kurdistan semi-feudal or capitalist?", "Must the Kurds (of Turkey, Iran, Iraq, and Syria) have a joint centralized structure or a separate political organization for each of the four parts?" . . .

One day (in 1978) when I was selling the (Kurdish) newspaper Roja Welat *in a café, three plainclothes policemen grabbed me by my arm when I walked out the door. Kicking and beating me, they took me to the central police office. I told them that a man whom I did not know had given me the newspapers to sell and that I was not aware that the paper was banned. After I had promised never again to sell the paper, they let me free the next day.*

In that same period we were given the task of shouting slogans at a meeting where (Turkish social democrat leader) Bülent Ecevit spoke. Positioning ourselves within the crowd, we loudly shouted, as a compact, enthusiastic group, "Freedom to the peoples." Ecevit's response then was severe: He called the guards and showed them where we stood. We dispersed ourselves among the crowd. Ecevit then interrupted his speech and turned to the crowd with the words, "There are no peoples in Turkey but one people; there is only the Turkish people!"

Yılmaz Odabaşı, *Bir Kürdün Eylül defterleri (A Kurd's September Notebooks)*, 1991, translated by Martin van Bruinessen

"Life at that time was hard and basic. Amenities were virtually nonexistent— rough winters and no luxuries. Tourists were seldom visiting during that period, and in some places we were the first foreigners the locals had seen. While they sometimes looked at us as if we'd stepped out of a rocket from Mars, we received extraordinary hospitality, and people always made us stay for dinner and preferably overnight." —Ad van Denderen

Ad van Denderen

TURKEY

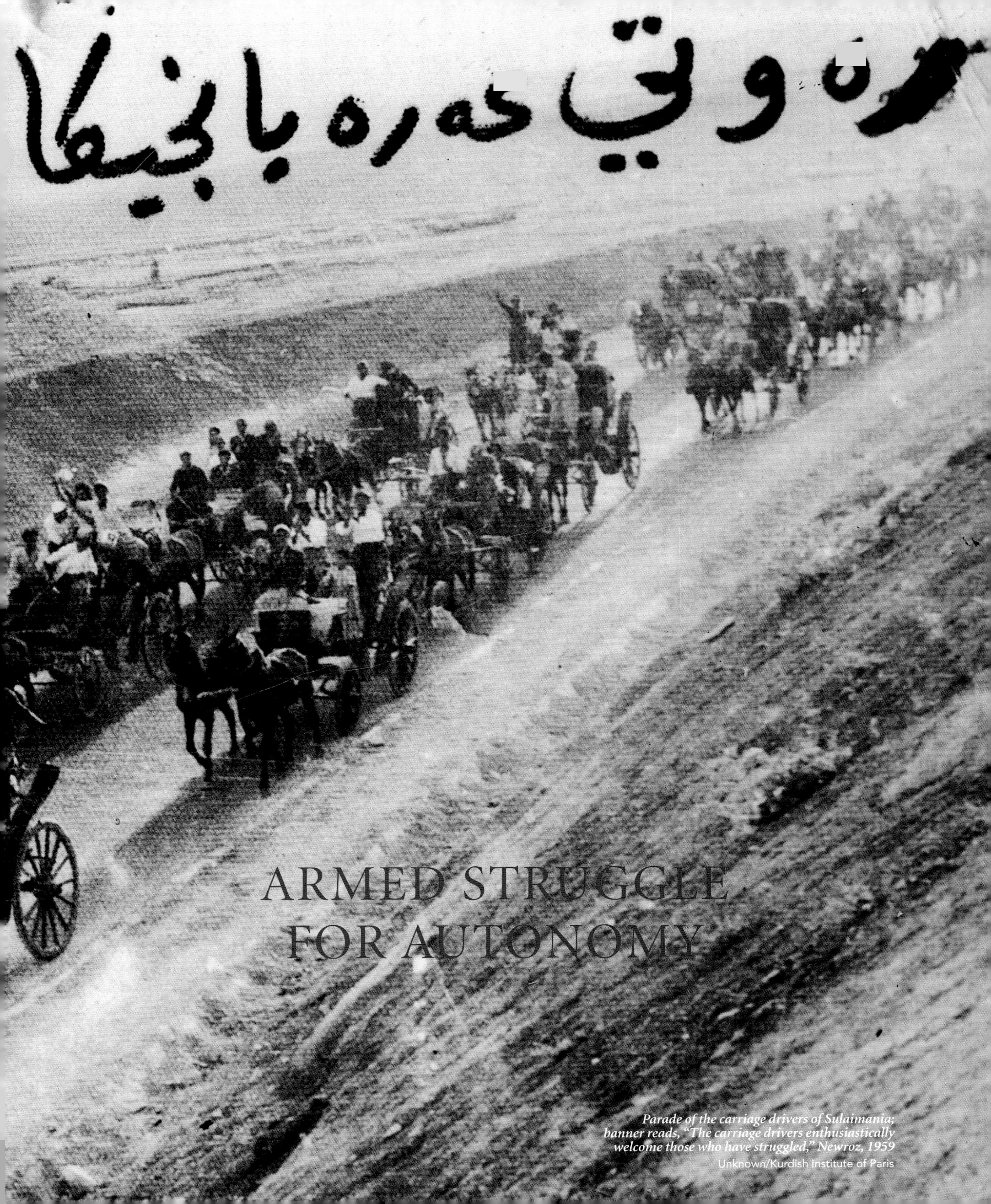

ونقی کادره یانیڤکا

ARMED STRUGGLE
FOR AUTONOMY

*Parade of the carriage drivers of Sulaimania;
banner reads, "The carriage drivers enthusiastically
welcome those who have struggled," Newroz, 1959*

The Republic of Iraq

A military coup by left-wing officers in 1958 overthrew the Iraqi monarchy and established a republic. The coup leader, Colonel Abdul Karim Qassem, promised the Kurds cultural and political rights and invited Mulla Mustafa Barzani to return to the country. Barzani's arrival greatly raised the Kurds' nationalist expectations. It also created a rift within the Kurdish movement, however, since both the KDP politburo, led by Ibrahim Ahmed, and Barzani himself, formally the KDP president, considered themselves the party's rightful leaders.

The relationship between Qassem and Barzani deteriorated as the latter developed a strong independent power base in the north of the country. By 1961, the first armed clashes between Kurds and government troops took place. Almost a decade of intermittent guerrilla war followed, in the course of which a series of Arab nationalist governments in Baghdad first made promises to the Kurds, then resumed the war and, weakened by the conflict, were brought down by the next regime.

Qassem was overthrown in early 1963 and succeeded by an (Arab nationalist) Baath Party government, which entered into negotiations with the Kurds on autonomy. This regime was unwilling to make concessions to the Kurds on the status of oil-rich Kirkuk, and the negotiations soon reached a stalemate. Hostilities resumed with a government operation in Sulaimania, in which numerous suspected peshmerga, Kurdish guerrilla fighters, were summarily killed. The army occupied large parts of Kurdistan, but before the year was over the Baath regime was also overthrown, and the cycle of negotiations, stalemate, and war, with the new strongman Abdussalam Arif, started all over again.

In this period the conflict between Barzani and the KDP politburo came to a head. Barzani negotiated a separate settlement with Arif, and Ibrahim Ahmed's politburo severely criticized Barzani's actions. Barzani then organized a party congress packed with his own delegates and had a handpicked new politburo chosen. His troops soon converged on the Ibrahim Ahmed group and virtually pushed them over the Iranian border. Ibrahim Ahmed was well received in Tehran, which perceived the Kurds as useful potential allies against Baghdad. Upon reaching a new settlement with Barzani, Ahmed returned to Iraqi Kurdistan. Tehran soon opted for Barzani as the more promising ally. Becoming marginalized, the Ibrahim Ahmed group sought accommodation with Baghdad and by 1966 was fighting Barzani alongside government troops.

Following yet another coup d'état in 1968, the Baath Party returned to power. Protracted negotiations with Barzani's Kurds led to a 1970 peace accord that promised the Kurds a significant degree of autonomy as well as participation in the central government. During the four years of preparation for autonomy, however, Baghdad reneged on several promises; Kurds were deported from the oil-producing Kirkuk and Khanaqin districts so that these would remain outside the autonomous region; and there were attempts on Barzani's life. Baghdad, on the other hand, and not without justification, accused the Kurds of plotting with its worst enemies: Iran, Israel, and America.

The Baath Party's ideology was a mixture of Arab nationalism and what they called socialism ("statism" is perhaps a better term). The party elite, who considered Iraq an integral part of the larger Arab nation, were not inclined to relinquish control of part of their territory—especially because they felt threatened by Barzani's ally, the shah. In the early 1970s, the British dismantled their navy presence in the Persian Gulf, which until then had protected the oil shipping lines. Iran in late 1971 filled the power vacuum by occupying three small islands controlling access to the Gulf (which Iraq insisted on calling the Arab Gulf). This happened at a moment when Iraq's relations with the West were approaching a new low over its granting the Soviet Union an oil concession and its ultimate nationalization of the (British-, Dutch-, and French-controlled) Iraqi Petroleum Company in 1972. Iraq, moreover, signed a friendship treaty with the Soviet Union in 1971, and the Baath leadership in 1972 invited the Iraqi Communist Party to take part in a government coalition.

These developments strengthened the bond between Iran and Barzani. The shah had not been the only neighbor to support the Iraqi Kurds in order to weaken the Baghdad government. Israel had also been providing arms and military training since the mid-1960s. By 1972 the United States also became directly involved. Barzani met Henry Kissinger in Tehran, and the CIA organized covert support for Barzani's Kurds on an unprecedented scale. Iran remained the go-between, however.

In March 1974, the Iraqi government proclaimed autonomy for the Kurdish region. Both the extent of the autonomous region and the degree of autonomy, as well as the share offered the Kurds in the central administration, fell far behind what the 1970 peace agreement had promised. Barzani scornfully rejected the government offer, and within days the war was resumed. Apparently, U.S. officials persuaded Barzani to go to war rather than make concessions to the Baghdad regime. For a year, the Kurds brought a vast part of northern Iraq under their control as "liberated territories," where they operated their own government, modeled on that of the Iraqi state.

Within a year, however, the shah and Iraq's strongman, Saddam Hussein, concluded an agreement by which Iran gave up its support of the Kurds in exchange for border concessions. Having become completely dependent on outside support, Barzani gave up the struggle and with his followers took refuge in Iran. The number of Iraqi Kurdish refugees in Iran, mostly peshmerga and their dependents, but also ordinary peasant families, rose well above the fifty-thousand mark. Barzani himself was very ill and went to the United States for medical treatment. His sons, Mas'ud and Idris, reorganized the party from their residence near Tehran, and by the end of the decade a small number of KDP peshmerga was again maintaining a token presence in northern Iraq near the Turkish border, apparently with Iranian connivance. A rival Kurdish party founded and led by Jalal Talabani, which had no Iranian basis but a liaison office in Damascus, carried on guerrilla activity from headquarters inside Iraq near Sulaimania.

—MvB

No. 52 - A Typical Kurd, Iraq

At the invitation of Abdul Karim Qassem, Mulla Mustafa Barzani returns from USSR to meet in Baghdad, October 7, 1958

Unknown/Courtesy Rafiq Studio

In Baghdad both Premier Kassem and the Communist Party laid claim to Barzani. Both wished to exploit the popularity which was reflected in the large and noisy reception he was given by the Kurdish community in Baghdad. . . . The Communists talked as though the twelve years in Russia had made Barzani a Communist. . . .

Barzani, who had no faith in Kassem and disliked the Communists, had to play a delicate political game. As long as Kassem showed any signs of carrying out the promises to treat the Kurds as partners, and as long as the Communists were tacit partners in Kassem's regime, he had to play along with both. Political statements he made during this period are full of praise for Kassem and gratitude to the Soviet Union for the hospitality it had shown his Kurds. In public he avoided ideological questions but in private he made no secret of his opposition to Communism. . . .

The Communists meanwhile tried to infiltrate the Kurdish Democratic Party and found that the hard core of anti-Communism within the KDP was Barzani.

Dana Adams Schmidt, *Journey Among Brave Men*, 1964

Russian boat carrying five hundred Barzani men [exiled after the Mahabad Republic] and their Russian wives, arriving in Basra from Odessa, Iraq, early 1959

Unknown/Courtesy the Rowanduzi family

Far-Off Red Flame

Red radio transmitters in Yerevan, Soviet Armenia, now beam four Kurdish-language broadcasts a week across the Caucasus Mountains, inciting their listeners against "those who for years have sucked the blood of the Kurds." In shaky Iraq, where Kurds make up nearly a quarter of the population, Soviet agitators preach the age-old dream of a unified, independent Kurdish nation: the great Kirkuk oil fields, they say, "will be your capital." An underground Kurdish "liberation movement" is at work.

In Iraq, Iran, Syria, and Turkey, where the proud Kurds form strong and dangerous minorities, Moscow's siren song has found a receptive audience. . . . Thanks to Soviet agitation since World War II, the pressure for an "independent" Kurdistan threatens to set the Middle East ablaze once more.

The signal for the Soviets' intensive new campaign was the return to Iraq last month, after fifteen years' exile in the U.S.S.R., of the legendary Mulla Mustafa Barzani, 60, fighting hero of the Kurdish Barzani tribe. . . .

Mustafa immediately set up shop in a Baghdad hotel room, telling all who would listen that "mass struggle" was needed to unify the Kurdish state. He gave praise to "our great and brave leader, Abdul Karim el-Kassem," but he also demanded expropriation of Western interests in the "Kurdish" oil fields—something el-Kassem had pointedly refused to do. Political insiders say he will soon move north to rally his followers.

The British predict that when this happens there will be a serious outbreak of trouble among the Kurdish workmen in the Kirkuk and Mosul oil fields (which supply one-sixth of Western Europe's oil). . . .

In seeking Kurdish support, Iraq's Premier el-Kassem is being pulled more and more to the left and has been forced to give important government posts to Soviet sympathizers. Radio Baghdad increasingly hews to the Moscow line.

What is Russia's real objective? The Kurdish nationalist movement, in a sense, runs counter to the Pan-Arab plans of Russia's other Mideast pawn, United Arab Republic President Gamal Abdel Nasser. But the Soviets' primary goal is to keep the whole area in continuous turmoil. Nothing could better serve this purpose than chronic unrest among the warlike Kurds.

Eldon Griffiths, "Far-Off Red Flame," *Newsweek*, November 10, 1958

Illustration by Clyde Magill, *Newsweek*, November 10, 1958

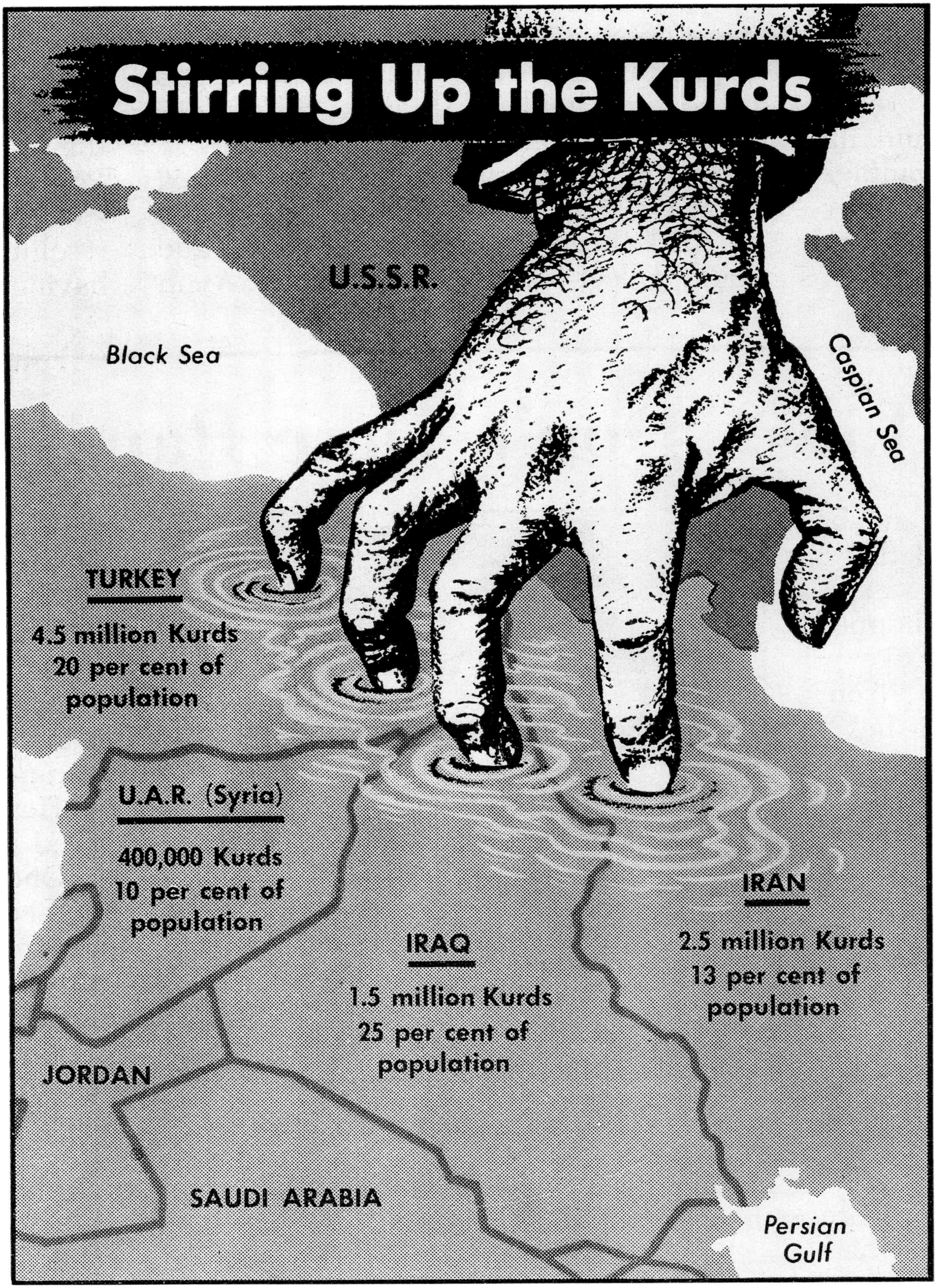

Stirring Up the Kurds

U.S.S.R.

Black Sea

Caspian Sea

TURKEY

4.5 million Kurds
20 per cent of
population

U.A.R. (Syria)

400,000 Kurds
10 per cent of
population

IRAQ

1.5 million Kurds
25 per cent of
population

IRAN

2.5 million Kurds
13 per cent of
population

JORDAN

SAUDI ARABIA

Persian
Gulf

Hajek Muhammed with his wife, Valentina

Family of Hajek Muhammed in Iraq   Unknown/Courtesy Hajek Muhammed

Hajek Muhammed
Kurdish Fighter

I was fourteen when I decided to become a peshmerga. We were extremely poor in Iraq. There were no hospitals or schools. If a relative was sick, I would spend days on a donkey looking for a doctor. We also wanted to defend ourselves. My father joined the peshmerga with me, but not my younger brother. We went to Iran and joined forces with Qazi Mohammad. We expected the Mahabad Republic to expand to all of Kurdistan. We didn't think the Russians would betray us. Our choices were to stay in Iran and surrender, go to Iraq to fight or surrender, or go to Turkey and be executed. We decided to accompany Barzani to the Soviet Union. Food was so scarce we wanted to kill a donkey and eat it. The Jalalis, an Iranian tribe, gave us bread and dried yogurt cakes. We crossed the Aras and went to Nakhichevan. We left most of our guns on the Iranian side and swam across the Aras. The Russians greeted Barzani well. We were given food and put up outside the city of Nakhichevan. My father stayed behind in Iran. I did not see him again until 1958.

My wife was a graduate of the technical institute. Six other Russian girls married Kurds. We stayed in Baku for a year, then moved to Uzbekistan. Then I went to Georgia alone to study to be an engineer.

In 1958, Mir Haj, one of Barzani's officers, gathered all the Russian women and told them, "We are going back." I told my wife, "I have nothing, no house. If you want to come, please do." We returned to Jameh, near Shirvan. My wife didn't know what to do in a Kurdish village.

Interview with Hajek Muhammed, Iraqi Kurd living in Iran, by Andrew Whitley, September 1991

1959

Zirar and Zoya Sulaiman Beg with their children

Zirar Sulaiman Beg and Zoya Ismailova
Kurdish Fighter and his Russian Wife

Zirar: When I was on the ship returning to Iraq, I told my father, who was the head of the tribe of the area, I want two things. First, I don't want anybody to ask my wife to dress in such-and-such a way. It's up to her. And the second thing is that I don't want my daughters to be married according to Kurdish tradition, where the father can offer his daughter to anybody.

For four months Zoya spoke no Kurdish. Then she began to learn.

I am ashamed that some of my friends, when they reached here, remarried. I had a lot of respect for my wife, because she was a stranger coming to our land.

I was sure I would come back to Kurdistan one day. I studied at a Russian secondary school, and I told the principal on the first day that I was a political refugee and that one day I would go back to my country.

Zoya: When I first saw the village, I said, "What is this?" Zirar's brother said, "This is the village where you are going to live." I thought, What have I done with myself? There was no road. They brought mules, but I didn't know how to ride, so I walked. At that time it was shameful to dress in a skirt, but my husband didn't tell me to change clothes. I had high-heeled shoes, and it was not easy to walk. There was no electricity. There were cows in the front of the house, and I was afraid. Zirar's sister passed by the cows twice so that I would not be afraid.

Maybe I looked at them as savages at the beginning. And they looked at me as a savage because we were so different. Maybe it was because I didn't wear a Kurdish dress. But, after a while, people came to respect me because I had graduated from the medical institute in Russia and I brought a lot of medicine with me, and I was like a doctor for the village. I taught the girls how to sew, how to be clean, and I became a teacher.

Interview with Zirar and Zoya Sulaiman, living in northern Iraq, October 1992

Zoya with relatives, 1959   Unknown/Courtesy Zirar and Zoya Sulaiman Beg

Kurdish Rebels Confident of Victory in Ir

Dana Adams Schmidt
American Journalist

In the spring and early summer of 1961 a series of delegations representing both the tribes and the Kurdish Democratic Party appeared in Baghdad to protest that the regime, far from having carried out its promises, was oppressing the Kurds in many ways. . . .

The Kurdish leaders complained that the government promise to recognize Kurdish as an official language in government offices in Kurdish districts had never been fully put into effect. Although the constitution assured them of their right to use their own language, not all Kurdish primary-school children and only a few in secondary schools could get education in the Kurdish language. . . .

A related complaint was that the Kurdish newspapers and magazines had been suppressed . . . [and] special Kurdish-language broadcasts on Baghdad radio had been cut down. . . .

In Kurdish areas signposts designating names of streets had been put up in the Arabic language in place of older signposts in Kurdish. . . . The Kurdish districts had not received their fair share of government revenues. Industrial and agricultural investments had been diverted from the Kurdish areas. . . .The Iraqi-Soviet technical assistance treaty included building radio and television stations all over Iraq, but very few in Kurdistan. . . .

Finally—Premier Kassem refused to receive the Kurdish delegations and ordered the staff of the Ministry of Defense not to receive petitions from the Kurds. Even post-office personnel were ordered not to accept letters addressed to the government.

Dana Adams Schmidt,
Journey Among Brave Men, 1964

1962

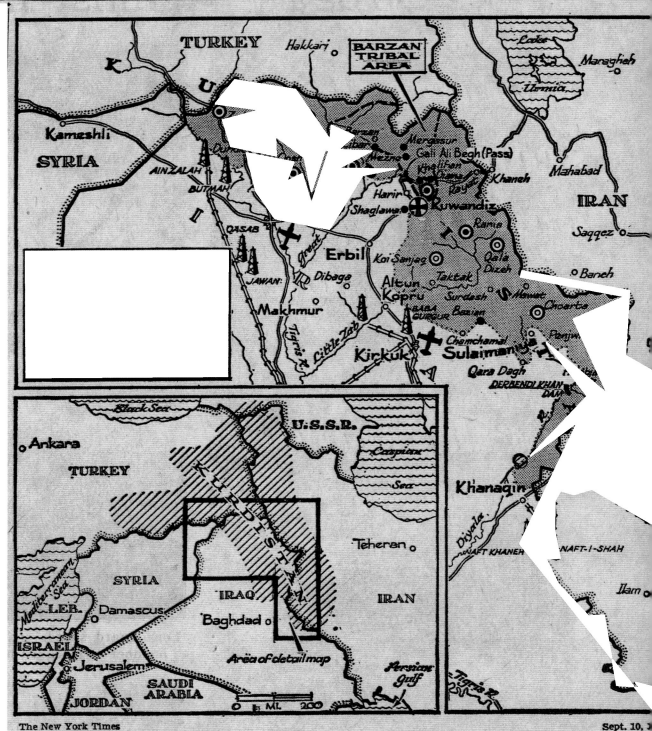

The New York Times   Sept. 10,
GUERRILLA STRONGHOLD: Kurdish rebels fighting to establish an autonomo
state of Kurdistan in Iraq control much of the northern part of the country. They are
ported to have 12,000 Iraqi troops surrounded in villages in the Rawandiz area (cross
The Kurds inhabit area overlapping four nations (diagonal shading on inset ma

In time of war you will need us. Look at our strategic location on the flank of any possible Soviet advance into the Middle East through the Caucasus and remember that, whether as guerrillas or as regulars, we are the best soldiers in the Middle East.

—General Mulla Mustafa Barzani

Kurdish Rebels Confident of Victory in Iraq

This is the first of four articles by correspondent Dana Adams Schmidt of
The New York Times, *who spent several weeks in the Kurdish-held area of Iraq.*

Kurds' Headquarters, Somewhere in Northern Iraq
It took forty-two days to reach the ever-moving headquarters of
Mullah Mustafa. Thirty-two days were spent riding mules and horses
or scrambling up and down trails too steep for riding. Several days
were passed waiting in a hideout for fighting to subside.

The 59-year-old general, who often has been in revolt, has for the
last year been leading the greatest Kurdish rebellion of modern
times.... Mullah Mustafa, grave in demeanor, hard and lean, coupled
his appeals for aid with warnings. If the Americans do not find a way
to help the Kurds, he said, the consequences could be "nefarious."...

"The danger is that we will be obliged by necessity to accept aid
from the Communists."...

Hospitality for the visiting American knew no limits. Goats,
chickens and lambs were slaughtered to supplement the basic diet of
rice, yoghurt and skimmed fermented milk. He was given the best
bedding, and even mosquito nets....

How the trip into Iraqi Kurdistan was carried out must remain
secret.... None of the surrounding countries would give permission
to enter the rebel territory nor would any other country help....

Visitor Supplied With Kurdish Garb
The correspondent was supplied with Kurdish clothing, including baggy
pants, a "pish" to be wrapped around the waist, and a red-and-white-
checkered turban. This was a security precaution to avoid detection.

The New York Times, September 10, 1962

*"In some areas Kurdish life is now confined to caves, where the
guerrillas set up headquarters."* —Dana Adams Schmidt

Kurdish Rebel Chief Says Force Is Only Way to Win Autonomy

This is the second of four articles.

Kurds' Headquarters, Somewhere in Northern Iraq
Between studying reports, issuing orders and interviewing commanders, Mullah Mustafa conversed at length over luncheons spread on
the ground, under the stars on the mountainside or in the light of an
oil lamp in the garden of a mosque in a newly captured village....

While the goal of the rebellion is autonomy for the Kurdish people,
Mullah Mustafa said that he was also fighting to overthrow Premier
Kassim. Until he accomplishes that, he said, Kurdish autonomy will
remain unattainable....

One danger he mentioned was that the Communists, who are
strong in Baghdad, might with Soviet support seize control of the
Government if Premier Kassim fell. He made this an argument for
strengthening the Kurds with American aid.

Rebellion Shows Mark on General
The rebel leader moves his headquarters daily. He never sleeps in the
same place twice. This is part of the elaborate precautions taken for
his safety. The appearance of the general has changed considerably
since an interview in December 1959. In contrast with his look of
self-confidence then, he now seemed grave, as though weighed down
by a sense of responsibility for the uprising he leads.

The New York Times, September 11, 1962

Kurdish guerrillas baking bread   Dana Adams Schmidt/Courtesy Tania Schmidt

IRAQ

A refugee winnowing wheat in the Guli Valley

The strength of the Kurdish women lies in the simplicity, vigor and healthfulness of their daily lives. . . . The household of the Kurdish woman is much like that of early American settlers. —Dana Adams Schmidt

A refugee woman weaving a cloth of mixed goat's and sheep's wool

Dana Adams Schmidt/Courtesy Tania Schmidt

Kurds' Guerrilla Tradition Aids Rebels in War on Iraqi Army

This is the third of four articles.

Guerilla fighting comes naturally to the Kurds. . . . Logistic problems are kept at a minimum. The army has some supplies—sugar, tea, grain and rice—tucked away in caves scattered across the country. Peasants are supposed to put aside 10 per cent of their produce for the rebel army. The army has the beginnings of an arsenal in caves where rifles and other weapons captured from the Iraqi Army are stored. . . .

In dress these soldiers do not differ from Kurds not in the rebels' service. They wear no uniform, insignia or badges of rank. . . .

The Kurdish man customarily sports a mustache since Kurds think it unmanly to shave the upper lip. Beards are frowned upon among the rebels because Mullah Mustafa is said to associate beards with conservative, and often pro-Government, religious leaders.

The New York Times, September 12, 1962

Kurdish Villages Suffer in Revolt
Women Bear Brunt of Iraqi Air War on Rebellion

This is the last of four articles.

A key question in the Kurdish rebellion against Iraqi rule may be: "How long can the Kurdish women and children stand the bombing?"

The Iraqi Government's most effective weapon against the Kurds has been the air force. The women and children in the Kurdish villages bear the brunt of the aerial attack much more than do the men scattered in guerrilla units on the mountainsides. . . .

The number of casualties was not as high as might have been expected, however. Many of the villagers take to the relative safety of the mountains and caves before sunup and do not return until after sunset. . . . The trip into Kurdistan provided first-hand experience of the Iraqi air attacks. The party had stopped in the village of Bindar when that village was attacked by three Iraqi planes—two Soviet-made MIG's and a British-built Fury. . . .

Eight other villages in nearby valleys were bombed that day, apparently because the Iraqi command guessed that Mullah Mustafa might be coming that way. . . .

Questions about how long the women and children can bear up under such attacks elicit defiant answers from the women. "Five, ten, fifty years," they declare. . . .

There are times when the usually stoic Kurdish women break down. Near the village of Halan, three women in black ran toward the visitors. One uttered a high-pitched sound as though she were beginning a song, then lapsed into a wail. She knelt beside the path, her head bobbing convulsively. . . .

To live in a cave represents no unacceptable hardship. The change merely makes life more uncomfortable. . . . Looking after children and animals is only the beginning of her duties. She milks cows and goats, makes milk into yoghurt, extracts fat for butter and makes the remainder into a drink called doh. She bakes flat bread in an oven in the ground heated by firewood. She spins wool and weaves cloth and makes most of the family's clothes. She keeps her family clean and healthy and herself attractive.

Her clothes are of many colors—perhaps a purple cloak and yellow shirt with a green skirt and a flowered sash plus some jewelry and a large red-and-gold hat. She dresses that way all day every day, as though forever ready for a ball.

The New York Times, September 13, 1962

1962

General Barzani during negotiations with Iraqi prime minister Tahir Yahya, Rania, 1963

Rafiq

Barzani always maintained what I regard as an aristocratic reserve. He might joke with a visitor but he never became intimate and, so far as I could discover, had no intimate associates. The men around him changed constantly so that no one could claim to have the master's ear or to influence him exclusively. There was no "right hand" man, no "ever present aide." His practice of constantly changing the circle of men around him, like his practice of moving from place to place, was probably partly security precaution and partly his political technique for maintaining contact with the widest possible number of his people, building his political fences with many individuals and many tribes. . . . He lacked the kind of experience and education that would have enabled him to analyze questions in a manner a Westerner would regard as logical. But at the same time he had a highly developed political intuition that enabled him often to penetrate to the heart and final conclusion of a matter while others were still immersed in the details.

Always his movements were secret. Although we were presumably quite closely attached to him we would awaken day after day to find that Barzani had "disappeared" during the night, moved on to some new camping place, the exact location of which was known only to a few intimates such as the men in his personal guard and those responsible for his personal welfare. . . .

I turned from the question of aid to the role of the Kurdish

Democratic Party. "What was its part in the struggle?" I asked. The question seemed to agitate him somewhat. We were sitting with at least twenty-five men gathered around within earshot. "Well," he replied, "what it can do it does." And then he raised his voice for all to hear: "But according to me, there is no party, only the Kurdish people. Those who will win will be the Kurdish people."

Behind this somewhat enigmatic remark lay a long, involved and painful relationship between Barzani and the KDP. Although he is president of the party and of its central committee, Barzani has little use for the generally leftist urban intellectuals who predominate in the party leadership. He contends that the presidency of the party was "forced upon me," without ever explaining who did the forcing. Nor do the party leaders have much use for the tribal chiefs, with their feudalistic attitudes and prerogatives, who surround Barzani. . . .

Barzani maintained that the revolution in Iraq was unique, that it had no relationship to any other part of Kurdistan in Turkey or Iran. . . . "Do you not think in terms of a greater Kurdistan?" I asked. He replied that all his efforts now were devoted to winning autonomy for the Iraqi part of Kurdistan. "This idea of a greater Kurdistan," he said, "I do not even dream about it. Without the consent of the United States and Britain such a thing is chimerical."

Dana Adams Schmidt, *Journey Among Brave Men*, 1964

Ibrahim Ahmed with peshmerga during conference of the KDP, April 1, 1964
L-R: Omar Dababa, Kaka Ziad, Ibrahim Ahmed, Ali Askeri, Jalal Talabani

Eric Rouleau

French Journalist

Iraqi Kurdistan on the Back of a Mule

If General Barzani is the head of the insurrection, the Kurdish Democratic Party is its soul; 75 percent of the resistance are members of the party; most of the other fighters are "sympathizers." All the command positions within the revolutionary army are in the hands of the "professionals" of the KDP, whose organization covers the whole country like a tight net.

"El parti," as its members refer to it with affection, centralizes the funds of the rebellion; mobilizes the masses in a real and figurative sense to intensify the war effort; and publishes the paper *Khabat (The Struggle)*, which it distributes publicly in liberated regions and clandestinely in the south of Iraq. It makes sure that food provisions are maintained for populations faced with blockades from Baghdad; maintains an intelligence service; and heads a terrorist operation in the cities charged with the execution of "traitors," as well as with sabotage missions.

A team of five men—members of the political bureau—supervise all its activities. Four of them fill various other military or adminis-

trative functions, whereas the fifth one concentrates on party matters. This is Ibrahim Ahmed, secretary general of the KDP.

Surrounded by more than a hundred partisans, Mr. Ahmed lives in a strange cave, dug into a rock surface, nestled between two high mountains. To get there one has to cross several streams, take a winding track, show one's credentials to well-hidden watchmen who surge out unexpectedly, at the bend of a road.

The small entrance of the cave is only visible from about ten meters. However, the refuge from the inside seems vast despite numerous boxes containing food supplies, weapons, and clothes that are stored there. . . .

The master of the house has been able to re-create an almost normal atmosphere within the large isolated cavity that he has transformed into a lodging. He has papered the walls with maps and multicolored magazines. Near his bed, two radios enable him to maintain contact with the outside world, and a tape recorder allows him to play the music of his choice. An avid reader, Mr. Ibrahim Ahmed is surrounded by books, two of which are placed at his bedside,

Peshmerga bringing supplies to Mawat

Rafiq

a collection of poems by the Persian poet Hafiz and Harrison Salisbury's masterpiece *Khrushchev's Mein Kampf.* His readings are eclectic. They range from Shakespeare to Bertrand Russell and from Dostoyevsky to Boris Pasternak, from Marx and Lenin to Harold Lasky. Mr. Ahmed prides himself on having read everything published in the Kurdish language in the last forty-four years (a total of around five hundred books, he specifies).

In his physical appearance the secretary general of the KDP also stands out from the rugged mountaineers who surround him. A fifty-year-old man, he is short and frail. His grey temples and his thin white moustache make him look distinguished. He speaks eloquently, in a clear harmonious voice not without the passion reflected in his intelligent eyes. One could imagine him very comfortable in an ancient Roman law court satisfied to give free rein to an inexhaustible spirit and enthusiasm. . . .

Mr. Ahmed insists on the fact that the "KDP has no intention of promoting anti-Communism" and that only political and tactical differences separate it from the Communist Party. The latter has for some time backed the national Kurdish claims. . . .

The major worry of certain leaders of the KDP is the future of their relationship with General Mullah Mustafa Barzani, whom they suspect of favoring the aghas. Among other things, he is reproached for his conviction that he alone "represents" the Kurdish people.

Those who have been able to converse with both General Barzani and Ibrahim Ahmed have noted the deep antipathy that separates the two men, whose social backgrounds, upbringing, and personalities are entirely opposite. Both will avoid conflict as long as the insurrection is not definitively over. It is feared that the return of peace in Kurdistan will only mark the beginning of another political conflict, this one within the nationalist movement. General Barzani has immense prestige in the country. The KDP also exerts a strong influence on the masses. A divorce between the party and its president would risk opening a dangerous era of instability.

Eric Rouleau, *Le Monde*, April 14, 1963, translated by Alexis Broben

Photographer's stamp reads "Photo Rafiq, Sulaimania"

Peshmerga sewing uniforms in the mountains, Mawat

Peshmerga packing up Tajan village

1960s

252

Crossing the river

My father told me not to go to the mountains, but I was young, so I went. It was 1961. In the mountains, with the peshmerga, I was taking photographs for history. Most of the pictures I took were portraits, and groups of peshmerga.

I couldn't take pictures of movement. If you have a movie camera or a video camera, you can go into the fighting, you can take all the movement, but with my camera I couldn't.

I stayed there until the end of 1963, the beginning of 1964, when Talabani and his followers retreated. I didn't want to be a refugee in Iran, so I said, "Mam Jalal, you are going to be refugees. I am not going with you." I put down my gun and came back to Sulaimania.

When I decided to come back and the peshmerga went on to Iran, I thought it would be safer if they took the negatives with them to Iran, because the government was very strict at the time. Unfortunately, the negatives were lost when they crossed the border.

I developed these four rolls of film when I came back, but I didn't make prints then, because if the Baathists saw them, they would have killed me.

Interview with Rafiq, living in northern Iraq, April 1993

Mule carrying Rafiq's traveling photographic studio

IRAQ

Margaret George
Kurdish Christian Fighter
Photographs by Zaher Rashid, Kurdish Photographer

I knew Margaret very well, and whenever she came to Qala Diza, she visited the studio because she loved photographs. She always liked to have new ones. A lot of people came and asked for photographs of Margaret, especially the Kurds of Iran. Margaret has been famous since the sixties, and her photograph is everywhere. The peshmerga in the mountains keep photographs of Margaret.

Margaret liked people to buy photographs so they knew she was a peshmerga. That way, other women would go to the mountains like her. But they didn't go, because they were Muslims. Muslims do not allow women to go out without the family. Margaret was allowed because she was a Christian and she was with her father, brother, and sister.

Barzani held the Sixth Congress of the KDP in Qala Diza. I took all the photographs. Unfortunately, none of these negatives remain. In 1963, the people of Qala Diza had to go to the mountains, so the materials and the studio were lost. During the bombardment of Qala Diza on April 24, 1974, my shop was attacked by a plane. One of my sons was killed, and I was seriously injured. I lost part of the shop and most of my negatives.

Interview with Zaher Rashid, living in northern Iraq, May 1993

Picture of Margaret George carried in Karim Zand's wallet

Margaret George in Kurdish dress with her sister

Margaret George with her father

Zaher Rashid

Margaret George

Zaher Rashid

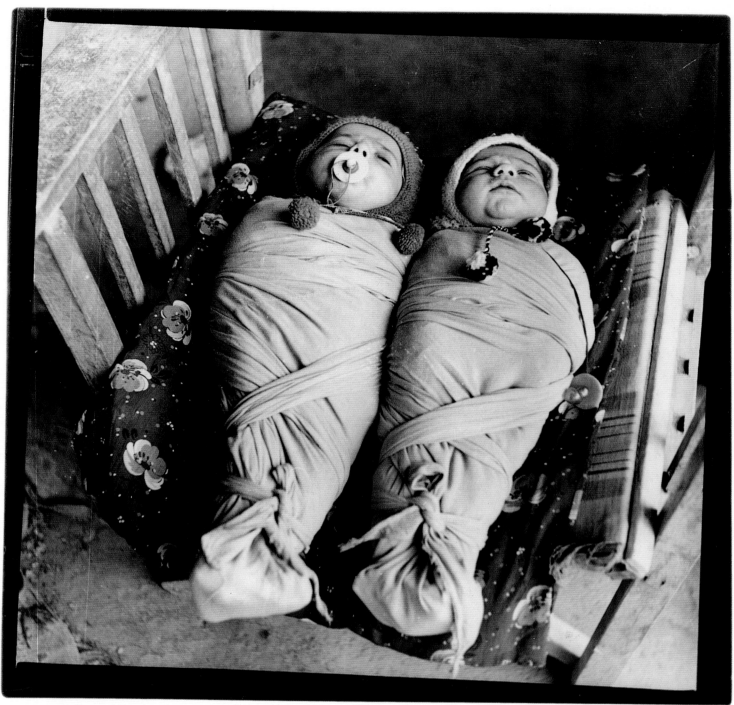

Infants swaddled in cradle, Rania

Jabar Abdulkarim Amin
Kurdish Photographer

The Iraqi police monitored shops selling three kinds of things—cassettes, photographs, and books. No one was allowed to sell a photograph or take a photograph that showed the tragedy of the Kurdish people. For example, a photographer in Sulaimania took a photograph of a poor baby with torn clothes and sold it as a postcard. The photographer was arrested for selling this photograph.

The government brought all the photographers to the secret police station of Sulaimania and ordered them to hand over all of their old negatives. We were called twice or three times a year, and they had very strict rules.

I never actually took photographs of the fighting in the mountains, but when the peshmerga took pictures they would send them to me

and I would develop them. You cannot imagine how difficult life was here. We were developing the negatives for the peshmerga in the mountains at the same time that we were being watched.

In 1962, my cousin was imprisoned for ten days for carrying a photograph. In 1963, when I came to Rania, I gathered the most important photographs of the Kurdish leaders, about seventy of them, and put them in a ceramic pot and hid them outside. But when they built the road there, the photographs disappeared. I had another group inside the house, but as the Iraqi police were searching house to house, I was afraid that they would come and find the photographs with me, so I burned them.

Interview with Jabar Abdulkarim Amin, living in northern Iraq, May 1993

1960s

Father

Jabar Abdulkarim Amin

Most of the photographs that are left are portraits taken for official documents, such as passports, and family photographs. After the exodus I stopped taking photos. I didn't have any money, and there was no work to do. Now, I no longer have my shop. —Jabar Abdulkarim Amin

Mamosta Ghafoor Amin Abdullah
Kurdish Teacher

At about midnight of June 19, 1963, the people of Sulaimania heard over loudspeakers, "No one goes out, on pain of death." They did not know who it was. Tanks and armored personnel carriers manned by the security police and military authorities appeared all over the city; small bridges going out of the city were destroyed to prevent anyone from escaping.

Most people were not informed. They went to their ordinary jobs in the morning. They were captured and executed on the way to work. They [the army] brought trucks and started capturing men from thirteen, fourteen to age seventy.

They took thirty thousand people captive. They did not take women. They captured many teachers and storeowners and students.

Four teachers [I was friends with] were executed. At first no one realized that men had been executed at the base. This was discovered [November 1963] after the fall of the Baath government when an old Kurdish man who baked bread for the Iraqi army came and told the townspeople about a mass grave near the base. The four teachers were in this pit. The soldiers put stones around the grave to mark it.

I took a Kodak camera and shot twenty negatives or photos, black

Site of exhumation of Ismael Ibrahim, outside Sulaimania

Mamosta Ghafoor Amin Abdullah

and white. There were ten photos on each roll. All the relatives of these people and other Sulaimania citizens went to the exhumation.

Yassin Mohammed was recognized because he had a gap between his two front teeth, which were slightly turned out. They found in his pocket a white silk handkerchief, which was used to give sweets to brides. Some of his friends had given it to him the night before he was captured. It was amazing: the body decayed but the handkerchief was not destroyed, not much changed.

There was one blindfold on one skull but not on the others. You couldn't tell if the hands were tied.

The second body to come up was Ismael Ibrahim, whose body appears on a pallet, decayed. They knew it was he because he had keys and a key chain that his wife recognized.

The third to be exhumed was Anwar Dartash. He was recognized by his shoes because the tops of the shoes were white.

The fourth to come up from the grave was Hamabour Mohammed Haj Saleh. His father is in a jamadani, standing straight, his son on a pallet, decayed, his head at his father's feet. His father said, "I have no photo of me with my son, so please take our picture together."

Interview with Mamosta Ghafoor Amin Abdullah, living in northern Iraq,
by Jemera Rone, Middle East Watch, August 13, 1992

Landscape near the Barzani headquarters

Chaim Levakov
Israeli Intelligence Officer

In April or May 1965, I was asked to go on a mission. I requested something to read to know where I was going: how are the people—what's the political problem? I found only one big book, Journey Among Brave Men, by Dana Adams Schmidt. But it was journalistic.

Yavne'el, the colony where I was born, is near Tiberias, and in Tiberias there is a community of Kurdish Jews.

A friend of mine makes roads in Tiberias, and he told me, "Twelve o'clock we stop the machines and we sit down to eat lunch. An old woman in Kurdish clothes and two little girls came to us with a tray with glasses and gave tea to all the people. Then at three o'clock she came with watermelon. Every day she did that. I didn't know who she was, and she didn't know who I was. When I finished my work, I wondered, What can I give these people? I stopped an old man and said, 'Tell me, you are wearing Kurdish clothes. What is your name?'

"'My name is David—Daoud Gabai,' he said.

"'What should I bring you? Your wife makes us wonderful things.'

"And he asked me, 'Are you a farmer?'

"He wanted wheat, so I brought them 120 kilograms of wheat, and they used stones to grind it and made a big festival."

I took my friend and formally presented myself to the biggest man in the Kurdish community, who turned out to be the same Daoud Gabai. I presented myself as a student and a journalist. I started to ask him questions about Kurdistan. What does the area look like? How do our hills and their hills compare? And Daoud started to tell me about his family and that his father was a friend of Mulla Mustafa Barzani's father. Barzani's brother, Shaikh Abdul Salam, was in prison, sentenced to be hanged. Daoud's father took a bag of gold and went to Sultan Abdulhamid to ask for Mulla Mustafa's brother's life, and Abdulhamid gave him an order to release Mulla Mustafa's brother. He came back to Barzan, but he was too late—two days earlier they had hung Mulla Mustafa's brother. Mulla Mustafa was then three or four years old.

Daoud used to be the richest man in northern Iraq. He had lived in Aqra, and all the villagers would come to him to get the money to

Chaim Levakov

make tobacco. And then when they sold the tobacco they would give him back the money.

I took a picture of Daoud with me when I went to Barzan in Kurdistan. I'll never forget the moment when Mulla Mustafa, who's like a lion, looked at the picture and kissed it. Then I knew that I had the man.

I felt myself going back three thousand years to the time of the Bible. All the poor men, everyone who had troubles, especially personal trouble, or family trouble, came to the big man to ask for help, like King Solomon. Every day, they had a bag of rice and everyone came through with a goat or a sheep. They ate there, they slept there, and waited until the day when they could see Mulla Mustafa Barzani. He was carrying the trouble of his nation. He knew everyone.

He didn't need maps, intelligence, information. He had a big brown radio. One Kurd walked behind him with the radio and he asked for Egypt, Iraq—he heard the news from all the stations on the radio.

But I think we gave him a window to the world. He wanted to send a note or a question or something to his men—they had people in Paris, people in Sweden, people in London—but they did not have a way to communicate with them. So they used our connections for communicating with their people.

When we were sitting or walking and he saw one of us with a camera in hand, he fixed his clothes, took a rifle, and was ready for a photograph. I asked him why he loved that. He told me, "Listen, I have never in my life gone to a photographer. All the photographers have come to me." So he had to do his best to help them.

I took panoramas, for strategic purposes. Once I brought back pictures with hills and water, and one of the boys saw it and said, "Very bad, very bad," because there was nobody in the picture.

What made me think like a Kurd was when we brought them guns that we had gotten from the Six Day War. Most of them were Egyptian submachine guns, which are good for attack. One old man asked why there was so much ammunition. One bullet in the head was enough. From that moment I started to think like the Kurdish people.

Interview with Chaim Levakov, living in Israel, May 1994

Just before the Six Day War, some Jews in Israel began taking an interest in Barzani. They wanted to help Barzani. But Mulla Mustafa refused to speak with any delegation from Israel unless he received a letter from our family, the Gabais, who had moved from Kurdistan to Israel in 1950. He demanded a photograph of Uncle David (Daoud) or a letter.

After Jerusalem was liberated, the government invited Mulla Mustafa to speak. He arrived in secret and asked to meet with David Gabai. It was April 17, 1968, and they met in a country club somewhere. My brother Zion remembers how Mulla Mustafa walked across the long hall until he reached David and how they cried to see each other again.

In Kurdistan, we had streams of people coming to visit us every day—Muslims, clerks, everyone.

In our city, Aqra, and in Mosul, conditions were excellent for Jews. The Jews and the Kurds identified with one another. They both had enemies, "sonim"— literally "haters"—nations that hate them. The Jews did not have a state and neither did the Kurds. We emigrated to Israel because we were Zionists, not at all because of what was going on in Kurdistan.

David was told that if he went to Israel, he would regret it. "Here you are like kings. There you will be like servants. Here you have lamb to eat; there you will barely have eggs. They will put you in the desert. . . ." When we finally left, they wept—the Muslims wept!

In Israel, it was difficult to adjust to poverty. Most of all I miss the respect our family had in Kurdistan. We have none of that here—the honor, the society, the trust, the honesty.

Interview with Magid Gabai,
Kurdish Jew living in Israel, May 1994

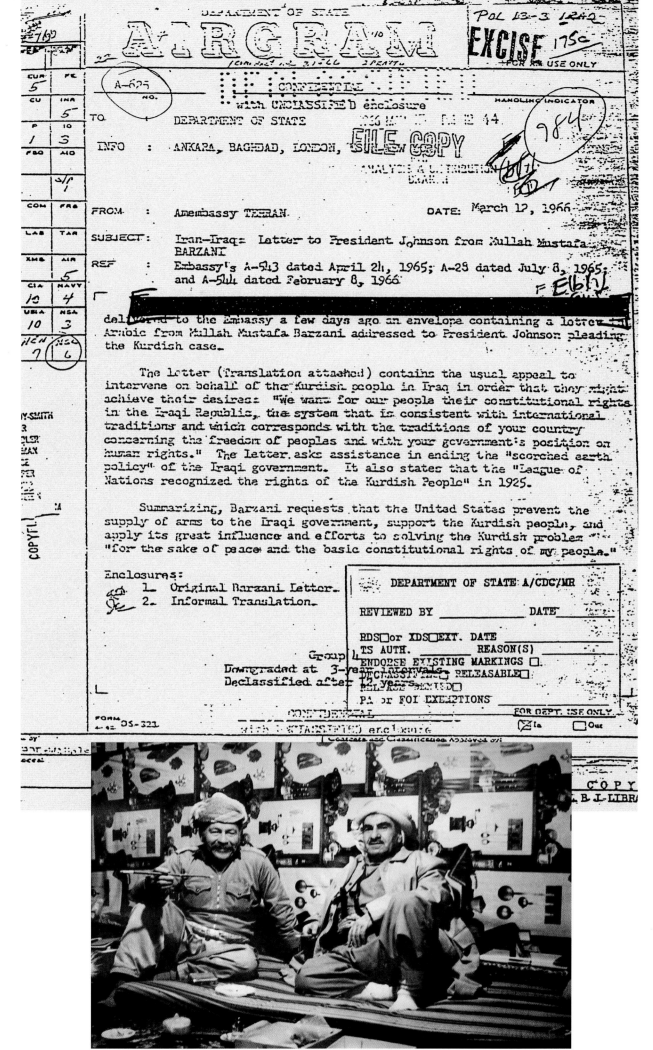

Chaim Levakov with Mulla Mustafa Barzani   Unknown/Courtesy Chaim Levakov

Tsuri Saguy

Israeli Military Officer

The framework of Israeli assistance to the Kurds included military assistance and extensive medical assistance. In the spring of 1966, the Iraqis prepared a large-scale attack on the Kurds. After a thorough study of the problems, I crystallized a defense approach that would withstand the Iraqi attack. I trained commanders and instructed the forces on the basis of a defense plan. I worked in close collaboration with the Barzani family—Mulla Mustafa Barzani, who was the undisputed leader, and his two sons, who helped him in the organization of the revolt. I built battalions and brigades and we used the ground to stop the Iraqi army without assault—only in good tactical places and high ground and very, very small units. The idea of entering into open defensive battle against the Iraqi army dismayed them, and rightly so.

The Kurds had big German rifles they got from the Iranians. They were from World Wars I and II. They are very good, but they aren't assault rifles—they're too long. The Kurds don't like assault. They like to take positions behind stones and to shoot. They're very good snipers. And I understood immediately that I could not go to the open field to attack the Iraqi army.

In May, after the thaw of the mountain snows, the Iraqis opened an extensive air and artillery attack throughout Kurdistan, and began a concentrated attack in the Rowanduz region on the road ascending to Haj Omran, and from there to Iran. The Iraqis concentrated most of the artillery in the Rowanduz region, and six brigades of infantry attacked our deployment. We were in an interior mountainous area in order to limit the capability of the Iraqi armor.

After six days of fighting, our forces began to collapse, and it was clear that we would not be able to hold out. I decided to launch a counterattack on the Fourth Mountain Brigade, which was attacking the heights of Mt. Natzran. The Iraqis halted their attack and tried to extricate the brigade, without success; the Iraqi Fourth Brigade was totally exterminated, and we were able to reorganize the defense. We deployed additional forces in order to execute a deep flanking attack and to surround the entire Iraqi forces in Rowanduz. The Iraqis sensed the danger, and proposed talks with the Kurds. That was how the talks of 1966 began. These talks went on for a few years without any results.

Interview with Tsuri Saguy, living in Israel, May 1994

Peshmerga training in the mountains

Chaim Levakov

263

"The village of Handela has a small dispensary. All of the peshmerga in our group wanted to be examined by the doctor. One man had his family in the village and brought his youngest son with him to the dispensary. Whatever the diagnosis was, a treatment was not possible; the dispensary had no medicine at all."

"Even the smallest village had a school, here a very simple and cold one. The stove was not working because of lack of firewood."

Gérard Klijn
German Photographer

I made my first contact with the Kurdish people in 1966 on an assignment about an earthquake disaster in east Turkey. At that time, it was no problem to meet Kurds, because the Turkish authorities were busier organizing help and finding housing for the earthquake victims than they were controlling journalists. I could move around freely.

I got very interested in the Kurdish people, so I decided to visit them in the only place where they live as free Kurds—in the liberated area of the northern mountains of Iraq.

A Kurdish friend in East Berlin told me to fly to Lebanon and contact friends in Beirut. On January 21, 1970, I arrived in Beirut. I phoned the number my friend had given me and handed over a letter from him to the person who came to my hotel.

After two days of waiting, a taxi picked me up and took me on a five-hour drive to Damascus. I was put up in a small hotel and locked in my room for another two days. The door was opened only so food could be brought in. Then finally I could leave my prison.

I was given Arab clothes to wear and, with three other persons (no names, no explanations), drove through the night to Aleppo, north of

Damascus. I was dropped off at the room of a Kurdish medical student, and didn't leave there for yet another two days. We left at night—another car, other guides, same Arab clothing—and arrived at sunrise at a simple farmhouse near the town of Qamishli, not far from the Turkish border in northeast Syria.

After three days of "imprisonment," Aziz, a new guide, appeared. We left in the dark—this time by tractor. After some miles the tractor got stuck in knee-deep muddy snow and we had to continue by foot. After hours struggling against the mud, the wet snow, and the cold creeping into our bones, we reached a poor one-room farmer's cottage filled with ten sleeping people. I found somewhere to lie down while Aziz went back to pick up the luggage and cameras we had left on the tractor.

The procedure was always the same: one night marching, guided by four or five Kurds, two days house arrest. During those two days the next trip was prepared, including a safe place to keep me. Fourteen days from when I arrived in Beirut, it was time. We would leave Turkey and enter the liberated zone in Iraq.

Letter from Gérard Klijn, living in Germany, October 26, 1994

"Six meters underground the Kurds worked the only printing press they had. A monthly newspaper was printed—circulation five thousand—and schoolbooks in the Kurdish language."

"In the same bunker as the printing press, the Kurds set up their own radio station, The Voice of Kurdistan. *For security reasons, the station, including the printing press, was moved to another secret location every two months."*
—Gérard Klijn

Gérard Klijn

"The hobby of the great strategist, General Mulla Mustafa Barzani, is playing chess"
Gérard Klijn/*Bild der Zeit*, December 1972

IRAQ

265

I was told we had to pass some small Turkish army posts (easy to spot by the campfires) and to cross some rivers. It was a beautiful night, incredibly clear, with a full moon so bright you could easily read a newspaper. To transport the luggage, the escort of twelve people had chosen a mule with a completely white hide. The animal could be seen from miles away.

The rivers were crossed with rafts made of the inner tubes of a truck and covered with branches. They were hidden between rocks at the river banks. One raft could carry two people using their naked feet as paddles. The white mule got to the other side by swimming.

When we arrived at the border-river to Iraqi Kurdistan, Aziz and I said goodbye to our escorts. The twelve Kurds embraced me heartily and told me they were proud to bring a foreigner to their Kurdistan.

I climbed behind Aziz on the white mule. The animal went into the ice-cold river without protest, obviously unaware of the big load it had to carry. In the fast moving current it began to have serious trouble—only its nostrils came out of the water. Wet up to our waists we were deposited safely on the ground of free Kurdistan. Immediately we were surrounded by a group of peshmerga armed with ammunition and weapons up to their armpits.

A wonderful time was ahead of me. Accompanied by five or six peshmerga, we were brought from village to village through magnificent Kurdish land to the headquarters of the Democratic Party of Kurdistan in the Iraqi town of Galala, not far from the Iranian border.

I was able to meet people in the villages, stay in their clay-roofed houses, discuss things with religious and military leaders during the long evenings, visit schools outside in the fields (school buildings were targets for the Iraqi Air Force), meet medical doctors with no medicine, listen to storytellers, and march and march.

The most impressive thing, however, was the hospitality in the mountains of Iraqi Kurdistan—hospitality of a kind I have never found again. After six weeks the expedition ended with a visit to Barzani. He ordered Aziz to buy me a peshmerga suit as a present of the Kurdish revolution. The next day Aziz drove me by Land Rover over the open Iranian border to Tabriz. From there we flew to Tehran. Two days later I passed the passport control with a brand-new visa, thanks to Aziz, and boarded the plane to Germany.

Letter from Gérard Klijn, October 26, 1994

I found a wonderful people, very gentle, proud, and very much aware of their tragic history—very different from the "mountain Turks who have forgotten their mother tongue" as the government in Ankara refers to them. —Gérard Klijn

"One of the biggest issues in the program of the Democratic Party of Kurdistan was school education in the Kurdish language. Boys and girls together would march into their classroom. The walls were decorated with banners and posters of the KDP." —Gérard Klijn

Gérard Klijn

1970

"Long live the first anniversary of the sacred March 11, 1971, agreement": sign carried at parade in Sulaimania

Rafiq

The March 11 Agreement, which came after six months of indirect and direct negotiations in which I chaired the Kurdish delegation, was a turning point in our history because autonomy for Kurdistan within Iraq was accepted for the first time, along with a lot of administrative, cultural and political rights. It's very unfortunate that it wasn't implemented as it should have been because of Baghdad's dictatorship and chauvinism and the illusion the Kurdish leadership (Barzani on top) had, that Kurds might get more from the USA with which we had official but secret relations in 1972.

Letter from Dr. Mahmoud Osman, Kurdish leader living in London, April 1997

The March 11 Peace Agreement

I arrived in Kurdistan on March 11, 1970, the day the autonomy agreement was signed between Iraq and the Kurdish leaders. It was the first time we saw freedom in Kurdistan. It had been a liberated region, but there had still been bombing. That day, everybody came out, not only the Kurds but also the Arabs. Arabs were shoulder to shoulder with peshmerga. There was kissing and embracing.

I had come from the Soviet Union to Tehran and then to Kurdistan. The Kurds in exile were active in Europe in the 1960s, and at the beginning of 1970 I wanted to go to Kurdistan. We had news that there was peace between Barzani and the Baathists, the ruling party in Iraq. The Kurds from Baghdad were allowed to come there. On March 21 it was Newroz, and everybody came.

That's where I saw Barzani. In their speeches, Barzani's sons said, "In Kurdistan, we are free. We can practice our culture and build schools, education, health, everything in Kurdistan. And of course, economically we can get 30 percent of the petroleum money to be spent in Kurdistan."

Barzani was not optimistic. "We have been fighting since 1961, for nine years, and the Arabs haven't given us peace. In 1963 and 1964 and later, sometimes we had a cease-fire, but they didn't give us peace. They have signed this agreement now because they had to do it. They couldn't fight us anymore. But they can fight us again. Therefore, I don't like it that we make big speeches to the people."

There was a committee that acted as a sort of parliament. They discussed everything that had to be done. And the peshmerga began to do many of the things that had to be done—opening newspapers and schools. They opened a university in Sulaimania where everything was in Kurdish.

Of course all the Kurds wanted a state, but it was not possible. There were two blocs. The Soviet Union was with Iraq, and the U.S. and European states were with Turkey and with the shah of Iran. There was no other possibility.

Interview with Hemres Reso, Kurdish activist living in Germany, October 1993

IRAQ

Saddam Hussein and Mulla Mustafa Barzani, March 20, 1970
Unknown/Rafiq Studio

Mulla Mustafa Barzani

"WE'VE got these beasts in Bagdad oppressing us: Arabs and Kurds alike." At the age of 69, Mulla Mustafa Barzani refused to be depressed about the future of the Kurdish National Movement he leads. He put his trust, he repeatedly insisted, "in the mercy of God and the will of our people."

It does almost seem that this grizzled old warrior, after a lifetime of hardship and danger, falls under some kind of divine protection, and there is something dour and irrepressible about the Kurds. But Barzani, as his harsh words show, is at present a nervous and disillusioned man.

It is perhaps unfortunate that he should have to say such things about an Arab Government, and decline, for tactical reasons, to say anything about the Turks and Persians, who have been the fiercest oppressors of his people.

But it is against the weaker, more tolerant Arabs that the Kurdish struggle is now mainly directed. Last March, Barzani achieved a major breakthrough with the signing of an agreement, ending long years of intermittent civil war, which gave the Kurds a greater degree of autonomy than an Iraqi Government had ever offered them before. Officially, the two sides still believe in each other's goodwill and determination that the agreement will eventually be fulfilled.

But all the signs are that it won't be. The ruling Ba'athists appear to have decided they can't go through with it. A war next spring is a serious possibility.

DAVID HIRST reports on the stru

The case of t

It was at Dilman, his winter headquarters, that Barzani — simple, shoeless, and without ceremony — received us in the one-floor house which, with its flat roof of wood and packed earth, resembles all those that his poor and backward people inhabit. Electricity, a fruit of the March agreement, was a newly acquired luxury.

Dilman, a small village, lay at the end of a precipitous journey up from the plains of Kirkuk, along a narrow track strewn with fallen boulders, through the towering gorge of Gali ali Beg, and out into a mountainous wilderness which is one of the world's natural fortresses.

But it was at his summer headquarters that we saw the real reason for Barzani's discontent. At Haj Umran, almost on the Persian frontier, and now way above the snow line, we saw the physical evidence of Barzani's latest, and luckiest, escape from death.

An eye-witness described how it happened. On September 29, nine religious sheikhs, some of them apparently bona-fide and some clearly not, came up from Bagdad to visit Barzani. They came in two cars: a Toyota belonging to the Islamic Cultural Association in Bagdad, and a Chevrolet belonging to a man who had lost it — along with his chauffeur, found dead in a ditch near Kirkuk — some 10 months before.

The Kurds conversed with their guests about religion and human brotherhood, and one of the sheikhs produced a gift of two holy books. Barzani came in, sat down, and began to talk. As he did so, Sheikh Ibrahim Khuzai, sitting directly opposite him, exploded.

He was sliced in two. His entrails still adhere to walls and ceiling. Unless one accepts the unlikely thesis that he sought a martyr's entry to Paradise — a thesis rendered more unlikely by the inferior erotic poetry found on his person — the explosive device had been planted on him without his knowing what it was.

How some evil genius managed to do that will probably never be known. But a favourite explanation is that the sheikhs, some of whom had been up there a fortnight before and had heard Barzani's grievances, genuinely believed they were playing a useful mediatory rôle, and the battery to convey Barzani's thoughts Sheikh Khuzai had been induced to hide what he imagined to be a tape recorder around his middle.

He therefore pressed the fatal button when Barzani began to speak. It was Barzani's guardian angel who decreed that at that very instant an unfortunate Pesh Merga (Kurdish soldier) should be serving tea to Sheikh Khuzai, therefore standing directly between him and Barzani.

Car remnants from attempt on Barzani's life, September 29, 1971
Unknown/KDP Archive

...e exploding sheikh

He died of his wounds, as did ... leading sheikh at Barzani's ...ide. At this point, the account grows confused. There was pandemonium. The sheikhs rushed out, some of them apparently drawing grenades from beneath their garments.

The Pesh Merga, some of them probably believing their leader dead, went wild. They slaughtered all nine sheikhs and the two drivers, who were apparently the leaders of the operation. I counted 40 bullet-holes in the steel door of the lavatory where one sheikh took refuge.

Half-an-hour later the Toyota exploded. Miraculously, no one was near. A brave man took the wheel of the Chevrolet and drove it away. It, too, had been rigged for an explosion. Thirty-seven sticks of dynamite lay beneath the back seats, and four blocks of TNT under the dashboard. But the *real piece ... resistance*, the Goldfinger touch, was the two home-made rockets, like drainpipes to look at, secreted in the tailfins and designed, at the flick of a switch, to shoot out via the rear lights and destroy a pursuing vehicle.

How any of the would-be assassins were led to believe there was a one-in-a-thousand chance of a getaway from this Kurd-filled wilderness is just another mystery.

This, of course, is the Kurdish side of the story, but it is impressively told and until the Government gives its version one must conclude, like the Kurds, that only the Government itself had the motive and resources for such an elaborate assassination bid. A joint Kurdish-Government committee is in theory investigating, but in spite of all the evidence available, and the Government's, it has failed to come up with conclusive results.

No one, from Barzani down, expects it to do so. The expectation is all the less in that to the Kurds the assassination attempt looks like an integral part of a growing campaign of provocation whose ultimate purpose, it is felt, is to crush the Kurdish movement.

Some aspects of the March agreement, the Kurds concede, have been fulfilled. The Government accepted, with certain reservations, the conversion of 6,000 Pesh Merga into frontier guards. Five thousand others have rejoined the army. Economic development is beginning. Fourteen thousand houses, to make up for those bombed in the fighting, have been built. Kurdish governors and high officials have been appointed in three Kurdish provinces.

But the debit increasingly outweighs the credit. There is the question of Kirkuk province, where Iraq's main oil-fields are. The Kurds say it is predominantly Kurdish and that they should enjoy the same autonomous rights (though with the oil revenues going, as always, to the central Government) as are enjoyed in the other three provinces. A census is supposed to be held there, and they accuse the Government of seeking by all sorts of devious means to settle the province with Arabs to tip the balance in their favour.

Kurds of Persian origin, even if they were born in Iraq, have been deported. Another army division has been moved up to Kirkuk. Some 6 members of Barzani's Kurdish Democratic Party (KDP) have been arrested.

The recently announced national charter is supposed to provide the framework for a front of "progressive parties" — the KDP was not even consulted. President Bakr insisted last week that the front would not extend to the army, where the Ba'ath would retain exclusive control : tantamount, in the Kurdish view, to undermining the whole point of the March agreement.

Most serious of all, perhaps, is the Government's failure to grant the Kurds any representative voice in ruling the country. They have five Ministers in the Cabinet, but these have no powers at all. They may resign at any time. The fact is that the Ba'ath, obsessed with security, cannot share power with any-one, let alone the Kurds, who, apart from them, are by far the strongest organised force in the country.

It would undermine the whole basis of their rule. The KDP would become a vehicle of opposition on which everyone would try to climb.

It is no accident that in a small way the Kurds already play a rôle. They give shelter in the North to political refugees. At the first KDP congress, Arab delegates attacked the Government — the Ba'ath were angry. The Arabic-language Kurdish newspaper, Ta'akhi (brotherhood), is the only one which speaks, however faintly, with a voice of its own and is therefore the newspaper which everyone, Arabs and Kurds, prefer to read.

They take risks, the journalists on Ta'akhi. A few weeks ago one of them, an Arab, was found dead, presumed electrocuted, in a Bagdad street.

It is not clear what the Government hopes to achieve in provoking the Kurds, and whether it is ready to go to the point of war. But the Kurds are bracing themselves for that possibility. One gathers that an important part of their strategy will be—if it is not so already — to present themselves as liberators, rescuing Arabs and Kurds alike from "the beasts in Bagdad."

So far, apparently, the results of their contacts in and out of Iraq have been disappointing, but as tension rises there may be a better response. There is little doubt that many Iraqis, whatever their misgivings about Kurdish "secessionism," would welcome any available means of overthrowing President Bakr and his followers.

Speech to local villagers, 1974

Rosy Rouleau/SYGMA

<u>"Fighting with the Pesh Merga rebels of Kurdistan", 13 April 74</u>   # 781
   General Mulla Mustafa Barzani and his Kurdish mountain troops continue
to wage their battle against the Iraqi garrisons stationed in northern
Kurdistan, part of the Kurdistan Democratic Party's struggle for freedom
from Baghdad.   The Pesh Merga rebels and Barzani roam around the plateau
regions of Kurdistan on mules, hiding during the day from Iraq Air Force
reconnaissance planes.   Their aim is to cut-off the Iraq military
garrison towns from their supply routes, there are about 8 such towns in
Kurdistan. Barzani demands that Baghdad hands over the oil installations
of Kirkuk to Kurdistan, as the town lies inside their boundary. It is
presumed that the Iranian government is helping Barzani and his men in this
struggle, as they too are interested in this oil rich border region of
their country with Iraq.

                    Photos by Rosy ROULEAU/SYGMA.

1974

Rosy Rouleau
French Photographer

Leave at 9:15 a.m. Not far away one can see an Iraqi camp in the valley. Weather is horrible. Constant rain. The light is very low. Storm. The good time to photograph is brief.

Lunch at Khate. In a house outside the village. It will take 4 hours, traveling quickly, to see another Iraqi camp.

Leave at 14:00 but stop a half hour later in a village named Toutma at the house of the chief of the village. Cannot leave again until tomorrow morning. . . .

Crude, low windows above. The house was bombed in '62. Two children died. Two rockets. It's the only house that was bombed. They were the children of the chief of the village. Before the bombing, Barzani came here for a few days. The man is a peshmerga, he belongs to the battalion we just saw. "In the summertime we live outdoors, we build houses. We are closer to our tobacco fields. There are approximately 100 families."

There is a school of 70 children, all boys, and 3 Kurdish teachers. A secondary school is at Rawanduz, a day's walking distance. No hospital, no nurse. We had to walk four hours to get to the first village and find a nurse.

"We plant mainly tobacco, but also wheat and tomatoes. Since the Voice of Kurdistan *started, we know everything. The French president, Pompidou, is dead. He died this morning. He was good for us."*

"Pompidou or de Gaulle?"

"Pompidou. We got things from him."

According to the news, the USSR helps the Arabs.

Telegram from Sulaimania: Iraqi troops have opened fire in the streets and killed a civilian factory worker. At Bani Kheylan, the Iraqis attacked a village with tanks but the Kurds pushed them back to their barracks at Dar Bedirkhan.

Visit with the women. Polygamy: very little. Two men in this village have married more than two women. It works very poorly for both the men and the women. What is done often is an exchange. For example: A man wants to marry a young girl; he picks her and gives his daughter away to marry the brother of the girl he wants.

They plant nuts, figs, grapes.

Excerpt from diary of Rosy Rouleau,
April 3, 1974/Courtesy Michel Raffoul

Peshmerga meeting

Kurdish child in Kurdish school

ADPO00
CO
PA
1C
AC
IN   3

                                                                        SP-03

R
FM
TO
INF
AMC
AME
AME
AMC
USI

Peshmerga on the Iran-Iraq border

C O N F I D E N T I A L TABRIZ 0007

E.O. 11652: GDS
TAGS: PINS, MOPS, IR, IZ
SUBJ: KURDISH WAR IN IRAQ: IRANIAN INPUTS

REF: TABRIZ A-10 OF APRIL 27, 1974

SUMMARY: IRAQI GOVERNMENT POLICY OF SUBDUING MULLA MUSTAFA
BARZANI'S KURDS THROUGH ECONOMIC BLOCKADE AND AIR STRIKES
APPEARS TO BE FAILING COMPLETELY, INSOFAR AS FIRST HAND
OBSERVATIONS AND INFORMATION FROM IRANIAN SIDE CAN DETERMINE.
KURDISH NON-COMBATANTS ARE MOVING INTO IRAN. IRANIAN SUPPLIES
AND SOME WEAPONS ARE MOVING INTO IRAQI KURDISTAN. THESE ARE
THE MAIN CONCLUSIONS DRAWN FROM VICE COUNSUL JUNE 4-6 TRIP
TO THE IRANO-IRAQI BORDER. END SUMMARY.

GENERAL OBSERVATIONS: IRAQ HAS DECLARED AN ECONOMIC BLOCKADE
OF KURDISH AREAS. NO ONE SHOULD BE UNDER ILLUSION THAT IRANIAN
BORDER IS A SEIVE; IT IS A FAUCET. HOTELS IN REZAIYEH,
MAHABAD, AND SARDASHT, ALL IN PROVINCE OF WEST AZERBAIJAN,
ARE WELL FILLED WITH BARZANI KURDS. HOTEL KEEPERS, BAZAAR
CONFIDENTIAL
CONFIDENTIAL

PAGE 02 TABRIZ 00007 090859Z

MERCHANTS, AND OTHERS UNIFORMLY SAY THAT IRAQI KURDS ARE WELL
SUPPLIED WITH MONEY AND ARE SPENDING FREELY. FABULOUS RUMORS
ARE SPREAD OF INDIVIDUAL KURDS DROPPING 100,000 OR 150,000
RIALS AT A CRACK. WHILE PROBABLY EXAGGERATED, THIS DOES GIVE

FEEL FOR VOLUME OF SPENDING GOING ON IN BORDER AREA. THOSE
DOING SPENDING ARE GENERALLY YOUNG MEN, WITHOUT WOMEN, WHO
IDENTIFY THEMSELVES FREELY AS IRAQI KURDS BUT WEAR NON-DIS-
TINCTIVE CLOTHING AND TURN UP FOR THREE, FOUR DAYS BEFORE
RETURNING TO WAR. THEIR VEHICLES, EITHER WITHOUT LICENSE
PLATES OR WITH IRAQI ONES, CAN BE SEEN AS FAR EAST AS REZAIKEH.

EXTENT OF IRANIAN COOPERATION QUITE CLEAR AT SARDASHT. STOCKS
IN GAS STATION NOW NUMBER MORE THAN 6,000 55 GALLON DRUMS OF
GASOLINE. APPROXIMATELY 50 VEHICLES OF IRAQI ORIGIN WERE SEEN
IN TOWN, MOSTLY LANDROVERS BUT WITH SPRINKLING OF RUSSIAN
AND AMERICAN JEEPS AND SOME SMALL TRUCKS OF THREE QUARTER TON
SIZE. ONE RUMOR, UNSUBSTANTIATED, FROM TRUCK DRIVER WHO RE-
GULARLY DRIVES SHORT STRETCH BETWEEN SARDASHT AND BORDER,
HAS IT THAT IRAN HAS RECENTLY GIVEN 25 RUSSIAN JEEPS TO KURDS
AND THAT TRUCKS CAPTURED IN IRAQ EXCEED KURDISH NEEDS. SINCE
RUMORS ARE FLYING FAST AND THICK THESE DAYS, THIS SHOULD BE
ACCEPTED WITH CAUTION.

DETAILS FROM   MORE DETAILS ON FIGHTING AND
IRANIAN SUPPORT WERE PROVIDED BY

                    ACCORDING TO HIM, IRAQI DECISION TO BOMB
ALL POSSIBLE TARGETS IN KURDISH AREAS WAS CONSIDERABLE MISTAKE.
SCHOOLS, HOSPITALS AND PRIVATE HOMES WERE ALL STRUCK. FIELDS
HAVE BEEN HIT WITH NAPALM. MAJORITY OF FAMILIES HAVE LOST
RELATIVES OR FRIENDS. THE RESULT HAS BEEN TO DRIVE EDUCATED
AND URBAN KURDS INTO UNITY WITH BARZANI, WHOSE PRESTIGE IS NOW
ENORMOUS THROUGHOUT KURDISTAN. TO SAFEGUARD FAMILIES, IN-
CREASING NUMBERS OF NON-COMBATANTS ARE MOVING INTO IRAN. SINCE
LAST VISIT FROM THIS CONSULATE, JUST OVER MONTH AGO, REFUGEE
CAMP OF OVER THOUSAND PERSONS HAS BEEN ESTABLISHED AT SARDASHT.
              STATED THAT TWO LARGER CAMPS, EACH OF 7-8,000
PERSONS HAVE BEEN SET UP NEAR KHANEH AND REZAIYEH. IRANIAN
GOVERNMENT IS PROVIDING AMPLE FOOD AND SOME CLOTHING TO THESE
PEOPLE. CAMP AT SARDASHT, WHICH REPORTING OFFICER SAW, HAD OVER
ONE HUNDRED FAMILY SIZE TENTS, WAS LAID OUT IN NEAT MILITARY
CONFIDENTIAL
CONFIDENTIAL

PAGE 03   TABRIZ 00007   090859Z

FASHION, AND APPEARED CLEAN. A RED LION AND SUN (IRANIAN RED
CROSS) TENT HAD BEEN SET UP NEXT TO IT TO FUNCTION AS A CLINIC.
BAZAAR RUMOR IN SARDASHT PLACED NUMBER OF REFUGEE CIVILIANS
IN IRAN AT 18,000; CLOSE ENOUGH TO GENERAL OTMISHI'S FIGURES
TO ACT AS PARTIAL CONFIRMATION.

AGAIN ACCORDING   FIGHTING HAS SLOWED IN RECENT
WEEKS. IRAQI GARRISONS HOLD ALL MAJOR TOWNS BUT DO NOT EXTEND
OUTSIDE TOWNS. BARZANI FORCES STILL HOLD MOUNTAIN TOPS AND RIDGE
LINES WITHIN ONE OR TWO KILOMETERS OF TOWNS SUCH AS SULAI-
MANIYA. IRAQIS, ACCORDING TO   DO NO NIGHT PATROLLING
OUTSIDE THEIR LINES. THE ROADS ARE OPEN IN TERMS OF LARGE
CONVOY MOVEMENT BUT CAN CERTAINLY NOT BE CONSIDERED SAFE.

John Stathatos
Greek Photographer

During the night of March 7, I crossed the border into the Chouman Valley in a blacked-out KDP jeep. Soon after midnight, I was woken by the muted roar of a heavy convoy. In the starlight, I could just make out the vast bulk of artillery pieces and their tractors toiling up the pass; less than twenty-four hours from the signing of the fateful Iran-Iraq agreement in Algiers, the Shah's 122 mm field guns were being withdrawn from the Rawanduz front. The Kurds were once again left to their fate, and I suddenly found myself with a major story breaking all around me.

Letter from John Stathatos,
living in England, March 1997

"Refugees with their belongings in the abandoned village of Haj Omran. When the Iranians stopped transport for three days, refugees had to find whatever shelter they could. Many were reduced to huddling under piles of bedding in the snow by the road."

EXCLUSIVE

APRIL THE FIRST IS TOO LATE : THE BETRAYAL OF A PEOPLE

OVER THE SNOWBOUND MOUNTAIN PASSES AND THE SWOLLEN RIVERS OF IRAQI KURDISTAN, AN ENTIRE NATION IS STRUGGLING TO REACH THE SAFETY OF THE IRANIAN BORDER BEFORE THE CEASEFIRE COMES TO AN END ON APRIL FIRST.THE HEROIC KURDISH DEFENCE OF THEIR MOUNTAIN STRONGHOLDS WHICH FOLLOWED THE ALL-OUT IRAQI ATTACK OF ~~2P~~ MARCH SEVENTH HAS PROVED INSUFFICIENT TO SAVE THEIR CAUSE IN THE FACE OF IRAN'S CRUEL POLITICAL BETRAYAL. SUDDENLY AND INEXPLICABLY ABANDONED BY THEIR ONLY ALLY, THE KURDS FACE AN AGONISING CHOICE BETWEEN STAYING IN KURDISTAN TO FIGHT A SAVAGE AND POSSIBLY HOPELESS PARTISAN WARFARE IN THE FACE OF OVERWHELMING ODDS, AND LEAVING THEIR BELOVED HOMELAND FOR AN UNCERTAIN EXILE IN IRAN.

THOSE PESH MERGA WHO HAVE ELECTED TO STAY BEHIND AND FIGHT KNOW THAT NOW THEY WILL REALLY BE JUSTIFYING THEIR NAME OF "THOSE WHO FACE DEATH". THE REST, MEN, WOMEN AND CHILDREN WHO ARE TRECKING OUT FROM THE REMOTE PROVINCE OF BADINAN UNDER THE TIGHTLY SEALED TURKISH BORDER, FACE AN IMPOSSIBLE DEADLINE: THE IRANIAN GOVERMENT HAS REFUSED TO KEEP ITS BORDER OPEN BEYONF APRIL FIRST. MANY THOUSANDS OF REFUGEE FAMILIES ARE STILL ON THE ROAD AT THIS TIME, SUFFERING FROM DISEASE AND ACCUTE MALNUTRITION. ON APRIL FIRST THE IRAQI ARMY WILL RESUME ITS ATTACK ON THE KURDISH LINES AT RAWANDUZ NEAR THE ~~DA~~ CHOUMAN VALLEY, THE ONLY ROUTE OUT TO IRAN AND SAFETY. IF THIS ROUTE IS CUT, THE REFUGEES CAN LOOK FORWARD TO NOTHING BUT DEATH, WHETHER OF COLD AND HUNGER IN THE CRUEL MOUNTAINS OR AT THE HANDS OF THE IRAQI ARMY. ~~NO FAITH WHATSOEVER IS~~ THEY HAVE NO FAITH WHATSOEVER IN THE IRAQI OFFER OF AMNESTY, AND REPORTS HAVE ALREADY REACHED JOURNALISTS IN TEHERAN OF CIVILIAN MASSACRES BY THE IRAQIS IN SOUTH BADINAN.

THE FLEEING KURDS, CIVILIANS AND PESH MERGA ALIKE, HAVE ONLY ONE QUESTION TO ASK THE WESTERN JOURNALISTS AND REPRESENTATIVES OF HUMANKNITARIAN ORGANISATIONS THEY MEET ON THE OTHER SIDE OF THE BORDER: "WHY HAS THE WEST ALLOWED THIS ~~Ø~~ TO HAPPEN TO US? WHAT CRIME HAVE WE COMMITED THAT WE SHOULD BE TREATED IN THIS ~~MATTER~~ MANNER?DOES NOBODY KNOW OR CARE ABOUT WHAT HAPPENS TO OUR PEOPLE?". WAITING AT THE TOP OF HAJ OMRAN PASS NEAR THE IRANIAN BORDER LAST WEEK, I FOR ONE COULD FIND NO ANSWER TO THEIR QUESTION.

197

JOHN STATHATOS

KEYSTONE EXCLUSIVE

INFO AMEMBASSY ANKARA
AMEMBASSY BEIRUT
AMEMBASSY DAMASCUS
AMEMBASSY TEHRAN
USMISSION USUN NY
USMISSION GENEVA
AMCONSUL ADANA
AMCONSUL KHORRAMSHAHR
USCINCEUR VAIHINGEN GER

C O N F I D E N T I A L TABRIZ 00

BEIRUT PASS BAGHDAD

E.O. 11652: GDS
TAGS: PINS, SREF, IR, IZ
SUBJ: IRAQI KURDISH WAR

John Stathatos

"Civilians arrive at the ruined Iraqi tower on the top of Haj Omran Pass. This is where they would, with luck, be collected by Iranian army lorries for evacuation."
—*John Stathatos*

Ronald E. Neumann to Secretary of State, March 31, 1975, Persian Gulf Collection, The National Security Archive, Washington, D.C.

SUMMARY: RECENT ALGIERS AGREEMENT APPEARS TO HAVE BROUGHT VIRTUAL END TO KURDISH WAR. TEN THOUSAND REFUGEES, INCLUDING MANY PISH MERGA FIGHTERS, ARE FLOODING INTO IRAN. ONLY FEW ARE PRESENTLY ELECTING RETURN IRAQ. IRAQI RED CRESCENT DELEGATION TRAVELED MARCH 26 TO MAIN REFUGEE CAMPS BUT FAILED PERSUADE MANY KURDS RETURN IRAQ. IRANIANS NOT ATTEMPTING FORCE KURDS RETURN IRAQ. PRESENTLY NO PLANS MOVE REFUGEES OUT OF CAMPS. SOME IRANIAN OFFICIALS EXPECT MAJOR REFUGEE RETURN MAY OCCUR AFTER SEVERAL MONTHS IF INITIAL RETURNEES NOT HARMED. KURDS BITTER ABOUT WHAT THEY REGARD AS IRANIAN SELLOUT BUT SEE NO POSSIBILITY OF CONTIN-UING WAR. EVERY INDICATION IS THAT IRANIANS ARE UPHOLDING AGREE-CONFIDENTIAL

Interview with General Barzani: Chouman, Iraq

A party consisting of Jim Hoagland and Nancy Moran for the Washington Post, *Leroy Woodson for* Time *magazine, Gwyn Roberts for* The Financial Times *and myself set out from Chouman on the evening of the Nineteenth for Haj Omran, near which Barzani was said to have his hideout.*

It was a sign of the times that the checkpoints along the Hamilton Road where we had expected to be held up for a long time, as we had no official invitation, were all deserted. Arriving at Haj Omran we had no difficulty in finding out the general's whereabouts and set off along a primitive track covered in mud, arriving after an extremely rough ride which almost defeated our Land Rover.

General Barzani's staff were obviously surprised at seeing an unannounced party arrive at eleven o'clock at night, but we managed to convince them of the urgency of the situation. Within minutes we were shown into a room where the general joined us along with his son, Idris Barzani, and politburo member, Doctor Mahmoud Osman, who acted as interpreter. The interview lasted for nearly two hours as the general turned out to be unusually tolerant of our questions. . . .

The future of the revolution was quickly out of the general's hands. The next day he announced that the peshmerga would not after all resume fighting in view of the crushing superiority of the Iraqis and the risk run by the civilian population. . . . Meanwhile, power within the KDP is passing into the hands of the newly formed revolutionary command council, which has renounced Barzani in favour of the principle of collective leadership.

John Stathatos' notes sent to *The Times* for Barzani interview article

John Stathatos,
The Sunday Times, London
March 23, 1975

Why are we treated like this? asks Kurd leader

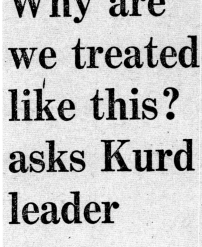

KURDISH rebels fighting for antonomy within Iraq had reached a crisis by the middle of last week. The Kurds' irregular army had pulled off a military miracle by holding back Iraqi troops on several fronts and the Bagdhad government had declared a ceasefire. But political isolation of the Kurds had become complete when their only ally, Iran, signed a treaty with Iraq and announced that its border with Kurdistan would be closed on April 1, the day the ceasefire was due to end.

It was at this point that JOHN STATHATOS interviewed Mullah Mustapha Barzani, chairman of the Kurdistan Democratic Party (KDP) and the rebels' military chief, at his mountain hide-out.

STATHATOS: *Do you feel betrayed by the recent agreement between Iran and Iraq?*

BARZANI: I would not like to word it like that. It seems the protagonists had their own interests at heart and that the agreement has been at our expense.

When the war began again in March last year, did the KDP have any encouragement from Iran?

We were given definite encouragement by Iran, as well as many promises which were not kept. We were offered full support in all aspects.

Has Iran explained to you why the Kurds were abandoned in this way?

We were not advised of the agreement. It has not been explained and we have still not been given the details.

On your recent visit to Teheran did you meet the Shah?

Yes.

Can you say how the conversation went?

I explained our position and spoke of the difficulties facing us. The Shah said the agree-

ment was made because it was vital to Iran. I asked what our future was to be, and the Shah said he would undertake to protect those Kurds who sought refuge in Iran

Do you think Iran stands to lose anything by this agreement?

The Baathists (the Iraqi ruling party) will not fulfil their obligations towards Iran. And the Iranians will soon see they have been deceived. The greatest loss to Iran would be the loss of the security they have had on the Iraqi border.

Is the KDP advising Kurdish civilians to stay here or go to Iran?

Some will stay and some are on their way. But the point is that the road is long and there are only ten days left. Then they will accept no more. That is why I have asked them to move the date to the end of April.

You have mentioned that you fear that the Kurds risk genocide at the hands of the Iraqi army. How many people do you think would be at risk if fighting resumed?

Perhaps as many as half a million.

If it would protect the civilian population, would you give yourself up to the Iraqis?

I have always been ready to give up my life for my people, but I have no doubt that if I hand myself over they will kill me and then go ahead with their plans. *Do you see the present situation as the end of the Kurdish national movement?*

Where there is a people and a nation, the national movement will never end. Maybe a phase will end, but the movement will always go on. At the moment, considering the situation we are in and the fighting we will have to do, I think it will be useless and we will risk genocide.

You have said you look to the United States for protection. Can you clarify that?

I look to the United States to protect my people and ensure that international humanitarian principles are met. But if through the threat of genocide we had to flee our country, then we would seek refuge there.

Have you had any indications that the United States is interested in the future of Kurdistan?

Through our contacts and those of our friends, we have always been given to understand that they are concerned with the Kurdish question at the highest level in the united States. Though they have given no definite written commitment, we always thought, through our talks with them, that they would never abandon this people.

How could the Americans protect Kurdistan?

If they decide to commit themselves to the rotection of a people, they can do it, whether through diplomatic pressure or outright aid. I think that if America were to come to such a decision, a way could be found.

You have lived through a year of bloodshed. How do you feel about the events of the past two weeks?

It has been a year of sacrifices. We have been fighting here and we have looked to other countries to protect us. Now I think that instead of getting our rights and seeing a good end to the year there will be a bad end to the year as a result of a strange sort of co-operation between certain countries. I do not know what crime we have committed to be treated in such a manner. *How do you view the immediate future of the revolution?*

The future is not bright for us. On one side the enemy has all the advantages and the support of the Russians, and on the other side we are all alone with no friends. I think dark times are coming.

Mulla Mustafa Barzani and Mas'ud Barzani in Washington, D.C.　　　Unknown/Courtesy Rafiq Studio

New CIA Tale:
Kurd Leader Was Secretly Flown to U.S.

Washington—Mullah Mustafa Barzani, the Kurdish leader whose autonomy movement was crushed by Iraq after Iran withdrew its support last month, was brought to the United States secretly by the CIA, given a medical checkup and a tour of the United States, was kept in total isolation, and then, over his protests, sent back to Iran.

Mr. Barzani begged to see Secretary of State Henry A. Kissinger and tolerated his total isolation up to the last moment in the belief that this was the condition of his meeting Dr. Kissinger and other American leaders.

At a house in the woods of McLean, Virginia, near CIA head-quarters, where he was kept with a joint escort of agents of the CIA and Savak, the Iranian secret police, Mr. Barzani met with Joseph J. Sisco, Under Secretary of State for Political Affairs, late in October. . . .

Mr. Sisco, in Florida with President Ford and President Sadat of Egypt, could not be reached for comment. Other high-ranking State Department officials said they knew nothing about the visit.

Dana Adams Schmidt, *Christian Science Monitor*, November 3, 1975

Background: *Mulla Mustafa Barzani*
Sven Simon/*Christian Science Monitor*,
November 3, 1975

the village VOICE

50c

EXCLUSIVE

Copyright © 1976 The Village Voice Inc.   VOL. XXI No. 7   THE WEEKLY NEWSPAPER OF NEW YORK   MON. FEB. 16, 1976

24-Page Supplement

THE REPORT ON THE CIA THAT PRESIDENT FORD DOESN'T WANT YOU TO READ

TEXT HIGHLIGHTS FROM THE SUPPRESSED HOUSE INTELLIGENCE COMMITTEE REPORT (P. 69)

"Barzani Tea" packaged in Iran for distribution in Iraqi Kurdistan during 1974–75 war
Courtesy Hassan Ghazi

In the [Pike] Committee report one manuscript page was missing. It is clear from the context that the missing material opened a discussion of a U.S. scheme, involving the Shah of Iran, to channel secret aid to the Kurds in their rebellion against the government of Iraq. . . .

The recipients of U.S. arms and cash were [said to be] an insurgent ethnic group fighting for autonomy in a country bordering our ally. The bordering country and our ally had long been bitter enemies. They differed substantially in ideological orientation and in their relations with the U.S.

Evidence collected by the Committee suggests that the project was initiated primarily as a favor to our ally, who had cooperated with U.S. intelligence agencies, and who had come to feel menaced by his neighbor. . . .

Documents in the Committee's possession clearly show that the President, Dr. Kissinger and the foreign head of state hoped that our clients would not prevail. They preferred instead that the insurgents simply continue a level of hostilities sufficient to sap the resources of our ally's neighboring country. This policy was not imparted to our clients, who were encouraged to continue fighting. Even in the context of covert action, ours was a cynical enterprise. . . .

All U.S. aid was channeled through our collaborator, without whose logistical help direct assistance would have been impossible. Our national interest had thus become effectively meshed with his. Accordingly, when our ally reached an agreement with the target country and abruptly ended his own aid to the insurgents, the U.S. had no choice but to acquiesce. The extent of our ally's leverage over U.S. policy was such that he apparently made no effort to notify his junior American partners that the program's end was near.

The insurgents were clearly taken by surprise as well. Their adversaries, knowing of the impending aid cut-off, launched an all-out search-and-destroy campaign the day after the agreement was signed. The autonomy movement was over and our former clients scattered before the central government's superior forces.

Despite direct pleas from the insurgent leader and the CIA station chief in the area to the President and Dr. Kissinger, the U.S. refused to extend humanitarian assistance to the thousands of refugees created by the abrupt termination of military aid. As the Committee staff was reminded by a high U.S. official, "covert action should not be confused with missionary work."

Excerpt of U.S. government document, *The Pike Report*, 1975, leaked to *The Village Voice* by Daniel Schorr, published February 16, 1976

Left: Cover *The Village Voice*/Courtesy Daniel Schorr

USA

279

The Islamic Revolution in Iran

The year 1978 was Iran's year of revolution. Throughout the country, mass demonstrations demanded the release of political prisoners and then, ever more loudly, an end to the shah's rule. Although most of the Kurds are not Shiite Muslims like the Persians but Sunnis, they also took active part in this phase of the revolution. Abdul Rahman Ghassemlou and other Kurdish political leaders returned from exile abroad and set about reorganizing the KDP-Iran (KDPI) and smaller Kurdish parties. By the time the old regime fell, in February 1979, mass meetings in various Kurdish towns called for autonomy for the Kurds in a federal Iran. The Kurdish provinces were the only part of Iran that resisted the establishment of an Islamic republic in the country.

In August 1979, Khomeini dispatched the army and revolutionary guards to bring Kurdistan under control. The cities were quickly occupied, and at some places such as Sanandaj summary executions took place. The Kurdish parties had expected this development and prepared for a prolonged guerrilla struggle. They took to the mountains and within a few months reconquered some of the cities.

Meanwhile, the relations between Iran and Iraq rapidly deteriorated. Although more than half of Iraq's inhabitants were and still are Shiites, they had no share in political power and were economically backward. This by itself was enough reason for the Baath regime (based in Sunni Arabs, who constitute at most a quarter of Iraq's population) to be wary of the demonstration's effects on the Iranian revolution. It clamped down on radical Shiites and executed leading clerics. Iranian military and politicians loyal to the shah were welcomed in Iraq and were permitted to prepare for a counterrevolution. Khomeini fiercely criticized Saddam Hussein and threatened that the next Shiite revolution might take place in Iraq. Iraqi Shiites were given military training, and Tehran also began supporting Idris and Mas'ud Barzani's KDP, in spite of their previous association with the shah's regime.

In September 1980, Saddam repealed the border agreement he had concluded with the shah in 1975 and sent his army into southwestern Iran, apparently believing that the Khomeini regime could be brought down by a quick strike. It was not his only mistake. The war was to last eight years and cost almost half a million lives, and its net effect strengthened rather than weakened the Khomeini regime. Part of the battles were fought along the Kurdish-inhabited northern half of the Iran-Iraq border. Both countries supported autonomist movements among each other's Kurdish populations. Iran, where many Iraqi Kurdish refugees lived, persuaded the KDP to help in suppressing its own Kurdish uprising and to cooperate militarily against Iraq.

By 1983, the KDPI lost the last bits of Iranian territory it had controlled and was definitively pushed across the Iraqi border. From then on, its guerrilla fighters only carried on hit-and-run actions from base camps inside Iraqi Kurdistan. Life, especially in the cities, returned to normal—except that those who had been too clearly involved in the Kurdish uprising had been killed, were imprisoned, or had fled abroad.

Iran's Islamic regime granted the Kurds limited cultural rights but kept the lid on the expression of political demands. It refrained from wholesale repression of the Kurds and instead hurt the political movement by assassinating its leaders. Abdul Rahman Ghassemlou, the popular leader of the KDPI, was in 1988 invited to meet in Vienna with representatives of Tehran to negotiate a settlement of the conflict. An assassination squad shot him and two colleagues dead while they were actually sitting at the negotiating table with their Iranian counterparts. In 1992, his successor, Mohammad Sadiq Sharafkandi, and three other party leaders were shot dead by Iranian gunmen in a restaurant in Berlin.   —*MvB*

U.S. Central Intelligence Agency memorandum,
"Iran's Minorities: The Kurds," February 2, 1979

Persian Gulf Collection, The National
Security Archive, Washington, D.C.

Recent Dissidence

████████████████████████████████████

██████████ recent incidents that have aroused Iranian
authorities' concern include:

- --Speeches at mosques by political and religious leaders
  calling for armed rebellion, and the discovery of
  weapons throughout the area. ████

- --Public displays of the flag of the "autonomous republic
  of Kurdestan," singing of its "national anthem," and
  separatist graffiti. (██

- --Formation of a "Kurdestan Solidarity Council" and alleged
  efforts to unite the tribes against the central
  authorities. ████

- --Attacks on local police and SAVAK representatives,
  their offices and homes, and another, by Iraqi Kurds,
  on an Iranian border post. ████

- --Demonstrations and clashes between "subversives" and
  troops. ████

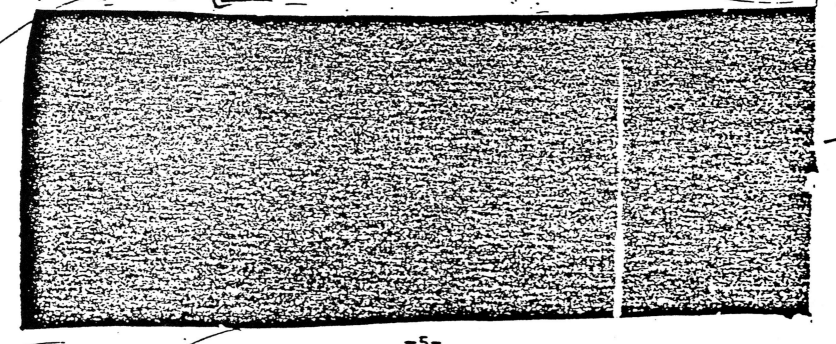

*Abdul Rahman Ghassemlou, secretary general of
the Kurdistan Democratic Party of Iran*

*Home of Aref Yasin, chief of the Doski tribe,
who fought with Barzani, Ziwa, Iran*

*Ghassemlou at public meeting, Chwar Chira Square,
Mahabad, November 20, 1979*

"It is the moment to negotiate. . . ."   *—Ghassemlou*

1979

The palace of Ishaq Pasha, Doğubayazit, Turkey, near the border with Iran

Chris Kutschera
French Writer and Photographer

*We started our journey from the palace of Ishaq Pasha, at Doğubayazit,
in Turkish Kurdistan, near the border with Iran. Beside the palace lies
the grave of Ahmed Khani, one of the most famous Kurdish poets and
the author of* Mem-û-Zin *(the Kurdish Romeo and Juliet). . . .*

*After kissing good-bye the bearded and mustached Kurdish smugglers
who helped us cross the border, we arrived in Iranian Kurdistan in a
village controlled by Iraqi Kurds. There we had one of our first real
contacts with the daily life of a traditional chief. Each time a new guest*

Chris Kutschera

came in, we all had to stand, shake hands with him, and sit down, cross-legged. We spent our time for several days standing, sitting, and drinking tea. . . . We went from village to village and met more and more people, most of them supporters of Ghassemlou.

At the end of three or four days, they told us, "No more Land Rover. We must go on foot." After a few hours, we reached Ghassemlou's headquarters, near the border between Iran and Iraq. Ghassemlou had left Paris at the end of 1978, at the beginning of the Iranian revolution, and now we were together again in Iranian Kurdistan. He said, "For the first time in my life, I have a house!" Everything had changed; the shah had left Iran forever, there was an Islamic republic, and

Ghassemlou, the exile, was living again in his country, the leader of a Kurdish party of twelve thousand fighters. . . . He had forgotten how to ride horses and use guns, and this man, who was so much at ease living like one of us in the European capitals where he got his Ph.D., was always a bit awkward when he had to share the daily life of peshmergas.

Later, during an informal cease-fire reached with the Iranian forces in November 1979, we snuck into Mahabad with Ghassemlou without any special escort. . . . A huge meeting was organized at Chwar Chira Square, the same square where Qazi Mohammad proclaimed the Kurdish Republic on January 22, 1946.

Letter from Chris Kutschera, living in France, 1995

THP032303 03/23/79-SANANDAJ, Iran: Gunmen wearing the Kurdish head dress take time off for a smoke during the shaky ceasefire in this battle-torn city. A few residents venture out in deserted street to buy food after being trapped indoors for four days, 3/22.
UPI   sr/Javad Bijarchian

Dr. Abdul Rahman Ghassemlou
Kurdish Leader

From August to November 1979 we had war with the central government. At the end of this period we forced them to negotiate with us. There was no central authority in Tehran. Added to this was the problem that Shiite theory does not accept the concept of nationality—we are all supposed to be united as Muslims. At one point I was negotiating with a religious leader over what term to use for autonomy. He would not accept the Persian word khodmokhtari *("self-choice"). I proposed that we use the European word* autonomia, *but that was rejected because it was foreign. I then suggested the Arabic term Hokm-i dhat ("self-rule"). But that was no good, and in the end he proposed "Islamic khodmokhtari." I willingly accepted. But there were others who were preparing a fresh offensive, and in the end their hard-liners won out. The central government insisted that the Kurds hand in their arms. If we had done so, they would have massacred us. It was a demand we could not accept. So, in March 1980, hostilities restarted, and we voluntarily withdrew from the larger towns to avoid causing destruction to the economic life of the people.*

Interview by Fred Halliday,
Merip Reports, July-August 1981

fighting between Kurds and Turkish-speaking residents, 4/25. A total of 200 bodies were collected from the battle-scarred town as efforts continued to retrieve bodies tossed in rivers.
UPI   sr/Kayhan

1979

THP032308 03/23/79-SANANDAJ, Iran: The Kurds may have plenty of firearms but, perhaps, not enough vowels, as this banner inscribed on a road block in Sanandaj shows 3/23. The Persian equivalent of the slogan in the tiny letters at the right side of barrier explains the Kurds want autonomy in the fullest sense of the term. Tension rode high in the city as the Kurds and Ayatollah Khomeini's representatives talked about the future control of the city, now held by the Kurds. UPI   sr/Jamshid Imani-Rad

Banner reads "We want a federal system"

UPI/Corbis-Bettmann, New York

Andrew Whitley
British Journalist

The first organized demonstrations took place at Tehran University— the first movements by intellectuals, writers, lawyers—to demand the establishment of the rule of law in Iran and the restoration of constitutional rights and of greater accountability by the executive. There was no teaching in Kurdish. Kurdish identity was not encouraged. They were treated as folkloric, but they were not allowed to express themselves.

I had come to Iran in late 1977. I came after a five-year absence of any BBC correspondent. One of the things about the Iranian revolution was that this was a revolution of communications. And it depended, like all revolutions, on various means of communications. In this case it was the cassette recorder, because of the cassettes of the speeches by Ayatollah Khomeini and by other religious leaders, that were transmitted clandestinely around the country. And the Xerox machine, which then was the high point of technology. The Xerox machine was used for underground newsletters or statements. I became one of the people who received these, because Iranian national radio and television were under central government control. I would receive phone calls from anonymous people. I received delegations of Kurdish tribesmen, who would come and camp outside the door of my house in Tehran and wait for me to wake up to deliver me petitions. I received various demands,

which were written on long medieval-type scrolls, with a list of names of all the signatories at the bottom, articulating their various demands. Demands started appearing like "the shah must go." The Kurds did not lead this in any way; they just picked up on an echo that they heard elsewhere in the country. It was only in the period after the establishment of the provisional government of Mehdi Bazargan in March 1979 that the Kurds began to organize and articulate themselves as demanding autonomy. It was at this time that Ghassemlou and his allies from the KDP reestablished bases back in Iran again. They began to articulate these demands on a national scale and demand their share of the prize. This was met with very fierce reaction, a very chauvinistic Persian reaction from Khomeini. He acted by sending in the troops and he sent in Ayatollah Khalkhali, the "hanging judge," known for his extreme brutality in ordering the wiping out of members of the old aristocracy and the old political classes. Ayatollah Khalkhali was sent to Kurdistan, together with the revolutionary guards, to pacify the Kurds.

They chose to make an example of the Kurds, to demonstrate to all the tribal peoples and the minorities of the country that there could be no challenge to this greater Persian Shia rule that was being established in the country.

Interview with Andrew Whitley, living in Switzerland, April 1994

Shaikh Ezzeddin Hoseini
Kurdish Leader

In the last years of the shah, many of the mullas who were prosecuted by the central government found refuge in the Kurdish areas.

There was enormous demand for a change of regime in the Kurdish areas as well. The Kurds didn't separate themselves from the mass movement which was developing to overthrow the monarchical regime. The Kurds were very ready to collaborate with the new regime.

During his exile both in Iraq and later in Paris, Khomeini spoke a lot about the rights of the Kurds. Even after he came back, in the beginning, there were some signs of accord, and I went to Tehran to meet him. I met Khomeini in a large room. He came in, shook hands and welcomed me.

We had discussions about the rights of the Kurds. And though the main demand was autonomy within the framework of Iran, we took up two questions during our meeting with him. The first demand from our side was that if an Islamic state were established, this Islamic state must not be called an Islamic state in the sense of a Shia state; the second one was the autonomy of the Kurdish nation.

During these meetings, Khomeini did not respond to anything concrete. He was just speaking in general terms, saying that everyone under the monarchy had been oppressed, without specifying anything about the fight of the nationalities. And then in the course of these meetings, I could feel that he was just trying to know people and that he was not going to give any rights or accept any rights. But in the initial stages, they just waited to see in order to consolidate their power base.

When I asked him what I could do for him, he said, "I want security and stability in Kurdistan from you." And then I took him by the collar of his garment, and I said, "Okay, for my part, I want the autonomy of Kurdistan from you."

From that meeting, in April 1979, I understood that he did not intend to give us anything.

Interview with Shaikh Ezzeddin Hoseini,
living in exile in Sweden, October 1993

Shaikh Ezzeddin Hoseini at prayer   Chris Kutschera

Kurdish gunmen on watch as chief mediator for Ayatollah Khomeini walks into mosque of Sanandaj

IRAN

Monir Nahid
Kurdish Mother

After the shah fell, everyone was happy and hopeful that things would change. Kurdishness and the Kurdish entity were emerging as a serious threat to the newly formed government. It was at the beginning of this period that my sons were arrested.

I found my son Hassan in a hospital bed, surrounded by pasdars and military personnel. I could only say two or three words and I was ordered not to speak Kurdish, only Persian.

Then I went to the gendarmerie station and waited, hoping that I could see my other son, Shahyar. One of the influential pasdars came and didn't know that I was the mother of the two. He started swearing, saying that he had been whipping and lashing the prisoners to extract information from them so they would give the names of their friends. It was impossible to see Shahyar; he had lost consciousness. I finally saw him at the Sanandaj airport, at twelve o'clock. At three, he was executed.

I was told later that Hassan was injured—three bullets in his leg. They put him in a cast and forced his younger brother to carry him to the execution site.

They said that they wanted five thousand tumans for my sons' bodies to be reclaimed. I said I couldn't pay that. Others paid the money. After two days, they gave me the bodies.

I was in Sanandaj for fourteen days and then I left the country. Someone called me and said they had a picture of the execution. That picture was published ten days after the execution. The first time I saw it was in a foreign magazine, Life.

It seems that some people disguised as pasdars took these pictures. Other than those people no one else was around.

Here in the U.S., a missionary from a church came to see me, and I showed him the pictures. Speechless, I tried to communicate a story that I felt he should know about.

It is important to me that people should know—it makes life more tolerable because I see this picture as an exposure of a reality. But unfortunately, I have never been able to put into words what is inside me.

Interview with Monir Nahid, mother of Hassan and Shahyar Nahid, living in the U.S., March 1992

July 1979. . . . . Eight condemned men in an empty lot. The "Executioner" [Ayatollah Khalkhali] is there, standing next to the helicopter that brought him from Tehran an hour earlier. "Shoot them," ordered Khalkhali. Everything happens very quickly. So fast indeed, that this assassination should slip through the grasp of history, its judgment, and its memory. There is the firing squad, composed of "Guardians of the Revolution," each one targeting "his own" prisoner. One can make out two men carrying cameras, but they belong to the Executioner's entourage. There is also a young soldier who stands discreetly with an Instamatic in his hand. His name is Mahmoud Abkhoran, he is nineteen years old and doing his military service. Then, there is the professional photographer. Having come to cover the Kurdish demonstrations, he is present at the Sanandaj airport that day only by chance. Because the regime is still ignorant of what images can do to it, they have not chased him away, but simply forbidden him to take pictures.

Eight bodies, broken by the impact of the bullets. The photographer works by instinct, with his camera against his stomach, taking advantage of the noise from the firing guns, and walking discreetly in a large circle behind the firing squad. He made six shots.

The next day, one of these photos is displayed on the cover of *Ettela'at*, the leading evening paper in Tehran. An editor opposed to the dictatorship managed to get around a still inexperienced censorship board. Khomeini, furious, stamps his feet. He starts by demanding the confiscation of the negatives. The imam's representative at *Ettela'at* has the material placed in the paper's safe. However, by some unknown means, the negatives are immediately smuggled out of the country. Everything happens as though these photos had taken on a life of their own, and now nothing seems to stop them. In the following week they appear more than two thousand times in dailies and weeklies around the world. An incredible rebounding effect brings them right back to Iran where, copied from foreign journals, they appear on posters that rapidly cover the walls in every major city.

What has become of their author? He isn't bothered. As a result of an error, Khomeini's wrath is directed against another photographer. *Paris Match*, a French weekly, published the photos in a six-page spread, but an error by the agency that held the rights attributed them to another Iranian photographer. The ayatollahs, who have been desperately seeking a scapegoat since the photos first appeared, rejoice in the news—but prematurely so. The wrongly accused photographer has been warned in time and manages to go underground. Luckily for him. In spite of telexes sent by *Paris Match,* by all the press agencies and journalists' unions to the Iranian authorities establishing the truth of the man's innocence, they are not enough to calm the wrath of Khomeini.

October 1980. The Iran-Iraq war has begun. The "Guardians of the Revolution" are sent to the front. Among these "volunteers," a certain ex-conscript named Mahmoud Abkhoran. With his Instamatic he too had taken several photographs of the airport massacre. Terrified by the extent of the scandal, he quickly hid the evidence. But circumstance has it that in his unit on the front is one of the members of the Sanandaj firing squad. This "Guardian of the Revolution" . . . recognizes Mahmoud, the soldier holding the Instamatic. He also knows of Khomeini's wrath and reports Mahmoud to an Islamic judge. The decision is immediate: death. Twenty minutes after being recognized by his fellow "Guardian of the Revolution," the young soldier is executed.

Today, the unknown photographer, the truly "guilty" man, is living in exile. He has not let the memory of Mahmoud die, however. He even managed to find the photos that cost the life of the young amateur photographer, and got them out of the country. As for those professional pictures, which to this day are the greatest slap in the face of a dictatorship a photographer has ever inflicted, they received the Pulitzer Prize in 1979. The only anonymous winner ever.

Yann Richard, "Islam: La Photo Hors-la-Loi? (Islam: The Photograph Outside the Law?)," *Photo*, June 1989

New York Times

NEW YORK, WEDNESDAY, AUGUST 29, 1979

25 cents beyond 50-mile zone from New York City.
Higher in air delivery cities.

United Press International

Army forces loyal to Ayatollah Ruhollah Khomeini executing Kurdish rebels and two former officers of Shah Mohammed Riza Pahlevi's army. The men were found guilty by Ayatollah Sadegh Khalkhali of crimes against the state.

Irish Police Search Coast for Clues To Blast That Killed Mountbatten

By WILLIAM BORDERS
Special to The New York Times

MULLAGHMORE, Ireland, Aug. 28 —

IRANIANS EXECUTE 20 IN KURDISH UPRISING

9 Soldiers Are Among the Victims

wing of the Irish Republican Army,

When the revolution happened I stayed in Iran and was punished for being a Kurd. The punishment was directed against the Kurdish Democratic Party, which was the biggest organized group in Iranian Kurdistan fighting against Khomeini's regime for Kurdish self-determination. The KDPI took some of our equipment, machines we were using for road building—bulldozers, tractors, graders, and other things. They took over some of our Land Rovers. And, most important, they took fifteen tons of dynamite. We used dynamite for breaking the mountains for roads; they used it against the Revolutionary Guards and the Iranian army. So here I was, accused of helping the Democratic Party—the guerrillas—against Khomeini and the Revolutionary Guards! That's why they arrested me.

My business partner wasn't Kurdish, so he didn't have as much of a problem as I did. The authorities wouldn't let me leave the country. Finally I collected what I had left—about twenty thousand dollars—and I gave it to the Iranian authorities as a bribe. And they let me leave.

I lost all my things, because the Kurds needed them. And the Khomeini regime took the rest. I was assumed to be an antirevolutionary.

My brother Hassan was a metallurgy student, but he spent most of his time in political activities in those years—antishah and Kurdish movements. After the revolution, Hassan trafficked armaments, guns, and rockets, from one part of Kurdistan to the other, and by coincidence, my other brother—the smaller one, Shahyar—was in that region. He went to see Hassan. He had a few days' vacation. So he was with Hassan when he was trafficking guns, and they got caught. My brother said that the Shiite official in charge of the trial had asked him three questions: "What's your job?" Shahyar said, "I'm a college student." "What's your religion?" "I'm Sunni Muslim." "And what's your nationality?" "I'm Kurd." And that religious person who was in charge of the trial said, "Each of these answers is enough reason to kill you. You have given all three." The trial had taken five minutes. Then he ordered both of my brothers, and nine other people who had been captured with them, to be executed.

Interview with Farhad Rashidian, brother of Hassan and Shahyar Nahid, by Ron Kelley, *Irangeles*, 1993

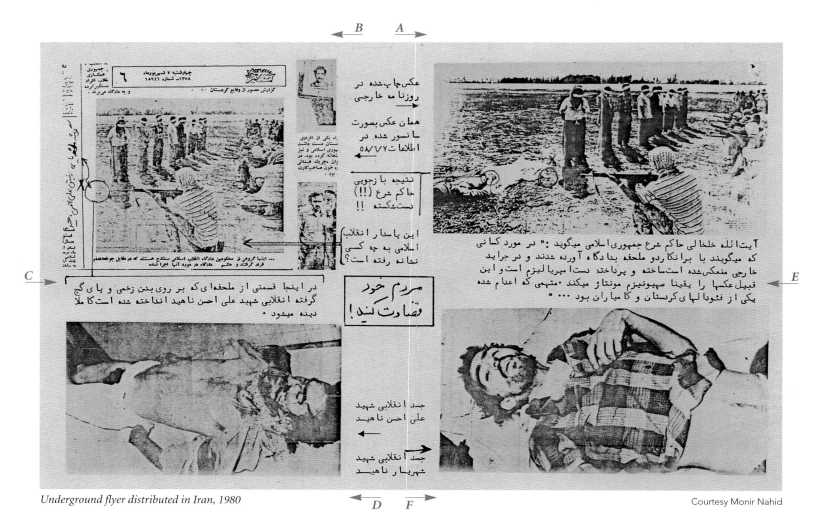

Underground flyer distributed in Iran, 1980

Courtesy Monir Nahid

A. "Picture printed in a foreign newspaper"
B. "The same picture in the censored form in which it appeared in Ettela'at" [Iranian newspaper]
C. "Who is this Islamic revolutionary guard aiming at?"
D. "Here you can plainly see part of a sheet which has been put over the wounded body and cast-encased leg of the revolutionary martyr Ali Hassan Nahid."

E. "Ayatollah Khalkhali, the religious judge of the Islamic Republic, says in connection with those who say they were brought to the court with a stretcher and two sheets, as reported in the foreign press, it is created by the hands of imperialism, and these kinds of photographs are surely montaged by Zionists. One of the accused who was executed was a feudal lord of Kurdistan and Kamyran."
F. "The result of the interrogation by the religious judge, a broken hand. Body of martyred revolutionary Shahyar Nahid."

Monir Nahid, holding a 1979 Paris Match *magazine, with her son, Farhad Rashidian, 1988*

Ron Kelley

Spot News Photography

The name of the photographer who won the 1980 Pulitzer Prize for spot news photography today is not known at this time. The picture, showing a government firing squad executing nine Kurdish rebels and two former police officers of the deposed Shah in Sananda, Iran, was distributed by United Press International August 28, 1979. In entering the photo, UPI managing editor Larry De Santis explained: "Standing by helplessly, armed only with a camera, this photographer did the only thing he could -- make a photo, get it distributed and hope it would arouse the world to react and put an end to bloodshed . . . . Because of the present unrest in Iran, the name of the photographer cannot be revealed at this time." If he won the Pulitzer Mr. De Santis said, "the prize can be forwarded to him as soon as the trouble in Teheran is history."

Press release on the Pulitzer Prize, from the Office of Public Information,
Columbia University School of Journalism, April 14, 1980

Courtesy Columbia University

Tehran-Vienna: Account of a Crime

After waiting twenty minutes, Azad begins to worry seriously. He knows well the Doctor's habits and his punctuality since the times of putting him up and serving as his chauffeur on his visits to Vienna. When they parted at five o'clock in front of the Hilton, the Doctor said, "Come back to get me at 7:15." . . .

When he speaks of Abdelrahman Ghassemlou, secretary general of the Kurdish Democratic Party of Iran (KDPI), Azad always says, "The Doctor." Settled in Austria for sixteen years, born in Mahabad, the "capital" of Iranian Kurdistan, Azad is first of all a disciplined and faithful KDPI militant. Even though the Doctor sleeps in his house and shares most of his meals when he comes to Austria, Azad would not take the liberty to ask questions.

He sensed that something exceptional was happening like he had already surmised in December and January when he drove the Doctor to mysterious meetings. But if the Doctor did not talk about it, it's because he had his reasons.

It is almost eight o'clock and still nothing. Azad decides to park the car and call his Kurdish friends who are awaiting Ghassemlou for a Party meeting.

Who knows, maybe the Doctor took a taxi to his next meeting. Azad doesn't really believe it, nor do his friends. It must be accepted that something abnormal has occurred. But what? Azad doesn't even know where the Doctor went after he dropped him off.

With his two friends joining him, Azad crossed police cars arriving with lights flashing and converging a hundred meters from the Hilton in the Linkebahngasse, a narrow street that snakes alongside the railroad tracks and is already closed to traffic. A terrible foreboding seizes them as they approach the policemen. Passing from one cop to another, it becomes a tragic certainty when an officer informs them that three people have been killed and a fourth wounded in a nearby building. . . .

On the fifth floor of 5 Linkebahngasse, a spectacle of horror awaits the three Kurds. At the end of the hall in a sort of salon to which the entry is barred by the police, they can see Dr. Abdelrahman Ghassemlou, immobile in an armchair, his shirt entirely red with blood. Two other men are stretched out on the floor. One is Abdullah Ghaderi. In shock, Azad doesn't identify the other, whom, nevertheless, he knows well. It is Dr. Fadhil Rasoul, also Kurdish but of Iraqi origin and a friend of Dr. Ghassemlou's.

It is 8:30. For Azad and his Kurdish friends

the saddest night of their lives has begun, and three weeks later they have not yet recovered. At this moment it is impossible to imagine who could be the authors of such carnage. . . . One killer, two killers? Where did they come from? What were their motives? Where did they disappear to? How? So many mysteries. . . .

In fact, the story had begun in 1987 while the Iran-Iraq war was dragging on eternally, and while a ferocious internal power struggle was going on in the anticipation of the "after-Khomeini" period. Militarily, the Iranian and Iraqi Kurds control from their respective regions most of the eastern border between Iran and Iraq. Tehran and Baghdad owe it to themselves to win over

the "other's" Kurds. In the perpetual and tragic game of alliance of political movements emanating from these people, the Iraqi Kurdish resistance found itself therefore in the Iranian camp, against the common enemy, Saddam Hussein, the Iranian Kurdish movement being, for symmetrical reasons, protected by Baghdad.

Concerning Iran, Ghassemlou's KDPI is not only a military force with which one must contend, since, despite eight years of war, it could not be weakened. But it is also the principal political force of the opposition to the Islamic regime, and the KDPI slogan, "Autonomy for Kurdistan, Democracy for Iran," constitutes a danger for the future. . . .

According to what one could find out about the discussions of December and January, for the first time in the history of the negotiations between the KDPI and Tehran,

the Iranian emissaries would not have rejected out of principle the claim for autonomy for Iranian Kurdistan. This would have included even accepting the reunification of the Kurdish region, the recognition of the Kurdish language, along with Persian as the official language in Kurdistan, the additional right to teach in Kurdish in school, the legalization of the KDPI, and the right to freely publish Kurdish newspapers. . . .

Abdelrahman Ghassemlou, assassinated in Vienna, July 13, 1989, was by all accounts an exceptional personality. . . . He was little known by the broad public, and many learned of his existence at the time of his assassination. . . . Not because he was a man in the shadows surrounded in deep mystery. . . . He was the passionate and tireless ambassador for his cause, traveling around the world to make it known. But he was never as happy as when he was with his peshmerga in a mud hut deep in an obscure valley on the Iran-Iraq border where, from one location to the next, he transported a library with him. . . .

Ghassemlou blended, at nearly sixty years of age—he would be fifty-nine next December—the serenity of an oriental sage with the dynamism of a young man, the curiosity of an encyclopedist and the appetites of a happy living person. Inflexible in his convictions as well as pragmatic in the conduct of his activities, Ghassemlou seemed to reconcile without distress the necessary harshness of political-military combat with the elegant skepticism of the academic that he had been for a long time. . . .

The death sentence was pronounced as early as 1979, when Abdelrahman Ghassemlou was elected, the only declared layman, deputy to the "Constituent" Assembly. For security reasons, he refused to go to Tehran. The Ayatollah Khomeini publicly regretted his absence before the television cameras and added: "What a shame; we would have arrested him and had him shot immediately." July 13, 1989, the day of Aid el Kebir, the "day of pardon" for Muslims, was also the fortieth day of mourning for the Imam, sacred celebration for the Shiites. Should one see only a coincidence? Or rather that, as assassins, disguised as peace negotiators with an official mandate from Hachemi Rafsandjani and passports signed by Velayati [the Iranian minister of foreign affairs], they came from Tehran in order to finally, on this ritual day, execute the sentence?

Marc Kravetz, *Liberation*, August 7, 1989, translated by Stuart Alexander

Above: *Commemoration following the assassination of Abdul Rahman Ghassemlou in Paris. Sign reads: "At the time of the Bicentennial of the French Revolution two democrats have been killed."*

Associated Press

Dr. Sadiq Sharafkandi, leader of the Iranian KDP, assassinated in Berlin, buried in
Père Lachaise cemetery with two associates, Paris, September 27, 1992

"There is a competition between the Iraqi Kurdish parties which makes me pessimistic about the future." Sharafkandi said this to me in 1992 in Kandil, at the headquarters of the KDPI. The relationship between the Kurds of Iran and Barzani was difficult in the sixties. Barzani felt Kurds from other parts of Kurdistan should stop their own activities until his revolution achieved a result. That created a problem with us and with the Turkish Kurds and has had its influence on later developments with the PKK and within Iraqi Kurdistan groups then with the KDPI in the 1990s. In contrast to Ghassemlou who was an Iranist, Sharafkandi was more Kurdistani—*he was in favor of a Pan-Kurdish movement.*

Interview with Bakhtiar Amin, Kurdish scholar living in the U.S., March 1997

I read about the burial at Père Lachaise cemetery on the 28th of September, but I didn't join the long march of hundreds of people who walked to the cemetery. I arrived late and walked directly up to the grave. Lots of people passed by, mostly Kurds, from exile in all different European countries. When I arrived at the graves, only the immediate families of the dead men were still there. I didn't want to take pictures and disturb them. It was such a very difficult and delicate moment. There were lots of security agents there, but nobody disturbed me while I was taking pictures of the graves. Shortly after, they took the paintings away and covered the graves. The place was wounded, wounded by hundreds of footsteps. I felt again sad and weak, as I always feel when I stand near a graveside, anywhere in the world. Another horrible killing and useless death.

Letter from Olivia Heussler, November 1994

The Military Takes Control in Turkey

Since the introduction of multiparty democracy after the Second World War, Turkey suffered three military coups, in 1960, 1971, and 1980, of which the last had the most pervasive effect on politics and society. All three interventions, although quite different in character and in motivation, were at least to some extent a response to Kurdish involvement in politics: the Democratic Party's use of Kurdish aghas and shaikhs as vote-getters in the eastern provinces in the 1950s; the left-wing Workers' Party of Turkey's advocacy of Kurdish cultural and economic rights in the late 1960s; and the proliferation of Kurdish nationalist associations and the radicalization of their demands in the late 1970s. These Kurdish activities were neither the sole nor the most important reason for the army to intervene, but military repression hurt the Kurds more than others.

In 1971, martial law was declared in the major Kurdish cities along with the industrial centers in western Turkey. In trials against Kurdish intellectuals, prosecutors stuck to the old line that there exists neither a Kurdish people nor a Kurdish language, and that all activities focusing on Kurdish identity are a direct threat to Turkey's existence. The Marxist Workers' Party of Turkey was banned because its 1970 congress had adopted a motion recognizing the existence of the Kurds and attributing the underdevelopment of eastern Turkey in part to anti-Kurdish policies of the past. The (Turkish) sociologist Beşikçi was sentenced to fifteen years imprisonment for a scholarly study of eastern Turkey that stressed the Kurds' ethnic distinctness.

It appears that these repressive measures had the effect of making young educated Kurds more aware of their distinct identity. After the return to civilian rule in 1973 and a general amnesty in 1974, the left and Kurdish movements reemerged. The Turkish left of the 1970s maintained great caution in referring to the Kurdish question, thereby strengthening the tendency for the Kurds to organize separately. Various Kurdish organizations became active, and not only found a much larger following than in the 1960s but also gradually radicalized in their analysis of the Kurdish question and their views of a solution. A wide range of political and cultural journals appeared (most of which were at once banned); some popular singers had the courage to sing an occasional song in Kurdish (for which they were severely punished); second- or third-generation assimilated Kurds rediscovered their ethnic roots and began learning Kurdish. The repression of these cultural activities fostered political radicalism. By the end of the decade there were a dozen clandestine Kurdish parties, some of which advocated armed struggle for independence.

The Kurds were not the only ones who radicalized. Militant trade unions organized strikes against deteriorating living standards and government policies that hurt the working class. There were strong though fragmented left-wing youth and student movements that believed in urban guerrilla and armed revolution. Extreme right-wing groups, aided by elements in the police and armed forces, waged civil war on the left and the nationalist Kurds. By 1980 polit-

ical violence demanded a death toll of eight per day. A divided parliament, incapable of making any decisions at all, paralyzed political life, as one unstable government coalition succeeded another.

The escalating political violence and inefficacy of the political establishment were the chief reasons the military adduced for their coup d'état in 1980. They moved against all radicals—the left, the right, and the Kurdish nationalists—with martial law, large-scale army operations, mass arrests, systematic torture, and mass trials before military courts. They also dissolved all existing political parties and briefly imprisoned their leaders, including the prime minister; they banned trade unions and purged the civil service (including the police and teachers) of suspected left or Kurdish radicals. There was a concerted, and largely successful, effort to depoliticize society and a renewed drive for assimilation of the Kurds.

Numerous Kurdish intellectuals and politicians spent time in prison. Most of those who managed to flee the country ended up in western Europe, where they found the freedom to establish associations and to publish journals and books that had always been absent in Turkey. By the mid-1980s, a Kurdish cultural revival was taking place in Sweden, France, and Germany. Of the various Kurdish organizations that had existed in Turkey before the 1980 coup, only the most radical and violent, the PKK, managed to maintain a presence in the country in spite of mass arrests of its supporters; all others practically disappeared.

The PKK's leader, Abdullah Öcalan (popularly known as Apo), and other members of the central committee had found a safe refuge in Syria, from there they succeeded in maintaining control of the party's network of sympathizers in Turkey. Like many other radical groups from the entire Middle East, the PKK acquired military training facilities in southern Lebanon, and apparently also other forms of Syrian aid. Syria, which felt seriously threatened by Turkey's damming of its major water supply, the Euphrates, was in need of means to put pressure on Turkey, and the PKK became its trump card. In August 1984, the PKK launched a guerrilla offensive inside Turkey, attacking military and police installations. It operated not only from Lebanon and Syria, but also had major base camps in Iraqi Kurdistan (where due to the Iran-Iraq War government control was weakened). It was soon to establish permanent bases inside Turkey as well.

The existence of the PKK has been the chief reason for extending martial law year after year, and it has provided the pretext for massive violations of human rights. The guerrilla war it has carried on since 1984 was countered with ever more heavy-handed repression. As early as 1983, Turkish troops had invaded northern Iraq in a vain attempt to destroy the PKK there, and there were to be regular Turkish bombing raids on suspected PKK camps inside Iraq. Nevertheless, the PKK kept growing, its guerrilla force increased from several hundred to several thousand, and in spite of its reputation for violence, it proved more successful than the military in the struggle for the hearts and minds of the rural population. *—MvB*

*Arrest of a woman of a nomadic
Kurdish tribe, near Diyarbakır, 1972*

Fikret Otyam

Mehdi Zana, ex-mayor of Diyarbakır (seated third from left), with other Kurdish detainees on trial, May 1981

Chris Kutschera

Mehdi Zana

Kurdish Mayor

In 1965, the pressure of the police and the agha was very heavy on our town. I was trying to figure out how we could get the Kurdish people to go out into the streets. One day, I went to the bazaar early in the morning and found that one of the shops had been robbed. There had been a series of robberies, and the state security forces knew who the guilty people were, but the police were getting their share.

I made a speech to the people around that shop and organized a march to the local government building. There were about five thousand of us, and we marched and occupied the building for eight hours. After that I told my colleagues that you cannot motivate people by writing. We should mobilize them with meetings and demonstrations.

In March 1971, there was a coup d'état and we were all arrested, all the revolutionaries, leftists, and patriotic people. In 1974, I was released from prison, and in 1977, I became an independent candidate for mayor of Diyarbakır. I criticized the former mayors of Diyarbakır, and spoke in Kurdish. The former mayors were also Kurds, but I was the first who affirmed my national identity.

On the fifth day I was mayor, the local government organized the bakeries to hold a strike against me. The strike lasted for twenty-eight days, and they tried to make me resign. Then they tried to block the services provided by the municipalities. For example, they stopped the garbage trucks. I wanted to repair the roads in the city, but they did not give me permission to break up the stones.

I was mayor for three years. In the coup d'état in September 1980, I was arrested and charged with being against the unity of the government, of being a separatist and a member of an illegal organization. While I was in prison, some other Kurdish people started to testify in Kurdish at the trials. A group of PKK people from Batman spoke in Kurdish, and they were beaten. And I told them, "Don't be afraid; I will avenge you. Tomorrow I have my trial." And the next day I went and spoke in Kurdish, but I was beaten and thrown out of court.

Out of principle almost everybody started to speak in Kurdish, but the authorities didn't bring translators. They beat me from 1987 until 1991. I never spoke another word in Turkish.

Interview with Mehdi Zana, living in Turkey, October 1993

1981

296

Leyla Zana
Kurdish Leader

When I was fourteen years old my father decided to marry me off to my thirty-five-year-old cousin Mehdi. I did not remember Mehdi although I was told I had met him years earlier when he visited my village campaigning for his party, the Communist Party of Turkey. Mehdi had been arrested in 1971 and spent three years in prison. On his release his mother asked for my hand for her son, and my father agreed.

I was very distressed, but despite my objections he gave me to Mehdi. I did not choose my husband and I knew that my life from then on would be a difficult one. We were so different. I was a child; he was a mature man. I had been living in a small world. Suddenly, I was transplanted to a far bigger one.

In 1980 Mehdi was arrested and sentenced to thirty-five years in prison, where he eventually spent the next ten years. I was just twenty, I had a small son, and I was pregnant. For the first year after his arrest I did not stop crying. I didn't know how I was going to survive.

When I went to visit Mehdi, I met many different people at the gate of the prison. I began to change, to question my own identity and to wonder exactly who I was. Until then I had no interest in the fact that I was Kurd. The ideal was to be a Turk.

For six months I was not allowed to see Mehdi. During this time they were torturing and beating him. Every week I would go to the prison to see him and be told "no visit." About that time I began reading books.

Everywhere in the world women are ill-treated by men but amongst the Kurds it is especially bad. A woman is not even treated as a servant; she is a thing, almost an animal. For a Kurd, the birth of a girl is nothing. Not long ago my father visited me and said: "I want your brother to marry." When I asked him why he told me it was because he wanted a grandson in case we do succeed and there is a free Kurdistan. I replied, "But you already have a grandson, my son." "No," my father replied, "your son is not interesting. He does not carry my name."

In 1988 I was arrested. I had gone to visit Mehdi. There were a lot of people in front of the jail. They took us into a garden, where it was announced that we would not be able to see the prisoners.

Then, on the other side of the wall we heard them beating the men we had come to see. We just revolted; we began shouting and throwing stones. I was arrested with another eighty-three people. A soldier said that I had tried to take his gun and finally I was accused of inciting people to revolt.

The first seven days in custody were terrible. I was blindfolded and led into the interrogation room, where I was stripped completely naked by a number of interrogators, all men. They hit me, I collapsed, and they splashed me with cold water to bring me round. They also tortured me with electricity.

It was about that time that I began to be a political activist.

Interview with Leyla Zana, by Chris Kutschera, *The Middle East,* October 1993

Mehdi and Leyla Zana, with their children, Rukan, three, and Ronay, seven, and his mother, Zemzema

It is thinking that has been put on trial.
—Ismail Beşikçi

EVIDENCE OF THE CRIME
Letter sent by Ismail Beşikçi to Mme. Boulanger, Chair, the Swiss Union of Writers, August 14, 1980
The official ideology in Turkey continues to maintain, insistently and obstinately, that there are no such people as Kurds and that there is no such language as Kurdish. A primary aspect of this ideology, which we can call Kemalism for short, is that it is unabashedly anti-Kurdish. It is racist and colonialist....

The universities, which are alleged to be autonomous; the judiciary, which is allegedly independent; the mass media, which are allegedly free; and the institutions, which are pointed out as particularly democratic, have one and all accepted that ideology without any discussion. These organizations have gradually become the builders and propagators of the ideology which is based on a lie....

University circles, political parties, unions, associations, mass media, etc., never touch on the Kurdish question. Subjects such as the division of Kurdistan, the application of the "divide and rule" principle after World War I, particularly between 1919 and 1923, are those which Turkish academics, Turkish thinkers, make special efforts not to see, not to study....

The real issue is one that supercedes that of a writer's freedom. The question is that of freedom for the Kurdish people.... The Kurdish people are in a nation partitioned by barbed wires and minefields as efforts continue to completely cut off the parts from one another. Under these conditions, the political status of the Kurdish people is even lower than that of a colony because, for example, in Turkey even their existence is not acknowledged. The Kurds in Turkey can have rights only to the extent that they become Turks. The alternative is repression, cruelty, prison. In light of such issues as these, it would be of great benefit if attention was focused on the question of freedom for a nation rather than of freedom for a writer. I wish to express my appreciation for your organization's letters.

THE INDICTMENT
Republic of Turkey, Chief of Staff Commander
Office of the Military Prosecutor
DATE OF CRIME: August 14, 1980
DATE OF DETENTION: June 19, 1981
CRIME: Publication in a foreign country
in such a manner as to diminish the State's
influence and prestige
THE DEFENDANT: Ismail Beşikçi

THE DEFENSE
A letter by a writer to a fellow writer and the views he expresses cannot diminish a State's prestige. The letter cannot harm national feel-ings. It cannot hurt the national interest. What does diminish the State's prestige is the making of this letter the subject of a trial. Criminal trial proceedings have been initiated over a letter and the views expressed in the letter. This is diametrically opposed to the concept of a democratic society. Suppression . . . [does] not secure any State's prestige.... Suppression of thought, putting it on trial and obtaining a conviction—is one of the most humiliating things for a State in a democratic, contemporary world....

Writing things that are known to everyone, that are talked about both in Turkey and around the world, cannot be described as "weakening national feelings" or as "casting shadows over the supreme interests of the nation." These are the basic realities of Turkey.... The defendant in this trial is not a person. I am not the defendant in this trial. Truly, thinking is. Science is.

Ismail Beşikçi in court   Fuat Kozluklu

SUMMATION
1: I am being tried because of my views since October 20, 1981. Nevertheless, I have never regarded myself as guilty. I feel that the State is attempting to put on trial scientific thought, scientific knowledge, the universally acclaimed values of our time.
2: Science provides . . . the most significant means humans have developed to understand nature, history, society, the human species....

Along with concrete facts there are official facts, ideological facts.... [Political] regimes demand that these "facts" be viewed as the most important and demand strict adherence to them. They deem thinking outside this [context] to be an offense punishable by imprisonment.

The existence of the Kurdish nation is a concrete reality irrespective of our will. But Turkish political administrations demand that this reality not be seen, not be expressed....

The main purpose of a trial is to do justice.... In my case, however, the principal aim of the trial is to suppress concrete facts, to prevent the expression of concrete facts with the threat of imprisonment. Its purpose is to ensure that the official ideology reigns supreme. Therefore, the trials are not legitimate....

One of the two prerequisites of a civilization is freedom of thought. The other is industrialization. Together these two conditions define "modern civilization." There is no possibility of achieving such a civilization by suppressing thought and preventing criticism. To counteract the power of ideas, brute force is applied; terror is resorted to. And then the use of force and terror becomes routine. The creation of a society that speaks with one voice does not lead to the development of a civilized society. One of the most important prerequisites of modern civilization is the creation of an environment in which different voices can be heard, different views can develop....

THE JUDGMENT
Republic of Turkey, Chief of Staff
The Navy and Martial Law Military Court
Gölcük/Koçali
March 23, 1982
Whereas foreign forces have for a long time engaged in covert and destructive activities whose purpose is to set up an independent state of Kurdistan in our southern provinces by achieving unity among our eastern Anatolian citizens as if they belonged to a separate Kurdish ethnic group, even though their Turkishness cannot be doubted, and to divide the country and thereby weaken it....

Whereas foreign organizations that gave him assistance and provided him with moral and material assistance sought to exert pressure for his release by sending telegrams and letters to the then President, the Prime Minister, and the Minister for Foreign Affairs....

Whereas by continuing with his lengthy criticism in this manner, he has published in a foreign country . . . baseless and exaggerated news and information about the internal affairs of the country so as to diminish the State's influence and prestige abroad and engaged in harmful activities....

Whereas his saying, "You are not Turks, you are from a different Kurdish ethnic group," for personal gain amounts to selling out his country to them and being at their command, it is necessary to reject the defendant's defense, which lacks sincerity and veracity....

UNANIMOUS JUDGMENT: Guilty

SENTENCE: 10 years in prison, 5 years banishment

Excerpt from *Kurdish Times*, Vol. 2, Fall 1986
The Kurdish Library, Brooklyn

1981

Şerafettin Elçi in military court, January 19, 1981

Turks Imprison Former Minister Who Spoke Up on Kurds' Behalf

By MARVINE HOWE
Special to The New York Times

ANKARA, Turkey, March 26 — A former Cabinet minister has been sentenced to two years and three months in prison for "making Kurdish and secessionist propaganda," it was announced today.

Serafettin Elci, who served as Minister of Public Works under Prime Minister Bulent Ecevit in 1978 and 1979, never hid his Kurdish origin and was critical of the Government's neglect of the Kurdish regions in eastern Turkey.

His conviction, the first against a high-level politician since the armed forces came to power in September, demonstrates the junta's determination to stifle any form of Kurdish nationalism.

The junta has announced the capture of 2,280 secessionists, the term used for Kurdish nationalists, since the Sept. 12 coup. Legal proceedings have been brought against six organizations.

The Ankara martial law court sentenced Mr. Elci under an article of the criminal code that makes "propaganda with a view to destroying or weakening national feelings" a crime.

Convicted on Basis of Interviews

The former minister was convicted on the basis of published statements in which he was quoted as having said: "I am a Kurd. There are Kurds in Turkey."

There are no official figures on the number of Kurds in Turkey because ethnic origin is not reported in the census, but they are known to be the largest ethnic minority, and they are estimated to make up about 12 percent of Turkey's 45 million people. The Kurds, like the ethnic Turks, belong to the Sunni branch of Islam, but linguistically they are related to the Iranians.

Turkey's Kurds live in the undeveloped eastern regions, adjoining Syria, Iraq, Iran and the Soviet Union, all of which also have Kurdish communities.

Several Kurdish revolts, between 1925 and 1939, were crushed. Since then Turkey has not faced the problem of Kurdish autonomy movements that have emerged in Iraq and Iran.

In the liberalism that flourished in Turkey in the 1960's, Kurds were attracted to leftist parties like the pro-Communist Turkish Workers Party that were sympathetic to Kurdish aspirations.

Some Clandestine Groups Formed

When the party was dissolved by the last military regime in 1971, some Kurds began to form their own clandestine organizations. Others, like Mr. Elci, joined the Republican People's Party, a Social Democratic group that shared Kurdish demands for social justice.

A graduate of the Ankara Law School, Mr. Elci gave a number of interviews while he was minister, stressing the need to help the Kurds. In one interview, published last July by the weekly Yanki, he declared that "the east has been left to underdevelopment, poverty and misery."

Although Turkey's oil comes from the southeast, he said, the local people do not benefit from it. Some steps, he said, have been taken to develop the region with hydroelectric power from the Euphrates River, but he added that the project had low priority and would take a long time.

Mr. Elci also criticized the authorities for failing to preserve the culture of the "eastern people" and in fact preventing their cultural development.

Questioned by Yanki about the activist organizations operating in the east, he said: "It is natural that there should be reactions in an underdeveloped society that is oppressed."

IT'S AN EMERGENCY: SAVE WATER!

Şerafettin Elçi
Kurdish Cabinet Minister

I am the first parliamentarian who declared openly that he was a Kurd. A reporter from Hürriyet *newspaper came to talk to me, and I told him that the government says that there are no Kurds in Turkey, but it is not true because there are Kurds and I'm a Kurd. And this sentence went on the front page as a headline. My words almost created an earthquake in Turkey. And I was accused of being a separatist.*

I said that the Kurdish problem must be solved within the borders of Turkey, not in a separatist way. My proposals were very mild things, like lifting the ban on the Kurdish language, broadcasting from the state-owned media in Kurdish, and educating the Kurds in Kurdish. These are very natural rights. The government, even today, is very far from giving these rights to the people.

If you deny your Kurdish identity in Turkey, all paths are open to you. If you appear with your Kurdish identity, all doors become closed to you.

At the time, I had parliamentary immunity. But after the coup d'état, I was charged. I was tried in the constitutional court because of my action during my ministry time. I defended my innocence. I was aware that according to the law I was not guilty. The things that I had done were legal. But the military leadership wanted me put in prison. The court followed the wishes of the regime, and they sentenced me. Their decisions were against the law. It was a kind of murder of the law.

Interview with Şerafettin Elçi, living in Turkey, October 1993

The New York Times, March 27, 1981

TURKEY

Siirt, southeast Turkey

1982

Ad van Denderen

Every person bound to the Turkish state through the bond of citizenship is a Turk.
—Article 66

General Ihsan Göksel: The statement in the first paragraph of article 75 [now Article 66] on Turkish citizenship . . . lacks the quality a definition should have and therefore appears to be at odds with reality. 'Citizen' is the general term for people living in the same fatherland. It is not possible to speak of belonging to a nation as long as there is not the combination of common language, custom and tradition, common descent and common history, the factors that give a nation its name. By accepting a person as a citizen we cannot change the blood in his veins and replace it with Turkish blood, we cannot take the values in his heart and mind and instead rebuild him physically and spiritually with Turkish culture, Turkish virtues, the rich history of the Turks and, if you wish, the racial superiority of the Turkish race. . . . You can make a person a citizen, but you cannot make him a Turk. . . .

Especially in Ottoman history there were numerous people who were not of Turkish race but welded each other together by their earnest adoption of the virtues of Ottomanness, Turkishness and citizenship. They had become not just citizens but Turks, and their contributions to the scientific, artistic and administrative life of our nation are unforgettable. In Turkey's republican period it is also possible to encounter people who thus adopted Turkishness. The Turkish nation has never, whether in the past or today, withheld anything from such persons who adopted Turkishness, and it has pressed them to its chest. But citizenship and Turkishness cannot be taken as equivalent. If the person who accepts citizenship has not adopted Turkishness you cannot call him a Turk but at most a Turkish citizen, no more than that. . . .

If one wishes to identify citizenship and Turkishness, one should definitely include the element of adoption of Turkish identity. The person who cannot call out from his heart the words 'Happy is he who calls himself a Turk' cannot be a Turk.

Serda Kurtoğlu: I wholeheartedly agree with the statements of our General (Göksel) on the first paragraph of the constitutional arrangements concerning Turkish citizenship, but I cannot support his proposal for an amendment. The formulation of this article is a legal formulation, and its words should be understood in the meaning they were meant to express. . . . The article was included in order to explain the concept of Turkish citizen, not that of Turk. . . . If we were to make distinctions between Turkish citizens by the loudness of their shouting 'Happy is he who calls himself a Turk', then we shall be divided according to the volume of the voices; the Fatherland will dissolve, the Nation will dissolve, Turkdom will dissolve. . . .

Kemal Dal: In the Commission we had extensive discussions about General Göksel's proposal concerning Turkish citizenship. We as the Commission do not wish to distinguish among Turkish citizens between those who are Turks and those who are not. Every person who has documents proving that he is a Turkish citizen is in our view a Turk. . . . In our formulation we were to a considerable extent inspired by Atatürk's words 'Happy is he who calls himself a Turk'. Everyone who has a Turkish identity card can quietly call himself a Turk. . . . The Commission cannot accept General Göksel's proposal.

From the deliberations on the definitive text of the constitution, amongst the members of the commission preparing the Draft Constitution, published as Appendix 16 in Osman Selim Kocahanoğlu, *Gerekçeli ve Açıklamalı Anayasa (The Constitution, with Explanations and Comments)*, 1982, translated by Martin van Bruinessen

TURKEY

Riza Ezer
Turkish Photographer

A captain and nine soldiers were killed in Hakkarı, so we went to the southeast. All the newspapers were there. I talked to the colonel in charge of the operation, and he told three of us that there was another operation going on and that he could send us there.

Our car was in the middle—with a military car in front and behind us. We reached the troops around six in the morning. We spoke with the soldiers walking from the mountain zones where they had received intelligence about a very small village with only three houses. When they checked the houses, they found Mekup sneakers. At the beginning the PKK guerrillas all wore Mekups, so the army confiscated them. Then they attacked another village close by.

Their general method was to watch, circle, and then enter the village. When they got in the houses, they checked IDs. In one village, there were maybe ten people with the same last name. There was a book in the hands of one of the soldiers and a list with the names of those who were being looked for by the government. They checked the book. If the name was the same, they took that man.

They collected about forty men and brought them to the main square of the village. When they finished checking houses, the soldiers came to the square. They made a line of the villagers, forcing them to put their hands on their heads. They checked IDs again, and when they were finished, the commander asked if we wanted anything else from them.

There was a man from Hürriyet newspaper with me. He put the soldiers in positions so he could get some different photographs.

The soldiers arrested only four people. This operation was a kind of show for us.

Turkish military operation in Hakkarı, southeast Turkey, October 1984

I told the commander, "If you violate them, I'll photograph you and put your picture in the newspaper." Maybe because we were there, the soldiers were not that cruel.

After our photographs ran, the commander who allowed us to take them was transferred to another place.

The situation is very different now. At that time, people could go on their own to the region and have contact with the people and the military. I had a very good dialogue with the local people. Before when I went and asked for food from them, they always invited me and offered whatever they had. They don't open their doors now, because so many police went there as journalists. I could not go there now as a journalist and tell them I would take pictures. They don't trust anyone anymore.

Interview with Riza Ezer,
living in Turkey, October 1993

"Kurdish Activity in Southeastern Turkey," July 16, 1987
Persian Gulf Collection, The National Security Archive, Washington, D.C.

Riza Ezer/*Cumhuriyet* Archive

1984

D.

PAGE 05 RUFI
2.

A.

B.

Turkish military operation in Hakkarı, southeast Turkey, October 1984

Riza Ezer/Cumhuriyet Archive

b1-
b2-
b7D

PAGE 06 RUFLWFA0652

COMMENTS///////////////////////////COMMENTS////////////////////////COMMENTS
COMMENTS:
(C/NF)
1.

2.   (U) THE PKK IS A VIOLENT SEPARATIST ORGANIZATION ATTEMPTING TO
CREATE A SEPARATE HOMELAND IN SOUTHEASTERN TURKEY.

Coşkun Aral
Turkish Photographer

Meeting Apo

For nine years PKK leader Apo [Abdullah Öcalan] had not seen a single journalist, foreign or Turkish. He invited Birand and me, and we arrived from Damascus by private car, which they hired.

As a photographer I was happy, because it was the first time that I entered the headquarters of an organization that was hurting my country. At first Apo was not pleased by my presence, especially my cameras. He said, "You can take a picture of me but please don't take any pictures of the other people and never of the outside of the camp."

When the interview with Birand was over, I told him that I had already photographed many political leaders of organizations like the PKK. One had to always show their military strength too. He first said no, but after a few minutes he spoke to several of his military consultants and said he was willing to let me take pictures of several militants, certain warriors. I told him that was not right either. I told him that if he wanted the PKK to look strong he had to also show their military strength. He asked me, "How?" I told him, "Why don't you mount a mock attack?" They made an offensive attack on a mock Turkish military barracks. But it was like a real attack. I was there shooting video and taking pictures at the same time.

Then I said, "Do you play football?" I asked whether he would play a game for me. At nightfall they played a football match for me. The next day I shot the drills of the women fighters.

After the coup d'état in 1980, the leftists went to Germany, Paris, and Syria and began to learn about national or international movements. The members of the PKK that I knew in Beirut were with the Palestinians and began to pursue military and theoretical studies.

The newspaper interview was the first time people learned things about Apo. Before that nobody knew anything except rumors: he was Armenian, he was gay, he was a criminal. They always showed the pictures of his arrest in 1979. He was young but his face had been disfigured, so nobody would have recognized him.

The Turkish government consider photography a form of espionage. Even in normal times when you are in possession of a camera and you come across a soldier, they stop you, steal your camera, and put you in jail.

You can't compare today to 1988. In 1988 when fifteen people died it was a scoop in the papers. Now there are twenty-five to forty people killed a day. It is a summary like a list, "Today twenty-five people were killed." There's a civil war going on.

Interview with Coşkun Aral, living in Turkey, October 1993

The newspaper used the report the first day as a scoop for the country, and the next day the government decided to confiscate one edition. Birand and I were sent to jail. The trial lasted a long time. I was considered a technician and I told them that I only took pictures and that I knew nothing. We were charged with publishing propaganda detrimental to patriotism in Turkey. —Coşkun Aral

Confiscated Milliyet *newspaper, published on June 15, 1988*

1988

Apo, Milliyet yazarı M.Ali Birand'a konuştu

Koyu Galatasaraylı

Abdullah Öcalan'ın PKK kampındaki uğraşlarından biri de futbol. Fanatik bir Galatasaray taraftarı... "Galatasaray'ın şampiyonluğu en mutlu olduğum anlardan biriydi" diyor. Takımı yenildiği zaman da çok üzülüyor. Galatasaray'ın maçlarını hâlâ heyecanla izliyor. Apo'nun futbol tutkusu, kampta düzenlenen gece ve gündüz maçlarıyla sürüyor.

"Apaçık konuşuyorum"

Öcalan, M.Ali Birand'la uzun söyleşisinde, en yakın örgüt arkadaşlarına bile söylemediklerini anlattı. "Ben bir Kürt milliyetçisi değilim" diyen Apo, en sıkışık dönemlerini anlatırken de şöyle dedi: "1977 - 1978 döneminde MİT, örgütümüzü çökertmek üzereydi. Yok olmamız an meselesiydi"

© Bu yazı ve fotoğrafların yayın hakkı Milliyet'e aittir, alıntı yapılamaz.

an teklif var

A FERVENT GALATASARAY FAN

Soccer is one of Abdullah Öcalan's hobbies in the PKK camp. He is a fervent fan of [the popular Istanbul soccer team] Galatasaray. He says, "One of the happiest moments in my life was when they won the championship title." He becomes very sad when his team loses. He still follows Galatasaray's games with excitement. Apo's passion for soccer continues with games that are arranged at the camp day and night.

"I AM SPEAKING VERY OPENLY"

In his interview with M. Ali Birand, Mr. Öcalan said things he would not even tell his closest associates in the organization. Apo says, "I am not a Kurdish nationalist." Talking about his most difficult periods, he says, "In 1977–1978 the Turkish Intelligence Service (MIT) was about to finish us up. We could have been destroyed anytime."

Translation of Turkish picture captions

TURKEY

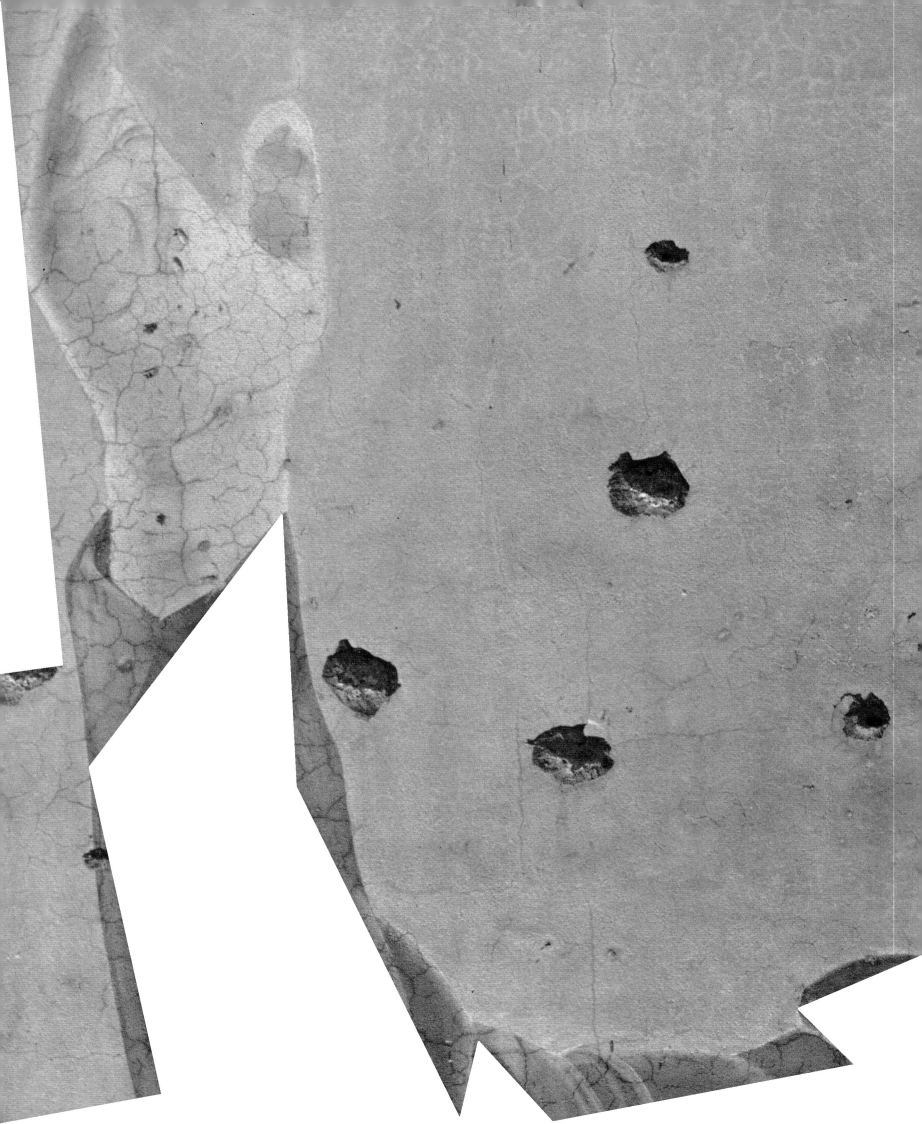

AFTER THE COLD WAR

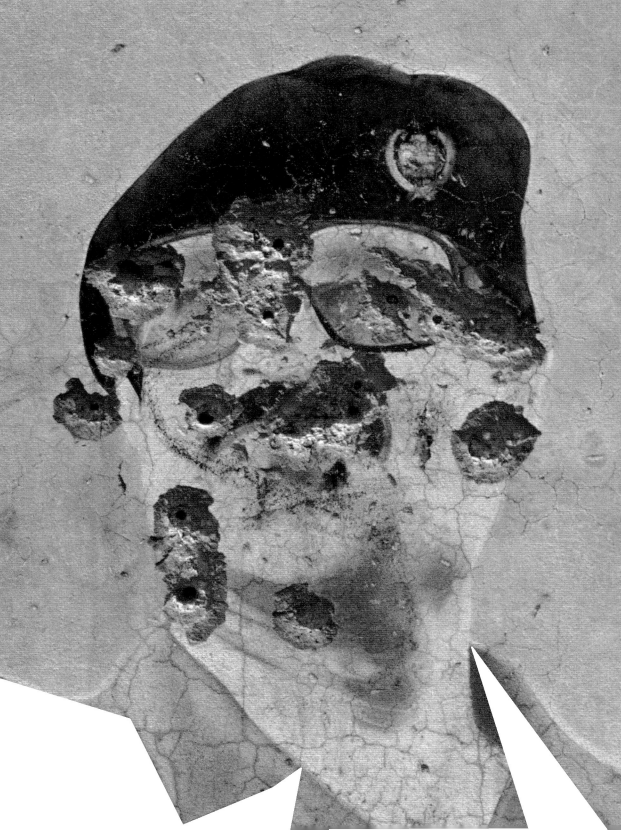

*Mural of Saddam Hussein, shot up
during the Kurdish uprising of 1991,
Zakho, northern Iraq*

Les Stone/SYGMA

From Genocide to Safe Haven in Iraq

Following the 1975 defeat of the Kurds, the Iraqi regime declared a forbidden military zone along the Iranian and Turkish borders, razed all villages there, and resettled their inhabitants in large camps. Spontaneous antigovernment guerrilla activity ensued. The Patriotic Union of Kurdistan (PUK), led by Jalal Talabani in Syrian exile, relocated to an inaccessible valley in the southern part of Iraqi Kurdistan's forbidden zone. In Iran, Barzani's sons Mas'ud and Idris reformed the Kurdistan Democratic Party, which established a presence close to the Turkey-Iraq border.

Supported by the new Islamic regime in Iran, the Barzanis and KDP peshmerga cooperated with Iranian troops against Iraq as well as against the KDPI and various smaller left-wing Kurdish rebel groups during the Iran-Iraq War. Talabani's PUK, initially allied with the Iranian Kurdish parties and with Baghdad, by the mid-1980s had also aligned with Tehran. In 1987 the feuding PUK and KDP joined with other smaller parties to become the Kurdish National Front, which claimed considerable liberated areas from the ineffectual Iraqi army.

Meanwhile, the Iraqi government recruited large Kurdish tribes into militia units (called *jash* by the Kurds) to police their own districts and to fight the Kurdish parties. In order to cut off the Kurdish insurgents from the civilian population, the regime destroyed ever more villages, resettled villagers into camps, and extended the forbidden zone. In the spring of 1987, chemical arms were used against peshmerga (Kurdish guerrilla) positions. In March 1988, the Iraqi town of Halabja, captured by Iranian troops aided by peshmerga, was bombed by chemicals, killing some five thousand, mostly civilians. This was followed by the Anfal ("Spoils") campaign, in which poison gas was liberally used against the population of peshmerga-held districts. Army units and jash attacked, looted, and razed the villages, captured the inhabitants, and dumped the women and children into camps without facilities. Most of the men—100,000 or more—were taken away; years later their bodies were found in mass graves in the desert.

After the 1990 Kuwait crisis and military defeat of Iraq, the jash, incited by President George Bush's appeal to overthrow Saddam Hussein, massively rose up, attacked the offices of the feared state security police, and disabled the Baghdad regime. The KDP and PUK, keeping low profiles during the Kuwait crisis, soon succeeded in taking the reins of the uprising. Much more of Iraq's military machine had remained intact than people believed, however, and after a few weeks of chaotic freedom the Kurdish cities were attacked by Iraq's elite Republican Guard. Brutal retaliations and fear of a repetition of the 1988 chemical bombardments drove the entire population in panic toward the Turkish and Iranian borders. More than a million Kurds attempted to reach safety. Turkey, fearing serious destabilization, refused to admit them, so that hundreds of thousands spent weeks on the border, exposed to snow and mud.

Public opinion in the West, mobilized by television images of this exodus, persuaded the United States and its allies to launch a humanitarian intervention and create a safe haven for the displaced Kurds in northern Iraq by pushing the Iraqi troops southward. Kurdish peshmerga expelled the Iraqi troops from a large zone further southeast as well. The refugees on the Turkish border were first relocated to camps inside Iraq and then persuaded to return to their homes, if they still had any. By the summer, a large part of Iraqi Kurdistan was again controlled by Kurds, under international protection. The various former jash tribes established alliances with either the PUK or KDP; some of the stronger jash chieftains became independent warlords.

The following year the Kurds held elections for a regional parliament in Arbil. The KDP and PUK received almost equal numbers of votes. The Christian minorities received a token representation in parliament as well as in the new regional government. The KDP and PUK agreed to divide all government positions equally, and to have each minister seconded by a deputy of the other party. Aided by mostly European, nongovernment organizations, the Kurds tried to reconstruct and revive the destroyed villages, infrastructure, and economy of their region. However, the UN embargo against Iraq and an additional internal embargo imposed by the Baghdad government against its Kurdish north made development nearly impossible. Throughout, Jalal Talabani and Mas'ud Barzani remained outside the government.

Deteriorating economic conditions and disagreements over the division of tolls and custom fees levied at the Turkish and Iranian borders led to tension between the two parties. In May 1994 an armed conflict broke out between the KDP and the PUK; attempts at mediation (by France, the United States, and Iran) led to temporary ceasefires but did not prevent an escalation of the conflict.

The neighboring countries as well as the Baghdad regime have in various ways tried to extend their influence in the region, by financing and arming proxies or by direct military intervention. In March 1995 Turkey launched a massive invasion of northern Iraq, ostensibly to purge the region of PKK guerrillas (without much success), but probably also to check the growing influence of Iran and Syria in the region. The following year, Iran sent a strike force deep into the region to destroy a camp of Iranian Kurdish refugees. Both the KDP and the PUK shifted alliances with these and other neighbor governments to weaken the hand of the other party.

In August 1996, even while American-sponsored KDP-PUK peace negotiations were resuming, Mas'ud Barzani's peshmerga joined the Iraqi army in a surprise offensive against PUK-controlled Arbil, the regional capital. A major setback for the PUK, it was an even more serious blow to the entire American-supported Iraqi opposition, also based in Arbil, which was practically eliminated by Iraqi security forces. For the first time since the establishment of the safe haven, Saddam Hussein's troops occupied a city that was under international protection. Mas'ud Barzani, hoping to finally destroy rival Talabani through this alliance with Baghdad, lost much of his remaining credibility among the Kurds and the international community. Both he and Jalal Talabani remain key figures in the ongoing negotiations for peace among the Kurds, a process increasingly shaped by the Turkish and Iraqi governments.   —*MvB*

Jalal Talabani

Kurdish Leader

The Kurdish people cannot live in isolation from the rest of the world, in the caves and valleys of this country. They are people like all other peoples of this world, who are affected by events of this world and affect the world too. The Kurds live in a region full of conflicts and contradictions in a rich and strategic part of the world. Our time has come and their plight and aspirations cannot be ignored for much longer.

Interview with Jalal Talabani, published in *Al-Sharara*, PUK newspaper published in Arabic from Syria, No. 6, June 1977, translated by Barham Salih

For nearly a year the Iraqi Army enjoyed the unusual experience of moving freely through the glens and valleys while the Baathist regime tried to forestall any rebellion by destroying Kurdish villages near the border and deporting the inhabitants far to the south....

While Barzani's old political opponent, Jalal Talabani, moved into the triangle to form the Patriotic Union of Kurdistan (PUK), the new KDP, renamed KDP (Provisional Leadership) but dominated by Barzani's sons Idris and Masud, tried to maintain a presence in their tribal base of Badinan....

Jalal Talabani's winter headquarters in Nawzang run far up either flank of a narrow valley overlooking the Nokan River, a tributary of the Lesser Zab. Peshmerga units are scattered up and down the river valley to provide cover—a big battle has already been fought against the Iraqi Army....

Plans are in hand to install a radio station, but Jalal Talabani has no intention of repeating Barzani's mistake of 1975 in attempting to defend the Rawanduz Valley, a mistake that committed him to a full-scale battle. Nawzang is an expendable position, one with no roads to facilitate attack but easily abandoned. The PUK's military activity consists of guerrilla hit-and-run actions far to the south and west....

The Kurdish supply line depends a good deal on the smugglers bringing in carpets, samovars and manufactured goods from Iran. The PUK makes use of that traditional activity by providing a bazaar in which goods are resold to Iraqi smugglers and the Peshmerga themselves....

Links with the Iranian Kurdish movement are informal.... Established in June, 1975, the PUK is a "semi-front" organization composed of four smaller groups. Its founders decided that the Kurdish struggle must be based on an alliance rather than one party because a number of trends and policies had to be reconciled....

Jalal Talabani is unambiguous: "The Kurds of Iraq are controlled by a fascist regime. We aim at the overthrow of this regime and the establishment of a coalition government of all democratic forces which will guarantee Kurdish autonomy."

The PUK's Arab allies are in full agreement with his programme of autonomy within an Iraq Republic, a programme that would leave responsibility for defence, foreign affairs and budgetary control in the hands of the Government. The "Iraqification" of the Kurdish revolution has already brought the PUK useful new allies, and it hopes it will prove a decisive card against President Saddam Hussein's regime.

John Stathatos, *The Times*, London, April 18, 1980

1980

Meeting of new recruits at PUK base camp, ...

Hero Talabani

Kurdish Leader

I was in Syria in 1979. The communications between the bureau in Damascus and inside were not good. I was always hearing rumors that there was nothing to eat and that the peshmerga were living in horrible conditions. I wrote a letter to Jalal, my husband, and I told him that I wanted to visit. At the beginning, he didn't agree. He said that the way was very difficult and that I could not come inside. The peshmerga who were coming and going through Syria also told me that they could not take me with them because it would be very hard for them to walk with a woman because I could not walk like they walked. Then I decided to go. I wrote another letter to Mam Jalal and said, whether you agree or not, I am coming.

I didn't plan to stay. I just wanted to go for a month or so. But when I saw the situation, I decided to stay.

In the mountains, you must prove that you can walk. You must eat what they are eating, and if there is a snake, you don't shout. If there is a scorpion, you kill it and don't say anything. Then they will accept you.

Jalal Talabani lecturing new cadres at his party's
mountain stronghold in Nawzang, Iraq   John Stathatos

Before going back to Damascus I told them that I would bring my video camera back with me. They laughed. "What will you do with a video?" they asked. "There is no electricity." I said, "We have a generator. We can manage." I told them I wanted to tape what was going on here and send it abroad so someone would know how they were living. Nobody believed me, but when I brought the video, it began something very special for everyone. Whenever they had a meeting, I always got an invitation to come. I told them that I knew it was not for me, it was for the video. I shot everything—how the peshmerga were working and washing plates, cooking and meeting, sitting together and speaking with the villagers, and how they spent their nights. At that time, the Iraqis were not bombing us; there was only fighting.

To be inside is better than to look from a distance. Because if you are inside at least you can do something. When you are outside you can't do anything but worry about it.

Interview with Hero Talabani, by Laura Hubber, April 1993

Nawzang market

Shorsh Resool
Kurdish Researcher

After the Anfal campaign in 1988, I asked many of my friends why nobody said anything about it or about Halabja to the international community and why the U.N. and the international human rights organizations didn't condemn or put pressure on Saddam Hussein.

Nawshirwan Amin, vice general secretary of the PUK, told me that people outside (I had never been abroad) need names, lists, and facts that you can tell them. If you say that four thousand villages were destroyed, you must have the names of the villages, the number of families deported, etc. And I said, "Okay, I have enough information. I can do this."

I asked people to give information about their villages—whether they had a school or not, whether they had a clinic center or not. I asked people about the number of families and the number of houses that had existed in their villages. I used my notes, my diaries, people's testimony, official documents, and other researchers' work.

Because I knew that people might exaggerate and were not precise in giving numbers—most of the people in the villages are illiterate—I took the lowest figure I was given by the villagers. Of course, there were other methods I used. For example, in traditional Islamic culture, there is a thing called Nezzer, where people slaughter a cow or a sheep and distribute the meat among all the families of the village. Everybody knew how many families were in the village because when they decided to do that, they needed to know how many families to distribute meat to.

Another important source for my research was a tremendous work done by Amin Mineh called Iraq's Strategy of Security and Ba'ath's Trine: Deportation, Arabization, and Ba'athization. *I also used Iraqi documents and maps.*

For the number of houses, I didn't need to ask the women and children, but for the disappeared people I had to ask them, because the men could not recall the names and the ages of the children who disappeared. But the children could recall the names of their friends. It was very fresh. It was still in their memories.

I asked them to imagine themselves walking through their village house by house, knocking on the door of each house, to give me the names of the people living in that particular house.

When I asked them how old the oldest boy was, they would answer, "He was born in the first year of the revolution" or "the year that Barzani came back from the Soviet Union" or "He was born in the year of Haras Qaumi," which was a militia group of the Baathist Party in 1963. These are dates that are important for the people. So it became history for them.

It turned out that the number of households and families that I put in my research was much less than the real number. I didn't want to exaggerate; I wanted to be precise. I didn't have access to the Dohuk-Badinan area. Even if I had gone back to the villages, I still could not have found out how many houses there were because they were virtually in ruins.

Although I published the research under the title "Destruction of a Nation" and put my own name on it, the international community and the human rights organizations never trusted me and never took any action. They said they could not rely on a member of a political party for evidence. But no one could make up a story of the destruction of 3,737 villages.

Interview with Shorsh Resool, living in England, April 1994

Right: Joint Chief of Staff to Defense Intelligence Agency, "The Internal Situation in Iraq," Washington, August 4, 1987, *Iraqgate: Saddam Hussein, U.S. Policy and the Prelude to the Persian Gulf War (1980–1994)*, ed. Joyce Battle, The National Security Archive, Washington, D.C.

کوردستان له دڵی تۆ دایەو
تۆش له دڵی هەموو کوردێکی
ئەمینداریّتی گشتیی رۆشنبیری و لاوان

Page from an Iraqi government publication showing Saddam Hussein in Kurdish dress

Courtesy General Secretariat of Youth Education, Bagdad

"Kurdistan is in your heart , and you are in the heart of the Kurds."
Translation of caption beneath photo

1988

IN ORDER TO COUNTNER THE SPREADING INSURGENCE, THE IRAQI
AUTHORITIES EMBARKED ON A RESETTLEMENT CAMPAIGN, FLATTENING
SOME 300 VILLAGES AND DESTROYING RESIDENTIAL AREAS IN
FREQUENT AIR RAIDS.

DESPITE THE
RUTHLESS REPRESSION, WHICH ALSO INCLUDES THE USE OF CHEMI-
CAL AGENTS, AND THE REINFORCEMENT OF THE ARMED FORCES BY
SEVERAL BRIGADES OF THE PRESIDENTIAL GUARD, IRAQI SECURITY
OPERATIONS, COORDINATED BY ALI HASSAN AL MAJID, HAVE
FAILED TO STIFLE THE KURD INSURGENCE SO FAR.

Streets of Halabja

Unknown/KDP Archive, Salahaddin

"The silent witness. That most horrible of fates: an adult clutches a child, both of them literally stopped dead in their tracks on a Halabja street." —Ramazan Öztürk

Uncle Omar had eight daughters and only one son, an infant, the last born. When the Iraqis began bombing Halabja with chemical bombs, Uncle Omar took his most precious child—the little boy—and ran away from his house to a neighbor's shelter; but he couldn't make it and died on the doorstep of the neighbor's house, holding his baby in his arms. What Uncle Omar never knew was that he had no chance anyway. All the members of the family who had gone to the shelter also died. The primitive shelter dug in their courtyard did not stop the deadly gases. —Chris Kutschera

Ramazan Öztürk

Turkish Photographer

As a war correspondent for the Turkish newspaper Sabah, *I had covered the Iran-Iraq War, so I knew both fronts where Saddam had fought against the Kurds. I first went to northern Iraq in 1987. A year later, we received a telex reporting that Saddam was using chemical weapons there, in Halabja.*

Everybody went. I was in the second group, of about forty journalists. It was a very difficult and dangerous trip. The bombardment was still continuing. A military plane took us to a city near Halabja. Then we took a helicopter. We landed in Halabja under difficult conditions. They kept bombarding the city. We had gas masks. Our guides were Iranian soldiers. And when we arrived in Halabja, my God, the corpses were scattered everywhere: women, children, old people. Everybody, everything was dead. The corpses were terrible. They were burnt. We arrived on the third day, and it stank.

When I saw "The Silent Witness," I was struck by him. I immediately understood that this picture would be the symbol of Halabja. I knelt down. I used an entire roll. I couldn't leave him.

I behaved sentimentally and not professionally. I did not send the

photographs to the paper. I did not want someone to make money by the blood of hundreds of people. I kept them with me. Then, after I returned to Istanbul, I was called by Sipa and the Gamma agency. They wanted me to send them some photos. I sent these photos to Sipa.

Hundreds of people came to see Halabja. Hundreds of people wrote books on it. In just one photograph, I could tell what they all tried to tell for pages and pages.

Kurdish people know me and trust me. Whoever sees this photograph remembers me and whoever sees me remembers this photograph. It was very influential in Iran. During the war between Iran and Iraq, the Iranians tried to publicize that Iraq was using chemicals. I succeeded at what they could not do. I made it publicly known.

I am from a Kurdish village near Pütürge, in southeastern Turkey, where there were no schools, no roads, no water, no electricity.

Interview with Ramazan Öztürk, May 1993

Background left: *The threat of chemical arms, Halabja*
SYGMA

CHEMICAL WEAPONS USE IN KURDISTAN: IRAQ'S FINAL OFFENSIVE

A STAFF REPORT

TO THE

COMMITTEE ON FOREIGN RELATIONS
UNITED STATES SENATE

Methodology:

To obtain as complete a picture as possible of recent events in Iraqi Kurdistan, we traveled over a 4-day period to each of the locations where significant numbers of Iraqi Kurds were present.

A refugee camp outside Diyarbakır . . .

A refugee camp at Silopi, about 1 mile from the only official crossing on the Iraq-Turkey border . . .

A refugee gathering point near Çiğli, close to the Iraq-Turkey border . . .

Two refugee camps, one to the west and the other to the south of the far eastern Turkish town of Yüsekova . . .

Weighing the Evidence:

Obviously, the leaders of the Pesh Merga, the Kurdish insurgents, have an interest in portraying Iraq in the worst possible light. To dismiss the eyewitness accounts, however, would require one to believe that 65,000 Kurdish refugees confined to five disparate locations were able to organize a conspiracy in 15 days to defame Iraq and that these refugees were able to keep their conspiracy a secret not only from us but from the world press. In any event, Iraq has a simple way to disprove the refugee accounts—it could invite neutral international investigators to the villages named by the refugees and allow them the time to make an independent investigation.

The eyewitness accounts occur in a context. This context is one of prior Iraqi use of chemical weapons and of ruthless oppression of the Iraqi Kurds. . . .

The eyewitness accounts also occur within the context of a brutal central government policy to suppress the Iraqi Kurds. . . .

Finally, doubters of the poison gas attacks would have to provide an alternative explanation for the very sudden exodus of the Pesh Merga from Iraq. The Pesh Merga are seasoned guerrilla fighters who have held out against various Iraqi regimes for 30 years. Suddenly, between August 25 and September 5, 1988, the resistance totally collapsed and the insurgents fled. Something catastrophic happened and every piece of evidence points to the use of poison gas. . . .

As described by the villagers, the bombs that fell on the morning of August 25 did not produce a large explosion. Only a weak sound could be heard and then a yellowish cloud spread out from the center of the explosion and became a thin mist. The air became filled with a mixture of smells—"bad garlic," "rotten onions," and "bad apples."

Those who were very close to the bombs died almost instantly. Those who did not die instantly found it difficult to breathe and began to vomit. The gas stung the eyes, skin, and lungs of the villagers exposed to it. Many suffered temporary blindness. . . .

The survivors who saw the dead reported that blood could be seen trickling out of the mouths of some of the bodies. A yellowish fluid could also be seen oozing out of the noses and mouths of some of the dead. Some said the bodies appeared frozen. Many of the dead bodies turned blackish blue. Most of the villagers quickly abandoned the contaminated areas, leaving the bodies unburied in the sun. In some cases, they later returned to the poisoned villages to bury the bodies. The few who ventured to look at the shattered pieces of the bomb casings said they were colored green.

The Iraqis continued to drop chemical weapons on Kurdish villages on August 26. Turkish villagers living less than a kilometer from the Turkey-Iraq border could see the Iraqi helicopters flying above a mountain ridge. . . .

On August 27 the chemical bombs continued to fall on villages in the Zakho, Dihok, and Amadiyah regions. . . . On August 28 villagers fleeing from areas farther from the Turkish border found their escape routes almost fully impeded by deployments of Iraqi soldiers. . . .

By September 5, however, the Iraqi troops had established camps all along the Turkey-Iraq border and the flow of refugees slowed to a trickle. More than 65,000 Kurdish refugees had arrived in Turkey. No one knows how many remain trapped on the other side.

A Staff Report from the Committee on Foreign Relations, United States Senate, Washington, D.C., October 1988

Printed for the use of the Committee on Foreign Relations

U.S. GOVERNMENT PRINTING OFFICE

It was 13 March 1988, and Iran had begun shelling the outskirts of Halabja. By the next day, the noise of the bombing was closer and a few shells hit the town itself. . . . The night of the 15th, things in Halabja were very unstable. We saw that many peshmergas from the PUK and from the Islamic Party led by Mella Ali had come into town. This was something very unusual as the Ba'ath officials of the Amn (Security) and Munazama (Ba'ath Party Political Headquarters) were nowhere to be seen. . . .

It was a warm spring evening and people were outside. We were talking with the peshmergas about developments. They spoke of liberating Sulaimaniya and other parts of Kurdistan, telling us, "Now you are free in Halabja." But they had only their Kalashnikovs, no heavier weapons. . . .

I went outside with my sister-in-law to wash the dishes under the garden tap, as there was no plumbing for running water in the kitchen. The family were inside drinking tea. I heard the sound of planes approaching. At almost the same moment, the bathroom adjoining the garden was struck by a bomb from above. One of our neighbours across the street had a shelter. We went straight there.

Down in the shelter we huddled together in a corner, motionless and silent, our heads buried in our laps, until the sound of the planes had gone. There were nearly a hundred people down there all trampling on each other and the air was suffocating. Small children were screaming and crying. . . .

Suddenly we began to smell something very peculiar, rather like household gas. But there was something different about it too. Soon it began to affect our breathing. I had heard that Saddam had used chemicals in Karadagh not far from Halabja. I had even read that if attacked by chemicals you should immediately soak a piece of cloth in water and cover your face with it. . . . We decided to try to escape from this shelter even though the planes kept on coming, bombing the town from every direction.

Outside everything had been transformed. . . . People were running through the streets, coughing, desperately. I too kept my eyes and mouth covered with a wet cloth and ran in the direction of a shelter we knew, which lay beneath a large public building away from the centre of town. A little further on we saw an old woman who already lay dead, past help. There was no sign of blood or any injury on her. Her face was waxen and white foam bubbled from the side of her mouth.

Interview with Şirwa, living in England, by Sheri Laizer,
Martyrs, Traitors, and Patriots, 1996

"Allah (CC)'ın arzında, Allah'ın verdiği nimetlerle hayatını sürdüren ve Allah'ın kullarına zulmedenleri Allah elbette ki cezalandıracaktır. Onlarla savaşmalıyız ki Allah (CC) bizim vasıtamızla onları azablandırsın..."

"Those who on God's earth lead lives in comfort granted them by God, but who oppress God's faithful servants— God will verily punish them. We must do battle unto them so that God may through us give them their just deserts."

Postcard produced in Turkey,
distributed by Islamic bookshops,
translated by Martin van Bruinessen

Mr. Perez de Cuellar, secretary general of the UN.

Kurds have through decades struggled with peaceful means to reach their goals, viz. national, cultural and democratic rights. These efforts have unfortunately not been successful yet.

The character of the kurdish problem is political. Therefore I strongly support an international conference on Middle East's conflicts where the kurdish question is also treated.

It is extremely important to emphasize that without solving the kurdish question in a just way there will be no real stability and peace in the Middle East.

Yours truly

Name:...

Address:...

Signature:..

Country:...

DON'T FORGET KURDS!

APRIL 15, 1991 $2.50

U.S. SCHOOLS: The Big Squeeze

TIME

Saddam's Latest Victims

Can Bush avoid a human tragedy?

Kurdish refugees near
the Turkish border

15

Who Are the Kurds?

Centuries of oppression have made them a people prepared to die for nationhood

It is not the first time Kurdish hopes for a homeland have ended in disaster. Their guerrillas call themselves *peshmerga*—those who face death—and over the years many have perished in aborted attempts to carve out a homeland of their own from the lands of rulers who despise them. In Iraq Saddam Hussein has for years tried to eliminate them.

Since 1975 four of every five Kurdish villages have been leveled; many of their residents have been moved to resettlement towns and detention camps in the southern deserts. When the U.S.-led coalition drove the Iraqi army from Kuwait, hundreds of thousands of displaced Kurds trekked north to reclaim their ancestral lands—only to be attacked by Saddam and forced to flee again.

A People Apart

The Kurds' ethnic roots reach back thousands of years to the dawn of Mesopotamia. They were not actually called Kurds until the 7th century, when most of them converted to Islam. Numbering between 14 million and 28 million, most Kurds are devout Sunni Muslims who speak a western Iranian language related to Farsi. Kurdistan has no official borders, but stretches from the Zagros Mountains in Iran through parts of Iraq, Syria and eastern Turkey. Most Kurds today are farm-

A Kurdish bodyguard, 1946

ers who live in small villages noted for their competitive clan structure and unruliness. They have at times even earned a reputation for brutality. The Turks provoked some Kurdish tribes to join in the massacre of Armenians near the end of the 19th century. Perhaps the most famous Kurd in history was Saladin, the legendary military leader who battled Richard the Lionheart and proved the wiliest and most effective defender of Islam against the invading Crusaders. ■

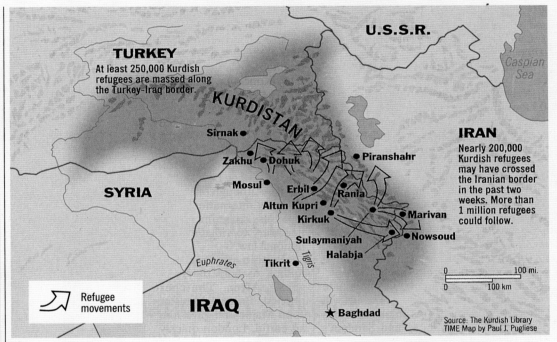

TURKEY
At least 250,000 Kurdish refugees are massed along the Turkey-Iraq border.

U.S.S.R.

Caspian Sea

KURDISTAN

Sirnak

Zakhu • Dohuk • Piranshahr

SYRIA

Mosul • Erbil • Rania

Altun Kupri • Marivan

Kirkuk

Sulaymaniyah • Nowsoud

Euphrates • Halabja

Tikrit • Tigris

★ Baghdad

IRAQ

IRAN
Nearly 200,000 Kurdish refugees may have crossed the Iranian border in the past two weeks. More than 1 million refugees could follow.

Refugee movements

0 ———— 100 mi.
0 ———— 100 km

Source: The Kurdish Library
TIME Map by Paul J. Pugliese

Years of Defeat

1920 Before World War I, the Kurds were split between the Ottoman and Persian empires. In the postwar Treaty of Sèvres, the colonial powers promised to create a unified independent Kurdish homeland, but the treaty was never ratified.

1925 Kurds rose up against the government in Turkey, but their revolt was soon crushed.

1946 A Soviet-backed Kurdish republic called Mahabad was formed in Iran. When the Soviets withdrew, leaving the Kurds to defend themselves, the republic was overthrown by Iranian troops.

1961 Under the leadership of Mustafa Barzani, organized armed resistance began against Iraqi rule.

1970 Iraq's Baath Party attempted to pacify rebellious Kurds with an offer of autonomy, but the agreement broke down.

1974-75 The Kurds resumed their fight, this time with the backing of the Shah of Iran. But they were abandoned when the Shah and Saddam Hussein cut a deal. Iran agreed to halt aid to the Kurds, and in exchange Iraq agreed to share sovereignty of the Shatt al-Arab waterway, which provides access to the Persian Gulf.

1988 Saddam avenged Kurdish support of Iran in the 1980-88 Iran-Iraq war. His army used poison gas against the town of Halabja, killing 5,000 Kurds, and destroyed thousands of villages.

Where They Live

Population estimates for Kurds vary widely, from 14 million to 28 million

52% TURKEY

18% IRAQ

24% IRAN

5% SYRIA | U.S.S.R. 1%

Sources: The Kurdish Library, World Factbook

Oil

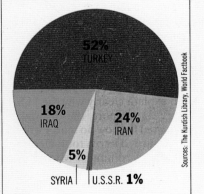

One-third of Iraq's total production is from its Kurdish region

Daily total: 3 million bbl.

Patrick Robert
French Photographer

Just after the reconquest of Kuwait and during the Kurdish offensive on the Iraqi troops, I spent three weeks in the region. I took this picture on the road from Dahuk to Mosul, before Saddam's army began to push back the Kurds. The Kurds had just retaken an ammunition warehouse from the Iraqis, a small military fort that you can see behind the characters in the picture.

But the next day the whole region was going to fall back into the hands of the Iraqis, and the great Kurdish exodus was about to begin toward Turkey and Iran. I followed fighters and families, all the way into Turkey, where the welcome by the soldiers was very brutal.

The conditions were very difficult and even painful: no food, little sleep, limited movement, entire days on foot. I even abandoned part of my equipment and all my luggage in order to continue on the path of exodus.

I have nothing to say about the Canon ad. It is of little interest. My work made the front pages of twenty magazines and about sixty double-page spreads around the world. I made two shipments of film (via Turkey and Syria) before seeing another photographer.

Letter from Patrick Robert, living in France, September 1995

PATRICK ROBERT/SYGMA. FORTIN DE L'ARMEE IRAKIENNE PRIS PAR LES PESH-MERGAS AUX ALENTOURS DE DUHOK. 30 MARS 1991.

1991

Patrick Robert, photographe chez Sygma depuis
quatre ans, est passé en Canon depuis
le début de l'année. Spécialiste du "news", il a
suivi l'exode kurde au début du
mois d'avril 1991, avec un équipement léger
et performant : deux boîtiers EOS 1
et deux zooms 20-35 L et 80-200 L
Qu'est-ce qui vous a séduit dans cet appareil ?
– L'un des gros intérêts de cet appareil
est la présence de fonctions personnalisées qui
permettent de configurer l'appareil en
fonction du reportage à couvrir.
En situation difficile, comme en Irak, la
discrétion est recommandée.
Il faut éviter le rembobinage automatique en fin
de film. En "news", c'est l'inverse :
le film se rembobine tout seul sans perte de
temps ni manipulation.
On adapte le boîtier au terrain.
Et l'autofocus, vous aimez ?
– En photojournalisme, la rapidité de
l'autofocus Canon est un atout essentiel.
L'appareil soulage l'œil, ce qui permet de
concentrer une plus grande
attention sur le sujet. Encore faut-il que celui-ci
soit opérationnel dans les situations
difficiles. Le système autofocus a très bien
fonctionné en basses lumières et dans les
conditions les plus difficiles pour ce reportage
de guerre sur les combattants kurdes.

What about this camera has seduced you?

"One of the great features of this equipment is that it has personalized features that allow you to set the camera in accordance with the type of reportage you're doing. In difficult situations, such as in Iraq, it's a good idea to be discreet. You have to avoid automatic rewind at the end of the film. But in the "news" mode it's the opposite: the film rewinds itself easily with no loss of time and no fuss. You adapt the camera body to the terrain."

And what about the autofocus? Do you like it?

"In photojournalism, the rapidity of the Canon autofocus is an essential feature. The camera fits the eye, which allows you to focus more attention on the subject. Again, the equipment needs to function in difficult situations. The autofocus functioned well in low light and the most difficult conditions for this war reportage on the Kurdish fighters.

Canon

v o i r   e t   é m o u v o i r

LIFE

MOMENTS

A Human Tragedy

As the Kurds' latest exodus turned into a nightmare that horrified the world, their faces made us feel their pain and made us marvel at the strength of the human spirit

■ On her road to an awful freedom, a woman pauses before taking up the burden of a lifetime

ANTHONY SUAU/BLACK STAR

Anthony Suau/*Life* magazine, June 1991

Anthony Suau
American Photographer

I was in Saudi Arabia during the Gulf War. It was an amazing scene as I witnessed the press dealing with this American military bureaucracy that was completely controlled and contrived. The military was most concerned with still photography because of the indelible image that a still photograph can put in somebody's mind. When the television pictures came out on the Kurdish situation, it looked biblical.

Interview with Anthony Suau,
living in France, February 1994

In the wake of the Iraqi defeat, my city rose up against the Iraqi government. Arbil stayed in the hands of the people and peshmerga forces for about twenty days. On the twentieth day, there was news saying that the Iraqi government was advancing from Kirkuk toward Arbil. All the people went to the streets; they couldn't sleep. Everybody had a gun in his hand. They were scared, but many people were determined to defend.

In the early morning I woke up to noises, people shouting, preparing themselves, packing their belongings. I told my wife and my mother, we should leave the city. We packed, putting our two daughters in a small cart with three wheels. Everywhere, people were running. It was chaotic. Some peshmerga were firing into the air to scare people, to make them stop running, to stay in the city. But it was useless. It was like an ocean, running to the north.

At the Arbil checkpoint, the shelling intensified. At this point I saw three helicopters in the sky. They were firing at people indiscriminantly. I saw some tanks coming toward the place where I was with my family. This was the first time I saw a live scene of an attack by an army. I had only seen this in movies. The soldiers were firing with their guns toward us and people started running. I lost my family because we went in different directions. I had been walking since the morning; I didn't have enough energy to run. The tanks were approaching, coming closer, and the soldiers were firing. I could hear the noise of the bullets passing by my ear. I was expecting to be hit at any moment. I said, "Come and take me: I can't walk, I can't run." I was exhausted from fear, not only from tiredness.

Interview with Mowlan Brahim, Kurdish lawyer
living in Germany, by Laura Hubber, January 1993

IRAQ

The Turkish soldiers made us climb this mountain. They wouldn't allow our vehicles to go up. When I arrived, there were only two or three other photographers there, but we had complete access. The Turkish military were surrounding this area, containing the people on the mountain at gunpoint, and what I saw was overwhelming. No motion picture could capture what was happening on that mountain. It was simply so overwhelming, and the amount of human tragedy was unfathomable. You could be standing here and an incredible incident could be taking place. Ten feet away there's another incredible scene, then one five feet away in the other direction. People being killed, a baby dying. It kept getting worse and worse.

We had to climb up this mountain every time. We couldn't spend the night, and the closest place to sleep was two or three hours away in a small hotel or in a house. So we would wake at two or three in the morning and start driving and arrive there just before sunrise. It was a poignant time to be there too, because it was when the funerals were being held. The nights were freezing on that mountain. Snow was coming down at a certain point. And these people had absolutely no protection; they were living under plastic tents. Dysentery was rampant and the ground was covered in nothing but mud.

Many people spoke English, so it was easy to connect with what was happening there. You had a sense of the pain they were going through and the problems that were put upon them, as opposed to a place like Ethiopia, where you had this distance of language and culture. People were able to describe what was happening, and at the same time, at point blank, the Turkish soldiers would shoot people who were trying to run out of the camp or attempting to grab something from an airdrop. I could work five hours and I was emotionally and physically drained. I just couldn't stay on the mountain.

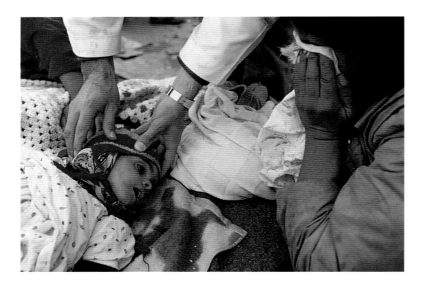

I never know whether I am going to make a difference as a photographer in these situations—I am in the middle of this thing, feeling the pain of these people, trying to get as close to it as I can. I tried to explain to the people what I was trying to do, but I never know if the magazine is going to publish my images or whether the world is interested, whether there can be a reaction to this.

The Americans arrived two days before I left and I started seeing the supplies coming in. The Americans literally said, "We wouldn't be here if you guys hadn't been." So that made me feel good and it's one of those very rare moments.

Interview with Anthony Suau, living in France, February 1994

Kurdish refugees on Işikveren Mountain, April 1991

Anthony Suau

A I D E   M É D I C A L E
I N T E R N A T I O N A L E

I, the undersigned, Doctor Johannés Littmann, président of
AIDE MEDICALE INTERNATIONALE (A M I), certify that:

NAME.... *KAPLAN   Jonathan*........

PROFESSION ... *Surgeon*............

NATIONALITY..... *British*.............

PASSPORT NO... *0453.74.U*........

is sent on a humanitarian médical mission by our organisation
to .. *North Iraq*.... for a duration of ... *2* .... months.

We ask that all civilian and military authorities to assist
him/her in this endeavor.

Jonathan Kaplan
British Doctor

I went as a surgeon to treat Kurdish battle casualties on the front line inside Iraq. But probably one of the most significant things I did out there wasn't in Iraq, and wasn't even medical; I stole a tent from the Turkish army and hid it in an ambulance going up the mountain to the camp, where people were dying of exposure. I gave it to the father of a family, a man I'd met the day before, and together we pulled it out of the ambulance, and it was so heavy that I couldn't even lift one end of it. This man was a teacher of mathematics from Zakho, and he loaded it onto his back and walked two or three kilometers along the mountainside to set it up. I later found him and gave him some medication for his family. And then the last time I walked across the border back into Turkey, I walked through the camp and he called to me and said: "Come with me!" I'd given him some tobacco whenever I'd pass by, and he said: "Come, I want to give you some tobacco." Inside the tent he said: "This is my family, this is the family of my brother who's lost his nine children, and my other brother and fourteen of his family." It was a big tent. He said: "These people are all alive because of you." That was a profound moment for me.

Interview with Jonathan Kaplan, living in England, June 1994

April 12, 1991
The howl of jet engines as the A10 "tank-busters" come in low up the valley. In the distance the drone of turbo-props and then the C-130's come in over the mountains to the north, slipping one by one into a drop-run. The cargo doors open, flaps down, and they fly over the ridge at 30 feet as the kickers go to work.... The people are galvanized, picking up rope, sacks and running for the drops. Sometimes the chutes don't open, and the panniers plummet into the trees.... Fights develop, swirling crowds around the panniers, and blood is shed.... People stagger up the hill like mules, [with] improvised packs of parachute cloth and line.

Page from Jonathan Kaplan's diary

DES MÉDECINS BENEVOLES AU SERVICE DE TOUS LES HOMMES

Aide Médicale Internationale, 119, rue des Amandiers, 75020 Paris · C.C.P. 45.44, V PARIS · Tél. : (1) 46 36 04 04
Télex : 211772 F AIDMEDI — Compte FONDATION DE FRANCE, AMI n° 06-0457 — FAX : (1) 46 36 66 10

Dear Jamal AL-sharafani
we are Now in Turkysh bowndary
[SABAH and his family and your
Father + mother and hoshyar +
his family and Adel + his family].
our situation is very bad there is
not water p food amd The weather
is very cold all of us are very
ill so please come to Turky and
meet with mr. Iskandar AL-sharafani
to save us from This place
quickly. our place is beside
(Bellah village The place of Koyd).

your broTher

SABAH AL-SHARAFANi

A note handed to me by a desperate
refugee, asking me to call his brother in Aberdeen
to get him out of this place. I sent a
fax to Paris + asked them to forward it toute
suite; as there was no answer on the phone.

أيها الشعب العراقي

تد وصلت قوات الجيش الأمريكي منطقة زاخو الآن
ـ ستتقدم قواتنا بتعاون مع قوات عسكرية دولية
ومنظمات الأعضاء الدولية الأخرى كثير من المساعدات
الأنسانية لكل من اللاجئين . لكي ستتقدم قواتنا
الأطعمة ـ المياه . كذلك الخدمات الصحية
ـ ستؤسس قواتنا لكم مؤقتاً المخيمات
ان نعمل هذا مطابق تماماً مع قرار الأمم المتحدة
المرقم ٦٨٨ والله هو الموفق
نضلاً حافظوا على قواتنا ومن معها تحت حمايتها
ـ ساعدوا هذه الجهود الأنسانية الهامة
وشكراً.

PEOPLE OF IRAQ!

    SOLDIERS FROM THE UNITED STATES OF AMERICA HAVE ARRIVED IN
ZAKHO. OUR SOLDIERS, AND OTHER INTERNATIONAL FORCES AND RELIEF
ORGANIZATIONS, ARE BEING SENT TO HELP YOUR BROTHERS WHO ARE
SUFFERING. WE WILL BE BUILDING TEMPORARY COMMUNITIES, PROVIDING
FOOD, WATER AND MEDICAL CARE. WE ARE DOING THIS IN ACCORDANCE
WITH UNITED NATIONS RESOLUTION 688, AND BECAUSE IT IS RIGHT IN
THE EYES OF ALLAH.

    OUR SOLDIERS WILL NOT HARM YOU UNLESS YOU ATTACK THEM, OR THE
PEOPLE THEY ARE PROTECTING. DO NOT TRY TO STOP THE HUMANITARIAN
ACTIONS OF THE WORLD! INSTEAD, JOIN US IN HELPING YOUR BROTHERS.

JOHN M.D. SHALIKASHVILI
LTG, USA
Commander, Combined Task Force

الفريق/جان ام دي شالكاشفيلي
قائد القوات المشتركة

WE ARE HERE TO FIND OUT WHAT YOUR NEEDS ARE
IF YOU HELP US WE CAN HELP YOU MAKE YOUR
LIVING CONDITIONS BETTER FIRST WE WOULD
LIKE TO EXAMINE YOUR CHILDREN THEN WE NEED
TO SEE WHERE YOU GET YOUR WATER WE WOULD
ALSO LIKE TO SEE YOUR CAMP TO ASSESS YOUR
NEEDS. WE NEED TO TALK TO ANY DOCTORS,
NURSES OR DENTISTS WHO ARE IN THE CAMP. WE
NEED INTERPRETERS SO THAT WE CAN BETTER HELP
YOU. IF YOU SPEAK ENGLISH, GERMAN OR ANOTHER
EUROPEAN LANGUAGE. PLEASE COME SPEAK TO
US!!!!!!!!

April 9, 1991

The camp is more terrible than I could have imagined. 250,000 refugees crowded into an area of sharp mountain crests by Turkish soldiers that keep them imprisoned. More pour over the border hourly—crossing high snowfields. There are Turkish troops along the border, who fire into the air to turn back this human tide. Only the fittest can avoid the soldiers by choosing the most inaccessible paths, so perhaps 200,000 remain behind in Iraq, unable to cross—women, children and old people. Those in the camp squat in a welter of churned-up mud, rotting entrails of slaughtered animals, and rivulets of liquid shit. Over 2,000 have already died, mainly children, but there is a steady flow of deaths from gunshot wounds when the soldiers fire into the crowds during the distribution of food. All they get is bread, which adds to thirst. The only source of water is snow, scooped by the handful from the highest valleys and melted down. It is gray, and tastes of petroleum—fallout from the oil field fires in Kuwait.

At the end of the road we stop the ambulance and are instantly overwhelmed. . . . Many of those wanting medication are well informed, know exactly what they are usually taking. Others are desperate, with tiny babies so dehydrated that they are unlikely to last the night. Our drugs are gone in two hours, and we leave in despair; it has made no difference. We cram three mothers and their dying babies into the ambulance with us to take them down the hill.

From the personal diary of Jonathan Kaplan

Jonathan Kaplan

I had lost my medical team somewhere in Syria, and when I first arrived at the camp I had no medical supplies, no backup. The one thing I could do was try to record what was going on. I knew that the pictures I took were important, that the accounts of what I was seeing were important, and for the first couple of days on the border I was sending back stories to the Dutch press and to the English press. As a doctor, the only thing that I can say that I might have seen with greater clarity was how close many people were to death. I'd find journalists trying to interview people that were dying, or unaware that in a group of people, some of the babies held in the women's arms were dead.

The difference between me and a journalist? In some areas I saw or felt more and in some areas I saw less or I felt less. A little later, when I started working as a surgeon at the front in Iraq, the differences were clearer. The experience of listening to shooting and knowing that I was going to get blood on my hands in the next short while was one that they probably wouldn't have had.

It was later, a couple of weeks after I got back to England, that I started having nightmares, of being woken from sleep on the floor of the fort by shooting and screams—but instead of two or three wounded men, bleeding, being brought in on people's backs, there'd be fifty or a hundred. And there I was, with my little box of medical equipment.

Interview with Jonathan Kaplan, June 1994

Pages from diary of Jonathan Kaplan

10,000 U.S. troops from Europe and the U.S. will join with British, French, Italian and Dutch forces to set up refugee centers in northern Iraq. Supplies arrive by sea at Turkish ports on the Mediterranean and by air at Incirlik and Diyarbakir air bases. They are then transported east to staging areas closer to the border.

TURKEY

U.S.S.R.

Staging areas for rail supplies

Forward staging area

KURDISTAN

Helicopter staging area

Diyarbakir •

• Misric

Hakkari •

450,000 refugees

Isikveren

Silopi •

Cukurca •

IRAN

Nusaybin •

Zakhu •

Amadiya •

Dohuk • 400,000 refugees

• Piranshahr

Mosul •

— 36° —

Erbil •   Rania •   1,000,000 refugees   — 36° —

SYRIA

500,000 refugees

Staging area

Possible area of refugee centers

Kirkuk •

Sulaymaniyah • • Marivan

Halabja • • Shushami

Euphrates

0 ———— 100 mi.
0 ———— 100 km

IRAQ

TIME Map by Paul J. Pugliese

Time, April 29, 1991

"On the mountain I didn't see Turkish soldiers shooting people, but they were very rough on the civilians. That's a troubling cycle in this business, one we're forced to live with."
—*Liliana Nieto del Rio*

Liliana Nieto del Rio
American Photographer

I felt a certain anger about the Gulf War, and I felt powerless sitting in New York looking at all these harrowing images. I was more interested in what the war had unleashed than in the disputes that had led to its outbreak.

The sheer numbers of refugees overwhelmed the military. The Turks were clearly caught off guard.

I communicated with the women the most. There were people dying every morning; you would hear the moans of women crying for their children. At dawn every morning the refugees would bring the bodies out and bury them, mostly the old and the children. This was all before the American army arrived.

The human cost was so great that it was sometimes difficult to absorb all that was going on. To be there was to be a witness at a crucial juncture in the tortured history of these people, and it's hard to convey that sense of devastation through pictures. I often felt that I'm not doing

enough, that I could help so much more if I were a doctor. I wonder if images are worth anything when it's a matter of life or death.

I've stopped believing that these kinds of pictures are going to change the world, though I may have felt that at some earlier, more idealistic, point in my career. I still believe, however, that documentation has an inherent value, and that, yes, some good can come of it. We're living in a moment of instant information, of information as a kind of currency. Unfortunately, human tragedies that unfold in obscurity or secret are even less likely to reach any kind of resolution.

When I returned to New York, there was very little interest in photographs of the refugees. Publications were mostly interested in the American part of it all, which I didn't concentrate on so much. Even that interest faded after a couple of weeks, as other news events moved onto the front pages.

Interview with Liliana Nieto del Rio, living in the U.S., April 1991

1991

330

ARAPÇA

Attention!

This Is a Warning!

Do not approach the border. The border of the Republic of Turkey is closed to any kind of entry. No form of asylum will be granted. If you make any attempt to cross the border your life will be in danger. Do not attempt. Retreat from the border line. We do not wish to harm you.

Leaflet dropped by Turkish helicopters on Kurds fleeing the uprising at Deshte Tak, Zakho, Iraqi border, March 1991 (written in Turkish, Arabic, Farsi, and "local dialect," i.e., Kurdish)
Courtesy Sheri Laizer

Liliana Nieto del Rio

Relatives search for the remains of those killed by the Iraqi military
during the Anfal campaign, Arbil cemetery, northern Iraq

1991

Susan Meiselas
American Photographer

Before the Gulf War, there had been reports that 4,000 Kurdish villages had been destroyed in Iraq by Saddam Hussein's forces during the "Anfal" campaign, yet there was no proof. Once the war was over in April 1991, Middle East Watch sent a mission to collect testimony from the Kurdish refugees who had fled Iraq.

As an American, my only way into the region was via Iran, but the processing of my visa was delayed and I missed joining up with the human rights team. Instead, I joined an entourage of journalists following Mme. Danielle Mitterand, the wife of the French president, who had just brought truckloads of supplies to the refugees and was now traveling to the Iran-Iraq border to meet with Mas'ud Barzani.

Some fifty peshmerga fighters came to greet her from the Iraqi side. She and Barzani sat and had tea in the middle of a minefield. Barzani reported that two weeks before, the Kurdish uprising had failed. Because of fighting in Kuwait, however, what remained of the Iraqi troops were pulled south. To Barzani's surprise, the Iraqi retreat left the Kurds in a liberated zone under their own command.

I knew I had to see what was happening on the Iraqi side. When the rest of the media flew back to Paris, I crossed the border with the Kurdish fighters. I spoke no Kurdish; I was a woman in a totally male, military environment. For four days, I was driven around by three young fighters and photographed every destroyed village I could find. I left the region knowing that though I had missed the Kurdish uprising and the traumatic flight of the hundreds of thousands of refugees, documenting the ruins fueled my desire to return.

Eventually, the Middle East Watch forensic team focused on the village of Koreme to systematically record sufficient detail of a single site so it could become the basis for an unassailable accusation of genocide. I documented the process of identifying the bones of townspeople, mostly male, who were lined up, shot dead, and dumped into open pits. After the 1988 massacre, Koreme, like so many other villages, had been taken over by the Iraqi military, who then dynamited it and bulldozed into the ground what remained. For me it was difficult to begin the encounter with the Kurds through their deaths.

Interview with Susan Meiselas, July 1997

IRAQ

333

Anfal began from the . . . assumption that, foreseeing a possible cease-fire in the Iran-Iraq war, it was time to settle the "Kurdish problem" once and for all. It was not intended as exemplary punishment of the Kurds for their presumed or actual collaboration with Iran or for supporting Kurdish guerrillas. Punishment is not exemplary if there is no one left to witness the lesson, and Anfal was thus not intended as punishment. Anfal was a "final solution," implemented by the Iraqi government, the Ba'ath Party and the Iraqi army. It was intended to make the Kurds of Iraqi Kurdistan and their rural way of life disappear forever. Only such an intent can explain the precise, neat, and thorough destruction of the already empty Kurdish villages, and the fact that Anfal encompassed virtually all Kurdish villages.

Draft for "The Anfal Campaign in Iraqi Kurdistan: The Destruction
of Koreme," Middle East Watch Report, January 1993

The front line between the Kurdish guerrillas and the government was extremely fluid throughout the summer of 1991. There was no line of control as there is today, but it was during that time that we first heard the story about somebody who had escaped miraculously from some mass killing that had taken place in the southern part of Iraq. Some journalists who were traveling in the area started to get accounts of mass graves.

The allegations began to come out from the Kurds that they had a lot of captured material from the time when the Iraqis withdrew, immediately after the Gulf War.

We wanted to be able to do at least one tentative dig to determine the timing of the deaths and be able to have some solid medical and forensic evidence. We had hopes of using new technology involving infrared equipment from a satellite to be able to look at disturbed earth. The idea was that we would be able to take a few sample sites from virgin areas out in the wilds and be able to use that to look at other areas still under Iraqi government control. Our first report, which had been originally designed as a reconnaissance, turned out to be more solid than we thought it was going to be.

Interview with Andrew Whitley, former director
of Middle East Watch, December 1994

Mass Murder Proven

Genocide and systematic murder of the Kurds in Iraq. Thirty-nine hundred villages and 180,000 inhabitants are missing. "Rumors," says Saddam Hussein. "There is no evidence at all."

Dr. Clyde Snow, the well-known U.S. anthropologist who, among other things, identifed Josef Mengele, thinks otherwise. He was in Iraq for an American human rights organization and did find evidence. In mass graves he found the skulls of young men between 15 and 18 with neck wounds from a small-caliber pistol and of women who were strangled, their skulls still blindfolded. Moreover . . . he has the testimonies of the gravediggers who say that they had to dig these graves on orders of Iraq's secret police.

In the meantime, the surviving Kurds remain in the mountains of northern Iraq without shelter, clothes, or food, and it still remains to be seen whether we will succeed in protecting these suffering people from the revenge of Baghdad.

Translation of text from Nieuwe Revu, Dutch
monthly magazine, January 30–February 6, 1992

Dr. Clyde Snow, forensic anthropologist, exhumes blindfolded skull of teenager from mass grave, Arbil, northern Iraq, December 1991

Susan Meiselas/Magnum

Clothing unearthed in the search for identification of those buried anonymously is now left to mark the graves, Arbil cemetery, northern Iraq

Taymour Abdullah Ahmad
Kurdish Boy

The army brought a large number of buses that looked like oversized ambulances, because they had no windows: it was all metal plating. Before the people were put in the buses, their names were called from lists, and then written down on a new list. I stayed with my mother and sisters. They drove from 6 a.m. until sunset. Then the bus stopped, and the guards opened the doors. They took everyone and told us to go into the trench that I saw in front of us, and they began pushing us into the trench. An officer and a soldier stood next to the trench and at once opened fire at us with Kalashnikovs. I was hit in the flesh just above my left armpit. After I received that bullet, I tried to climb out of the trench, toward the soldier on my right. I saw that the soldier was moved to the point of crying. But then the officer standing on my left-hand side gave an order to the soldier (in Arabic, which I did not understand at the time), and the soldier pushed me back into the trench, and fired at me in the lower right back.

Then the shooting stopped. It was dark. The soldiers left, and I could hear them talking with one another far away from the trench; I could not see them. I climbed out of the trench by myself, in the opposite direction of where the soldiers were, and climbed on top of the pile of dirt next to it.

I either fell unconscious or asleep, but the next thing I remember is that I woke up in the hole I had dug on the dirt mound. The empty trenches that I had seen were still open, and there were perhaps some twenty more on my left side, which is the direction in which I began to walk, into the darkness. There was no moon.

After a while I saw the shadow of a tent. The whole journey from the execution site to the tent took me two and one half hours.

Close to the tents, dogs tried to attack me; they were barking. I threw stones at them. The noise alerted the owner of the tent who came out with a flashlight. When the man saw this boy in Kurdish dress who was bleeding, he pulled me by the arm straight inside the tent.

After three days, the man took me in his truck to his brother's family in Samawa. I stayed two and one half years in Samawa. After nine months, I was able to speak Arabic fluently, and could tell my host family what had happened to me.

Interview with Taymour Abdullah Ahmad, by Joost Hiltermann,
adapted in "Genocide in Iraq," *Human Rights Watch,* July 1993

Right: *Taymour Abdullah Ahmad, December 1991*

The New York Times Magazine
JANUARY 3, 1993 / SECTION 6

IRAQ
A CASE OF GENOCIDE
ACCUSED
BY JUDITH MILLER

Woman next to exhumed grave of her brothers, Koreme, June 1992

Susan Meiselas/Magnum
The New York Times Magazine, January 3, 1993

When we identified the people from Koreme, the exhumation team and Clyde were excited because we'd been able to identify everybody. That doesn't happen very often. But the relatives with other sons or daughters who had disappeared said, "Well, what about the others who disappeared? Can you do something about that?"

You can do very little. The Iraqis dynamited four thousand towns and killed between sixty thousand and eighty thousand people, and we just identified twenty-seven. Of course you have the explanation that this one case is an example for the other ones, and I believe in that. But at the same time you feel you are just doing this little thing that takes months of work, and particularly for these people we don't have an answer. And no, there is nothing more we can do.

When the women were crying by the sides of the grave and would get too emotional, one of the men would say something that we didn't understand and throw her out of the grave. This happened a few times, and then we finally intervened with the translator and asked what

the problem was. They said, "Well, they're disturbing you by crying so loud," and we said, "It's okay. It's fine." I learned that the women were not allowed to be with the men at the time of the reburial, but once the ceremony was over the women were allowed to come into the area of the grave.

I am always very surprised by the need for clear signs to realize that the person is dead. Freud talks of the test of reality. When someone dies, the first reaction is denial, then the external signs arrive from the outside confirming that that is what happened. That's strongly reinforced in cases of disappearances or cases where people were not able to see. They heard the screams. It's so desperate. The image of being on the other side of the hill, hearing the screams and the machine guns. You get stuck on that image and you can't go beyond it. You need to see the body.

Interview with Mimi Doretti, Argentine anthropologist,
living in the U.S., December 1994

338

The Destruction of Koreme

Oral Testimony and Physical Forensic Evidence

Whether or not all of the men and boys taken aside were carrying weapons when they were captured—and it is irrelevant to the legal assessment of the crime that followed—survivor accounts are uniform that these men were made to form a line. A lieutenant told them to sit down, and they did so, squatting on their heels rather than sitting in the dirt. The other villagers, including those men not singled out, were led away behind the hill near the partly ruined village schoolhouse. . . .

The thirty-three detained men . . . wept and pleaded for their lives, although the soldiers insisted that nothing would happen to them. One of the lieutenants offered them cigarettes and water; meanwhile, some twelve to fifteen soldiers had taken up positions facing the line. . . .

The commander, they said, was going to call for orders from Mengish, so they would know what questions to ask.

Immediately upon receiving a reply from headquarters in Mengish, the officer ordered the soldiers guarding the line of Koreme men and boys—approximately fifteen soldiers armed with automatic rifles—to open fire. . . .

Of the thirty-three men and boys in the line, twenty-seven died. Six survived the execution, one of whom later disappeared.

The dead men and boys were left unburied for some time, and were eventually deposited in two mass graves near where they fell. . . .

Prior to Anfal, Koreme had some 160 houses made from mud bricks or from stone and cement; it also had a school and a mosque made from stone and cement. It had limited irrigation works attached to its springs. Electricity was installed in 1987. Following Anfal, nothing was left. . . .

Between 1988 and 1992, vegetation had overgrown the site so that only the rubble of the school and mosque suggested to the uninitiated that there had once been a village there. Wildflowers that grow best in disturbed earth sprang up, and in the spring, much of the flattened village was covered with mustard flowers, dandelion, and Queen Anne's lace. The orchards had been burned, and the vineyards uprooted.

Draft for "The Anfal Campaign in Iraqi Kurdistan: The Destruction of Koreme,"
Middle East Watch Report, January 1993

Finding the I.D.'s

As we waded through 18 metric tons of Iraqi government documents in the U.S. National Archives in 1992–94, pulling bunched-up files out of boxes and bags, small I.D. pictures would often come rolling out onto the floor. Others would still be in their proper place: attached with pins to the tops of file pages that provided biographical information about persons questioned by the Iraqi secret service, the Amn. More often than not, the person on the form had been detained or executed for "belonging to the saboteurs," a euphemism for alleged membership in one of the Kurdish rebel parties. The regime also kept records on government employees, listing their ethnicity and declared loyalties. A separate set of files brought together information on government informers infiltrated into Kurdish society and rebel groups. In the final analysis, it appeared that every single Kurd—informer, detainee, suspected rebel, political activist, or ordinary citizen—sooner or later would have a file with the Amn and would be under constant scrutiny from colleagues or relatives working for the regime—persons they might never even have suspected of collaboration.

Letter from Joost Hiltermann, living in the U.S.,
researcher for Human Rights Watch, June 1995

Abandoned schoolhouse, former battle site at Mawat, near Iranian border with Iraq

PUK storehouse for land mines and captured Iraqi intelligence documents

Documents prepared for loading at Zakho airstrip for allied forces in Operation Provide Comfort, northern Iraq

Andrew Whitley

I think no one, not any of the Kurdish groups, knew the full dimension of what they had in their own hands. Eighteen tons of Iraqi intelligence documents were stored away in various locations. Xeroxes of documents were being brought out by individual Kurdish leaders and shown to us.

We realized in early 1992 that there was a considerable likelihood that the liberated zone could be overrun again by the Iraqi government forces and that this material would be lost to posterity. We thought it important for the Kurds' sake and for the sake of a potential case against the Iraqi government—we had no idea about the scale. Whenever we started thinking about being able to get access to it, the question of scale was always difficult to work out with the Kurds. We wanted the documents kept under secure conditions to research quickly. We didn't want them to become the Dead Sea scrolls.

We had to enlist the cooperation of the U.S. government because the Turkish government refused to allow materials they considered military records to cross through their land. I take some satisfaction from the fact that I was able to push the U.S. government to persuade the Turkish government to allow an airlift. We wanted to get it out as completely as possible. Not just samples of it; we wanted to see the whole picture.

When I traveled to northern Iraq in February 1992, my underlying goal was to see for myself some of the Iraqi military documents we'd heard about. It was quite a dramatic moment to actually get to Mawat and this abandoned schoolhouse. The PUK had taken it over to store land mines and grenades along with these documents. We found the documents in gunnysacks and rice sacks and Jordanian army ammunition boxes. It was like going into Aladdin's cave! Suddenly I saw the entire contents of the secret police summons files that went back twenty years or so. I was taking measurements so that I could give the Pentagon some idea of volume, weight—to figure how we were going to get this stuff out. I wanted to get some sense of authenticity. But it was very clear that there was no way, as the Iraqi government claimed subsequently, that these were forgeries.

It's a great pity that those sacks of pictures of the victims didn't come out. I believe that Jalal Talabani kept back quite a lot of material. They were looking for material about themselves. They wanted to find out the degree to which they had been infiltrated, which of their people might be spies. But what they were handing over was part of the Iraqi government's secret records about a very important, very sensitive military campaign. And they handed them over to the Americans and to a foreign human rights organization. It was a brave act.

We had eleven or twelve helicopters that took the material out, and then a transcontinental plane took it on to Washington. We were finally able to see that this campaign had probably been conceived of by the Iraqi government as a pure military campaign to destroy an insurgent movement and its supporters. But, because Kurds were taken away and killed for being Kurds and for living in a certain region, it became genocide.

Bringing a case of this kind to the World Court would strengthen the Kurdish claim for self-determination, which is a no-no word as far as the Western governments are concerned. It could increase the pressures on them to stay in the area longer to provide protection. Under the Genocide Convention, you cannot abandon a case where there are people who potentially stand to be murdered again. I think we're in a holding pattern in Iraq because the United States does not want to be drawn in any deeper.

Interview with Andrew Whitley, former director
of Middle East Watch, December 1994

Photograph of Iraqi military officers seen with an executed prisoner, recovered along with Iraqi intelligence documents

> *It is not easy to find a smoking gun document saying "Kill all the Kurds," but what [documents] we find every day about the Iraqi policy toward the Kurds and the other minorities, if we gather them all together, becomes just like a puzzle and gives us very good evidence of genocide.* —Shorsh Resool

While screening the eighteen tons of captured Iraqi documents, we found documents about the fate of the people disappeared during the Anfal, and a very straightforward directive saying, "From now on, if anyone asks about the fate of their relatives or friends who disappeared in Anfal, don't say that we captured them and they disappeared. Say we have no information about them."

Among the many documents, we have photos of every individual who was interrogated, and peshmerga forces or returnees who came back or were arrested in clashes with the government. Whatever people had in their pockets, it's there. For example, any picture they had. We found other interesting photos of people whom the Iraqis were chasing. For example, if they wanted to go after someone, they photographed these people while they were meeting someone on the street or when they were going home.

Although the documents are about the destruction of villages, the killing of people, and interrogation, I enjoyed reading them because they gave me a clear view of how directives were issued by high-ranking officials and how the lower-rank officers implemented them. One of the audiotapes even insults the Kurdish collaborators who were with the government. I thought at least the Iraqi government would be faithful to people who had been collaborating with them for decades. But I found that they were against all Kurds, regardless of their being with them or against them.

Interview with Shorsh Resool, living in England, April 1994

1992   L   3

on Iraqi Torture of Kurds

Provide Comfort Coalition rebuilds homes in villages destroyed by Saddam Hussein, 1992

Colonel R. M. Naab

Colonel R. M. Naab
American Military Officer

Operation Provide Comfort was a complete success in terms of encouraging the Iraqi Kurds to return to their homes. We relocated approximately 400,000 people from the north in a short period of time. We arranged for them to return to their abandoned villages, and began to help the NGOs address the serious problems with resettlement. Once we got them all back, we had major problems getting the needed support and materials because they no longer fit the UN definition of refugee status.

I thought from the very beginning about the Vietnam Syndrome: we had to get rid of this "Tar Baby." At every high-level meeting, the military wanted to make this go away as quickly as possible, without getting bogged down in Iraqi and Kurdish politics in the north. We always thought that Saddam felt time was in his favor. That had a good and bad side to it. Because he regarded it as a stone on his heart, if we could convince him that we weren't there for a long-term presence, he would probably be more cooperative with us, and in fact he was. But in the final analysis, if you allow someone like that to understand that you are just there for a short term, he will bide his time, wait till you get out, and then hope that things will go his way.

In May 1992, Iraq was having an election. I said, "What is this going to solve?" And in fact, while Kurds participated in it very actively, the U.S. gave very little help officially. It didn't make the problem of the rivalry between the two major parties in Kurdistan go away. I mean Jalal and Massoud are still at it. It still goes hot and then cold for a

while. It gives people in the West the opportunity to say, "Well, there they go again. They're all tribal. They can't manage their own affairs. They're killing each other. That's too bad for the Kurdish people."

I don't know whether we now have a U.S. policy toward Iraqi Kurdistan. I know we did not at the time. We have never had a Kurdish expert. It was always some junior state department officer who worked in Iraq. Or the Turkish desk, which had the Ottoman Empire view from the guy in Ankara who saw Kurds as a problem for Turkey. We never had a person who consistently tracked the Kurdish issues, except maybe at the UN.

The Kurds often ask what would happen if the Iraqis would attack Erbil? And they get silence from senior military officials. I'm not sure what the allies would do, frankly, because, after all, it's not a violation of anything we laid down in terms of our exit agreement or in terms of safe havens. If there is a ground attack to the north, what will we do about it? Who will respond?

In a way the Kurds need Saddam. They need to keep him alive because after Saddam, there will be an agreement with "son of Saddam," whoever that may be. That ultimately will not help the Kurds in their quest for an autonomous region within an Iraqi state or some sort of independent Kurdistan. They need to keep Saddam alive to keep themselves on the international "media map."

Speech by Colonel R. M. Naab, War College, Virginia, 1994

Autonomy, Federation, Independence

Early on the morning of May 19, a multitude of men and women lined up patiently to vote in Dohuk, the chief town of Badinan province, as they were doing all over Iraqi Kurdistan. . . .

All the contesting parties, even the Iraqi Communist party, despatched motorcades through the towns bedecked with flags and carrying supporters shouting their slogans. . . . If some Western observers were bewildered by the frenzy, its meaning was all too clear to one East European guard attached to the UN forces. "I understand their exaltation so well," he declared. "Like us, they have been forced to remain silent for so many years.". . .

Calling the elections "a farce and a crime organized by their American masters and implemented by Kurdish lackeys," Saddam Hussein tried hard to disrupt them. . . . In the end, the Iraqi leader was powerless. Only a shortage of ballot boxes prevented all the voters from taking part. "I never believed that one day I would vote in Kurdistan," said Mumtaz, an Iraqi Kurd living in Britain who had returned for the occasion. "It's like a dream.". . .

In a separate vote, all had to choose a "president.". . .

The real object of the exercise was to bring an end to the endemic rivalry between the 46-year-old [Massoud] Barzani, who claims the inheritance of his legendary father Mustafa, and 59-year-old [Jalal] Talabani, who poses as a revolutionary leftist leader embodying the spirit of progress. The voters would have to choose between the two and, in doing so, cast their verdict on the extent of freedom to which Kurdistan can aspire. . . . Barzani is by nature prudent and feels that the Kurds should not go beyond their traditionally modest objectives of autonomy simply because world opinion is momentarily (and unusually) in their favour.

Talabani is altogether more ambitious in advocating a federal set-up in Iraq which would give Kurdistan many of the attributes of statehood as well as more territory. He accuses Barzani of selling out Kirkuk and its population by limiting Kurdish claims to autonomy over a smaller area. The logic of Talabani points implicitly to full independence (though he certainly does not say as much). This, however, would win little support in the West (and none regionally) which would also be wary of a federal solution for Iraq after the sorry experiences of Yugoslavia and Czechoslovakia. . . . "Either we fight or we go to the polls," explained one KDP leader. . . .

Many observers have expected a social explosion in protest against the administrative vacuum left behind by the withdrawal of the Iraqi army and civil service last October. . . .

What happens next depends as much on Saddam Hussein as on the Kurds. If the Iraqi leader sticks to his refusal to make any concessions to Kurdish demands, he could lose any chance of regaining even limited control of the region. "It looks as if we are forming a republic without announcing it," remarked one of Barzani's aides. "Maybe we should redefine it as 'external autonomy'!"

Chris Kutschera, *The Middle East*, July 1992

Rivals for power Mas'ud Barzani (left) and Jalal Talabani battled each other to a draw on the May 1992 ballot for the position of paramount leader of Iraqi Kurdistan.

Ed Kashi/National Geographic Society

R. Maro
German Photographer and Aid Worker

When I left Iraqi Kurdistan in 1994, I felt that the Kurdish parties, or what remained from the Liberation movement, were unwilling and also unable to satisfy the needs of the population. They were too busy fighting for power.

No journalist or photographer could know in 1995 where to look to take a picture of Talabani on his satellite phone trying to reach the White House to find out what the US foreign policy wanted, or to look at Barzani with his military commanders, when he is playing with tanks and military toys to beat his enemy. One day the question was, is the PUK backed by Iran or not, on the next day the support of Saddam Hussein for the KDP became the focus of the international media. Who could know what was really happening, but the conflict is very old. It began in the 1960s when Mulla Mustafa returned from Russia to Iraqi Kurdistan.

After the uprising in 1991 and the 1992 elections, the Kurdish Regional Government was not able to solve this fight for political power. Beside the old conflict between Barzani and Talabani, the Kurdish Parliament was not able to build a Kurdish administration to rule the country and depended totally on the existing social infrastructure of the Iraqi regime and the international support for important sectors like health and education. The only alternative for the parties to expand their influence, was to build up their militias. For most inhabitants of Kurdistan, joining the party militia became their only income possibility, if they didn't find an alternative working illegally as smugglers or something else outside the state-controlled sector.

To increase their influence, the parties made a lot of dirty alliances with the former collaborators (known as "jash") and their militias who were established by the Iraqi Regime to fight the Kurdish Liberation movement. The "jash" came into power again and controlled key positions of the weak local economy. In this war economy, it was necessary for everyone to search for protection and a kind of social insurance through their clan structures.

Houses were reconstructed in the destroyed villages, and the traditional lifestyle, devastated by the Iraqi deportation policy, was revived with international humanitarian aid. Only villagers who returned to their homes were supported to reestablish agriculture, but none of the international organizations or the Kurdish parties took care about the difficult question of land ownership. By then, the majority of Kurds were living in urban centers without any international aid.

Before the uprising Iraqi society had become dependent on oil money, and even basic food items were not produced inside the country. Everything was imported. Kurdish farmers in Iraq were prohibited from cultivating the land and were forced to move into big collective towns under military supervision. After the uprising, the international aid mechanism just replaced the former Iraqi system of distribution to beneficiaries, which had become part of the Iraqi social system. Now, the whole economy became dependent on the only economic input into Iraqi Kurdistan—international humanitarian aid.

Humanitarian intervention was an external interference which also played an important role by distributing help to certain favored beneficiaries. The distribution of international aid helped destabilize Kurdish society.

The Kurdish leadership is responsible for the internal conflict by collaborating with the neighboring states. Both parties were supported by their former enemies with weapons, money and infrastructure and were fighting like soldiers of fortune for the interest of their neighbors.

Letter from R. Maro, February 1997

An Iranian rocket attack against the headquarters of the Iranian Kurdish Opposition movement, Komala/Iran, at 10 a.m. on October 24, 1993, between Halabja and Sulaimania. Two houses were destroyed and three people wounded.

R. Maro

Polarization in Turkey

The year 1991 was not only a major turning point for the Iraqi Kurds, it also brought important changes for the Kurds of Turkey. Turkish president Turgut Özal, who in the Kuwait crisis had placed his country unambiguously into the Western alliance, and who had been among the first to plead for a safe haven for the Kurds in northern Iraq, also favored a certain measure of liberalization toward Turkey's own Kurds. Early in 1991 the ban on publishing in Kurdish was lifted, as were some other restrictive laws, and some political prisoners were released. The abolished laws were replaced, however, by a comprehensive anti-terror law, which soon proved more repressive than the previous laws had been. Under these laws numerous writers and publishers were sentenced to long prison terms and issued high fines for no other offense than disagreeing with the government's Kurdish policies. Around this same time, Turkey's counterinsurgency strategy shifted from military operations against PKK guerrillas and their hideouts to tough measures against civilians suspected of harboring pro-PKK sympathies.

There was a significant degree of liberalization during the 1990s; but it went, paradoxically, hand in hand with an unprecedented decline in human rights standards. Still, for the first time it became possible to mention the Kurds in public and to publicly debate the Kurdish question in a context other than that of banditry or terrorism.

In 1990 the first local Kurdish party, HEP, was established by Kurdish deputies of Turkey's Social Democrat Party. This party, and its successor the DEP, had from 1991 on a number of deputies in Turkey's parliament. The government considered these parties to be fronts of the PKK (although, in reality, they represented a wider range of Kurdish political opinion) and subjected them to much harassment. In 1994 the parliamentary immunity of five—and, later, of all—DEP deputies was lifted and they were brought to trial on the accusation of contacts with the PKK. Several of them, including the only woman, Leyla Zana, are still in prison at the time of this writing.

The HEP and the DEP suffered more than legal harassment. In 1991, death squads, obliquely associated with police authorities, made their appearance in Turkey. They targeted human rights activists, lawyers, Kurdish community leaders, persons suspected of working for the PKK, and business rivals of certain well-connected people. By the time the DEP was banned in 1994, at least sixty-four party activists, including one member of parliament, had been assassinated by these unidentified assailants. The Ankara offices of the DEP's successor, the HADEP, were bombed and dozens of its members assassinated.

The sharpening of repression in the 1990s was a response to the PKK's success in winning the hearts and minds of increasing segments of the Kurdish population. Probably more effort went into organizing the civilian population through local committees than in the physical guerrilla struggle. By the beginning of the decade, the PKK had come to enjoy such widespread popular support in certain regions, especially those near the Iraqi border, that it believed it could change its strategy from guerrilla warfare to intifadah-type popular insurrection. In 1990 such popular uprisings took place in the cities of Cizre and Nusaybın. The Turkish authorities responded with concerted efforts to cut the PKK off from the civilian population on which it depended. Villages suspected of supporting the PKK were forcibly evacuated and destroyed. In the years 1990-92 more than three hundred settlements were at least partly evacuated; in the following years this number rose to almost three thousand. Not only villages were targeted: In 1992 an alleged (but possibly nonexistent) raid by PKK guerrillas on Şırnak was the pretext for wholesale shelling of the city that left tens of thousands homeless. Numerous inhabitants of Cizre and Nusaybın, too, were pressured to leave their homes.

As in Iraq, an important part in the conflict is played by government-recruited Kurdish militias, called village guards in Turkey. They are tribesmen, usually operating under their own traditional chieftains but integrated into the military command structure. The village guard system was established in 1985 with the recruitment of some tribes that were believed to be loyal to the state and hostile to tribes that supported the PKK. In the first years there were many volunteers for these jobs—carrying arms gives prestige, and this was one of the few possibilities of earning an income in the region. Because they knew the mountains at least as well as the PKK guerrilla fighters, the village guards were much more effective than regular military units. The PKK retaliated with brutal attacks on the guards' villages in which women and children were killed indiscriminately.

This violence gave the PKK bad press in the West but served its purpose well: It made people reluctant to become village guards. As the village guard system kept being expanded, the military authorities had to exert increasing pressure to make people join the guards. In many cases, villagers were told that they either had to accept arms and fight the PKK or would have to evacuate their villages and see them destroyed. Many yielded to pressure—the number of village guards has gone on rising—but much larger numbers, unable or unwilling to choose between the state and the PKK, fled the region and ended up in the squalor districts of the large cities of western Turkey.

The PKK differs considerably in several respects from all earlier Kurdish organizations. It not only speaks much of (national and class) oppression, but it has actually recruited many if not most of its militants from among the poorest and most oppressed strata of Kurdish society—including large numbers of young women. Violence has a prominent place in the party's discourse; this concerns both the repressive violence of the state, which produces awareness in the oppressed, and the liberating violence of the nationalist revolutionary, which is believed to bring about a new man and a new society. The PKK has deliberately provoked harsh reprisals by the army and police against civilians, and thereby successfully alienated them from the state. Self-sacrifice and martyrdom have become the object of an almost religious cult, which reached its most extreme form in the veneration for several young women who immolated themselves in acts of protest or who carried out suicide attacks. Their violent deaths, and those of all other martyrs, are made into symbols of the expected rebirth of the nation.   —MvB

Bridegroom dancing in the street, Diyarbakır
Ad van Denderen

Şırnak

Kurdish Town

By day, Şırnak looks like any small town in Turkey. . . . But as night falls on this town, which overlooks a large military garrison housing some 15,000 troops, shop lights are shut, streets empty out and soldiers take position in a small park in the center of town. By 10 p.m., an unofficial curfew has set in. . . .

In a hotel late one night, as a handful of people sat around waiting for gunfire, a Kurdish journalist working for a Turkish paper pulled out a cassette from his pocket and put it in the tape recorder. From a fuzzy noise emerged the distinct sounds of gunfire and cries in Kurdish: "This," he said, "is from the first battle the PKK fought in 1984." Slipping the tape back into his pocket, he remarked, "This tape is very popular among people."

The next morning, local residents were talking about the PKK's exploits of the previous night—two village militia were killed in an attack on a village on the road towards Hakkari, and the PKK spirited away seven boys from Toptepte village a few miles south of Şırnak. A relative of one of the boys was anything but worried: "They'll release him in a few days because he's already done his military service in the Turkish army." The "forcible kidnapping" of young boys, as it is called in the Turkish press, is one of the PKK's recruitment methods. What remains unclear, however, is how many of these young boys want to join the PKK and how many are forced to become guerrillas. . . .

In southeast Turkey, information is shrouded by fear, secrecy and the difficulty of questioning people who know neither Turkish nor what lies a few miles beyond their village. What is clear, however, is that people are frightened, and more often than not it is the army they fear rather than the PKK. . . .

While power lines now bring electricity to villages, and even the most remote areas are now accessible by road, this means little in a region where people do not have money for lightbulbs or cars. The schools that are built do not have enough space or teachers for the children, and residents of the region say that at night these schools are turned into military barracks, making them targets of the PKK. . . .

The growing public discussion of the Kurds in cities such as Istanbul and Ankara has had little real effect on the lives of the people in the southeast. Increasingly, the PKK is seen as the only group that is concerned with and fighting for the Kurds. Back in Şırnak, a television is constantly on in one of the restaurants frequented by journalists. . . . One night, amid reports of army plans to conduct a massive raid on the Cudi Mountains before winter sets in, General Chief of Staff Necip Torumtay appears on the screen. "It is not easy to crush the guerrillas, but the people love their nation and the fight to protect it will go on," he says. "All the people of the region are on the side of the nation." The camera cuts to another story.

Aliza Marcus, *Middle East Report*, March–April 1990

Background: *Welcome sign to Şırnak reads*
"Happy is he who calls himself a Turk"

Chris Kutschera

Soldiers came to the village of Üçkiras one June day to take these pictures. . . . On one side, the military photographer works. On the other side, notes are taken. What is the name of number 1? And number 2? The photographs are taken in order to make files of the villagers. The man who gives the orders is the major commanding the gendarmerie unit at Cevizdudu. In his possession, he has file cards with the photographs of all villagers in the region. . . . The reporter for Yüzyıl spoke with the villagers of Üçkiras because the other villages had been evacuated.

Yüzyıl, Turkish weekly magazine, November 4, 1990

These pictures were taken by a soldier who brought them to us at 2000'e Doğru, a Turkish weekly magazine. After the military coup, there were three taboos in the Turkish press: criticizing the army, talking about the Kurdish problem, or even using the word "Kurd" (you had to say "people of Turkey," not even "peoples" of Turkey). We didn't have much money, but we had correspondents all over the country—even a shepherd who once sent us a pamphlet the military had dropped from planes. We didn't ask him anything·about how he got the pictures. I think he took them, but it would have been very dangerous even to ask.

Interview with Şule Perinçek, picture editor, Yüzyıl, October 1993

It's impossible to look for these people now. So many people have been forced to flee from their villages you couldn't find them, and even if you did find someone they'd probably be too terrified to speak. I talked to local journalists and people at the Human Rights Association. They said it was impossible. Since these pictures were taken, hundreds of villages have been evacuated. You can't go into Şırnak and ask any questions. Şırnak was destroyed in 1992 and there's no one left to ask.

Interview with Aliza Marcus, American journalist, New York, April 1995

Unknown/Courtesy *Aydınlık* Archive

Opposite: October 31, 1990, Persian Gulf Collection, The National Security Archive, Washington, D.C.

1990–91

KURDISH WORKERS PARTY (PKK) STOPPED A DOLMUS TRAVELING BETWEEN
ULUDERE AND BEYTUSSEBAP TOWNS OF SIRNAK PROVINCE, TURKEY. (FIELD
COMMENTS: 1. A DOLMUS IS A SMALL BUS OR VAN USUALLY UTILIZED WITHIN
TURKEY FOR PUBLIC TRANSPORTATION WITHIN CITIES OR BETWEEN CITIES AND
VILLAGES THROUGHOUT TURKEY. 2. THE TOWNS OF ULUDERE AND
BEYTUSSEBAP ARE LOCATED IN THE TURKEY'S SIRNAK PROVINCE, WHICH WAS
RECENTLY ESTABLISHED. SIRNAK IS LOCATED IN SOUTHEASTERN TURKEY AND
IS PART OF AN AREA CONSIDERED AS THE EXTRAORDINARY SITUATION AREA,
WHICH IS REFERED TO AS SUCH BECAUSE OF THE INTENSE PKK ACTIVITY
WITHIN THE AREA.) THE PKK MEMBERS KILLED THREE VILLAGE GUARDS, AND
KIDNAPPED THREE OTHERS., SECURITY FORCES (BOTH TNP OFFICERS AND
JANDARMA SOLDIERS) FROM SIRNAK WERE SUBSEQUENTLY ADVISED OF THE
INCIDENT AND SHORTLY THEREAFTER CONFRONTED THE PKK MEMBERS WHO WERE
HOLDING THE THREE VILLAGE GUARDS. THE TURKISH SECURITY FORCES
OPENED FIRE ON THE PKK MEMBERS, WHO RETURNED FIRE KILLING ONE
JANDARMA SOLDIER. THE PKK MEMBERS SUBSEQUENTLY RAN OFF, EVADING THE
SECURITY FORCES, TAKING THE THREE VILLAGE GUARDS WITH THEM. (FIELD
COMMENT: THE TURKISH JANDARMA IS A PARA MILITARY FORCE RESPONSIBLE
FOR LAW ENFORCEMENT IN THE RURAL AREAS OF TURKEY.)

3.

4.

5.

6.

Dietrich Hackenberg
German Photographer

A close friend of mine, a Turkish photographer born in Germany, asked me if I wanted to accompany him to the east of Turkey. On the main road to Hakkari, we reached a camp situated in a hostile valley. The people there had been living in the mountains. On order of the Turkish army, they had to move from the village to this camp. When we asked about the circumstances of the village, the agha invited us for a cup of tea and explained how things happened.

All had begun with the decision of the agha to cease boarding the PKK fighters in the village. It was very tempting to receive payment from the government to become "village guards." The local PKK fighters were members of tribes he had considered enemies for decades. The government realized that it could take advantage of the traditional hostilities between the different Kurdish tribes. The village received weapons and ammunition from the Turkish government. As locals who know the land, they had to support the army in the fight against the PKK.

From then on, the villagers feared revenge of the terrorists. For the shepherds, it became too dangerous to be on the remote pastures. There, they had to face the attacks without any shelter. For men in the mountains, there was no other possibility for making money other than sheepbreeding. Thus they became dependent on the government's payment.

When the attacks against the villagers increased, the Turkish army decided that the village could no longer be protected due to the unfavorable strategic situation, so the villagers were moved to a camp beside the road. The young men invited us to a shooting contest. When they presented their weapons, the depressed mood disappeared from their faces for a moment. The Kurds are prohibited to carry knives with a blade longer than their middle finger. The greater temptation is to possess a machine gun as a village guard.

The sun sets and it is time for the men to assume their guard posts. One guard tells us how the PKK took revenge on a village guard. They ambushed a man who had collected his payment in Cizre. He was found hanging on a telegraph pole, the money stuffed in his mouth. Later our Kurdish taxi driver told us how the people hate these village guards. He considers them traitors of the Kurdish nation. But at the end of our journey, even he realized that these people were only victims.

Letter from Dietrich Hackenberg,
living in Germany, November 1995

A threshing place on the Mesopotamian plain, Mardin, Turkey

1991

Dietrich Hackenberg

After the burial of Kudret Filiz, at the cemetery in Dabulo, Lice

Olivia Heussler/Impact Visuals

Olivia Heussler
Swiss Photographer

*From the 10th until the 19th of December,
1990, I accompanied an independent Swiss
delegation to Turkish Kurdistan, invited by
the Turkish Human Rights Office.*

*On December 13, we drove in a minibus
towards Lice, north of Diyarbakır, where the
day before, during a demonstration against
the expulsion policy, a 27-year-old woman
farmer, Kudret Filiz, and a young man were
killed by policemen.*

*We traveled past Kızıltepe to the Turkish-
Syrian border area. Here, heavily guarded,
directly next to military barracks, Iraqi Kurds
who escaped from Saddam Hussein's troops
and poisonous attacks have lived for two
years. Now they live in tents, where it is too
hot in the summer and too cold in the winter.
I'm not allowed to photograph, and a creepy
nervousness dominates the civil policemen,
who stand around us. Without permission
from the government, we are also not allowed
to visit the Kurds who live here. Even if we
would have gotten permission, it would have
been impossible to talk to the people.*

*Our trip should continue to Cizre;
however, the local military patrols don't let us
into the town and try to force us to turn back.*

*In Siirt, a small town with a large military
presence, we visit the office of the Human
Rights Organization. Within a very short time
the room is filled with displaced farmers from
the region who want to tell us their stories. But
we are also visited by two policemen in civilian
clothes. They register us and ask us to leave the
city within an hour.*

*When we reached Diyarbakır, we were
inspected, followed and harassed every day
and as usual again thrown out. The National
Information Service (MIT) and the press police
accompany us to the airport. From there we
flew on to Ankara where I witnessed the trial
against Kurdish lawyer Vedat Aydın for
speaking in Kurdish in a meeting. He was
released and seven months later found tortured
and dead in a street in Diyarbakır-Elaziğ.*

*In Kurdistan, an undeclared war prevails.
People are pushed here and there partly
because their houses lie in militarily strategic
places, partly because their villages are to be
flooded with water for the purpose of dam
construction. . . . Kurdish, Turkish and
foreign journalists are gagged through
intimidation and torture.*

*Never in my professional life have I been
so severely restricted as I was on this trip.*

Letter from Olivia Heussler,
living in Switzerland, January 1991

Yıldız Alpdoğan, State Security Court, Diyarbakır

1991

Ed Kashi
American Photographer

I was in Diyarbakır for about a week working with a human rights lawyer who was representing the two subjects of this photograph. I stumbled into the courtroom with him. I turned to my right and there was this scene. I was immediately struck by this woman's pride and strength. Although I didn't know her name or the circumstances which put her in this predicament, her powerful presence still resonates in my memory. I shot off a frantic six or seven frames and I knew I got it, and then the judge said: "Sit down!" and that was it. I took no more pictures in that situation. And then I was just worried when we shuffled out that somebody was going to stop me and ask me for my film. Fortunately nothing happened.

It seemed that since the need for access by the international community had expired with the end of the refugee crisis, the Turks felt there was no reason for foreigners to be sniffing around the southeast, exposing the degree of their overt military campaign against the Kurds, especially the PKK.

I felt that the PKK presence in Turkey had incredible sympathy and support. It was as if the Kurds were rediscovering themselves in their identification with the PKK. I also felt very protected when I was with the Kurds. I found they viewed me as a symbol of the West through whom they could get their message out.

I was told that after the issue of National Geographic *with these pictures initially appeared in Istanbul, even receiving a mention in the pro-government daily* Hürriyet, *all the copies were confiscated and the issue was banned.*

Interview with Ed Kashi, living in the U.S., June 1994

Yıldız Alpdoğan, a Turk from the city of Denizli, was convicted, at the age of 21, for directly participating in the Kurdish struggle. She was sentenced to 12 years and 6 months in jail.

In her trial in Diyarbakır at the State Security Court it was stated that Alpdoğan, a student of Izmir Higher Nursing School, had joined the PKK and was nursing wounded PKK guerrillas in the country-side outside of the town of Cizre, Şırnak district.

Yildiz Alpdoğan met a Kurd when she moved from Denizli to Izmir to start her study in the university in 1988. Later they got married. Now her husband cannot visit her because he is also wanted by the authorities. Communication is only through writing.

Aydınlık newspaper, July 31, 1993

The Anti-Terror Law (Law 3713)

... any kind of action conducted by one or several persons belonging to an organization with the aim of changing the characteristics of the Republic as specified in the Constitution, its political, legal, social, secular and economic system, damaging the indivisible unity of the State with its territory and nation, endangering the existence of the Turkish State and Republic, weakening or destroying or seizing the authority of the State, eliminating fundamental rights and freedoms, or damaging the internal and external security of the State, public order or general health by any one method of pressure, force and violence, terrification, intimidation, oppression or threat.

Helsinki Watch, "Turkey: New Restrictive Anti-Terror Law,"
A Human Rights Watch Short Report, Vol. 3, No. 9, June 1991

Ed Kashi/*National Geographic*, August 1992

Birand: Speaking face to face with Abdullah Öcalan in the camp, I wished to learn how he saw the recent developments—how far he would go with the armed struggle, why he had not been able to get the full support of the people, and what the future of this struggle would be, now that they were suffering increasing losses. . . .

Apo: Violent actions are only one percent (of our activities). The main task (of our cadres) is to educate. That is, to organize on the basis of persuasion. This is what really worries me. They have important organizational tasks ahead of them, and the people are in fact quite ready for this. It worries me that they cannot do this. This is what I am most occupied with these days, to make us freer in inventing new types of action and propaganda. . . .

Birand: Do you mean to say that you cannot go very far by armed action alone?

Apo: It won't do all by itself, of course. What result could we get? In terms of weapons the Turkish state is far stronger than we are. It is far more important how you organize the struggle politically; and note that if we had not had this sort of leadership, we could not have established this degree of rapport with the masses. There were many other armed groups in Turkey, but they were eliminated in a very short time. One must be very firm in giving priority to the political line. We too had people who thought they could finish the job in two days. A group that only believes in armed struggle survives at the most six months.

Birand: Do you believe that you can defeat the Turkish armed forces?

Apo: It would be wrong to make exaggerated claims about defeating the Turkish army militarily. We do not make such claims, we do not see this as a struggle where two armies oppose one another and where either they will win or we [will]. We wanted to achieve a situation where we have a people carrying on a struggle, and we are reaching that phase. Putting the national question on Turkey's agenda is more important than defeating an army. . . .

Birand: Do you mean that your show of armed force is part of a plan to gain more supporters?

Apo: The effect of armed propaganda is obvious. It brings you prestige and honor. That's a well-established fact. . . .

Birand: Speaking of relations with the people, the first thing that comes to mind is the relations with the tribes. The PKK used to fight some of them but had good relations with some others. Did it, in other words, wish to use the tribes?

Apo: We definitely do not have much respect for tribal organization.

Birand: But you also want to use some tribes.

Apo: The Kurds constitute a tribal society. Everyone has tribal loyalties; that is an inescapable fact. You cannot call what we do "using" the tribes. Everyone comes from some tribe. . . . When he joins you, you become associated with his tribe too. . . .

Birand: You say that for you, education comes first, before armed struggle. But the human material that you get is after all a very ignorant raw material, isn't it? You attempt to teach this ignorant raw material, people who are still illiterate, communist ideology. Isn't that difficult?

Apo: I develop the strategy, and . . . principles of leadership. This is what we give the militant into his hands. He then works with it according to his own character. Sometimes he behaves like an agha. . . . He sees that while he used to be a serf he now can command thousands, and he goes mad. If the man is uncultured, if he has grown up with feudal norms and values, he will develop the attitudes of an agha. If he is educated he will turn into a cheap bureaucrat. These phenomena are widespread among our people, and I have been using all my energy to combat them.

Mehmet Ali Birand, Turkish journalist, *APO ve PKK (APO and the PKK)*, 1992

Live ammunition focuses the minds of trainees for the PKK at the Mahsum Korkmaz Academy in the Bekaa Valley of Lebanon.

1992

Ed Kashi/ *National Geographic,* August, 1992

LEBANON

359

Reza
Iranian Photographer

According to Zoroastrian tradition, Kurdish people believe the New Year begins with the first day of spring—Newroz.

March 21, 1993
The city of Cizre in Turkish Kurdistan is closed to journalists. Gathering and celebrating are forbidden by Turkish authorities. Cizre should have been a "death city." However, Cizre is not. Lighting fires, like in their ancestral tradition, becomes a mark of rebellion against oppression. Only a few journalists are in Cizre to witness and commemorate the massacre of last year. The army shoots; three hundred people are wounded and some of them are killed. This year, like all years, tires are burned and children dance around fires. Revolt is in the street against this New Year of repression. Tanks, bought by Turkey from NATO, try to disperse the people. Tension is present amidst the mud and fire.

I move cautiously from one house to another. At nightfall, everyone returns home. Curfew takes effect. Cizre is plunged into an alarming silence. Alone in my hotel room, I wait. Suddenly, the whizzing of bullets breaks the silence. Still in my memory is the black and incandescent sky.

Letter from Reza, living in
France, March 1996

"The use of German armored vehicles against the Kurdish population in Cizre on New Year's Day, 1992, where about a hundred civilians were killed, created tension between the German and Turkish governments."　　—Reza

Reza

*Tracer bullets blaze past a hotel window
as the police and PKK exchange night fire
in Cizre, Turkey, March 21, 1993*
Reza/National Geographic, May 1994

Destroyed homes in Ormaniçi, southeast Turkey

1993

Richard Wayman

Richard Wayman
British Photographer

It took two days of walking to reach the village of Ormaniçi (the Turkish name given to the Kurdish village of Bane by the authorities in 1960). We travelled by night in order to avoid Turkish army patrols. There are no roads to the village, people arrive on foot or donkey. The Turkish soldiers came in by helicopters to blow up houses, make arrests and threaten the population.

Ormaniçi was constructed from stones, hewn from the scraggy hills nearby and looks as if it had grown from the ground. Hardy sheep and goats survive on the sparse covering of grass and scrub and provide the village with its only income.

The smell of burnt timber and rotting meat hung in the air as I was helped over rubble to one of the surviving houses. Inside, warmed by a stove, we drank sweet, black tea and talked about the day in February 1993 when the soldiers came.

An old man knelt on the floor with his head pressed to the ground to show how a soldier had forced his face into the mud in the village 'square' where everyone was ordered to gather. Four younger men showed feet wrapped in dirty bandages stained with a yellow/orange pus. Their feet had been beaten by the soldiers. An officer accused the people of giving food and shelter to guerrillas of the PKK (Kurdish Workers' Party).

As the villagers stood, surrounded, in the drizzle and mud, other soldiers threw grenades into homes. Explosions brought down roofs, and paraffin, used for lamps, ignited. A grenade was tossed into the communal barn killing livestock. Before they left, five people were taken to the waiting helicopters—accused of being members of the PKK. Two-thirds of the houses had been totally or partially destroyed in the action. Sheep, goats and two donkeys had been killed. Villagers didn't expect to see the arrested five again. Not surprisingly half of the families left the village shortly after the attack. They will join the many thousands now living in squalor around regional cities in southeast Turkey such as Diyarbakır, whose population has increased twofold in the past three years.

I left Ormaniçi with two young men who were off to join the PKK in nearby hills. The old man said, "This is my home. If I was younger I would fight for it too."

Letter from Richard Wayman, living in England, June 1995

TURKEY

The Dark Cloud Over Turkey

Apart from a couple of hesitant voices, no one is standing up and demanding to know what the Turkish government is doing, what this destruction means. No one is saying: "After all your signatures and promises you are riding towards doomsday, leaving the earth scorched in your wake. What will come of all this?"

Turkish governments have resolved to drain the pool to catch the fish; to declare all-out war. Only the people of Turkey have been kept in ignorance; newspapers have been forbidden to write about the drainage. Or maybe there was no need for censorship: maybe our press, with its sense of patriotism and strong nationalist sentiment, chose not to write about it, assuming the world would neither hear nor see what was happening. . . .

During the War of Independence we fought shoulder to shoulder. We established this state together. Should a man cut out the tongue of his brother?

The most horrific aspect is the inhumanity of outright war for the sake of a few fish. They have burnt almost all the forests of eastern Anatolia because guerrillas hide out in them. Turkey's forests have been burning for years. . . . Turkey is disappearing in flames along with its forests, anonymous acts of genocide, and 2.5 million people exiled from their homes, their villages burnt, in desperate poverty, hungry and naked, forced to take to the road, and no one raises a finger.

Some of my friends, my old journalist colleagues, friends whom I love and who don't want anything to happen to me, are anxious. Some say I am taking sides. . . . I am on the side of the Turkish, the language in which I write. . . .

Of course I take sides. For me the world is a garden of culture where a thousand flowers grow. Throughout history all cultures have fed one another, been grafted onto one another, and in the process our world has been enriched. The disappearance of a culture is the loss of a colour, a different light, a different source. I am as much on the side of every flower in this thousand-flower garden as I am on the side of my own culture.

Yaşar Kemal, Turkish writer living in Turkey,
Index on Censorship, No. 1, 1995

Leyla Zana, one of eight Kurdish members of the Turkish parliament accused of backing the banned Kurdistan Worker's Party, delivers her final defense speech. Leyla Zana was sentenced to fifteen years along with four of her codefendants.

Burhan Ozbilici, Turkish writer/Associated Press

I object to everything that the court accuses me of. Our ideas are known to all; we fight within the framework of democracy, for human rights and brotherhood among people. We will continue until the end of our life.

Leyla Zana's statement to the State Security Court,
Ankara, December 8, 1994

1993

Kurds Creating a Country On the Hostile Soil of Iraq

By CHRIS HEDGES
Special to The New York Times

ERBIL, Iraq, Aug. 5 — For the third time this century, a fledgling Kurdish state has risen out of the havoc of war.

Largely as a result of the American-led intervention on their behalf at the end of the Persian Gulf war, the four million Kurds in northern Iraq have been able to form their own government, as their forebears did brief[ly] and 1946.

to run a government, we can be self-sufficient within a year," said the prime minister, Fouad Masoum, dressed in a beige linen suit and sitting in his air-conditioned office here. "But if we cannot, we will face catastrophe."

Kurdistan, land-locked wedged into a mou[ntain]

KURDS RETURNING TO RAZED VILLAGES

Refugees Head Back to Ruins of the Towns Demolished by the Iraqis in 1989

By CHRIS HEDGES
Special to The New York Times

QALA DIZA, Iraq — The tug of mem[ory] draws them through the snowy

Turkey threate[ns] to bomb Kurdis[h] guerrilla camp[s]

A CHARGE by Suleyman De[mirel], the Turkish Prime Minister, [that] foreign nations are involved [in the] Kurdish Worker's Part[y] guerrilla uprising [is a]

his troops against Kurdish insurgents in 1988, while used chemical weapons against Kurdish civilians.

Further, the Kurds have long found themse[lves] enmeshed in the sort of byzantine political complex[ity] for which this region is well known. It is not ea[sy to] keep a scorecard.

During its eight-year war with Iraq ending in [1988] the Iranian Government offered sanctuary and su[pport] to Iraqi Kurdish leaders even as it attacked s[trong]holds of Iranian Kurdish rebels.

Today, for their own individual reasons, th[e] ernments of Iraq, Iran and Syria back the [Kurdish] rebels fighting in southeastern Turkey.

For its part Turkey has acquiesced to th[e] security zone, despite misgivings, in part to av[oid a] refugee crisis and in [...]

As Kurds Enjoy Freedom, They Wake the Neighbors

By CHRIS HEDGES

ERBIL, Iraq [—]

THE Kurds of northern Iraq, who have managed to create the third de facto Kurdish state of this century, are [trou]blesome not only to the Iraqi Government [but to Turkey and] Iran as well.

The new Gover[nment, after] elections in May, is [busy] filling the administ[rative] withdrawal from [the] intervention of Am[erica and] the neighbors, the [Kurds'] new domain the p[...]

But to the Ira[qi and] Kurdish minoritie[s] dangerously clos[e...] Kurds across all [...] been fig[hting...]

the American-led intervention of March 1991 in the aftermath of the Persian Gulf war. Taking heart from the allied rout of President Saddam Hussein in Kuwait, the Kurds had risen in revolt only to be crushed by the regrouping Iraqi Army. To coax home 1.5 million Iraqi Kurdish refugees in Turkey and Iran, 15,000 allied troops moved into the north to set up a security zo[ne.]

The zone, whose southern boundary roughly cor[re]sponds to the 36th Parallel, is now monitored by [mil]itary observers stationed in the border town [...] to [keep] Iraqi forces at bay, there are al[lied planes] based in Turkey.

Turks 'used Kur[ds] as mine detecto[rs]'

By Amberin Zaman in Tekevler villa[ge]

ALLEGATIONS that Kurd[ish] villagers were [used as] human mine detec[tors by] troops fighting K[urdish] Workers Party se[paratists] are being investiga[ted by] Turkish parliament[ary] MPs from t[he] rights commiss[ion] investigated the [...] to disclose thei[r] report next we[ek ...] kevler, a tiny [vil]lage in the r[...] man, believ[es the] difference t[...]

"Nothin[g ...] horror of [...] forced to [...] Hadji M[...] in his lat[...]

"It w[as] ing. Th[...] to the [...] 30 of [...] into [...] were [...] woo[...] to [...] ful[...]

Batman MP fr[om the] Islamist Welf[are party] who said [...]

The Kurds victims or terrorists?

Sir: The letter (22 January) [about] the Atroush refugee cam[p gives a] shockingly one-sided and [...] account. This is not a case [of the] United Nations High Commissioner for Refuge[es closing] down a sanctuary for genu[ine] refugees, but one of an international humanitarian [...] operation being sabotaged [by] militant terrorists.

The camp was originally [set up] by the UNHCR in co-opera[tion] with the Kurdish Democrati[c Party] of northern Iraq. Those stay[ing] there fell into two distinct categories.

One group was of villager[s from] south-eastern Turkey who sa[id] they had been forced by the [PKK to] leave their homes. They wan[ted to] go back as soon as condition[s] permitted. A number of thes[e have] already done so and others [have] emphasised to the UNHC[R and its] visitors to Atroush that this [is what] they wanted.

A second, smaller group we[re the] armed members of the PKK [who] systematically tried to conver[t] Atroush from a refugee cam[p into] an operational base. In partic[ular] they seized food and relief su[pplies] from the UNHCR and distrib[uted] them to their followers. They [...]

U.S. DECIDES TO ACT AGAINST THE IRAQIS FOR RAID ON KURDS

MILITARY STRIKE EXPECTED

Officials Dismiss Pullout From Kurdish City and Say Iraq Is Expanding Its Attack

By STEVEN LEE MYERS

WASHINGTON, Sept. 2 — The [C]linton Administration took steps to[day] toward military action to punish [P]resident Saddam Hussein for Iraq's [mi]litary campaign in the northern [Kur]dish enclave. The Administration [officials] [...] Iraq appeared to be pressing [...]

Pressure renewed on Turkish author

TURKEY'S best-known author, Yasar Kemal, left, was given a 20-month suspended jail sentence by an Istanbul court yesterday for "spreading separatist propaganda". His publisher, Erdal Oz, right, got a suspended fine. The 72-year-old writer, whose most famous novel, Mehmet My Hawk, has been translated into more than 10 languages, was charged for an article he wrote about the Kurdish problem.

His lawyer, Enver Nalbant, said: "I can't believe it and we are going to appeal. They are tightening up again now, because we have a rightist government."

A conservative coalition government of the Motherland and True Path parties was approved by President Suleyman Demirel this week, and yesterday the prime minister, Tansu Ciller, handed over power. The outgoing human rights minister, Adnan Ekmen, criticised True Path leaders for ignoring his reports on human rights violations.

The cases of four former Kurdish MPs facing separatism charges were adjourned. — Chris Nuttall, Ankara.

[Map: KURDISH REGION — IRAN, TURKEY, Qala Diza, Kirkuk, 36th PARALLEL, SYRIA, IRAQ, Tigris, Euphrates, Baghdad, 0 Miles 100 — The New York Times]

Tens of thousands of Iraqi Kurds have returned home to rebuild villages like Qala Diza.

[their] lives, the threa[t is] palpable. His forces hav[e in the] north and continue t[o...] [Ku]rds wonder how long thi[s] peace can last.

[pe]ssimist, but I am very [...] [Ab]dul Rahman, an Iraqi Kurdish [...] [...] we have allied protection. [...] every six months. What [...] and our allies decide not to [...] [h]ow can we survive?"

[...] it will be difficult.

[...] who has dealt more ruthlessly [...] [any]one since Mustafa Kemal [...] modern Turkey, was even able [to...] [Kur]dish militias to fight alongside [...]

refugees in Iran and Turkey, who ha[d...] [after] an abortive Kurdish uprisi[ng ...] [...] was safe to retur[n ...]

Late Edition

New York: Today, mostly sunny, cooler, less humid, breezy. High 81. Tonight, clear. Low 65. Tomorrow cloudy

THE DAILY TELEGRAPH

23 May 1995

Turkey protests as Kurds beam TV from Britain

in Ankara and Kathy Marks

TURKEY has c
the Governmen
vision regula
about a Londo
lite television
beams Kurd
programmes
defiance of d
MED-TV,
tional Ku
channel, ha
turous wel
in Turkey
TV progr
language
But th
ties are
station
uled b
day to
East a
The
the "
the
pas
rity
re
W
a

1997

he ruling
Party. Mr
ated the
here have
es, but it's
e ever
sed as

oincide
e Turk
win ove
include
s for mi
ast and
cibly d
ear confli
has al
ith its me
numan ri
other cri
g traffi
ggling.
gue of
forced
e milli
than
he killi
ty
cused
s to or symp
rebels.
Commissio

NYT 7/5/96

Turkish Kurds Go on Rampage, Battling the Police in Germany

By ALAN COWELL

BONN, March 17 — For the second
ne this month, Kurdish protesters
manding a separate state in south-
stern Turkey rampaged against
German police over the weekend,
mpting calls from politicians for
tant Kurds to be deported.
urdish demonstrators, barred by
urt ruling from holding a rally in
mund to celebrate the Kurdish
Year, blocked major highways
urs on Saturday and encircled
erman police officers, beating
ticking them before stealing
ervice weapons.
man officials singled out the
h Workers Party — an organi-
banned in both Germany and
— for initiating the violence
e Dutch-German border as
in the cities of Münster and
The clashes followed vio-
n Kurdish

the hard-line Kurdish Workers Party
at around 7,500, drawing on a much
wider network of sympathizers.
Interior Minister Manfred
Kanther called the movement a
"criminal organization" after the
latest violence, which started when
the German police sought to prevent
thousands of Kurds from converging
on Dortmund. At least 2,000 entered
the city and 1,300 of them were temporarily detained. Seeking to lower
tensions, the police finally allowed

Melees prompt German officials to call for militants to be deported.

A Fiery Protest by a Kurd in Germany
A Kurd running toward police officers after setting fire to himself yesterday in a protest calling for a homeland. He survived the ordeal.

Reuters

Kurdish Suicide Bomber Kills 9 Turkish Soldiers

By STEPHEN KINZER

ANKARA, Turkey, July 1 — On
Friday, less than 48 hours after the
head of Turkey's Islamic Party, Nec-
mettin Erbakan, took office as
Prime Minister, Kurdish rebels sent
him a harsh message.
As Turkish soldiers were marching in a military parade through the

tack, and hope that Allah will show
compassion to our martyrs."
The official Syrian newspape
Tishreen, however, suggested th
relations between the two countri
might soon improve.
"After the formation of the Tu
ish Government headed by Mr.
bakan," the newspaper said in

Kurdish dream of nationhood dies

Sunday Times 8 Sept 96

The Iraqi dictator has taken full adv
of tribal division

*Protest by a Turkish Kurd in
Germany, March 23, 1994*
Still from video,
Reuters/Corbis-Bettmann, New York

Portraits from southeast Turkey
William Coupon

EPILOGUE

In the poem "Ey raqib!," which the Iraqi and Iranian Kurds adopted as their national anthem, the lines that are always sung with the greatest intensity are those of the refrain: "Let no one say that the Kurds are dead; the Kurds are still alive; never shall our flag be lowered!" The poem is a challenge to the Kurds' enemies (*raqib*), who would prefer them not to exist, and it proudly proclaims that the Kurds will always remain Kurds and attached to their national symbols. In Turkey, where the survival of Kurdish culture and identity has been even more under threat than in Iraq and Iran, recognition was the first objective of the new Kurdish movement that emerged in the 1960s. Kurdish intellectuals, prosecuted in 1971 for "separatist activities," wrote as their defense pleas essays on Kurdish history and culture, which were later published abroad under the title "Listen Well, You Fascist Prosecutor: There Are Kurds in the World!"

The would-be nation-states among which Kurdistan was divided in the aftermath of the First World War have, each in its own way, made great efforts to assimilate and integrate their Kurdish citizens. They have had a certain measure of success: the Kurds of Turkey, Iran, and Iraq are more different from one another now than they were three quarters of a century ago. Many persons of Kurdish descent, especially in Turkey, have come to identify with the dominant nation. From the 1960s on, however, growing numbers of Kurds took part in movements for cultural revival and demanded the right to maintain and develop Kurdish language, literature, and culture in general. The repression of these cultural movements strengthened the hand of those Kurdish leaders who spoke of Kurdish rights in political and military terms. The Kurdish movement became almost identical with armed struggle for autonomy.

Decades of such struggle have strengthened the Kurds' sense of national identity, but the costs have been extremely high. It is true that no enemy can say that Kurdish identity is dead; it is very much alive indeed. But much of traditional Kurdish society, including its economic base, has been destroyed. Not only did Iraq physically destroy four thousand villages; in resettling their populations in large townships without economic resources, the Iraqis made them dependent on government handouts and destroyed their self-esteem and moral sense of community. The war and the genocide of 1988 left hundreds of thousands of widows behind, and several times that number of fatherless children without much prospect for the future. The guerrilla war in Turkish Kurdistan has also forced many to leave their villages and resettle in large cities, where they have joined the unemployed underclass.

The armed struggle has repeatedly had the effect of turning the Kurds—or at least their political leaders—into hostages of the interests and power conflicts of states in the wider region. Mulla Mustafa Barzani received significant support from Iran and Israel, and later also from the United States, because these countries wished to weaken the Iraqi regime. His increasing dependence on this support changed the character of the Iraqi Kurdish movement and was the cause of its collapse as soon as the shah reached an understanding with Saddam Hussein in 1975. The PKK owes much of its military capacity to the support of Syria, which needs means of turning the screws on Turkey. The geopolitical struggle for control of Euphrates and Tigris water, which is of vital importance for Syria, has given the PKK a major strategic ally as long as the guerrilla war continues. A peaceful settlement of the Kurdish question in Turkey, however, appears not to be in the interest of Syria. The conflicting strategic interests of neighboring states, and their direct as well as indirect interventions, are also a major factor exacerbating the intra-Kurdish conflicts in Iraqi Kurdistan.

Another effect of the armed struggle has been a shift in the social composition of the Kurdish movement, the urban intellectuals who were its most prominent leaders being replaced at least in part by military men, often of rural backgrounds. The Iraqi and Turkish governments have recruited tribal chieftains as militia commanders to fight the Kurdish guerrillas and have thereby strengthened tribal social structures that had been dissolving. The Iraqi Kurdish leaders, too, have concluded alliances with militarily powerful tribal chieftains, infusing Kurdish politics with tribal loyalties and tribal conflicts. The reemergence of the tribes is, in a sense, a return to a more traditionally Kurdish past, a reversal from assimilation to the Turkish or Iraqi nation-states. The strengthening of tribal loyalties, however, is also a serious impediment to the emergence of Kurdish unity.

Especially since 1980, numerous educated Kurds have had to flee Kurdistan and the wider region and have sought asylum abroad. In Europe they joined a large Kurdish community that had earlier migrated there as workers (an estimated 400,000 Kurds live in Germany alone). The arrival of these refugees speeded up the emergence of a Kurdish diaspora network of various cultural, educational, and political associations communicating through a steadily growing number of print and electronic media. Liberated from Turkey's suppression of the Kurdish languages, writers in Europe started publishing in their mother tongue and have engineered a revival of northern Kurdish as a literary language, producing a considerable output in books and journals. Several Kurdish-language films have been produced in Europe (and could be seen in Kurdistan on video). A rapidly growing number of Internet sites connect Kurdish individuals and groups across the world. In 1995 a Kurdish television station began broadcasting by satellite from Europe to the Middle East, making the Kurds the first nonstate nation to have access to this powerful modern means of nation building. The destruction and oppression that forced many Kurds to leave their homeland has had the unintended effect of regenerating Kurdish culture.

—MvB
July 1997

Mother holding memorial to her dead son,
cemetery of Sulaimania, Iraq, 1992

Susan Meiselas/Magnum

BIOGRAPHIES

ABDULHAMID II (ABDUL HAMID II), sultan of the Ottoman Empire (1876–1909), slowed the pace of westernizing reforms and struggled to hold the empire together despite increasing European interference and the rising nationalism of the Christian minorities. In 1892 he established the Kurdish tribal militias (Hamidiye) named after him. In 1908 a military coup, the Young Turk "revolution," forced him to adopt a constitution and install a parliament; in 1909 he was deposed. Abdulhamid was a great patron of nineteenth-century photography. He believed traveling to view his empire firsthand was too dangerous, and thus commissioned a photographic survey of its people, its topography, and the results of his reforms. In 1893 he presented fifty-one photograph albums to the Library of Congress, mostly by the Armenian photographers Abdullah Frères.

GHAFOOR AMIN ABDULLAH is a schoolteacher in Sulaimania, northern Iraq.

MOHAMMAD ALI SHAH, the last shah of the Qajar dynasty, succeeded his father, Muzaffaruddin Shah, in January 1907, less than a year after the country had received its constitution. Hostile to constitutionalism, in June 1908 he dissolved parliament and jailed or executed many popular deputies. Discontent, the large Bakhtiari tribe marched on Tehran and brought him down in July 1909. His twelve-year-old son Ahmad was proclaimed shah, the constitution was restored, and parliament reconvened.

ALIŞÊR (ALISHER), a poet and Kurdish nationalist politician. Born in the Koçgiri district into a family of seyids (hereditary religious leaders of the Kurdish Alevis), Alişêr was probably the real organizer behind the first postwar Kurdish uprising in Turkey, in Koçgiri (1920). He also took a leading part in organizing the Dersim rebellion in 1937, together with Seyid Riza. During these events he was treacherously murdered by fellow Kurds. His wife, Zêrifa, who fought alongside him, killed one of the assailants before she herself was killed. Alişêr also composed many poems of religious and nationalist inspiration, in Kurdish as well as in Turkish.

JABAR ABDULKARIM AMIN learned photography from Ghafoor Mulla Najim, and photographed in Iraqi Kurdistan from the 1960s, when he opened a studio in Koisanjak. He was killed in an accident in 1995.

TAYMOUR ABDULLAH AHMAD was born in 1976, a member of the Rohzay tribe in Iraq. In 1988 his village Kulajo was evacuated and destroyed by the Iraqi army, and at age twelve he became the only known survivor of the mass execution of women and children during the Anfal campaign. He lost twenty-eight relatives, including his parents and three sisters.

IBRAHIM AHMED, a prominent poet and politician, was born in Sulaimania in 1914. When studying law in Baghdad in the early 1930s he joined a Kurdish cultural and political association, which had a formative influence on him. From 1939 to 1949 he published and wrote poetry for the Kurdish literary journal *Gelawêj.* Although opposed to Barzani, he joined the KDP in 1947, was elected its secretary-general in 1953, and served until the mid-1960s, when a definitive break with Barzani occurred. He retained some influence in the Kurdish movement through close contacts with Jalal Talabani (who became his son-in-law). Since the late 1970s he has lived in Great Britain.

APO: see Abdullah Öcalan.

COŞKUN ARAL, a photojournalist from Turkey, has covered wars on the front lines from central Asia to Central America. He spent over ten years in Lebanon and covered the Gulf War from Baghdad. He is coauthor of *The World's Most Dangerous Places.*

HASSAN ARFA was born in 1895 in Tiflis, where his father was the Persian consul. He made a brilliant military career in the Persian army, and under the Pahlavi shahs he took part in various campaigns against the Kurds and other tribal groups. In 1921–22 he fought against Simko, and in 1927 he led a regiment in a campaign against tribes in the Merivan-Hawraman region. From late 1944 to mid-1946 he was chief of staff of Iran's armed forces; he was dismissed from the army for political reasons. In 1957 he was appointed Iran's ambassador to Turkey, and from 1961 until his retirement in 1963 he was ambassador to Pakistan.

ATATÜRK: see Mustafa Kemal.

EMMA BARNUM, the daughter of missionaries, went to Harput with her parents in 1858. The Armenian massacre of 1895, which she witnessed, became known, in part, through letters written by her and other missionaries who lived in the region.

CAPTAIN BARRY traveled with Ernest Chantre, the assistant director of the Museum of Lyon, and was the photographer for all of Chantre's work, most notably two albums about the Diyarbakır and Bitlis regions.

SHAIKH AHMAD BARZANI was the hereditary religious leader of Barzan in northern Iraq, a district with a long tradition of resistance to government control. There were repeated "rebellions" in Barzan in the 1920s and 1930s until he was bombed out of his district in 1932 and fled to Turkey, where he was held in detention. After declaring his loyalty to the Iraqi king, he was eventually allowed to return to Iraq. He joined his younger brother, Mulla Mustafa, who lived in the Barzan region in defiance of the government. After military operations against them in 1945, the brothers and thousands of followers crossed into Iranian Kurdistan. After the fall of the Mahabad Republic, Shaikh Ahmad returned to Iraq and was banished to internal exile in the south. He died in the late 1960s.

MAS'UD (MASSOUD) BARZANI, son of the third and most influential wife of Mulla Mustafa Barzani, was born in 1946 in Mahabad. After Mulla Mustafa's final defeat in 1975, Mas'ud and his elder brother Idris, then based in Iran, reorganized the KDP. Since Idris's death in 1988, Mas'ud has led the party alone. After a decade of armed clashes with the rival PUK and its leader Jalal Talabani, in 1986 the two parties joined with other smaller parties to form the Iraqi Kurdistan Front, Barzani and Talabani its cochairmen. In the 1992 elections in the free Kurdish zone of Iraq, Mas'ud Barzani and Talabani received almost equal numbers of votes. Both have, however, refused to accept formal positions in the regional government. As the de facto leaders outside the democratic structures, since 1994 they have been in armed confrontation.

MULLA MUSTAFA BARZANI was a younger brother of Shaikh Ahmad and, from 1932 on, the military leader of all Barzan uprisings. Banished to Sulaimania with his brother, he returned to his home village in 1943, which led to the eruption of another local rebellion. In 1945 he took refuge in Iran with a large group of followers, who in the following year were the backbone of the armed forces of the Mahabad Republic. After the republic's collapse, he fled to the USSR with five hundred men. In 1958, he was pardoned by President Qassem and returned to Iraq. During his absence, the Kurdish Democratic Party had made him its president. Growing alienation between the Kurds and Qassem's government led to guerrilla war in 1961, which escalated throughout the 1960s. The ongoing war strengthened the Kurds' sense of nationhood and culminated in a peace agreement with the government in March 1970, by which the Kurds formally achieved autonomy. When the government did not implement all promises, Barzani, who had received promises of considerable CIA support via Iran, led a final offensive in 1974–75. When the shah reached a major agreement with the Iraqi government and gave up his support of the Iraqi Kurds, Barzani's movement collapsed. Mulla Mustafa, with tens of thousands of followers, took refuge in Iran. Seriously ill and disillusioned, he gave up politics and went to the U.S. for medical treatment. He died there in 1979; his body was flown to Iran and buried in Iranian Kurdistan.

BEDIRKHAN CLAN, the descendants of Bedir Khan, the last ruler of the Kurdish emirate of Jazira Bohtan, who brought a large part of Kurdistan under his control in the early 1840s and was deposed by the Ottomans in 1847. The family remained highly respected, and many of its members achieved high office in the Ottoman state; others lived in exile in Egypt or Russian-controlled Georgia. In the early twentieth century numerous Bedirkhans lived in Istanbul; the leader of the clan then was Emin Ali Bedirkhan (died 1926), who played a key role in the first Kurdish associations established there in 1908 and 1918.

CELADET BEDIRKHAN (died 1951), one of Emin Ali's sons, was one of the founders of the Kurdish National League,

Khoybun, from his exile in Syria. Here he also published *Hawar,* a literary and patriotic journal, from 1932 to 1935 and from 1941 to 1943. Written in the Kurmanji dialect of Jazira, it introduced the Latin alphabet for Kurdish and developed what came to be widely accepted as standard written Kurmanji. Celadet Bedirkhan also wrote, together with Roger Lescot, the most influential grammar book of the Kurmanji dialect.

KAMURAN ALI BEDIRKHAN (1895–1978), another son of Emin Ali, collaborated with his brother Celadet in Khoybun and the journal *Hawar.* From 1943 to 1946 he published in Beirut the weekly *Roja Nû* (in Kurdish and French). In 1948 he moved to Paris, where he taught Kurdish at the National Institute of Oriental Languages and Civilizations and published a bulletin of Kurdish studies.

LEILA BEDIRKHAN was the daughter of Abdurrazaq Bedirkhan and his Polish wife, Henriette. Born in 1908 in Istanbul, Leila studied ballet in Germany, and performed in Europe and the United States. She died in Paris in 1986.

MIQDAD MIDHAT BEDIRKHAN, together with his brother Emin Ali, figured in an abortive attempt at a Kurdish uprising. In 1898 he lived in exile in Cairo and published there the first Kurdish journal, *Kurdistan.* After the first five issues he returned to Istanbul for health reasons and left his brother Abdurrahman in control of the journal.

SÜREYA BEDIRKHAN, an elder brother of Celadet and Kamuran, published the journal named *Kurdistan* in Istanbul in 1908, following the Young Turk revolution. Accused of supporting an anti–Young Turk uprising in 1909, he was jailed. Later he lived in exile in Cairo, where he published a few more issues of *Kurdistan* and several tracts in French, Arabic, and English stating Kurdish claims for independence.

GERTRUDE BELL, born in England in 1868, set Alpine mountaineering records before she made her first trip to Iran in 1892. From 1910 to 1913 she undertook expeditions throughout the Middle East and was one of the first female archaeologists to engage in field research there. Fluent in Persian and Arabic, she was assigned to the intelligence service in Cairo during World War I, and, after the British occupied Baghdad, served as Oriental secretary under Sir Percy Cox. Her travel books include *Amurath to Amurath* and *The Desert and the Sown.* Strongly pro-Arab, she used her influence to shape British policy and helped bring King Faisal to power. She remained in Iraq until her death in 1926.

ISMAIL BEŞIKÇI, a Turkish sociologist, has spent more than thirteen years in jail for his public criticism of Turkey's policies toward the Kurds, beginning with his 1969 study of social and economic conditions in eastern Turkey. He published numerous important works on the sociology and history of the Kurds. All his books are banned in Turkey. A tireless advocate of freedom of the press, he is presently in prison for publishing his latest work on the Kurds.

ISABELLA L. BIRD, the daughter of a clergyman, was born in Yorkshire, England, and began her travels when she was twenty-two. A philanthropist, she built five hospitals and an orphan asylum in the Far East. She was the first woman to be elected a Fellow of the Royal Geographical Society. In 1889, at the age of fifty-eight, she set off alone for Persia. She spent nine months traveling from Basra to Baghdad to western Iran, where she spent most of her time among the Bakhtiari nomads, then through eastern Turkey and the Black Sea region. She published accounts of her travels in *Journeys in Persia and Kurdistan* and in an album of photographs. She died in 1904.

MEHMED EMIN BOZARSLAN was born in 1934 in Diyarbakır province. He began his public career as the mufti of Kulp district, but his critical attitude (he wrote a book denouncing the feudal order and superstitions behind the shaikhs' authority) forced him to give up this position. Later, he was imprisoned several times for his writings. His books include *Alfabe,* a children's primer on Kurdish; important translations of two classics, the Kurdish history *Sharafname* and Ahmad-i Khani's *Mem û Zin;* and a few collections of short stories. Since 1978 he has lived in Sweden as a political refugee and produced some twenty new books, including annotated reeditions of Kurdish journals from the beginning of this century.

Martin van Bruinessen is a Dutch social anthropologist who has done extensive fieldwork in the Turkish, Iranian, Iraqi, and Syrian parts of Kurdistan as well as in Indonesia and has published widely on various aspects of Kurdish society and history. His major works in english are *Agha, Shaikh and State: The Social and Political Structures of Kurdistan* and the historical study *Evliya Celebi in Diyarbekir.* He presently teaches Kurdish and Turkish studies at Utrecht University in the Netherlands and at the Free University of Berlin.

Kamil Chadirji was born in Baghdad in 1897 into a wealthy, influential family. An avid photographer, he documented Iraqi cultural life from the 1920s through the 1940s. An advocate of democracy, liberalism, and socialism, Chadirji founded and was president of the Iraqi National Democratic Party until it was abolished in 1963.

Sir Austen Chamberlain was born in Birmingham in 1863. After graduating from Cambridge, he traveled to France and Germany before entering politics as a member of parliament. Before the outbreak of the First World War, Chamberlain played a key role in persuading the opposition to pressure the government to stand by France and Russia. In May 1915, he was named secretary of state for India. He resigned when the campaign in Mesopotamia was charged with mismanagement, but remained active in government until 1931. He died suddenly in 1937.

Ernest Chantre, assistant director of the Lyon Museum of Natural History, traveled through Central and Eastern Europe and the Middle East beginning in the 1870s. An ethnographer and archaeologist, he was an expert on the Caucasus, Armenia, and Anatolia. His publications include *Recherches anthropologiques dans le Caucase* (1885–87); *Rapport sur une Mission Scientifique en Arménie Russe* (1893); and *De Beyrouth à Tiflis.*

Melville Chater wrote fiction for magazines before he became the *Red Cross Magazine*'s field correspondent in 1917. He filed for the Red Cross from France, Italy, Turkey, and Asia Minor and acted as publicist for Near East Relief in Asia Minor, Syria, and Palestine until 1922. Back in the U.S., Chater wrote for *National Geographic,* covering the United States, Asia, Europe, and southern Africa. He also lectured widely on his travels and published four books, including *Little Love Stories of Manhattan* (1906) and *Two Canoe Gypsies* (1932). He died in 1936.

Winston Churchill was born in 1874 in Oxfordshire, England. After attending Sandhurst Royal Military Academy, he served in Cuba, India, Egypt, and South Africa, where he also served as a war correspondent. After the 1918 armistice, Churchill was secretary of state for war (1918–21) and colonial secretary (1921–22). From 1924 to 1929 he served as chancellor of the Exchequer, but lost power along with the government at the onset of the Great Depression. Churchill was a vocal opponent to appeasement during the Second World War, and two days after Chamberlain declared war, Churchill was invited to serve as First Lord of the Admiralty. After the Germans attacked Norway, Chamberlain resigned and advised King George VI to appoint Churchill prime minister; he led the country through most of the war. From 1951 to 1955, he again served as prime minister. Churchill wrote over forty volumes before his death in 1965.

Joseph Plumb Cochran was born in Urmia in 1855, the son of an American Presbyterian missionary doctor. He received his medical education in the U.S., and in 1878, at twenty-three, he returned to Urmia, where he befriended Shaikh Ubaidullah, the Kurdish chief, whose letters, some of the earliest documents of the Kurdish claim for a nation, were forwarded to the British government. He remained in Persia until his death in 1905.

William Coupon is a portrait photographer whose subjects include aboriginal peoples and U.S. presidents, rock stars and international leaders. He has won numerous awards for his work in *Esquire, The New York Times Magazine,* the *Washington Post Magazine, Rolling Stone,* and *Time,* and has exhibited his work in the United States Senate Rotunda. Coupon has also recently begun to direct French television commercials. A selection from his series *Social Studies Sixteen: Turkish Kurds* was exhibited at FotoFest '96 in Houston, Texas. Coupon presently lives in Santa Fe, New Mexico.

Sir Percy Cox joined the British army in 1884 and rose quickly through the ranks. In 1914 he was appointed secretary to the government of India in the Foreign Department; in the First World War he was sent to the Gulf as chief political officer. He established his headquarters at Basra until 1917, when he moved to Baghdad. There, he assembled a team that included Sir Arnold Wilson and Gertrude Bell. After the armistice in 1918, Cox briefly served as Her Majesty's Minister to Persia but was recalled to England when Iraq was made an independent Arab state under a mandate from the League of Nations. In 1920, Cox returned to Baghdad and formed the government headed by Faisal, enthroned on August 23, 1921. In 1923, Cox retired to England.

Lord George Curzon traveled widely throughout the Middle East and Asia from 1887 to 1894. In 1891 he was named undersecretary at the India office; in 1895 he became undersecretary of foreign affairs. In 1898 he was made Viceroy of India, returning to England in 1905. In 1911 he was appointed president of the Royal Geographical Society, and in 1916 became a member of the inner war cabinet under Lloyd George. As foreign secretary, he was the British representative at the European Conference at Lausanne in 1923. He died in 1925.

Martha Dahl, born in Norway, emigrated to America in 1911. At sixteen, she vowed "to devote herself to the Master's service." In 1922 she graduated from the Lutheran Deaconess Hospital in Chicago; in 1925 she joined the Lutheran Orient mission hospital in Mahabad. She left the mission to marry Mirza Hussein, a Kurdish resident of Mahabad, where she brought up a family and remained for the rest of her life. In addition to her work as a nurse, she was reported to have worked as a translator for Qazi Mohammad during the Republic of Mahabad.

Leslie A. Davis entered the American foreign service in 1912 and was sent in 1914 to Elazığ, Turkey, where he served as American consul until 1917, when the United States broke diplomatic ties with Turkey. During the Armenian deportations, he sheltered a number of Armenians within the grounds of the consulate and arranged transportation for others. In 1918 he wrote a report of the deportations and massacre of the Armenian people, which he witnessed, for the State Department. Davis later served in Archangel, Helsinki, Zagreb, Lisbon, and Glasgow before retiring to the United States, where he died in 1960.

Ad van Denderen is a freelance photographer whose photographs on prison life, miners, Palestinians, the Kurds, and South Africa have been published in magazines throughout Europe. His books include *24 Hours of Amsterdam* and *Welkom in South Africa.*

M. Nuri Dersimi was born in Hozat in Dersim in the early 1890s, into one of the few literate families. Nuri became involved in the Kurdish associations (1911–14) and spent the war years as a military veterinarian in Erzincan; he then moved to the Koçgiri district, taking part in the Koçgiri uprising of 1920. In the 1930s he was a veterinarian in Dersim and in close contact with Seyid Riza (whose secretary his father had been). Just before the outbreak of the 1937 resistance movement in Dersim, he had to flee the area. In Syrian exile he wrote *Kürdistan Tarihinde Dersim (Dersim in the History of Kurdistan),* a major work on this part of Kurdistan. His *Memoirs (Hatiratım)* were published posthumously.

Sir Henry Dobbs was born in London in 1871. Educated at Oxford, he entered the civil service in 1890 and was transferred to the political department in 1899. During the First World War, Dobbs was a political officer with the Expeditionary Force in Mesopotamia. From 1923 to 1929 he was high commissioner for Iraq, during which time he consolidated the state of Iraq. After overseeing the election of a constituent assembly, the Iraqi parliament, the ratification of the Anglo-Iraqi treaty, the control of the Kurdish districts, and the Mosul frontier question, he retired to his family home at Cappoquin.

William O. Douglas, associate justice of the United States Supreme Court, was a champion of individual freedoms and a strong advocate for the protection of America's wilderness areas. He traveled widely and wrote about his Kurdish experiences in *Strange Lands and Friendly People.*

William Eagleton was a U.S. Foreign Service officer from 1949 to 1988. His first experience in Kurdistan was as public affairs officer with the United States Information Service based in Kirkuk, Iraq (1954–55), following Lee Dinsmore. As the American consul in Tabriz (1959–61), he met frequently with Iranian military officers, Kurds, and tribal leaders in Iranian Kurdistan. During his second year in Tabriz, he began to gather information and interviews about the founding and history of the Mahabad Republic, which he later published in *The Republic of Mahabad.* In 1980 he returned to take charge of the U.S. interests section in Baghdad, where he renewed his contacts with Kurds of Iraq. Ambassador to Syria from 1984 to 1988, he was recently the U.N. special coordinator for Sarajevo. He has since retired to Taos, New Mexico.

Cecil John Edmonds served as the British assistant political officer in Mesopotamia and southwest Persia before being appointed in 1922 to special duty in southern Kurdistan, where he became involved in fighting Shaikh Mahmud. In 1925, Edmonds served as liaison officer with the League of Nations Commission of Inquiry into the Iraq-Turkey frontier, and later as an advisor to the Iraqi government. Upon retiring in 1950, he became a lecturer in Kurdish at the University of London and compiled the first extensive Kurdish-English dictionary (1966) with the Kurdish politician and scholar Taufiq Wahby.

Şerafettin Elçi was born in 1938 in Cizre, Turkish Kurdistan, where he later practiced law. In 1977, he was elected to parliament as deputy for the largely Kurdish province of Mardin. He helped topple the conservative Demirel government and became minister of public works under Ecevit's new government (1978–79). After the 1980 military coup he served two years in prison for stating in a public speech, in 1979, that Kurds exist and that he himself was a Kurd. In 1996 he established a new legal, conservative Kurdish party, the Democratic Mass Party.

Muzaffer Erdost was a military veterinarian in the Kurdish district of Şemdinan (Şemdinli), in Turkey. He published his experiences and observations in a series of articles in the leading left-wing journal *Yön* in 1966 and was the first person in Turkey to attempt to analyze tribal society in Marxist terms. He was successful as a publisher of leftist books and an essayist. When his brother Ilhan, a poet and publisher, was killed by police, he added his brother's name to his own and adopted his brother's publishing house. His writings on Şemdinan were reprinted as a book, *Şemdinli Röportajı,* by this publishing house.

Lotte Errell was born in 1903 in Münster, Germany. In 1924, she married a photographer and accompanied him on a film expedition to West Africa. The photographs from this trip were published in numerous magazines in 1930. In 1934 she traveled to Iran for the Associated Press and continued to Iraq and Kurdistan. In the same year, the press office of the Third Reich prohibited her from practicing journalism in Germany; she moved to Baghdad, where she remarried and again traveled to Kurdistan and Iraq. When the war broke out, she was arrested in Iraq as a suspected Nazi spy; simultaneously, the National Socialist government took away her German citizenship. In 1946, she and her second husband returned to Munich. In 1959 her Kurdistan photographs were published in *Atlantis.* She died in 1991.

Riza Ezer was born in 1951 in Ankara. After learning photography from his father, a newspaper photographer, Ezer took up photojournalism in 1967; he has since worked for *Ulus, Yenigün, Hürriyet, Cumhuriyet,* and the Turkish News Agency. He photographed the Iran-Iraq War and has won numerous awards in Turkey for his photographs.

King Faisal I was the son of the Sharif Husain, the traditional ruler of Mecca, who in 1916 launched the "Arab Revolt" against the Young Turk regime. Faisal led the Bedouin forces that conquered Damascus in 1918. He set up an Arab government and administration, but meeting French resistance to an independent Arab Syria, he was forced to flee Syria in the 1920s. At the request of T. E. Lawrence, Winston Churchill secured for Faisal the Kingdom of Iraq in August 1921. He died in 1933.

Abd al-Hosein Farmanfarma, born in Tehran in 1859, was the grandson of the Qajar crown prince Abbas Mirza. He was sent to Austria for military training, and later became governor of many provinces and served in various cabinets. He led the Iranian forces against Ottoman invaders in Azerbaijan and against the forces of Salar al-Dowleh (who was opposing Tehran) in Kermanshah. He died in Tehran in 1939.

HENRY FIELD was born in the United States and trained at Oxford University. As curator of the physical anthropology department at the Field Museum of Natural History in Chicago, he made numerous trips to Iraq in the 1920s and '30s. He left the museum in 1941 to become an advisor to President Franklin Roosevelt and later engaged in largely private research while working at the Peabody Museum of Harvard University. Assisted by the physical anthropologist Winifred Smeaton, Field traveled to the southern and northern regions of Iraq to study Kurds.

M. ŞERIF FIRAT was from the leading family of the Hormek tribe in Varto, which during the Shaikh Said rebellion actively fought against the Kurdish rebels. The Hormek, who are Alevis, had frequently been oppressed by their Sunni neighbors and considered the Kemalist regime their liberator. Fırat, a village schoolteacher, wrote an apologetic history of his tribe and region (1948), in which he attempted to prove that all Kurds are really Turks. A year after he published this book, he was murdered. The book was repeatedly reprinted with government endorsement and became part of Turkey's official view of the Kurds.

ROSITA FORBES, writer and novelist, drove ambulances on the Western front during the First World War before traveling to the Middle East. Her writings emphasized the position of women in these countries. She received, among other awards, the Gold Medal of the French Geographical Society. She died in the Bahamas in 1967.

MARGARET GEORGE, the first woman to go to the mountains with the peshmerga, became a symbol of women's participation in the Kurdish struggle. An Assyrian Christian, she was able to travel with men more easily than her Muslim sisters, though she was accompanied by her father. She was killed in the 1960s under mysterious circumstances.

ABDUL RAHMAN GHASSEMLOU was born in Urmia. He studied sociology in Paris and political economy in Prague. In 1967 he became a member of the revolutionary committee of the Democratic Party of Iranian Kurdistan (KDPI) and in 1971 he was nominated secretary-general. Leaving Czechoslovakia after the suppression of the Prague Spring in 1968, he lived in Paris, where he taught Kurdish at the university. In 1978 he returned to Iranian Kurdistan to rebuild the KDPI, which for several years following the Iranian revolution came to constitute the de facto government of a large part of Kurdistan and carried on a guerrilla struggle against the central government. Invited to negotiations with Iranian government representatives in Vienna, he was assassinated at the negotiating table on July 13, 1989.

ZIYA GÖKALP was born in Diyarbakır in 1876. A Kurd, he became the most influential ideologue of Turkish nationalism. As a student in Istanbul, he joined the Young Turk underground; he spent ten months in prison in 1898–99 for spreading revolutionary ideas and was then exiled to Diyarbakır. Following the Young Turk coup in 1908, he moved to Salonika, where his writings made a great impact. In 1915, he lectured on philosophy at the University of Istanbul. After the war he was briefly exiled to Malta by the Allies. In 1921 he returned to Diyarbakır, where he continued publishing. In 1923 he became a member of Turkey's parliament. He died in 1924.

AUGUSTA GUDHART was born in Poland in 1884. At sixteen, she moved to America, where she trained as a nurse. In 1911 she was called by the Lutheran Orient Mission Society as missionary to Persian Kurdistan, where she founded a home for the elderly and established an orphanage. She stayed in Saujbulaq (Mahabad) until she was forced to leave due to war and starvation in 1916. In 1920 she joined the Near East Relief party to Armenia and was recommissioned as a missionary to Kurdistan in 1920. She died in Philadelphia some time after 1965.

DIETRICH HACKENBERG was born in Birkesdorf, Germany, in 1964 and studied political science before he began to photograph. He has worked as a freelance photographer since 1993.

A. M. HAMILTON was born in New Zealand and spent five years in Kurdistan (1928–32) building what became known as the Hamilton Road from Arbil through the Rowanduz and Berserini gorges. In 1932 he settled in England, where he consulted on military bridges and developed a joint patent for the unit construction bridge, the standard heavy-duty bridge of the British army. He died in 1939.

HAPSA KHAN was born into a prominent family of Sulaimania in 1881. After the death of her father, she made the family house a public meeting place and founded an evening school to educate Kurdish women. Her husband, Shaikh Qadir, was a brother of Shaikh Mahmud. She established what is considered the first Kurdish women's organization in Iraq. After her death in 1953, her home, as she had intended, became a school.

JAMES HARBORD was born on a farm in Illinois in 1866. He became a general in the First World War, and in 1919, as chief of the American Military Missions, he traveled to the Middle East to study the situation of the Armenians. In 1923, after his retirement from the army, he was named president of the Radio Corporation of America.

HASAN HAYRI, from the leading family of Dersim's Karabal tribe, was an officer in the Ottoman army during the First World War and a Kemalist supporter. A believer in the common interests of Kurds and Turks, he was made a member of Turkey's parliament. By 1924, disaffected with Mustafa Kemal, he joined the opposition Progressive Republican Party. Not feeling safe in Ankara, he returned to Elazığ. Following the Shaikh Said rebellion—in which he was not involved—he was apprehended, tried by the Independence Court, and hanged.

RAFIQ HILMI, a Kurdish intellectual of Sulaimania, was secretary to Shaikh Mahmud. After Mahmud was exiled from Sulaimania, Rafiq Hilmi entered Iraqi government service as director of a secondary school and, later, as inspector for the ministry of education. When in the early 1940s urban nationalists established the Kurdish association Hiwa, Rafiq Hilmi became its secretary-general. Considered too pro-British, he played no part in the more radical KDP that later replaced Hiwa. He died in 1962.

SHAIKH EZZEDDIN HOSEINI was born in Bane in Iran in 1921. As a young mulla in 1942 he joined the first Kurdish nationalist organization in the Mahabad region, Komala J-K, which later merged into the more broadly based Kurdistan Democratic Party of Qazi Mohammad. In 1967 he became the imam of Mahabad's principal mosque. During the Iranian revolution he emerged as a charismatic leader speaking for Kurdish rights. In 1979 he negotiated with Tehran on behalf of the Kurds. The government offensive of 1980 forced him to flee Iran. He currently lives in Sweden.

OLIVIA HEUSSLER was born in Zurich and trained as a medical technician before becoming a photographer. Since 1980, she has devoted herself to photography, documenting progressive movements in Switzerland and throughout the world. She has recently photographed in Eastern Europe, Turkish Kurdistan, Palestine, and Central America.

SADDAM HUSSEIN, born in 1937 in Takrit, central Iraq, was a leading member of the Iraqi Baath Party that took power in a coup in 1968. Second in command, he signed the 1970 peace agreement with the Kurds. In a series of internal coups and purges he eliminated all actual and potential rivals, becoming the sole leader of one of this century's most bloody regimes. As an opponent of Iran's Islamic regime, he was a favorite U.S. ally. Even the Anfal operations against the Kurds in 1988, with some hundred thousand killed, did not result in any sanctions. Only his invasion of oil-rich Kuwait in August 1990 changed his status in the West.

IBRAHIM PASHA, chief of the large Milli (or Milan) tribe, was a powerful Hamidiye commander. He subjected neighboring tribes and took tribute from ever-wider territories. When the Young Turk revolt ended Sultan Abdulhamid II's rule in 1908, Ibrahim Pasha remained loyal to the sultan and tried to incite Syria to revolt. Failing in his effort, he fled south, dying shortly thereafter.

JA'FAR AGHA, leader of the Shikak confederation in Iranian Kurdistan, was assassinated by the Iranian government in

1905. Upon his death, his younger brother, Ismail Agha, "Simko," assumed his position of leadership.

ALBERT KAHN was born in 1860 in Alsace. He studied in Paris and made his fortune in international loans and South African mines. In 1893, he launched his project "The Archives of the Planet." Between 1910 and 1931, geographer Jean Brunhes (1869–1930), along with eight photographers and three cameramen, traveled to forty-eight countries and created 72,000 autochromes, 4,000 stereoscopic plates, and 170,000 meters of film. After the stock market crash of 1929, the local government bought all of Kahn's property, including his photography and films, and maintained their integrity. The Albert Kahn Collection is now housed on the grounds of his home and gardens in Boulogne-Billancourt, just outside of Paris.

JONATHAN KAPLAN was a doctor in South Africa until he was called up for army service. He then emigrated to England, where he worked as a surgeon for nine years. He used the money he earned as an air ambulance doctor and a ship's medical officer to subsidize his volunteer work as a trauma surgeon and physician in conflict zones and underdeveloped countries. He treated Kurdish battle casualties in northern Iraq during the 1991 uprising, and has also worked as an investigative journalist for British and European television, and as a photojournalist in the Far East. He is currently an emergency room physician in a central London hospital.

ED KASHI is a photojournalist whose work has been published internationally. His photo essays have depicted the heroin problem in Poland, the nightlife of Berlin, Soviet veterans of the Afghanistan war, and the City of the Dead in Cairo, Egypt. His photo essay on the Kurds was published in National Geographic. A book, When the Borders Bleed, followed. He lives in San Francisco.

MUSTAFA KEMAL PASHA, known as Atatürk, came to fame as the Turkish commander who won the 1915 battle of Gallipoli. Sent to eastern Turkey to supervise the demobilization of the Ottoman army in 1919, he organized local opposition to the further dismemberment of the Ottoman Empire. Establishing parallel government structures based in Ankara, he won massive popular support, destabilizing the Istanbul-based government. After defeating the Greek occupation armies, he proclaimed the republic in 1923 and made himself president. Instituting programs to transform Turkey into a modern, westernized, secular state, he also brutally suppressed all opposition to his reforms, turning the state into a one-party dictatorship. He died in 1938, and was succeeded by his old associate Ismet Pasha (İnönü).

YAŞAR KEMAL, one of Turkey's most widely read and internationally best-known novelists, was born in the Adana region to a family of Kurdish origins. Prior to 1950 he held a variety of jobs, including day laborer, watchman, and teacher; in 1951 he moved to Istanbul and began a career as a journalist. He was arrested in 1950 for alleged Communist propaganda, and in later life remained politically active on the left. His early literary work is strongly influenced by the oral traditions of Turkey's countryside, integrating Turkish and Kurdish themes. Later novels reflect his involvement with Turkey's emerging socialist and labor movement. At least thirteen of his novels have been translated into English, including his most famous, Ince Memed (Memed, My Hawk).

ADELA KHANUM was born into a leading Kurdish family in the former principality of Ardalan, the major center of Kurdish culture in Iranian Kurdistan. When she married Osman Pasha, head of the Jaf tribe in Halabja, she set up her household in Persian aristocratic style, with mansions and gardens. In 1919, when Shaikh Mahmud rebelled against the British, Adela Khanum sided with the British, perhaps due to the influence of her longtime friend E. B. Soane. She continued to exercise her influence through her son, Ahmad Beg, until her death in 1924.

AHMED KHWAJA, a member of a prominent Sulaimania family, fought in Shaikh Mahmud's revolt in 1919. His memoir, Çim Di (What I Saw), is one of the few first-person accounts of the events of the period.

GÉRARD KLIJN was born in 1940 and began his career as a professional photographer in 1963. He made his reportages of the Kurds in 1970, after photographing government clashes in Northern Ireland and Czechoslovakia. Three-time winner of the World Press Photo prize, Klijn has most recently worked in Burundi, Rwanda, and the Sudan.

Naci Kutlay was born in 1931 in a village in Kars province in eastern Turkey, and studied medicine in Ankara. After serving time in Istanbul's military jail for his involvement in the activities of the "49" (a group of Kurdish intellectuals arrested by the Turkish government in 1958 for "separatist" activities), he worked as a physician in public service. Following the military coup of March 1971, he was put on trial again for "separatist" activities and sentenced to seven and a half years in prison. He was released under the general amnesty of 1974 and returned to medicine, becoming head surgeon of state hospitals in Ağrı and Mardin. Following the 1980 coup he was arrested again; after his release he emigrated to Sweden, where he is now a general surgeon.

Chris Kutschera, a French writer and photographer, publishes articles and photographs in the French and foreign press. He has covered Biafra (1969), the Persian Gulf (1970–90), the Sudan (1971–89), Kurdistan (1971–96), Chile (1976), and Palestinians (1976–78). His *Le Mouvement National Kurde* was updated and recently reissued as *Le Defi Kurde.*

Chaim Levakov was born in Yavniel, Palestine, in 1916. He acted in the Special Night Squad under Captain Charles Orde Wingate in 1938 and participated in a special mission against the Nazis in Syria and Lebanon in 1941. He joined the Israeli Intelligence Service as an officer in 1954, and from 1966 to 1972 he headed the Israeli mission in Kurdistan.

Sir Percy Loraine, after studying at Eton and Oxford, served in South Africa until 1902 and then worked for the diplomatic service in Constantinople, Tehran, Rome, Peking, Paris, and Madrid before being employed at the Paris Peace Conference. From 1933 to 1939, he was British ambassador to Turkey, and close friends with Atatürk. After Atatürk's death, Loraine was ambassador in Rome from 1939 until the Italians entered the Second World War. In retirement Loraine bred horses and helped innovate the photo-finish. He died in 1961.

Henry Finnis Blosse Lynch, educated at Eton and Cambridge, first traveled to the East in 1889. His first trip—on horseback and by raft—inaugurated a new service on the Karun River (Persia) under the British flag and laid the groundwork for a 270-mile trade route into Persia. Later trips—scientific, political, and commercial in purpose—were to the Caucasus and Armenia.

Shaikh Mahmud, in the early part of the twentieth century, was the leading personality of the Barzinji family of religious scholars and shaikhs, which wielded unparalleled influence and power in southern Kurdistan. The British named him governor of southern Kurdistan upon their occupation of the area in 1918, but in 1919 he led an uprising against the British for greater independence; they exiled him to India for three years. He was repatriated and reappointed governor of the Sulaimania region in 1922. He defiantly proclaimed himself King of Kurdistan. An army and air force offensive drove him to the mountains and, later, behind the Iranian border. After a failed revolt in 1931, Mahmud remained under house arrest in southern Iraq until his death in 1956.

Mahmud Efendi was a prisoner of war in Jerusalem before opening a photo studio in Sulaimania, northern Iraq. Efendi made portraits of the Sulaimania townspeople for more than three decades from the 1920s through the 1950s, at which time he left his studio to his son, Rafiq.

G. Eric Matson and his family joined the American Colony, a Christian community in Jerusalem, in 1896. In 1934, he and his wife, Edith, took over the Colony's large photo department, which became the Matson Photo Service. The Matsons photographed throughout the Middle East for *National Geographic* until 1946, when actions aimed at ending the British mandate compelled them to leave Palestine. They settled in the United States, where they continued to collaborate. He died in 1977.

Susan Meiselas began photographing in the early 1970s, and is particularly known for her work in Central America throughout the 1980s. She has been a member of Magnum Photos since 1976. She received the Robert Capa Gold Medal for her work in Nicaragua in 1978, and was named a MacArthur Fellow in 1992. She has authored two books, *Carnival Strippers* and *Nicaragua,* and edited three books of collective work.

Qazi Mohammad (Ghazi Mohammad) was a member of a prominent Mahabad family. He served there as a religious judge and by the 1940s was recognized as one of the most influential, politically astute of the region. In 1945 the initially left-leaning nationalist association Komala J-K recruited him as a member. Qazi Mohammad transformed Komala J-K into the "national-democratic" Kurdistan Democratic Party, which in early 1946 proclaimed the Kurdish republic. The Mahabad Republic lasted for less than a year. Qazi Mohammad, his brother Sadr Qazi, and their cousin Seyf Qazi were publicly hanged on March 31, 1947.

Mohammad Mokri was born in Kermanshah, Iran, in 1923 and worked in the ministry of education as head of the section of tribal affairs and, in 1949, the ministry's director general. In the early 1950s he taught at the University of Tehran. He traveled widely among the Kurdish tribes in Iran, taking photographs and collecting manuscripts and rare historical documents. A sympathizer of Mosadeq's National Front, he emigrated to France following Mosaddeq's fall. As a researcher at the Centre National de Recherches Scientifiques, he published widely on Kurdish and Iranian subjects. After Iran's Islamic revolution, he was made Iranian ambassador to the USSR, but soon came into conflict with the new Tehran regime and returned to France.

Mohammad Mosaddeq was a European-educated Iranian aristocrat. Fiercely independent and opposed to Reza Shah's dictatorial powers, Mosaddeq became in the 1940s an outspoken defender of Iranian democracy and national self-reliance. He led a broad coalition, the National Front, that fought for the nationalization of Iran's oil. Against the wishes of Mohammad Reza Shah but supported by mass demonstrations, parliament appointed him prime minister in early 1951. He carried out the promised nationalization of the country's oil, for which Iran was punished with a crushing international boycott. He also legislated land reform for the peasants. In August 1953 he was overthrown by a CIA-engineered coup d'état. He spent the last years of his life in enforced residence in his home village, where he died in 1967.

Giw Mukriyani, from Mahabad, Iran, learned photography in Syria from his older brother, the Kurdish historian and journalist Husain Huzni Mukriyani. Following the reformation of the Iraqi government after the English mandate, Giw followed his brother to Iraq in 1923. In Rowanduz they published the Kurdish magazines *Zarê Kurmancî* (1926–32), *Ronakî* (1935–36), and *Hataw.* Giw became a professional photographer in 1933 and continued to do studio photography in Arbil until his death in 1968.

General Richard M. Naab, after postings in Germany, Russia, and Belgium following the Gulf War, was appointed the first chief of the Humanitarian Coordination Center in Zakho, Iraq, for Operation Provide Comfort. During his time in the Kurdish region, he managed the resettlement of Kurdish refugees in cooperation with UN agencies and nongovernmental organizations. From April 1991 to June 1992, he oversaw the building of more than 2,000 houses, the renewal of 250 schools, and directed mine-clearing operations in the Kurdish areas. He lives in Virginia.

Nadir Nadirov was born in Soviet Azerbaijan and as a child was deported, along with many Kurds of Azerbaijan, Armenia, and Georgia, to Central Asia. He studied engineering and became a member of the Academy of Sciences of Kazakhstan. After the Soviet Union's breakup, he was among the first to draw attention to Stalin's mass deportation of Kurds in the years 1937–44.

Monir Nahid is the mother of Hassan and Shahyar, executed in August 1979 in Sanandaj, Iran. She now lives in the United States with her son Farhad Rashidian.

Liliana Nieto del Rio is a photojournalist residing in California. In addition to her work on Kurdish refugees in the Gulf War aftermath, her work includes reportages in El Salvador, Chile, and the Mexican Zapatista uprising.

Edward William Charles Noel, a career military officer, served as a British intelligence agent in Turkish Kurdistan. His reports urged British support for the cause of Kurdish autonomy, and at least until the middle of 1919, when Shaikh Mahmud's aspirations for an entirely independent state became apparent, British policy was influenced by Noel's sympathies. Awarded the Companion Order of the Indian Empire and the Distinguished Service Order, he continued to serve in Mardin and Kermanshah until World War II.

Ihsan Nuri, born in Bitlis, was a Kurdish career officer in the Turkish army in the early 1920s. When his involvement in the Shaikh Said rebellion was found out in 1924, he took refuge in Iraq. A few years later he reappeared and became military leader of the Ararat rebellion (hence his title Pasha, "general"). After the 1930 suppression of the Ararat rebellion, he and his Turkish wife, Yashar Khanum, were given asylum in Iran, where they lived for the rest of their lives.

Abdullah Öcalan, known as Apo, was born into a poor peasant family in a village in the Halfeti district of Urfa province in Turkey in 1949. Educated in Ankara, in 1969 he was sent to work at the cadastral survey in Diyarbakır. After a year, he returned to Ankara to study political science, where he became involved in left-wing student politics. In 1973 he joined Turkish and Kurdish friends to form a clandestine group that ultimately became the PKK. In 1976 the group left Ankara to create a base in Kurdistan, and in 1978 PKK was formally established. Their first armed activities took place in 1979. Öcalan moved that same year to Syria, where he set up political contacts so that the PKK could acquire military facilities in Lebanon. He remains the PKK's unrivaled leader.

Marian O'Connor, the wife of a British officer, traveled extensively through the Middle and Far East, eventually donating her negatives and album to the Royal Geographical Society. Little else is known about her.

Yilmaz Odabaşi, a Kurdish poet and journalist, was born in Diyarbakır in 1960 and is the author of several books, including *Bir Kürdün Eylül Defterleri.*

Mahmud Osman, a medical doctor, was a member of the political bureau of the KDP from 1964 to 1975, a close colleague of Mulla Mustafa Barzani, and one of the most powerful men in the Iraqi Kurdish movement. After its collapse in 1975, he parted ways with Barzani over his dependence on Iran and the U.S. He then established the Preparatory Committee of the KDP, which in 1979 merged with another minor party into the Socialist Party of Kurdistan. In 1987 he was among the founding members of the Iraqi Kurdistan Front, which united KDP, PUK, and the Socialist Party.

Fikret Otyam, born in the Anatolia town of Aksaray in 1926, studied art at Minar Sinan University. For three years he worked as a journalist in east and southeast Anatolia. Writing for journals such as *Dunya* and *Cumhuriyet,* he settled in Gazipasa in Antalya province, where he continues to write and paint. He has exhibited his art in Turkey and abroad, published forty-three books, and written a screenplay and a play.

Ramazan Öztürk was born in a Kurdish village in southeastern Turkey without schools, roads, water, or electricity. He continued his education in Diyarbakır and did factory work in Istanbul. He worked for an Istanbul newspaper as an office boy while attending university and bought a Zenith camera. In 1975 he went to Cyprus to work as a war correspondent. He has photographed throughout the Middle East and Latin America for the Turkish newspaper *Sebah* and was among the first journalists to arrive in the Halabja region after the Iraqi government's gas attack.

Mohammad Reza Shah Pahlavi was born in 1919, the only son of Reza Khan, who became Reza Shah in 1925. After Reza Shah was forced to abdicate in 1941, Mohammad succeeded him as ruler of Iran. During an internal power struggle with the nationalist and more liberal politician Mosaddeq, who nationalized Iran's oil in 1951, the shah temporarily left the country, but in 1953 was brought back by a CIA-supported coup. The following year, American oil companies acquired significant control of Iranian oil. Mohammad Reza Shah destroyed the left and liberal opposition and established an authoritarian rule. In the 1960s he embarked upon his "White Revolution," distributing land among the peasants; establishing literacy, sanitation, and development corps; granting women greater rights; and proposing profit-sharing plans for workers. He had major clashes with the powerful religious establishment, whose economic backbone he attempted to break, and he also lost the loyalty of most intellectuals and students. His regime became notorious for imprisoning, torturing, and executing dissidents. Massive, violent protest demonstrations throughout 1978 threw the regime into crisis. On January 11, 1979, the shah left Iran, after having appointed a regency council to rule in his name. Three weeks later the Ayatollah Khomeini triumphantly returned to Tehran from exile in France, and within weeks a revolutionary Islamic government was installed. The shah, shunned by his former allies including the U.S., retired to Egypt and remained there until his death.

Reza Shah Pahlavi, formerly Reza Khan, was an Iranian gendarmerie officer of common descent who successfully staged a coup in 1921, appointing himself army commander in chief, minister of war, and, in 1923, prime minister of Iran. In 1925 he arranged to have the last shah of the Qajar dynasty, Ahmad Shah, deposed by parliament; he then proclaimed himself shah, taking the name Pahlavi for his dynasty. After pacifying restive tribes and regions, he set upon a course of modernization from above, inspired by Atatürk's reforms in Turkey. In the 1930s he was pro-Germany, if only out of distrust of Russia and Great Britain, major threats to Iran's sovereignty. For his refusal to take their side in World War II, Britain and the USSR occupied Iran in 1941 and forced him to abdicate in favor of his eldest son, Mohammad, exiling Reza Shah Pahlavi to Mauritius and then to South Africa, where he died.

Piremêrd (pen name of Tawfiq Beg Mahmud Agha) was one of the most illustrious poets of southern Kurdistan. Born in Sulaimania in 1868, following his well-to-do family tradition, he made a career in Ottoman government service. Later he was active in Kurdish nationalist circles and wrote nationalist poetry. From 1926 to 1938 he edited the weekly Kurdish newspaper *Jiyan.* He died in 1950.

Morgan Philips Price traveled in Central Asia, Siberia, Persia, and Turkey from 1908 to 1914. He became a correspondent for the *Manchester Guardian* in Russia and served as correspondent of the *Daily Herald* in Berlin from 1919 to 1923. Back home in England, he became a Labour Party member of parliament and pursued a political and journalistic career until his death in 1973.

Abdul Karim Qassem was a career soldier who in 1958 led the coup that overthrew the monarchy in Iraq and established a left-leaning populist military regime. Seeking Kurdish allies, he courted especially Mulla Mustafa Barzani but failed to arrive at a mutually satisfactory definition of the status and rights of the Kurds in Iraq. The Kurdish war, which broke out in 1961, seriously weakened his regime. In February 1963, a coup d'état led by the Arab nationalist Baath Party brought down Qassem. Together with a number of loyal officers, he was executed.

Rafiq, known as "Rafiq-i-Wenagir" (Rafiq, the photographer), is the son of photographer Mahmud Efendi. He has maintained his father's photographic studio in Sulaimania and recorded life in Iraqi Kurdistan for more than forty years. His brother, Muhammad, fought in the Mahabad army and was one of the four officers killed upon their return to Iraq after the collapse of the Republic of Mahabad.

Sardar Rashid, a Kurdish leader from the Ardalan family in Iranian Kurdistan, united several Kurdish chieftains against the central government of Iran and was imprisoned until 1922. After Reza Shah came to power, however, Rashid lost the support of many tribes and sought shelter with Shaikh Mahmud in southern Kurdistan. He was promised pardon in Iran in 1928; but when he returned, he was imprisoned. After his release in 1941, Sardar Rashid was barred from Kurdistan and spent his remaining days in Tehran.

Zaher Rashid is a photographer from Qala Diza, Iraq, who first learned his craft while in Iranian exile from 1959 to 1961. He returned to Qala Diza to open a photography studio, which he ran until it was destroyed by the Iraqi government in 1988. Rashid photographed townspeople, Jalal Talabani, and Margaret George, and pursued his own documentary photography. After moving to a resettlement village, Rashid saved as many of the negatives as he could; he intends to return to Qala Diza once it is rebuilt.

Shorsh Resool was born in the town of Koisanjak, in Iraqi Kurdistan, graduated as a civil engineer, and joined the Kurdish movement in 1979. In 1989 he completed three papers on the destruction of the Kurds by Saddam Hussein's regime: "Destruction of a Nation: Villages and Towns Destroyed by Iraq," "Mass Killing: Kurds Killed Between 1975–1988," and "Mass Disappearance: Kurds Arrested by Iraqi Troops in Anfal, 1988." A refugee in Britain since 1990, Resool worked for Human Rights Watch on the Anfal documents and recently completed a master's degree in water engineering. He is now a college lecturer in London.

Reza, a photographer born in Tabriz, Iran, worked during the Iranian revolution for Agence France Press. Reza gave up his studies in architecture to pursue photography full-time, becoming a *Newsweek* correspondent in Iran and then *Time* magazine's Middle East correspondent. Reza has photographed Afghanistan, Pakistan, Israel, Turkey, Berlin, and Azerbaijan. He lives in Paris.

Seyid Riza (Seyyid Riza), the leader of the Dersim revolt of 1937, belonged to an influential Dersim family (the title "Seyid" indicates that his family was of the saintly lineages that monopolize major ritual functions among the Alevi community). Like his father, Seyid Ibrahim, Seyid Riza enjoyed worldly authority over the tribes of central Dersim. More than other traditional leaders of the region, he was influenced by modern ideas of Kurdish national identity. After the rebellion broke out and illustrated that Dersim could not easily be subjected, Seyid Riza was lured with promises of a negotiated settlement. He was apprehended and, without trial, hanged on November 16, 1937, along with his son and five other tribal leaders.

Percival Richards accompanied Major E.W.C. Noel through Kurdistan, and his photographs were published in Noel's diary. Years later, on his deathbed, Richards believed he had returned to Mesopotamia with his grandson, and bequeathed to him his forty-foot turban of pure silk, an unused ticket for a rail journey from Baghdad to Nepal, two daggers and an amulet, and his white Arab stallion, Satan.

George Riddell, born in Brixton, London, in 1865, became a solicitor in 1888. Riddell became the legal advisor for *News of the World,* and later traded law for journalism when he was elected its chairman. Lloyd George appointed Riddell liaison officer between the British delegation and the press at the Paris Peace Conference in 1919. He was made baronet in 1918, and in 1920 became Baron Riddell, of Walton Heath, Surrey. He died in 1934.

Patrick Robert graduated in agronomy and began his career as a photographer's assistant in fashion and advertising. Since 1982 he has covered the Palestinian uprising, the revolution in Romania, and the wars in Afghanistan, Bosnia, Chad, Georgia, and Rwanda. He received two awards for his photographs of the Kurdish exodus after the Gulf War.

Archibald Roosevelt, grandson of President Theodore Roosevelt and cousin of President Franklin D. Roosevelt, rose through the American intelligence service to become prominent in the CIA. In 1946, as military attaché for the American Embassy in Tehran, he was one of the few foreigners to visit the short-lived Mahabad Republic. As a military intelligence officer, he worked in North Africa, Egypt, and the Levant. He ended his army career as assistant military attaché in Iraq and Iran and retired from the CIA in 1974. He later became director of international relations for Chase Manhattan Bank. He died in 1990.

Eric Rouleau, born in Cairo in 1926, was chief reporter for the Middle East and editorial writer for *Le Monde* from 1955 to 1985. During 1985–86, he was France's ambassador in Tunisia. Since August 1986 he has been a roving ambassador. He wrote two books about the Palestinian question, and continues to publish in Europe and America.

Rosy Rouleau, born in Cairo in 1934, traveled with Gorden Troeller and Marie Claude Dessauge, from whom she learned photography. She worked with her husband, Eric, on assignments for *Le Monde*. In the 1960s and '70s, she worked in Iraq, Egypt, North and South Yemen, Madagascar, Oman, Kuwait, and Bahrain.

Wolfgang Rudolph is a German anthropologist who served in World War II before studying cultural anthropology in Berlin. Rudolph did fieldwork in Kurdish areas of Turkey and Iran in the late 1950s and early '60s, and taught at the Free University in Berlin. He was the editor of the journal *Sociologus* from 1975 to 1995.

Sir Horace Rumbold joined the diplomatic service in 1891 and was posted in Cairo, Tehran, and Vienna. During the negotiations with Turkey after the Treaty of Sèvres, he became high commissioner and ambassador at Constantinople. Rumbold served as deputy to Lord Curzon during the first Lausanne conference and as chief British delegate at the second Lausanne conference, signing the peace treaty with Turkey on July 24, 1923. After postings in Madrid and Berlin, he retired from diplomatic service in 1933. During World War II, Rumbold served in the Ministry of Economics.

Tsuri Saguy was born in Herzliya, Palestine, in 1934. At the age of eighteen, he enlisted in the Israeli paratroops and rose to division commander. Saguy graduated from the National Security Academy and the U.S. Marine Corps Commanding Staff College and helped train the Shah of Iran's special forces. Retired from the military, he is now an agriculturist.

Shaikh Said was born in 1865 in Palu, Turkish Kurdistan, the son of an influential shaikh of the Naqshbandiya mystical order. He had a traditional religious education and upon his father's death inherited his position. A charismatic religious leader, he established his authority among all the Zaza-speaking tribes of the districts between Diyarbakır and Erzurum. Because of his influence, nationalists against the Turkish republic sought him out. When the uprising broke, in February 1925, the shaikh inevitably became its leader. After the bloody suppression of the rebellion, Shaikh Said was sentenced to death by the Independence Court and hanged on June 29, 1925.

Dana Adams Schmidt served as a foreign correspondent for *The New York Times* in Germany, Greece, Israel, and Czechoslovakia from 1944 until 1961, when he became Middle Eastern correspondent based in Lebanon. In 1963, he won the George Polk Award of the Overseas Press Club for his stories on his visit to the Kurds in northern Iraq.

J. Pascal Sebah, a photographer probably of Turkish descent, had studios in Constantinople and Cairo. The Ottoman imperial court appointed him to document the regional costumes of the empire for an exhibition in Vienna in 1873, and throughout the latter part of the nineteenth century he created studio portraits, often using exotic costumes in his sittings.

Antoin Sevruguin, from Russian Armenia, ran a photographic studio in Tehran from the 1870s to the 1920s. One of the official photographers of the Iranian imperial court, he also had a large following among European travelers, for whom he provided scenes and portraits as souvenirs of their Oriental adventure. His interests ranged beyond the studio to the countryside of Persia, where he documented its ethnography, architecture, and landscape.

Arab Shamo (Ereb Şemo, Arab Shamilov), the first Kurdish novelist, was born in 1898 in a village near Kars (now Turkey, then Russian-controlled), the son of a shepherd. In World War I he served the Russian army as an interpreter. After the war he joined the Bolsheviks and worked as a teacher among the Kurds of Armenia. At the Oriental Institute of Leningrad, he assisted in developing an alphabet for the Kurdish language, and became a member of the editorial board of the Kurdish newspaper *Riya Taze,* published in Yerevan from 1930 to 1937. His first and most celebrated novel, *Kurdish Shepherd (Şivanê Kurd),* was published in 1935 (in Russian only, and after serious censorial edits). Like many Kurds, he was banished during the years of Stalinist paranoia, spending nineteen years in Siberia. He published two more novels after his return to Armenia, where he died in 1978.

Sherif Pasha, born into an aristocratic Kurdish family in Istanbul in 1865, was the Ottoman ambassador in Sweden from 1898 to 1908. Following the Young Turk coup, he resigned and settled in Paris, where he published an anti–Young Turk journal. In 1919 he attended the Peace Conference as representative of the Kurdish people and pleaded for an independent Kurdistan. The passage of the Treaty of Sèvres allowing for the possibility of a Kurdish state was his doing. Placing his hopes in Shaikh Mahmud, he briefly visited Iraq in 1922. In 1923 he settled in Cairo, where he appears to have remained until his death in 1944.

MOHAMMAD SADIQ SHARAFKANDI was born in the district of Bukan, Iranian Kurdistan. He studied chemistry, and joined the KDPI after meeting Ghassemlou in Paris. Following the Iranian revolution, he was elected to the KDPI leadership; after Iranian troops reoccupied parts of Kurdistan, he took part in the guerrilla struggle. When Ghassemlou was assassinated in Vienna in 1989, Sharafkandi was named his successor. He and three associates were assassinated by hit men of the Iranian regime in Berlin in September 1992.

"MAR SHIMUN" is, since the mid-sixteenth century, the hereditary title of the Nestorian church patriarchs who used to reside in the mountain village of Qotchanis in Hakkari. Mar Binyamin Shimun (acceded in 1903), during the First World War, led 30,000 Ottoman Nestorians from Hakkari to the relative safety of Urmia and Salmas (now in northwestern Iran, but then occupied by Russian troops), which already had a partly Nestorian population. This change in the local balance between Muslims and Christians caused much hostility. In March 1918 the Mar Shimun was ambushed and assassinated by Kurdish tribal leader Simko, with whom he had arranged to negotiate.

SIMKO, or ISMAIL AGHA, the chief of the large Shikak tribe in Iranian Kurdistan, led a large-scale rebellion after the First World War. During the war he had been in contact with the Ottoman army as well as the Russian army but also with Kurdish nationalist intellectuals. Taking advantage of the weakness of Iran's central government and coordinating his actions with other tribes of the region, Simko brought a large part of Iranian Kurdistan under his control. Only in 1922 was the central government strong enough to send an army that was a match for Simko, and he fled to Iraq. Pardoned, he returned to Iran in 1924, led another rebellion in 1926, and was forced again to flee. In 1929 the Iranian government lured him back with the promise of a governorship. On his return, he was ambushed and killed.

ELY BANNISTER SOANE worked for a British bank in Persia for several years before traveling through Kurdistan in 1909 disguised as a Persian—ostensibly to save costs. Adela Khanum, the celebrated female ruler in Halabja, hired him as her scribe. After meeting and marrying Lynette Lindfield in Australia, he returned to southern Kurdistan in 1919 as an administrator for the British government, and used his earlier connections to obtain the loyalty of surrounding tribes. He died at sea in 1923 of tuberculosis.

LYNETTE LINDFIELD SOANE, wife of E. B. Soane, traveled with her husband throughout Kurdistan at age nineteen. In 1935, after her husband's death, she traveled alone to Kurdistan and later lectured on her travels at the Royal Geographical Society. She retained a strong connection with the Kurdish people until her death in 1994.

RALPH SOLECKI, an archaeologist, first went to Kurdistan in 1950 with a University of Michigan expedition. He discovered Shanidar Cave, where he later found Neanderthal skeletons and evidence of a child burial in ancient Mousterian deposits. He was in Shanidar in 1960 when the conflict between the Kurds and the Iraqi government halted his work. Solecki went on to direct excavations in Syria, Iran, and Lebanon, all discontinued for political reasons. Now a professor of anthropology at Texas A&M University, he has resumed his investigations in Syria.

FREYA STARK was born into a bohemian family and began her travels at age two and a half, when her parents carried her across the Alps in a basket. Troubled by ill health in her twenties, she learned Arabic while convalescing, and her ensuing journey to Baghdad led to a series of articles for *The Baghdad Times* and, later, to *Baghdad Sketches.* During the Second World War, she worked as a South Arabia expert for the Ministry of Information, assisting in the spread of Allied propaganda. She returned to Turkish Kurdistan in the 1950s, and died at the age of 100 in May 1993.

JOHN STATHATOS was born in Athens in 1947. Working as a freelance photojournalist between 1972 and 1982, he covered the liberation struggles of the Polisario in the ex-Spanish Sahara, the New People's Army in Mindanao and Northern Luzon, and the Kurdish peshmerga in the mountains of Iran and Iraq. His work has appeared in *The Times* (London) and *The Guardian.* He lives in London, where he is an exhibitor, critic, and curator of contemporary visual art.

ANTHONY SUAU won the 1984 Pulitzer Prize in feature photography for a series about mass starvation in drought-stricken Ethiopia. Since 1991 he has been a contract photographer for *Time,* for whom he covered the Gulf War and the Kurdish exodus from Iraq. In 1992 he received Picture of the Year for his coverage of Kurdish refugees. He is working on his first photography book, *Revolution,* about the global democratic moment, 1986–91.

ZIRAR AND ZOYA SULAIMAN have been married since they met in the Soviet Union in the 1950s and presently live in Diyana, Iraqi Kurdistan.

SIR MARK SYKES was the British honorary attaché in Constantinople from 1905 to 1906, at which time he traveled to Mesopotamia and Syria to do mapping for the War Office. Sykes's political duties during the First World War took him to Serbia, Bulgaria, Egypt, and India, and it was his knowledge of French diplomatic training and familiarity with Kurdish tribes in the Ottoman Empire that prompted Lord Kitchener and the Foreign Office to admit him to formal conversations with the French. After 1916, Sykes virtually single-handedly carried on the negotiations with France's representative, Georges Picot, which resulted in the Sykes-Picot agreement that divided the Middle East among the Allies.

HERO TALABANI received her B.A. in education and psychology from Baghdad University, and is the wife of PUK leader Jalal Talabani and the daughter of the writer and former KDP secretary Ibrahim Ahmed. She left Iraq in 1973, returning in 1977 to join the Kurdish peshmerga, whose movement she documented on video in the 1980s. Elected to the regional parliament in 1992, she remained in Arbil until fighting between KDP and Iraqi troops began in August 1996.

JALAL TALABANI was from his youth involved in Kurdish politics. In the 1960s, with his father-in-law, Ibrahim Ahmed, Talabani was a member of the politburo of the KDP, and the two repeatedly clashed with Mulla Mustafa Barzani. Talabani and Ahmed led a breakaway section of the party that in 1966 even fought Barzani alongside government troops. After Barzani reached a peace agreement with Baghdad, Talabani and Ahmed returned to the ranks and remained loyal until Barzani's final defeat in March 1975. Later that year, Talabani established the Patriotic Union of Kurdistan (PUK), initially based in Damascus but soon carrying out low-intensity guerrilla struggle inside Iraqi Kurdistan. From 1978 on, the PUK was in serious, often armed conflict with the KDP of Idris and Mas'ud Barzani, and only in 1986 did the parties reach an agreement to cooperate against Baghdad. In the 1992 elections in the Kurdish-controlled part of Iraq, Talabani and Mas'ud Barzani got equal popular support. The precarious economic situation has brought old conflicts to the surface again, and since 1994 the self-governing Kurdish districts have been divided into Barzani- and Talabani-controlled zones.

SHAIKH UBAIDULLAH descended from a long line of influential religious leaders based in Nehri, in the Ottoman part of central Kurdistan. The most respected shaikh of his day, his authority was recognized by most tribes of the region. In 1880 he led a revolt in which his tribal followers occupied a part of Iranian Kurdistan. Iranian troops defeated the shaikh's men, and an Ottoman force captured the shaikh and took him to Istanbul in 1881. After a few months, he escaped and made his way back to Nehri, where he was again captured by the Ottomans and exiled to Hijaz. He died in Mecca in 1883.

RICHARD WAYMAN, a British photographer, first visited Turkish Kurdistan in the summer of 1987, investigating changes in traditional Kurdish society, for which he won the Observer/David Hodge Award for Young Photojournalists. He documented the plight of Iraqi Kurds fleeing chemical attacks in northern Iraq in 1988, human rights

abuses in Turkey in 1990, the Kurdish uprising in northern Iraq in 1991, and the first democratic elections in northern Iraq in 1992. In the fall of 1992, he returned to southeast Turkey to document human rights violations and the PKK's struggle for independence. His photographs have been published in *The Independent, The Guardian, The Times,* and *The Telegraph.* He is presently based in London.

JEAN WEINBERG was a studio photographer in Istanbul in the early decades of the twentieth century. In 1923 he was the first of his colleagues to go to Ankara to take Mustafa Kemal's portrait. He went on to create portraits of other prominent persons of the new Turkey, which he published in an album entitled *Gazi'nin eseri/L'oeuvre du Gazi* in 1933. He also contributed photographs illustrating the process of Turkey's modernization to some fifty European and American newspapers and magazines.

ANDREW WHITLEY is a writer on the Middle East. In the 1970s he was the BBC's staff writer on Iran and, later, its correspondent in Tehran. From 1990 to 1994, he was director of the U.S. human rights organization Middle East Watch, which is now part of Human Rights Watch.

SIR ARNOLD TALBOT WILSON was a British administrator in southwest Persia from 1909 to 1913, exploring and surveying districts in Luristan and Fars. When the British formed a civil administration for the Ottoman territory occupied in 1916, Wilson was appointed deputy civil commissioner under Percy Cox. When Cox became temporary British minister in Persia in 1918, Wilson was made civil commissioner, and for the next three years was largely responsible for running the British civil administration. In 1920 Cox returned, and Wilson became director of the Anglo-Persian Oil Company. Later in England, he was a member of parliament.

YAHYA EFENDI was one of the first Kurdish photographers in Iraqi Kurdistan. Trained by the British after World War I, he opened his first studio in Sulaimania in 1919. Because he was a translator for the British and on friendly terms with foreigners, the Iraqi government believed he was a British spy and arrested him in 1934. Four years later, he was allowed to return to his work in Sulaimania. The Baath Party looted his shop in 1963, and though he continued to photograph until his death in 1976, virtually all his negatives have been lost.

DIMITRI YERMAKOV, a photographer from Tiflis (now known as Tiblisi), Georgia, began his trade in the early 1880s. He crossed Georgia from one end to the other in a specially fitted covered wagon, shooting inaccessible mountain villages. He sent these photographs to institutions for the arts and humanities and to the press. During the Russo-Turkish War (1877–88), Yermakov worked with other photographers in the Field Photographic Section of the General Staff of the Caucasus Army. In 1883 he was appointed art photographer to the Moscow Archaeological Society, and in 1889 he produced a "Georgian Historical Photo Album" of Georgian churches. He won awards from Persia, Turkey, and Italy for his images. From 1880 until his death, he ran a photographic studio in Tiflis.

LEYLA ZANA, the first Kurdish woman elected to the Turkish parliament, was born in the Diyarbakır region of Turkey. She married Mehdi Zana and was still very young when her husband was imprisoned in 1980. She could neither read nor write Turkish then, but energetically taught herself all she needed to take care of her husband's affairs, gradually becoming a public figure in her own right. She was among the twenty-two deputies of the first legal Kurdish party elected into parliament in 1991. In the middle of her term, she and a number of other Kurdish members were charged with separatism and contacts with the PKK. In March 1994 they were arrested. Tried and convicted, she is now presently serving a fifteen-year sentence in an Ankara prison. She received the European Parliament's Sakharov Prize in 1996.

MEHDI ZANA was a tailor in the Kurdish city of Diyarbakır before he was elected mayor in 1978 as an independent candidate supported by Kurdish nationalists. Following the military coup of September 1980, he was imprisoned for over a decade because of his commitment to Kurdish rights in Turkey. Released in 1991, he served another two-year prison sentence for a speech he gave in the European parliament in 1994.

GLOSSARY

AGHA—Kurdish tribal leader or member of landed aristocracy

ALEVIS—Islamic sect, regarded by many Muslims as heretical

AMIR (EMIR, MIR)—Prince, ruler of a Kurdish (semi-independent) principality in the Ottoman Empire and Iran until the mid-nineteenth century

AMN—General security directorate of Iraq

ANFAL—Literally, "the spoils of war," title of a chapter in the Qur'an; a destructive military campaign against Kurdish-controlled areas in northern Iraq in 1988 resulting in some 100,000 Kurds being killed

ASHIRET (ASHIRA)—Tribe

ASSYRIANS—Christian ethnic minority in central and eastern Kurdistan speaking an Aramaic dialect. Originally, all Assyrians adhered to the eastern Syrian or Nestorian Church. (See *Nestorians, Chaldeans*)

BAATH PARTY—Pan-Arab Socialist party, founded in Syria in 1943 with branches in Iraq and other Arab countries, advocating Arab unity and socialism. The present Syrian and Iraqi regimes represent rival wings of the Arab Baath Party.

BAHA'IS—A religious sect that emerged from Shia Islam in nineteenth-century Iran and considers itself the latest world religion. Its adherents are considered apostates by Muslim religious authorities.

BEDOUIN (BEDAWIN)—Nomadic Arab

BEG (KHAN)—Feudal lord; ruler of Kurdish principality

BEY—Variant form of Beg, corresponding to Turkish pronunciation

CALIPH—Successor of the Prophet Muhammad, temporal and spiritual head of all Sunni Muslims. The Ottoman sultans claimed the title of caliph, never seriously contested by other Muslims.

CALIPHATE—The dominion of the caliph (claimed by the Ottoman state)

CHALDEAN—Christian minority of Kurdistan who speak an eastern Aramaic dialect and are Roman Catholics converted under the influence of Italian and French missionaries

CARAVANSARAI—Fortified lodging for travelers

C.U.P.—Committee of Union and Progress (Ittihat ve Terakki Cemiyeti): the Young Turk Party

D.C.P.O.—British reference for a District Civilian Personnel Officer

DIWANKHANE—Guest house or room in which prominent persons entertain followers and guests

EMIR—See *Amir*

EFENDI—Title of respect for urban notables and officials

G.O.C.—British term for General Officer Commanding

GURKHA—Member of one of the dominant races in Nepal of Hindu descent, especially famous for prowess in fighting; general term for British crack units recruited in Nepal

H.E.—His Excellency

HAMIDIYE—Kurdish tribal militia regiments established by Sultan Abdulhamid II in 1892 to protect the eastern provinces of the Ottoman Empire against external (Russian) and internal (Armenian) threats

HAN—Variant form of Khan, corresponding to Turkish pronunciation: lord, prince

HARAM—Everything that is forbidden and unlawful according to Islamic law

HIWA (HEWA)—Meaning "hope," one of Iraq's Kurdish nationalist parties based in Sulaimania, Arbil, and Kirkuk, active in the late 1940s. It followed a pro-British line, and was led by Rafiq Hilmi.

HODJA (HOCA)—Title of respect for a religious teacher in Turkey

HUKMDAR (HOKEMDAR)—Literally, "one who has authority to rule"

IMAM—Among Sunni Muslims, this term refers only to prayer leaders; Shi'is reserve the term principally for Ali (the son-in-law of the Prophet Muhammad) and eleven descendants in the direct line; a general term for major religious and political community leaders

IRADEH—Decree or order by a ruler

JAMADANI—Kurdish men's headdress

JASH (JAHSH)—Literally, "donkey foal," a term of abuse used by Iraqi Kurds for those Kurds who collaborate with the ruling government

JIHAD—Holy war waged on behalf of Islam

KALASHNIKOV—Soviet-made automatic weapon (AK-47) favored by guerrilla movements

KAZA (QAZA)—Administrative district in the Ottoman Empire, a county, subdivision of a liwa

KDP—Kurdistan Democratic Party (of Iraq), established 1946. Mulla Mustafa Barzani was made party president in the 1950s and led it through the guerrilla struggles of the 1960s until his defeat and exile in 1975. His son Mas'ud Barzani now leads the party.

KDPI—Kurdistan Democratic Party of Iran, established in 1945 under the leadership of Qazi Mohammad. The party formed the backbone of the Mahabad Republic in 1946 and maintained a quiet underground presence until the Iranian revolution, when it became the largest Kurdish movement in Iran under Abdul Rahman Ghassemlou.

KHAN—Title for feudal lord or prince

KHANUM or KHATUN—Title of respect used for a woman, corresponding to the male Khan

KIZILBASH—Literally, "red-headed," a term of abuse for the heterodox sects in Turkey known as Alevi

KOLKHOZ—Russian collective farms

KOMALA—"Society"; used in the name of a number of political parties

KURMANJI—The major Kurdish dialect group of northern Kurdistan (See *Sorani, Zaza*)

LEVA—See *Liwa*

LEVIES—Troops of Assyrian soldiers formed in 1921 in Iraq, led by British officers

LIWA (LEVA, LIVA)—An administrative district, subdivision of vilayet; also known as sanjaq (sancak)

MAIDAN—Open city square or plaza

MIR—See *Amir*

MOHAMMEDAN—Western term for Muslim, follower of the Prophet Muhammad, now obsolete

MUFTI—Expert of Islamic law who issues authoritative answers or verdicts (fatwa) in response to queries

MUKHTAR—Elected village headman

MULLA (MOLLA)—Muslim religious functionary; prayer leader, preacher, or teacher

MUSSULMAN—An obsolete term for Muslim

MUSLIM—A person who professes Islam

MUTASARRIF—Chief administrative official of Ottoman district (liwa)

NAHIYAH (NAHIYE)—District (subdivision of kaza)

NAQSHBANDI—Follower of the Naqshbandiya, one of two Sufi orders that have a large following in Kurdistan. Each of these orders has its distinctive mystical techniques (of recitations, meditation, etc.).

NESTORIANS—An Eastern Christian denomination, found as far as India and Central Asia. Most of the Assyrians belonged to this church before many were converted to Western churches.

NEWROZ—The New Year festival of all Iranian peoples, celebrated March 21; the Kurds have adopted Newroz as their major national holiday.

PAHLAVI—The name chosen by Reza Shah for the new ruling dynasty he founded in Iran

PASDAR—"Revolutionary Guard" (in postrevolutionary Iran)

PASHA—Ottoman title for high military and civilian officials; presently used only for generals

PESHMERGA—Kurdish guerrilla fighter, literally, "one ready to give his life"

PKK—Kurdish acronym for Kurdistan Workers Party, led by Abdullah Öcalan ("Apo")

PUK—Patriotic Union of Kurdistan in Iraq; presently one of the two major Kurdish parties in Iraq, led by Jalal Talabani and established in 1975.

QADI—Judge in Muslim court of law

QADIRI—Follower of the Qadiriya sect (mystical) order, one of two popular orders in Kurdistan (See *Naqshbandi*)

QAJAR—The dynasty that ruled Iran during the nineteenth century, finally overthrown in 1925 by Reza Khan

QUR'AN—(often spelled in English as Koran) The holy book of Islam

REBENDAN—A Kurdish month in midwinter, corresponding to the period from January 21 to February 19

SARAI (SARAY, SERAI)—Palace

SAVAK—Iran's secret police. The acronym stands for "National Information and Security Organization"

SEYID (SEYYID, SAYYID)—Descendant of the Prophet Muhammad. Among the Alevi Kurds, seyids are hereditary religious leaders without whom major rituals cannot be performed.

SHAIKH (SHEIKH, SHAYKH)—Islamic religious leader, especially the leader of a Sufi (mystical) order

SHARIF (SHERIF)—Descendant of the Prophet Muhammad (also seyid)

SHIITE—Follower of the Shia branch of Islam, which considers Ali (Muhammad's cousin and son-in-law) to be the true successor of the Prophet rather than Abu Bakr, who was elected by the (Sunni) majority

SORANI—One of the two major dialect groups of Kurdish, spoken in southern Kurdistan (in northern Iraq and Iran). Kurmanji and Zaza are spoken by Kurds in central and northern Kurdistan (eastern Turkey).

SOWAR—Horseman

S.S.O.—Special Service Officer serving as intelligence for the British RAF

SULTAN—Ruler of Muslim states, especially the Ottoman Empire

SUNNI (SUNNA)—Literally, "a person who adheres to the practice (sunna) of the Prophet Muhammad himself." The term designates the majority branch of Islam, as opposed to the Shia.

TEKIAH (TEKYE, TEKKE)—A building used for religious rituals of sufi (mystical) orders

TUMAN—Iranian currency unit

UMMA—Religious community; especially, the community of Islam

VALI (WALI)—Governor of a province of the Ottoman Empire or in present Turkey

VILAYET—Province of the Ottoman Empire (in present-day Turkey more commonly called "il")

WALI—See *Vali*

YEZIDI—A non-Muslim minority religion and community in Kurdistan

ZAKAT—Islamic alms tax, or the agha's share of dues paid by villagers

ZAPTIEH (ZABTIYE)—Ottoman police force

ZAZA—Kurdish dialect spoken in various regions of the northwestern part of Turkish Kurdistan, differing considerably from Kurmanji

SOURCES CITED

Alakom, Rohat. *Ziya Gökalp'in Çilesi Kürtler (Ziya Gökalp's Ordeal: The Kurds).* Istanbul: Fırat Yayınları, 1992.

Arfa, Hassan. *The Kurds: An Historical and Political Study.* London: Oxford University Press, 1966.

Atatürk. *A Speech Delivered by Mustafa Kemal Atatürk.* Ankara: Başbakanlık Basımevi, 1981.

Beddoe, Dr. F.R.S. *Notes and Queries on Anthropology.* London: Royal Anthropological Institute, 1874.

Bedirkhan, Kamuran Ali. *Elfabeya Min: Elfabeya Kurdi (My Alphabet: the Kurdish Alphabet).* Damas: Çapxana Teraqi, 1938.

Bedirkhan, Süreya. *The Case of Kurdistan Against Turkey.* Philadelphia: Kurdish Independence League, 1928.

Bell, Lady, ed. *The Letters of Gertrude Bell,* Volume II. New York: Boni and Liveright, 1927.

Bell, Gertrude. *Amurath to Amurath.* London: W. Heinemann, 1911.

Beşikçi, Ismail. *Doğuda Değişim ve Yapısal Sorunlar (Social Change and Structural Problems of the East).* Ankara: Doğan Yayınevi, 1969.

Bishop, Mrs. Isabella L. Bird. *Journeys in Persia and Kurdistan,* Volumes I and II. London: John Murray, 1891.

Cağlayangı, Ihsan Sabri. *Anılarım (My Memories).* Istanbul: Yımaz Yayınları, 1990.

Chaliand, Gerard, ed. *People Without a Country: The Kurds and Kurdistan.* London: Zed Books, 1980.

Chantre, Ernest. *Les Kurdes: Esquisse Historique et Ethnographique.* Lyon: Alexander Rey, 1897.

Chantre, Ernest. *Archives du Museum d'Histoire Naturelle de Lyon,* 6th Edition. Lyon: Henri Georg, 1895.

Davis, Leslie A. (Susan K. Blair, ed.). *The Slaughterhouse Province: An American Diplomat's Report on the Armenian Genocide.* New Rochelle: Aristide D. Caratzas, 1989.

Dersimi, M. Nuri. *Kürdistan Tarihinde Dersim (Dersim in the History of Kurdistan).* Aleppo: Ani Matbaası, 1952.

Dersimi, M. Nuri. *Hatiratım (My Memories).* Ankara: Öz-Ge Yayınları, 1992.

Douglas, William O. *Strange Lands and Friendly People.* New York: Harper, 1951.

Edmonds, C. J. *Kurds, Turks and Arabs.* London: Oxford University Press, 1957.

Eagleton, William. *The Kurdish Republic of 1946.* London: Oxford University Press, 1963.

Erdost, Muzaffer Ilhan, *Şemdinli Röportajı.* Ankara: Onur Yayınevı, 1987.

Field, Henry. *The Anthropology of Irak II.* Chicago: Field Museum, 1940.

Field, Henry. *Arabian Desert Tales: Between the Two Great Wars.* Santa Fe: Synergetic Press, 1977.

Fırat, M. Şerif. *Doğu Illeri Ve Varto Tarihi (The History of Varto and the Eastern Provinces).* Ankara: Türk Kültürünü Araştırma Enstitüsü, 1983.

Forbes, Rosita. *Conflict: Angora to Afghanistan.* London: Cassell, 1931.

Genelkurmay Belgelerinde Kürt Isyanları (Kurdish Rebellions in Documents of the General Staff), Volume 2. Istanbul: Kaynak Yayınları, 1992.

Hamilton, Archibald Milne. *Road Through Kurdistan.* London: Faber & Faber, 1937.

Hassanpour, Amir. *Nationalism and Language in Kurdistan.* San Francisco: Mellen Research University Press, 1992.

Hawar, M. R. *Shêkh Mehmûdî qareman û dewletekey khwarûy Kurdistan (The Heroic Shaikh Mahmud and the State of Southern Kurdistan),* Volumes 1 and 2. London: Jaf Press/Black Rose, 1990–91.

Hurewitz, J. C. *Diplomacy in the Near and Middle East, A Documentary Record.* Princeton: Van Nostrand, 1956.

Kutlay, Naci. *49'lar dosyası.* Istanbul: Fırat Yayınları, 1994.

Laizer, Sheri. *Martyrs, Traitors and Patriots.* London: Zed Books, 1996.

Lynch, H.F.B. *Armenia: Travels and Studies.* Volume II, London: Lonmans, 1901.

Moorehead, Lucy, ed. *Freya Stark: Letters.* Salisbury: Compton-Russell, 1975.

Nikitine, Basile. *Les Kurdes: Étude sociologique et historique.* Paris: Imprimérie nationale, 1956.

Odabaşı, Yılmaz. *Bir Kürdün Eylül defterleri (A Kurd's September Notebooks).* Broy Yayınları, 1991.

Price, M. P. *A Journey Through Turkish Armenia and Persian Kurdistan.* Journal of the Manchester Geographical Society, Vol. XXX, 1914.

Roosevelt, Archibald. *For Lust of Knowing.* Boston: Little, Brown, 1988.

Schmidt, Dana Adams. *Journey Among Brave Men.* Boston: Little, Brown, 1964.

Sharaf Khan Bidlisi. *Sharafname: Tarikh-i Mufassal-i Kurdistan (Extensive History of Kurdistan).* Tehran: Ilmi, 1343/1964.

Şimşin, Bilal N. *British Documents on Atatürk,* Volume II. Ankara: Turk Tarih Kurumu Basimevi, 1975.

Soane, Ely B. *To Mesopotamia and Kurdistan in Disguise.* London: John Murray, 1912.

Solecki, Ralph S. *Shanidar: The First Flower People.* New York: Knopf, 1971.

Stark, Freya. *Riding to the Tigris.* New York: Harcourt Brace and Company, 1959.

Speer, Robert E. *"The Hakim Sahib," The Foreign Doctor: A Biography of Joseph Plumb Cochran, M.D., of Persia.* New York: Fleming H. Revell, 1911.

Sykes, Sir Mark. *The Caliph's Last Heritage: A Short History of the Turkish Empire.* London: Macmillan & Co., 1915.

Wilson, A. *A Clash of Loyalties.* London: Oxford University Press, 1931.

Wratislaw, A. C. *A Consul in the East.* Edinburgh: W. Blackwood, 1924.

SUGGESTED READING

Ahmad, Kamal Madhar. *Kurdistan During the First World War.* London: Saqi Books, 1994.

Brauer, Erich. *The Jews of Kurdistan.* Detroit: Wayne State University Press, 1993.

Bruinessen, Martin van. *Agha, Shaikh and State: The Social and Political Structures of Kurdistan.* London: Zed Books, 1992.

Çem, Munzur. *Gülümse ey Dersim (Smile Dersim).* Köln: Özgürlük Yolu, 1990.

Farouk-Sluglett, Marion and Sluglett, Peter. *Iraq Since 1958,* 2nd Edition. London: I. B. Tauris, 1990.

Kreyenbroek, Philip G. and Allison C. *Kurdish Culture and Identity.* London: Zed Books, 1996.

Kreyenbroek, Philip G. and Sperl Stefan, eds. *The Kurds: A Contemporary Overview.* London/New York: Routledge, 1992.

Kutschera, Chris. *Le défi Kurde.* Paris: Bayard Éditions, 1997.

McDowall, David. *The Kurds.* London: Minority Rights Group, 1992.

McDowall, David. *A Modern History of the Kurds.* London: I. B. Tauris, 1996.

Olson, Robert. *The Emergence of Kurdish Nationalism and the Sheik Said Rebellion, 1880–1925.* Austin: University of Texas, 1989.

Olson, Robert, ed. *The Kurdish Nationalist Movement in the 1990s.* Lexington: University Press of Kentucky, 1996.

Randal, Jonathan C. *After Such Knowledge, What Forgiveness?* New York: Farrar, Straus and Giroux, 1997.

Sabar, Yona. *The Folk Literature of the Kurdistani Jews: An Anthology.* New Haven: Yale University Press, 1982.

INDEX

385

ACKNOWLEDGEMENTS

This book is like a family album, gathered with the support of those who generously contributed and collaborated in its creation, including the many travelers, both acquaintances and strangers, who discovered Kurdistan long before me. Beyond the authors and photographers, there are many people who dedicated valuable time, helping me to uncover material and evolve a greater understanding of Kurdish history.

I owe a large and particular debt to Martin van Bruinessen, for patiently enduring endless questions while inviting my exploration and, most important, for the critical thinking he continually brought to this project. I am also grateful to Amir Hassanpour, who was deeply supportive both as a scholar and a friend, challenging me through these years with a Kurdish perspective. From the early stages, Charles Merewether shared his insight and contributed invaluable help to the complex selection process. There are many other scholars who offered their expertise concerning specific periods or geographies; my thanks especially to Rohat Alakom, M. R. Hawar, Dr. Liora Lukitz, M. Malmîsanij, and Robert Olson.

For six years, during our visits to Kurdistan and to the exile community, many families generously welcomed us. I am grateful to all, though I cannot list them by name here because of the consequences they might suffer. Special thanks to Hassan Ghazi, As'ad Gohzi, and Aytul Gurtas for their kind guidance and expert translation.

This project could never have been realized without the enthusiasm of a large network within and around the Kurdish community and particular reassurance from the following: Bakhtiar Amin, Joyce Blau, Munzur Çem, Omer Erzeren, Dr. Ahmed Ferhadi, Mustafa Khezry, Sheri Laizer, Aliza Marcus, Paul and Edith Maubec, Nuri Medyali, Omar Sheikhmous, Kumru Toutamis, and Memo Yetkin. I would especially like to thank Kendal Nezan for generously incorporating me into the life of the Kurdish Institute of Paris.

I am most grateful to Aryeh Neier, former director of Human Rights Watch, whose integrity has always been an inspiration to me, and who recognized the enormity of this project early on and opened many doors. My thanks to Andrew Whitley, who sent me on my first trip to Kurdistan while he was director of Middle East Watch, and with whom the first seeds of this book were sown.

I am deeply indebted to the John D. and Catherine T. MacArthur Foundation for awarding me a fellowship a year after I'd begun this project, making it financially possible for me to do extensive research, crisscrossing between Kurdistan and the exile community in Europe.

I am also indebted to Marcia Schiff and the Polaroid Foundation, who supplied film and a special camera for the photographic reproduction work in Kurdistan; the Hasselblad Foundation, whose grant enabled further research assistance; and Anthony Richter and the Open Society Institute, for sponsoring my travels to the former Soviet Union.

I would like to express my gratitude to Random House, Harold Evans, and my editor, Ann Godoff, for their patient confidence. I would also like to acknowledge Mark Holborn, for his masterful eye and indispensable counsel on the difficult process of integrating editorial concepts within the design; Kathy Rosenbloom, for her vigilant watch over the production process; and Benjamin Dreyer, for whom no detail was unimportant and who led me to Gail Bradney, with whom the arduous task of assuring the book's consistency was diligently pursued.

There were few straight paths in this collection process, and I very much appreciated the commitment of researchers Stuart Alexander, Alexis Broben, Nicky Cull, and Gabrielle Lyon, as well as their intuition and persistence. Following their efforts was a team of interns who often took on tedious but necessary work: Baptiste Lignel, Galina Kharkover, and Astrida Valigorsky deserve special mention for the considerable time and skill they brought to the digital preparation of images.

My sincere thanks to Bob Gardner and Dana Bonstrom of the Harvard Film Study Center for generously facilitating the production of a color rendition of the book, such that I could begin to imagine the impact of its design; as well as to Jim Lanahan at Apple Computer, who made possible a loan of equipment so that our design could be achieved, and Bob Stein, who lent me his very own laptop with which I began my travels to Kurdistan.

Particularly, I would like to single out three people who have been most intimately involved with this project. Collectively they made it possible for this very complicated vision to become a reality. The great pleasure of this endeavor is in large part due to the extraordinary dedication of Laura Hubber, Meryl Levin, and Dolly Meieran, each of whom engaged with remarkable faith and endured this unpredictable process throughout its many stages.

Laura appeared just as the necessity for assistance overwhelmed me. Her letter writing led to more extensive archival research and finally to the field alongside me as a wonderful companion, collecting stories and images throughout Kurdistan. I am especially appreciative of her perceptive and selective reading of the multiple memoirs she discovered. I will always value her early and continuing passion for this project.

Meryl came soon after and progressively moved from coordinating the management of material to becoming fully integrated into the final design process. She brought tremendous energy and inventiveness, as well as her own remarkable talent. There were many days I could not have faced my studio without knowing that she would join me.

Dolly was hired to work alongside Michael Callaghan, who literally lived in the studio as he sketched out the book's form and style. She then continued, with ferocious focus, to carry us through the extensive and exhausting tyranny of digital detail, often at the midnight hour.

I am also especially grateful to Roslyn Shloss, whose great clarity and careful editing helped shape the first draft, and who believed that this could be a book when I, myself, was not so sure.

Thanks to the staff of Magnum Photos, and particularly to Ernie Lofblad, who kept track of the assorted negatives and incoming material throughout the process.

I could not have persisted all these years without the many close friends who patiently suffered with me through my consuming preoccupation with this project.

I am inexpressibly thankful to my sister, Nancy Meiselas, my first reader, whose optimism and belief in me provided moral support; to my father, for his unwavering encouragement and affection; and to my partner, Dick Rogers, my most trusted critic, who has sustained me throughout this long journey.

—SCM
July 1997

General security prison,
Sulaimania, Iraq
Chris Kutschera

This book has been made possible through the generosity of countless individuals, families, archives, and publishers worldwide. While I am not at liberty to name all those who have contributed material, I would like to acknowledge the following collections and publishers who have granted permission for reproduction of material free of charge:
The Atlantic Monthly   Burhan Jaf   Canon Europa   Central Zionist Archives   Clarkson, Wright & Jakes   Columbia University   Corbis-Bettmann
Deutsches Archiologisches Institut   Evangelical Lutheran Church   FDR Library   The Evening Standard   The Field Museum   Freer Gallery of Art
Foreign Affairs ©1946 by the Council on Foreign Relations   Pierre de Gigord   Human Rights Watch   Illustrated London News Picture Library   KDP Archive
Kurdish Institute of Paris   The Kurdish Library   Library of Congress   Little, Brown and Company   Luther-Northwest Seminary, Region 3 Archives
John Murray Publishers   Melissa Media Associates   MERIP   Le Monde   Museum Folkwang   National Anthropological Archives, Smithsonian Institution
The National Security Archive   National Archives   The New York Times PHOTO   Project Save   PUK Archive   Rafiq Studio
The Robinson Library and the Department of Geology at the University of Newcastle-upon-Tyne
Royal Geographical Society   Sipa Press   SYGMA   Time/Life, Inc.   The Village Voice   Wall-to-Wall TV

Library of Congress Cataloging-in-Publication Data
Meiselas, Susan.
Kurdistan : in the shadow of history / Susan Meiselas.
p.   cm.
Includes bibliographical references and index.
ISBN 0-679-42389-3
1. Kurdistan—Pictorial works. 2. Kurds—Pictorial works.
I. Title.
DS59.K86M44   1997
956.6'7—dc21   96-53931

Random House website address: http://www.randomhouse.com
Printed on acid-free paper by Arnoldo Mondadori Editore, S.p.A., Verona, Italy

2   4   6   8   9   7   5   3
First Edition

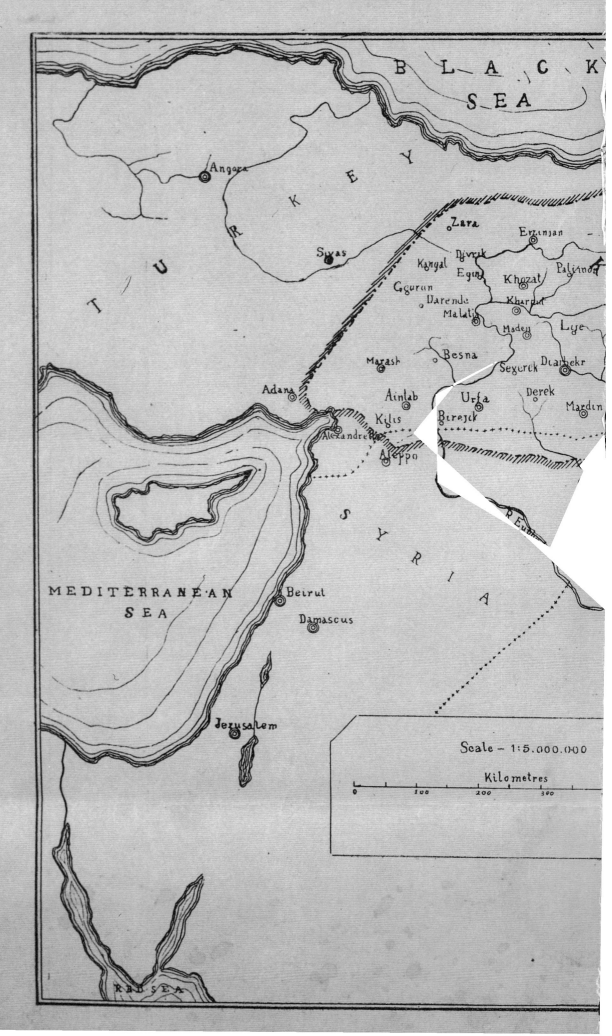

KURD

BLACK SEA

Angora

TURKEY

Zara
Erzinjan
Sivas
Kangal
Djvrik
Egin
Palinon
Khozat
Gcgurun
Varende
Kharput
Malati
Maden
Lye
Besna
Marash
Seyerek
Diarbekr
Adana
Aintab
Urfa
Derek
Kilis
Birejik
Mardin
Alexandretta
Aleppo

SYRIA

Euph

MEDITERRANEAN
SEA

Beirut
Damascus

Jerusalem

Scale — 1:5.000.000

Kilometres

0   100   200   300

RED SEA